Handbook of Employee Benefits and Administration

PUBLIC ADMINISTRATION AND PUBLIC POLICY

A Comprehensive Publication Program

EDITOR-IN-CHIEF

EVAN M. BERMAN

Huey McElveen Distinguished Professor
Louisiana State University
Public Administration Institute
Baton Rouge, Louisiana

Founding Editor

JACK RABIN

Professor of Public Administration and Public Policy
The Pennsylvania State University—Harrisburg
School of Public Affairs
Middletown, Pennsylvania

Available Electronically

Principles and Practices of Public Administration, edited by Jack Rabin, Robert F. Munzenrider, and Sherrie M. Bartell

PublicADMINISTRATION*netBASE*

Handbook of Employee Benefits and Administration

Edited by

Christopher G. Reddick
The University of Texas
San Antonio, Texas, U.S.A.

Jerrell D. Coggburn
North Carolina State University
Raleigh, North Carolina, U.S.A.

 CRC Press
Taylor & Francis Group
Boca Raton   London   New York

CRC Press is an imprint of the
Taylor & Francis Group, an **Informa** business

CRC Press
Taylor & Francis Group
6000 Broken Sound Parkway NW, Suite 300
Boca Raton, FL 33487-2742

© 2008 by Taylor & Francis Group, LLC
CRC Press is an imprint of Taylor & Francis Group, an Informa business

No claim to original U.S. Government works
Printed in the United States of America on acid-free paper
10 9 8 7 6 5 4 3 2 1

International Standard Book Number-13: 978-1-4200-5192-6 (Hardcover)

Library of Congress Cataloging-in-Publication Data

Handbook of employee benefits and administration / editor(s), Christopher G. Reddick, Jerrell D. Coggburn.
    p. cm. -- (Public administration and public policy)
    Includes bibliographical references and index.
    ISBN 978-1-4200-5192-6 (hardback : alk. paper)
    1. Employee fringe benefits--United States. 2. Personnel management--United States. 3. Public administration--United States. I. Reddick, Christopher G. II. Coggburn, Jerrell D.

HD4928.N62U63529 2008
658.3'25--dc22   2008007019

Visit the Taylor & Francis Web site at
http://www.taylorandfrancis.com

and the CRC Press Web site at
http://www.crcpress.com

Dedicated to
Rachel and Abigail—CGR
Jackson—JDC

Contents

PART III: HEALTH AND RETIREMENT BENEFITS

PART IV: FINANCIAL MANAGEMENT
AND EMPLOYEE BENEFITS

PART V: CONTEMPORARY EMPLOYEE BENEFITS ISSUES

Preface

The *Handbook of Employee Benefits and Administration* is one of the first books that comprehensively covers the administration of employee benefits in public sector organizations. There is a rich array of chapters from leading scholars and practitioners in the field examining the contextual issues of employee benefits, health and retirement benefits, financial management and benefits, and contemporary issues in employee benefits. This book is unique as it covers both the social aspects of employee benefits and the financial elements. It will provide excellent reading in a course on human resource management, or as a stand-alone book in a course on employee benefits in both MBA and MPA programs.

Editors

Christopher G. Reddick is an associate professor and department chair in the Department of Public Administration at the University of Texas at San Antonio. Dr. Reddick's research and teaching interests are in all areas of public administration, with a focus on electronic government, public sector financial management, and employee health benefits. Some of his publications can be found in *Public Budgeting & Finance, Government Information Quarterly, Financial Accountability and Management, Social Science Computer Review, e-service Journal, Journal of e-government, International Journal of Electronic Government Research, Municipal Finance Journal*, and the *Review of Public Personnel Administration*.

Jerrell D. Coggburn is an associate professor and chair of public administration in the School of Public and International Affairs at North Carolina State University. His research interests include human resources management, public management, and public procurement. He is a past recipient (with Sandra K. Schneider and William G. Jacoby, 1997) of the William and Frederick Mosher award for the best public administration review article written by an academician. His research has appeared in *Public Administration Review, Journal of Public Administration Research and Theory, Review of Public Personnel Administration, Public Performance & Management Review*, and other scholarly outlets. He is a coeditor, with Khi V. Thai and Dianne Rahm, of *Handbook of Globalization and the Environment* (CRC Press, 2007). A life member of the American Society for Public Administration (ASPA), he serves on the editorial board of the *Review of Public Personnel Administration* and the executive board of ASPA's Section on Personnel Administration and Labor Relations. He received a BA (1992) in political science from Oklahoma State University and MPA (1994) and PhD (1999) degrees from the University of South Carolina. He previously served as a faculty member and department chair at the University of Texas at San Antonio.

Contributors

Ann Beck
Department of Government
   Law and International Affairs
Murray State University
Murray, Kentucky

James S. Bowman
Askew School of Public Administration
   and Policy
Florida State University
Tallahassee, Florida

N. Joseph Cayer
School of Public Affairs
Arizona State University
Phoenix, Arizona

Jerrell D. Coggburn
School of Public and International
   Affairs
North Carolina State University
Raleigh, North Carolina

Roddrick Colvin
Department of Public Management
The City University of New York
New York, New York

Elsie B. Crowell
Askew School of Public
   Administration and Policy
Florida State University
Tallahassee, Florida

Dennis M. Daley
Public Administration Department
North Carolina State University
Raleigh, North Carolina

Ilka M. Decker
Carl Vinson Institute of Government
University of Georgia
Athens, Georgia

Cary Elliott
Bates White, LLC
Formerly United States Congressional
   Budget Office
Washington, DC

Doug Goodman
Department of Political Science and
   Public Administration
Mississippi State University
Starkville, Mississippi

Charles W. Gossett
Department of Political Science
California State Polytechnic University
Pomona, California

Orla Gough
University of Westminster
London, United Kingdom

Rod Hick
University of Westminster
London, United Kingdom

Joseph H. Holland
Department of Political Science
and Public Administration
Mississippi State University
Starkville, Mississippi

Albert C. Hyde
Center for Executive Education
The Brookings Institution
Washington, DC

Justin Marlowe
Department of Public Administration
University of Kansas
Lawrence, Kansas

Dean Michael Mead
Governmental Accounting Standards
Board
Norwalk, Connecticut

Mark Musell
Robert F. Wagner Graduate School
of Public Service
New York University
New York, New York

Eddy S.W. Ng
Department of Management
and Human Resources
California State Polytechnic University
Pomona, California

Joan E. Pynes
Department of Government and
International Affairs
University of South Florida
Tampa, Florida

Christopher G. Reddick
Department of Public
Administration
The University of Texas at
San Antonio
San Antonio, Texas

Charlene M.L. Roach
School of Public Affairs
Arizona State University
Phoenix, Arizona

David Torregrosa
United States Congressional Budget
Office
Washington, DC

Jonathan P. West
Department of Political Science
University of Miami
Coral Gables, Florida

Anthony G. White
Division of Public Administration
Urban and Public Affairs
Portland State University
Portland, Oregon

OVERVIEW

I

Chapter 1

Employee Benefits Administration: An Introduction and Overview

Christopher G. Reddick and Jerrell D. Coggburn

CONTENTS

1.1 Introduction

"The pay is lousy, but the benefits are good!" So goes conventional wisdom on public sector compensation. Whether empirically justified or not (Reilly, Schoener, & Bolin 2007), public sector salaries and wages are commonly portrayed as lagging those of the private sector. To help offset this and retain competitiveness, public employers have developed relatively generous employee benefit packages (Schneider 2005). Together, this combination of direct compensation (pay) and benefits represents total compensation. In devising a total compensation strategy, employers follow one of the three compensation strategies: to lead, lag, or match the market (Society for Human Resource Management [SHRM] 2002).

From a public sector human resource management standpoint, conventional wisdom on public sector benefit presents both opportunities and challenges. On the one hand, having a widely perceived advantage should prove advantageous in a competitive market for human capital. To the extent that potential employees are attracted by generous benefit packages, public employment opportunities should appear attractive. On the other hand, maintaining such competitive advantage (assuming that it exists) may work to constrain public employers. In other words, ensuring that public employers maintain the image of the leader in benefits militates against adopting a strategy of lagging the market in this area. This, in turn, can create difficult choices for public employers as they attempt to reconcile rising costs and strained budgets with employee expectations and heightened demands for public services.

1.2 The Multiple Roles and Growing Importance of Benefits

Total compensation systems aim to achieve multiple goals, including attracting employees; retaining solid performers; motivating performance; spending compensation dollars wisely; aligning employees with organizational goals; and rewarding behavior the organization wants to encourage (SHRM 2002, p. 55). Because benefits are integral to the total compensation equation, they are inextricably linked to fundamental human resource purposes.

The magnitude of benefits continues to grow, with benefits (health, pension, and other benefits) constituting upwards of 40 percent of employee compensation (see Daley's chapter). Research indicates that public employees receive larger portions of their compensation in the form of benefits (Zorn 1994; Peterson 2004). Benefits have grown as a proportion of total compensation for a variety of reasons, including competition for employees, meeting an increasingly diverse set of employee expectations, favorable tax treatment, and the lower visibility of benefit enhancements relative to wage and salary increases (Kearney 2003; Roberts 2004).

1.3 The Cost Issue

Traditionally, government leaders have been reticent to provide large salary increases, opting instead to enhance employee and retiree benefit packages. This strategy has been favored because it is less visible and less likely to raise a public backlash (Moore 1991; Kearney 2003; Reilly, Schoener, & Bolin 2007). As this suggests, public sector benefits have been a relatively obscure topic. Such obscurity, however, has been replaced in recent years by scrutiny (Coggburn & Reddick 2007; Reilly, Schoener, & Bolin 2007). Fueled by widespread concern over spiraling healthcare costs and by high-profile pension fund troubles in places like San Diego and Milwaukee, employee benefits have emerged as a salient issue on the public agenda. In general, the dialogue centers on reducing costs.

Containing benefit costs is not a new goal (Bergmann, Bergmann, & Grahn 1994), but the means employed to attain that end have taken on a harsher tone in recent years. Private sector companies (e.g., automobile manufacturers, airlines) are backing away from previous commitments to employee and retiree health and pension plans on the grounds that their long-term costs cripple competitiveness and threaten survival.

The public sector is not immune to these pressures. Spiraling benefit costs have strained budgets and led to cost-containment efforts. Evidence from the local level suggests that governments are more likely to reduce their total workforces, cut or eliminate services, or increase taxes and other fees than they are to reduce employee salaries or benefits (Reilly, Schoener, & Bolin 2007). Governments have also responded by exploring ways to cut costs, share costs with employees and retirees, or perhaps even eliminating some benefits (Perry & Cayer 1997; Kearney 2003). Examples of such cost-containment strategies include introducing managed healthcare (e.g., health maintenance organization [HMO], preferred provider organization [PPO]), increasing employee co-payments and co-insurance rates, and shifting from defined benefit (DB) to defined contribution (DC) pension plans (Reddick & Coggburn 2007). The net result, as discussed in West and Bowman's chapter, is that employees are now shouldering greater burdens in securing their income security.

1.4 Overview of the Contents

The publication of the *Handbook of Employee Benefits and Administration* signals the growing importance of employee benefits from both policy and administrative standpoints. From a human resource policy perspective, decisions about which benefits to offer, to whom, and when have direct bearing upon the ultimate performance of public organizations. From an administrative perspective, organizations face practical challenges of skillfully managing an increasingly complex array of benefit offerings. These realities underscore the need for systematic inquiry into a host of questions related to employee benefits. The original chapters contained in this volume, written by respected public administration scholars, represent an attempt to contribute to understanding of employee benefits in the public sector. This book is unique because it brings together both scholars and practitioners in public human resource management and financial management for an understanding of the policy and administration of employee benefits. The handbook's goal is to shed light on current practice, enduring issues, and prospects for employee benefits in the public sector. In pursuing this goal, this handbook begins to address an important void in the public administration literature, where there remains a paucity of benefits-related research (Fredericksen & Soden 1998; Kearney 2003).

Part II, "The Context of Public Employee Benefits," opens with Daley's chapter on "Strategic Benefits in Human Resource Management." This chapter sets an important and pervasive theme for the handbook, namely, that employee benefits are an integral component of an effective human capital strategy. On the one hand, organizations need to recognize the various benefit needs and expectations of a diverse workforce. On the other hand, organizations need to be aware of how benefits can be structured so as to support important organizational purposes. In pursuing these arguments, Daley develops a "strategy–motivation matrix" which usefully frames employee needs (i.e., existence, relatedness, and growth) and organizations' strategic human resource purposes (i.e., attraction, retention, and motivation). This chapter then turns to a discussion of the array of benefits included in the matrix.

In "Employee Benefits: Weighing Ethical Principles and Economic Imperatives," West and Bowman explore two sets of values, economic and ethical, that underlie judgments about the provision of employee benefits. The authors describe how rapidly escalating benefit costs, particularly for health benefits, have tended to elevate economic considerations over all others as organizations cut back their benefits to contain costs. West and Bowman attempt to refocus decision makers' analytical approach. They do so by introducing a decision quadrant comprised of economic (good/bad) and ethical (right/wrong) axes, with best practice associated with decisions that are both economically good and ethically right. The authors examine a selection of employer-offered benefit programs through the lens of their analytical tool, thereby demonstrating its practicality and usefulness to decision makers.

Given the strategic importance of a competitive and comprehensive employee benefits package, an important question for public employers relates to the comparability of their benefit offerings with other employers. Making such comparisons, however, is not a straightforward task as specific benefit provisions may have differing value across types of workers and sectors of the economy. In "Comparing Federal Employee Benefits with Those in the Private Sector," Musell, Elliott, and Torregrosa report findings on one approach, developed by the United States Congressional Budget Office, for comparing public (federal) and private (nonfederal) benefits. The chapter is important reading for a number of reasons. First, it shows that the federal government's benefits tend to be more generous and due to benefit cuts (particularly in pension and healthcare), may be growing relatively more generous with time. Second, the chapter vividly demonstrates the often daunting challenges facing human resource researchers in making meaningful comparisons about the value of benefits.

Returning to the strategic theme introduced in Daley's chapter, Decker explores generational issues associated with employee benefits. Decker stresses the importance of organizations assessing the needs of their workforces, developing benefit programs that meet identified needs, and doing so within an overarching emphasis on aligning benefit programs and practices with operational goals and missions. This imperative is complicated by the growing diversity within organizations, including generational diversity. As Decker points out, the presence of workers from multiple generations—including matures, baby boomers, Generation X, Generation Y—yields a one-size-fits-all approach to employee benefits obsolete. In its place, organizations need to be more analytical, gathering data on workforce demographics, employee needs, and employees' awareness and utilization of benefits. Decker's chapter is important for practitioners in that it offers practical strategies for meeting the benefit challenges posed by intergenerational differences within the workforce.

In the final chapter of Part II, "The Social and Economic Context of Employee Healthcare Benefits," Beck examines factors affecting the provision and cost of healthcare benefits. Beck argues that the provision of employer-sponsored health benefits is unique compared to many other industrialized nations. Health insurance can be used to attract and retain employees. However, high healthcare spending in the United States limits the ability of citizens to address other priorities. Some of the factors that influence contemporary health insurance design decisions are the health insurance quality, quantity, costs, political culture, unionization, labor market, and salary.

In Part III, "Health and Retirement Benefits," the focus turns to the two pillars of employee benefits, healthcare and pensions. In "An Overview of Federal Retirement Benefits," Torregrosa, Elliott, and Musell provide a detailed examination of the United States federal government's pension and retiree healthcare programs. The authors draw important distinctions between the earlier Civil Service Retirement System (closed to new participants since 1983) and the Federal Employees' Retirement System, which covers most employees hired since January 1984. Echoing a theme from Chapter 4, the authors discuss certain federal benefit attributes, like inflation protection for defined benefit pensions and nearly identical healthcare premiums and coverage for plan participants (i.e., active employees and retirees), that make federal benefits more attractive than the typical postemployment benefits found in the private sector. This chapter also considers funding issues, drawing distinctions between the federal government's approach and that of subnational governments and private employers.

Picking up on the important differences in retirement benefit funding, Hyde's chapter states that the public pension issues in state and local governments focus on two core themes. The first theme, can state and local governments cope with the unfunded pension liability. Second, will state and local governments' public pension systems remain the last bastion of DB plans or will there be a movement to exclusively offering DC plans. Hyde makes the important conclusion that appropriate reward systems are at the heart of public sector employment, with these tough fiscal choices that state and local governments have to face will impact the future workforce in terms of retention.

Gough and Arkani chapter discusses retirement planning in the United Kingdom. These authors note that the United Kingdom's pension system is considerably less successful at replacing preretirement income than many other European Union countries. The authors note that there has been a shift in the United Kingdom like many other countries from DB to DC plans to transfer risk from employers to employees. There is a general under savings for retirement in the United Kingdom and a lack of trust by the British people with 24 percent of those surveyed do not trust government in relation to their pension. The voluntary pension system does not work well in the United Kingdom; therefore there is retirement under savings in the United Kingdom.

Beck's second contribution to the handbook, "Comparing Public and Private Sector Wage and Health Benefit Compensation," uses a variety of federal and other data to describe existing aggregate wage and benefit level information for both public and private employees. Beck believes that to understand employer costs and benefits one must first understand the wage compensation because most employers' health benefit costs are directly tied to employee wages. Overall, it appears that the typical public employee earns comparable wages than the private sector employees, supporting Baumol's hypothesis. Evidence shows that healthcare costs are much higher for public and private sector organizations because of the greater participation rate which drives up costs. Average wage and salary data from a variety of sources suggest that they are comparable between sectors, there appears to be some convergence.

Part IV, "Financial Management and Employee Benefits," begins with Marlowe's discussion of other postemployment benefits (OPEB) and the long-term costs of providing these benefits and accounting standards. Financial reporting of OPEB is used to understand the long-term financial implications of providing health benefits. The Government Accounting Standards Board (GASB) statements argue that state and local governments must account for these liabilities. All jurisdictions have in common is that financial management decisions about OPEB are made in a political environment. Critics have all raised concerns about the sticker shock of the possibility of disclosure of a large, unfunded OPEB liability, will prompt policy makers to take drastic action, including eliminating OPEB altogether to reduce their liability and protect their financial position.

White's chapter discusses the benefits and costs of the National Guard and Reserve, or the so-called citizen soldiers. This chapter discusses some of the costs and benefits to both the society and the individual faced with the prospect of being mobilized and to the organizations being impacted by the mobilization. The National Guard and Reserve component back up the traditional military force. The National Guard and Reserve create more of a job ready military personnel, as opposed to the active duty soldiers of the Armed Forces. This chapter outlines some of the important employee benefits from federal and state governments for this important component of the military.

Crowell's chapter provides a concise overview of the privatization (including outsourcing) movement, as embodied in New Public Management and championed by public choice theorists. The effects of this broad movement are then related to the specific case of public sector human resources. Human resources are the fastest growing area in outsourcing (Gay & Essinger 2000). The rationales underlying human resources outsourcing range from the mundane (e.g., cost savings) to the elegant (e.g., allowing organizations to focus on core human resources strategy) (Rainey 2005). In the specific area of benefits, outsourcing promises to improve employee access and flexibility (e.g., through automated self-service applications) and choice. Crowell draws upon her decades of public service experience in Florida to focus attention on that state's People First outsourcing initiative. As she illustrates, the road to outsourcing is fraught with danger, including inflated expectations, unrealized benefits, unanticipated consequences, technological glitches, and lost institutional knowledge and expertise. She concludes by noting that outsourcing is not a panacea and calling for additional research in this area.

Mead's chapter discusses the types of financial information that state and local governments need. The opaque nature of government transactions between taxpayers and government calls for extraordinary efforts by government to demonstrate their accountability to the public that they are proper stewards of resources through financial statements. The GASB has specific standards that exist for pensions and OPEB, which this author discusses.

Finally, in Part V, "Contemporary Employee Benefits Issues," the handbook examines several benefit issues facing public sector employees and employers. Cayer and Roach's chapter on "Work–Life Benefits" provides a fitting introduction to these issues. The authors describe important shifts in demographics and societal expectations that are affecting the workplace. For instance, the workforce is becoming increasingly diverse in a number of respects, including, gender, race and ethnicity, age, marital status, and sexual preference. At the same time, employees are working more hours than ever before, a fact that can create stress as the time and energy needed for activities and issues outside of the workplace dissipate. Given this, many organizations have developed work–life benefits which, as Cayer and Roach note "reflect the need for adjusting benefit packages to differing needs of employees and to their lifestyle concerns." This chapter examines a number of typical work–life benefits, including flexible work schedules, dependent care, employee assistance programs, and wellness programs. Such offerings are important from the standpoint of increasing employee job satisfaction, effort, and commitment, decreasing their stress over unmet personal roles and responsibilities outside the workplace, and improving the organization's employee retention and productivity.

Rapid technological changes and an increasingly global environment are among the forces creating the need for knowledgeable and adaptive workforces. This need is challenged by rising tuition costs, declining access to affordable financial aid, and changing population demographics, which see increases in the number groups and individuals historically underrepresented in higher education. These are among the issues explored in Pynes' chapter on higher education benefits. Pynes argues that individuals, organizations, and society benefit from investments in higher education, hence, higher education benefits should be factored into organizational human resource planning. Such benefits represent strategic investments in employees, investments that signal employer commitment to employees and accrue performance benefits to the organization. Recognizing that not all public organizations can support tuition reimbursement, Pynes identifies several other strategies that aim to promote this most important of employee benefits.

Holland and Goodman's chapter examines differences between DB pension plans—predominate in the public sector—and DC pension plans, and the implications for transitioning to DC plans. The shift to DC plans is easier to administer because employees have the responsibility for retirement planning. The purpose of their research is to determine if transitioning to DC plans employees can make better decisions about their retirement planning given their level of financial literacy. The overall conclusion from this empirical study is that employees need to be more familiar with the financial world to make intelligent decisions on employee benefits.

Gossett and Ng's chapter examines what has been, at times, a controversial employee benefits issue—domestic partner benefits. Private sector employers have adopted domestic partner benefits at an impressive rate relative to the public sector, largely on the grounds that it is important from a human capital perspective (e.g., being competitive in the labor market for new talent, improving employee retention, etc.). In the public sector, these same human capital considerations are important, but so too are more fundamental concerns like fairness and equal treatment under the law. Gossett brings needed clarity to what is meant by "domestic partner," highlights the challenges facing human resource professionals in implementing domestic partner benefits, and examines both financial and legal implications facing policy makers and employers who have decided to recognize domestic partners in their respective benefit programs.

Colvin in his chapter discusses that employees who are interested in creating transgender friendly workplaces must change or implement policies that do not discriminate against those employees. Work environments will continue to become more diverse and the demand for more specialized benefits to meet these needs of all employees should increase. There is a new realm of specialized benefits for gender identity, medical benefits for transgender employees remain the most underutilized components of a comprehensive transgender inclusive workplace.

References

Bergmann, T.J., Bergmann, M.A., & Grahn, J.L. 1994. How important are employee benefits to public sector employees. *Public Personnel Management* 23(4): 397–406.

Coggburn, J.D. & Reddick, C.G. 2007. Public pension management: Issues and trends. *International Journal of Public Administration* 30(10): 995–1020.

Fredericksen, P.J. & Soden, D.L. 1998. Employee attitudes toward benefit packaging: The job sector dilemma. *Review of Public Personnel Administration* 18(3): 23–41.

Gay, C.L. & Essinger, J. 2000. *Inside Outsourcing: An Insider's Guide to Strategic Sourcing.* London: Nicholas Brealey Publishing.

Kearney, R.C. 2003. The determinants of state employee compensation. *Review of Public Personnel Administration* 23(4): 305–322.

Moore, P. 1991. Comparison of state and local employee benefits and private employee benefits. *Public Personnel Management* 20(4): 429–439.

Peterson, J. 2004. Retirement rage. *Governing Magazine* 62.

Perry, R.W. & Cayer, N.J. 1997. Factors affecting municipal satisfaction with health care plans. *Review of Public Personnel Administration* 17(2): 5–19.

Rainey, G.W., Jr. 2005. Human resource consultants and outsourcing: Focusing on local government. In Condrey, S.E. (Ed.), *Handbook of Human Resource Management in Government* (2nd ed., pp. 701–734). San Francisco, California: Jossey-Bass.

Reddick, C.G. & Coggburn, J.D. 2007. State employee health benefits in the United States: Choices and effectiveness. *Review of Public Personnel Administration* 27(1): 5–20.

Reilly, T., Schoener, S., & Bolin, A. 2007. Public sector compensation in local governments: An analysis. *Review of Public Personnel Administration* 27(1): 39–58.

Roberts, G.E. 2004. Municipal government benefits practices and personnel outcomes: Results from a national survey. *Public Personnel Management* 33(1): 1–22.

Schneider, M. 2005. The status of U.S. public pension plans. *Review of Public Personnel Administration* 25(2): 107–137.

Society for Human Resource Management (SHRM). 2002. *The Fundamentals of Human Resource Management*. Alexandria, Virginia: SHRM.

Zorn, P. 1994. PPCC survey results. *Government Finance Review* 10(8): 46–48.

THE CONTEXT OF PUBLIC EMPLOYEE BENEFITS

Chapter 2

Strategic Benefits in Human Resource Management

Dennis M. Daley

CONTENTS

Success is ultimately dependent upon people. This is the task set for strategic human resource management. All human resource practices can be framed within a strategic focus. Each needs to be linked to how best to achieve organizational goals. Strategic compensation links all pay and benefits to attracting, retaining, and motivating employees. Although some pay and most benefit options will be inflexible (i.e., equally provided to all employees), these can be designed to aid in recruiting desired employees and for encouraging their continued commitment. Other pay options (e.g., the various pay-for-performance schemes) are flexible devices for motivating or enticing added effort.

Every manager and employee knows how important individuals are to success. Despite our machinelike analogies, the positions described with their listed responsibilities and requisite qualifications are not a set of interchangeable parts. People make a difference. Attracting individuals and keeping them is the foremost ingredient in creating a successful organization.

Adequate compensation is one of the factors that can attract individuals. Adequate compensation also helps to retain them once they have been hired. A vacant position (or one filled with the wrong individual) is not costless. Work is not being done (or done poorly), and a mission is going unfulfilled. More importantly, by focusing employees' attention on a desire for continued employment, it also focuses their attention on the long-term health and well-being of the organization (so it will be able to offer them that much-desired continued employment).

2.1 Benefits and Motivation

Although public sector pay has often lagged behind than in the private sector, its benefits (especially the pensions, due process, and job security) have compensated for that in their ability to attract and retain employees. Because governments discriminate less than private sector companies do, even its pay policies have often been attractive.

Benefits are a major component in compensation. They can compose from 20 to 40 percent of the total compensation package. Yet, benefits are a hodgepodge. Mainly composed of healthcare and retirement pension programs, benefits also include a vast array of miscellaneous services. Further complicating matters is the fact that not all benefits are tangible; many offer intrinsic incentives that are difficult to place a dollar value on. Furthermore, the value of benefits, even those with clear price tags, actually will vary from individual to individual depending upon the actual use. However, benefits still serve the same set of purposes that pay does—to attract, retain, and motivate employees.

Because benefits compose a growing proportion of the total compensation package, it is necessary to treat benefits with the same strategic considerations as wage and salary decisions are subjected to. Although benefits are more likely to satisfy attraction and retention needs than to be motivational, this latter role should not be overlooked. Hence, organizationally specific information on benefits desired by employees, whether public and private is important (Moore, 1991; Bergmann, Bergmann, and Grahn, 1994; Davis and Ed Ward, 1995; Streib, 1996).

Clayton Alderfer (1972) in his Existence-Relatedness-Growth (ERG) theory has modified Abraham Maslow's needs hierarchy. Maslow's five stages have been "turned on their side" and regrouped into three concepts. No longer are we dealing with a vertical hierarchy of "lower" and "higher" level needs, but with a horizontal arrangement of equal needs. Existence combines Maslow's physiological and safety needs. Relatedness encompasses the social and esteem needs. Growth represents the self-actualization stage (with the emphasis perhaps placed a bit more upon its training and development components). In Alderfer's motivation model relatedness assumes a pivotal role in balancing and adjusting the mix between existence and growth needs. In addition, Alderfer recognizes growth as an asymmetric component whose satisfaction does not lead to satiation. These models posit that individuals offer "motivation" in a voluntary exchange for need fulfillment.

Combining the Maslow–Alderfer needs model with our three strategic purposes of attraction, retention, and motivation creates a strategy–motivation matrix. This matrix outlines how various benefits can be used to both meet employee's needs and the organization's purposes.

	Attraction	*Retention*	
Existence	Pay	Pay	Pay-for-performance
	Health insurance	Health insurance	
		Retirement pension	
		Disability income	
Relatedness		Wellness programs (gyms)	Professional conferences
		Cafeterias, health services, etc.	
		Social events (sports, parties, etc.)	
		Family-friendly policies	
Growth		Employee assistance programs	Educational and training benefits
			Professional conferences
			Recognition awards

2.2 Healthcare

One of the two primary benefits sought by employees is health insurance (Perry and Cayer, 1997). Modern medical costs for hospital care will run into the tens of thousands of dollars in a matter of a few days for even a minor illness. Something that requires intensive care indeed truly merits the name catastrophic not only in terms of its life-threatening nature but also in respect to its exponential costs. Fears of illness and the subsequent devastating financial burdens that they can impose are quite disquieting. Health benefits are an invaluable tool in recruiting and retaining employees.

2.2.1 Health Insurance

Health insurance is the means by which these fears can be allayed. In addition to major medical expenses, health insurance can also inexpensively aid in alleviating other health-related threats to motivation and productivity. Health insurance plans may include additional provisions for prescription drug, mental health, dental, and eye care benefits. What is included and the extent of that coverage varies substantially from plan to plan.

The basic healthcare covered under insurance plans is likely to be separated into segments requiring different levels of co-payments. Preventive care as found in an annual physical examination and periodic eye and dental checkups is often fully reimbursed (directly paid by the insurance company to reduce paperwork and delays) and exempt from any deductible provisions. Relatively common, minor medical procedures may be reimbursed at a 90 percent level. More serious or long-term (but not catastrophic, life threatening in nature) illnesses may require a 50/50 match. Catastrophic care (e.g., cancer and heart disease) whether as part of the general policy or as an additional or optional benefit again provides something about 80 or 90 percent reimbursement. Because the cost of catastrophic care quickly escalates into the hundreds of thousands of dollars, even at these reimbursement levels the co-payment requirements are substantial.

Employer-provided health plans usually provide options for family coverage (paid in full or part by the organization or entirely at the employee's expense). Concerns about the health of family members can adversely affect an employee's productivity. Hence, the extension of health benefits to family members is necessary (Gossett, 1994; Hostetler and Pynes, 1995).

Health insurance is an essential item in recruitment. Whether searching for basic employment or professional positions individuals are aware of the healthcare dilemma. A compensation package with health benefits (including family coverage) is second only to salary. In addition, health benefits can be a strong retention factor. This is especially true where pre-existing conditions are involved.

2.2.2 Disability Income

Although health insurance covers the costs of obtaining medical care, it does not itself address the loss of income that also occurs due to illness. Workmen's compensation legally covers employees for job-related accidents. Sick leave provides an employee with pay during short-term illness. This encourages employees to take care of themselves when necessary, instead of attempting to "gut it out" only to lapse into a more long-term illness. It also removes potentially infectious individuals from the workplace. In addition, sick leave can be used for medical appointments and caring for ill family members (Garcia, 1987; Kroesser, Meckley, and Ranson, 1991).

Although part of the social security program covers long-term disability, the amounts may not be enough to fully or adequately replace the lost wages and salaries. Disability insurance for replacing the lost income (enabling one to continue paying for the ongoing expenses that that level of income was financing) is often provided. Short-term disability policies can often provide 100 percent of pay replacement for up to a month and replace 50 percent of pay over the next six months. Long-term disability (often integrated with, i.e., reduced by, social security) can replace two-thirds of pay until the disabled employee reaches age 65. In case of permanent disability, long-term medical care insurance for home healthcare and nursing homes may be necessary (albeit this is quite expensive and seldom provided as an organization-paid benefit).

Sick leave is used and thereby costs an organization. Patterns of use should be examined with the thought for the introduction of cost-effective preventive action. Unfortunately, sick leave abuse also does occur. This needs to be treated. However, it must be first established that there is indeed a case of abuse. Anti-abuse policies where there is no abuse or only a few cases can undermine employee morale and trust.

Disability income is not as readily recognized among employees as an important protection. Hence, it serves primarily as a retention device. Because market-based disability policies can be purchased, it probably receives less weight than other factors.

2.2.3 Wellness

Wellness programs focus on preventative healthcare. They undertake to encourage behaviors that lead to good health and ease stress. They encourage individuals to exercise, eat healthily, and give up hazardous habits. Many of these activities are geared to behaviors that are associated with the risk of cancer and heart disease—two of the costliest insured illnesses (Erfurt, Foote, and Heirich, 1992).

As part of such efforts, organizations may actually establish gyms or health spas for their employees or, alternatively, subsidize memberships (with reimbursement linked to actual spa/club attendance). Many large organizations construct walking trails around and build their parking lots at the edge of their campuses. As a social activity, employee sports teams may be encouraged.

Cafeterias help insure that employees eat a proper diet. They also insure that employees are readily available for lunchtime emergencies. Vending machines can be stocked with fruits and other acceptable snacks. Nutritional information is made available to employees. Because obesity is a major problem among Americans (and contributes to heart disease and stroke), weight loss programs are also sponsored.

Wellness programs may be viewed by employees more as perquisites than a part of the overall healthcare benefit. As such, their availability can be a retention factor. This is especially true where they help to establish social relationships among individuals.

2.2.4 Employee Assistance Programs

For individual employees the availability of counseling, drug and alcohol treatment, and other aspects of employee assistance programs (EAP) can be quite encouraging (Johnson, 1986; Johnson and O'Neill, 1989; Perry and Cayer, 1992). Employee assistance programs represent the personnel function in its most positive, humanistic mode. The initial success with alcohol treatment led to the expansion of EAPs. Today they not only deal with other serious illnesses such as drug dependency and psychological disorders but also with family and financial problems. In addition, some EAPs include career counseling, weight control, and related wellness activities.

Employee assistance programs treat the whole person. Organizations are cognizant that nonwork behaviors and personal problems can adversely affect an employee's work. They also recognize that their individual employees are valuable resources. Each employee represents a substantial human investment in job training and organizational socialization. Although termination and replacement is an option, it is often the least preferred and last resort. Hence, efforts spent in helping employees solve their problems are worthwhile for the organization.

Employee assistance programs have also been the source of economical personnel functions. Family and marriage counseling services have formed the nucleus for alternate dispute resolution and mediation processes. Their very independence and confidentiality has helped in resolving conflicts. Family finances and budget planning have opened the door to financial planning for retirement (and other major life goals).

Employee assistance programs address problems. Helping people resolve their problems and pursue a successful career can contribute greatly to employee loyalty and retention.

2.2.5 Retirement and Pensions

Modern medicine has for the first time created a world in which there are substantial numbers of "older" people. This is actually a relatively new phenomenon. Until the twentieth century, old age was a rarity and an exceedingly short affair. Today, there are not only more people living into their 60s and 70s, but also one in which life expectancies well into the 80s and 90s are not at all uncommon. In fact, the baby boom generation (those born between 1946 and 1964) is actually creating a permanent age shift in the population demographics.

Psychological perceptions are slowly adjusting to these changes (over 50 is still seen as old). With today's health standards and life expectancies now between

75 and 85 years, individuals are quite capable of productive work for far longer than those of a generation or so ago are.

Not to provide the individual with some form of postemployment financial security would cause the same worries and resultant adverse effects on productivity as failing to provide for health insurance. To insure employees' current commitment and attention on productivity, future security must be guaranteed.

2.2.6   Retirement Income

Retirement from employment need not mean that an individual ceases to work. Although many individuals need to continue working to supplement their retirement income, many also undertake new employment for the enjoyment or activity it affords them. Voluntary and nonprofit organizations become the focus attention for many of the still active elderly. Dynamic, public service careers are often the result. However, to engage in such pursuits requires financial security.

Although all projections are subject to the vagaries of individual preferences and inflationary changes, general estimates suggest that a minimum figure from 80 to 85 percent of preretirement income is necessary to maintain one's lifestyle during retirement.

The money to provide this future stream of income during retirement is derived from social security, pensions, and individual savings. It is highly unlikely that any individual will be able to enjoy a financially secure retirement without contributions from all three sources.

The Social security system provides a foundation for retirement. Social security guarantees a basic pension to virtually every American worker. Social security is a defined benefit plan with redistributive provisions for poorer workers. On average social security replaces 40 percent of preretirement income. This will vary from 50 percent of preretirement income for salaries under $20,000 to 25 percent of preretirement income for salaries over $50,000. This makes the pension and savings components of the retirement equation all the more important. These will be expected to assume an even greater role in underwriting future retirement benefits.

Pensions are categorized either as defined benefit or defined contribution plans. Pensions are funded through salary reduction contributions from the employee and matching payments from the employer. The Employee Retirement Income Security Act of 1974 (ERISA) establishes a ten year vesting requirement for private sector organizations (five years is more common); in general, its procedures have been voluntarily adopted among public organizations.

The Baby Boom generation desired defined benefit programs that implied lifetime careers and rewarded such loyalty. Generations X and Y envision a career involving multiple job changes that enhance their personal growth. For them the portability of defined contributions is valued.

Most plans require that the employee obtains the age of 65 (earlier retirement beginning at age 55 or 62 at a reduced benefit level may be available) before receiving benefits. Police and firefighters are commonly required to retire at 55 due to the physical (and psychological) demands involved in their jobs. The Tax Reform Act of 1976 requires that pensions begin paying-out by age 70 and a half (even if the employee is not formally retired).

Equally important in many cases is the need to retain employees past "retirement" or to have phased retirement option. Critical shortages and higher salaries can pose serious barriers. Deferred retirement option plans (DROP) are being introduced to address this concern. In DROP, an employee continues working. However, their retirement is now calculated differently. Instead of continuing in the regular pension plan (whose benefits may be capped or minimal), the employee is provided a "new, defined contribution plan" into which the organizations "drops" what would have been the regular plans retirement payouts. Hence, on retirement the employee receives both their regular payments (calculated based on years of service and salary prior to entering the DROP, i.e., the same amount that has been dropped into the new account) and the DROP account. The DROP can be paid out either as a lump sum or as an additional pension (Calhoun and Tepfer, 1999a,b).

Traditionally, pensions were defined benefit plans. Under a defined benefit plan, an individual is guaranteed from 50 to 75 percent of their highest salary upon retirement. Alternatively, their retirement benefit may be calculated based on 2 to 3 percent of the highest salary multiplied by the number of years of service. Most systems also define "highest salary" in terms of a three to five year average.

Defined benefit plans are not readily portable from one employer to another. Hence, they can somewhat discourage job changes that might otherwise be beneficial to both the individual and the organization. Under a uniform system that provided pensions calculated on 2 percent of highest salary multiplied by years of service, two individuals who shared identical salary histories would receive different pensions if one had changed jobs. Assume two individuals were paid $20,000 at the end of ten years, $40,000 after twenty years, and $60,000 on the completion of thirty years. An individual who had been employed for the entire thirty years by one organization would be eligible for a pension of $36,000. An individual who changed jobs every ten years, on the other hand, would qualify for three separate pensions of $4,000, $8,000, and $12,000—a total pension of only $24,000 (Hegji, 1993).

The defined contribution plan does not suffer from a portability problem. It is based entirely on each year's employee and employer contribution. These funds are invested, and their growth and accumulation is the basis for future retirement income. The defined contribution plans are less generous to long-term employees as they dispense with the multiplier effect found in the defined contribution plans.

Although cash-balance plans combine features from both defined benefit and defined contribution plans, they are closer to the latter in their overall effect. Like defined benefit plans, the money (made up entirely of the employer's contribution; a separate employee 401k may also be available) placed in the pension fund is guaranteed to return a predetermined benefit regardless of actual performance. If the fund (which is theoretically invested) fails to achieve this growth, the organization "makes-up the difference." Because cash-balance plans usually set their rate of return at a conservative money market level (4–5 percent), a short fall is unlikely. In fact, most cash-balance plans earn a substantial return on investment. Cash-balance, like defined contribution, plans avoid the longevity bonus that a defined benefit plan entails.

The major retirement arena for individual savings is the 401k and 403b tax-sheltered, supplemental retirement accounts. The tax code (from whence the 401k and 403b terminology is derived) encourages this form of retirement savings. In addition to employee–employer funded retirement pensions, individuals may also make tax-deferred contributions to a retirement account. Income tax on the principle (and the interest it earns) is deferred until it is withdrawn from the account during retirement (when the individual is usually in a lower tax bracket). As mentioned above, at age 70 and a half the distribution of retirement benefits must begin.

Although psychologically discounted as being something "a longtime away," employees are aware of retirement pensions. They are a third factor in recruitment and can be a major consideration in retention (especially with regard to defined benefit programs).

2.2.7 Health and Family Considerations

Providing income for the individual employee in retirement is not the sole concern of pensions. With retirement projected to last from ten to twenty years, healthcare is also a concern. Many individuals see Medicare as a basic, minimum level of service. Supplemental health insurance and long-term care insurance (home healthcare and nursing home coverage) may be included in ongoing employee benefit packages.

Family concerns prior to and during retirement are also important matters. Many organizations provide employees with life insurance (in multiples of their salary, usually about 1½ times earnings). Optional group life insurance policies may also be available for purchase (with a benefit ranging from one to three times earnings). In the event of their early death, the life insurance will provide for their families. Although the family would receive some benefits from the accumulated pension fund, these might not yet amount to much (or become available only later). Hence, life insurance serves as a financial bridge. Terminally ill employees may also be provided with the option for a "living benefit." A living benefit allows the employee to borrow against (or sell the rights to) the policy's death benefit to cover expenses during their terminal illness. Such options assume that the surviving family, if any, is not denied support.

Adequate retirement income is not usually the concern of just one person; in many cases, there is a spouse and perhaps dependent children involved. Although many spouses will have pension rights of their own, others will not. Benefits to take care of the survivor in their retirement are also an issue (Nielson and Beehr, 1994). Under the Retirement Equity Act of 1984, pensions must include provisions for a joint-and-survivor annuity within the plan itself or through an insurance option.

2.3 Other Perks and Rewards

Perquisites and rewards primarily serve to retain employees. These provide an array of "creature comforts" that although less important than salary, healthcare, and pensions are still highly valued. Many of these other rewards can be used for motivational purposes, as there is no need to automatically provide them to everyone.

Although clearly designed to make the organization better able to cope with its environment, employee development is also a major individual benefit. The knowledge-based organization must invest in its people if it is to exist. Yet, that very investment in people improves and adds value to those people. Education, training, and professional conferences are all means of enhancing organizational productivity. Because it is more economical to hold conferences in major locations, they also serve the social benefit of providing the employee with a "paid vacation."

Employee development has the added advantage of not only enhancing technical skills but also psychologically motivating the individuals involved. The organizational investment is recognition of the employee's worth. The added skills although paid for by the organization belong to the individual. For the organization to fully obtain the benefits of its education and training programs, it must keep the individual. This implies a long-term relationship and fosters organizational commitment and loyalty.

Tuition reimbursement and educational leave are two means of encouraging employees to add to their knowledge and skills. Prior approval of course work is required in tuition reimbursement programs. They also usually stipulate that courses are job-related and that the minimum of a "B" letter grade (or equivalent) be earned. Educational leave may vary from a flextime arrangement (with work hours made up) to granting paid time-off for courses. A few public organizations (such as the military) even send employees to school as their duty assignment.

Business expenses are also paid for or provided by the organization. Employee equipment, parking, transportation, and vehicles can be furnished or subsidized. Uniform or clothing allowances can be included. On-site childcare (including sick baby care) facilities may be available (Suntrup, 1989; Kossek and Nichol, 1992). All of these items help defray the direct costs of going to work.

Indirectly, organizations can subsidize living expenses. They can provide housing allowances and underwrite mortgages. They may actually provide the housing itself (in locations convenient to the organizations offices). Commissaries and cafeterias can reduce food costs. Other retail services may also be made available to employees at discounted rates. In recruitment relocation and temporary housing expenses are often paid. In some cases, the organization may even assist in the sale (including buying) of an existing house.

Social activities designed to build teamwork and a sense of "family" loyalty can be undertaken. The organization can create clubs (and even build or help the community build various sport facilities); it can organize parties and outings. Even a newsletter can be used to allow employees to place short ads.

Family-friendly benefits recognize the demographic changes that have made women a permanent part of the modern workforce. Because women in the workforce still bear the major brunt of family responsibilities, organizations are finding that they must make adjustments to accommodate these requirements. Flextime schedules (geared to school hours) and daycare are only two of the most well-known benefits. Educational assistance (tutoring, scholarships, school matching, etc.) for dependents may be offered. Trailing spouse programs are used in recruitment ranging from assisting in job searches to actually creating a job for the spouse.

Although family-friendly benefits are much in vogue, their actual existence is rather sparse. Most organizations go little beyond healthcare assistance and flexible work schedules (Osterman, 1995; Durst, 1999; Newman and Mathews, 1999). Because the mostly male upper-level managers primarily design benefit packages, the need for family-friendly options has not registered as a priority. In part, this is also due to the lack of empirical evidence supporting the benefits of family-friendly benefits. Durst (1999) notes that personnel managers perceive a relationship between family-friendly benefits and an organization's recruitment (albeit the causal direction of this relationship remains uncertain). These personnel managers also see the provision of family-friendly options as successfully affecting employee satisfaction and organization results. However, they are unable to produce concrete, empirical evidence in support of these contentions.

Cafeteria benefit plans attempt to fine-tune the benefits offered by allowing the individual to allocate their benefit dollars among those options that they themselves deem most useful. Some benefit programs are obviously mandatory for all employees. However, many others are merely in the desirable category. Although many employees may often desire them, for others they are clearly inappropriate. To provide these benefits to all employees is a waste of resources (Barber, Dunham, and Formisano, 1992).

2.4   Conclusion

Benefits compose a substantial 20–40 percent of the compensation package. To ignore their strategic potential for attracting, retaining, and motivating is reckless. Healthcare and pensions are items that every individual knows to be concerned with. Hence, they serve a major role in attracting individuals to an organization. Once hired, these and the other benefit options are important tools in retaining valued employees.

References

Alderfer, C. 1972. *Existence, Relatedness, and Growth: Human Needs in Organizational Settings.* New York: Free Press.

Barber, A.E., R.B. Dunham, and R.A. Formisano. 1992. The impact of flexible benefits on employee satisfaction: A field study, *Personnel Psychology 45*,1 (Spring): 55–75.

Bergmann, T.J., M.A. Bergmann, and J.L. Grahn. 1994. How important are employee benefits to public: Sector employees? *Public Personnel Management 23*,3 (Fall): 397–406.

Calhoun, C.V. and A.H. Tepfer. 1999a. Deferred Retirement Option Plans ("DROP" Plans), part 1. *IPMA News* (August): 13, 15.

Calhoun, C.V. and A.H. Tepfer. 1999b. Deferred Retirement Option Plans ("DROP" Plans), part 2. *IPMA News* (September): 13, 15.

Davis, E. and Ed Ward. 1995. Health benefit satisfaction in the public and private sectors: The role of distributive and procedural justice, *Public Personnel Management 24*,3 (Fall): 255–270.

Durst, S. 1999. Assessing the effect of family friendly programs on public organizations, *Review of Public Personnel Administration 19*,3 (Summer): 19–33.

Erfurt, J.C., A. Foote, and M.A. Heirich. 1992. The cost-effectiveness of worksite wellness programs for hypertension control, weight loss, smoking cessation, and exercise, *Personnel Psychology 45*,1 (Spring): 5–27.

Garcia, R.L. 1987. Sick-time usage by management and professional employees in the public sector, *Review of Public Personnel Administration 7*,3 (Summer): 45–59.

Gossett, C.W. 1994. Domestic partnership benefits, *Review of Public Personnel Administration 14*,1 (Winter): 64–84.

Hegji, C.E. 1993. A note on job transfer, pension portability, and compensating salary differentials, *Review of Public Personnel Administration 13*,1 (Winter): 76–86.

Hostetler, D. and J.E. Pynes. 1995. Domestic partnership benefits: Dispelling the myths, *Review of Public Personnel Administration 15*,1 (Winter): 41–59.

Johnson, A. 1986. A comparison of employee assistance programs in corporate and government organizational contexts, *Review of Public Personnel Administration 6*,2 (Spring): 28–42.

Johnson, A. and N. O'Neill. 1989. Employee assistance programs and the troubled employee in the public sector workplace, *Review of Public Personnel Administration 9*,3 (Summer): 66–80.

Kossek, E.E. and V. Nichol. 1992. The effect of on-side child care on employee attitude and performance, *Personnel Psychology 45*,3 (Autumn): 485–509.

Kroesser, H.L., R.F. Meckley, and J.T. Ranson. 1991. Selected factors affecting employees' sick leave use, *Public Personnel Management 20*,2 (Summer): 171–180.

Moore, P. 1991. Comparison of state and local employee benefits and private employee benefits, *Public Personnel Management 20*,4 (Winter): 429–440.

Newman, M. and K. Mathews. 1999. Federal family-friendly policies: Barriers to effective implementation, *Review of Public Personnel Administration 19*,3 (Summer): 34–48.

Nielson, N.L. and T.A. Beehr. 1994. Retirement income for surviving spouses, *Public Personnel Management 23*,3 (Fall): 407–428.

Osterman, P. 1995. Work/family program and the employment relationship, *Administrative Science Quarterly 40*,4 (December): 681–700.

Perry, R.W. and N.J. Cayer. 1992. Evaluating employee assistance programs: Concerns and strategies for public employees, *Public Personnel Management 21*,3 (Fall): 323–333.

Perry, R.W. and N.J. Cayer. 1997. Factors affecting municipal satisfaction with health care plans, *Review of Public Personnel Administration 17*,2 (Spring): 5–19.

Streib, G. 1996. Specialty health care services in municipal government, *Review of Public Personnel Administration 16*,2 (Spring): 57–72.

Suntrup, E.L. 1989. Child-care delivery systems in the government sector, *Review of Public Personnel Administration 10*,1 (Fall): 48–59.

Chapter 3

Employee Benefits: Weighing Ethical Principles and Economic Imperatives

Jonathan P. West and James S. Bowman

CONTENTS

3.1   Introduction

Despite claims of increased economic empowerment by political and corporate leaders, the shift of economic risk from employers to employees and their families has left large segments of society feeling financially insecure (Hacker, 2006). Unpredictable healthcare premiums and retirement benefits, fear of job loss, catastrophic medical costs, partial health insurance coverage, an uncertain future for Medicare (and to a lesser extent Social Security), and an increase of part-time and temporary work undercut personal responsibility advocates (Norquist, 2005) who extol the virtues of individual economic management in an "ownership society."

As employers focus on the economics of managing human resources, notably employee benefits in the public sector, economic values can often subsume other values. In highlighting ethical considerations in benefit policy and administration, this chapter first examines background material pertinent to the issue, including an analytical tool that makes explicit ethical and economic values. The central portion of the chapter considers selected benefit programs and their ramifications. Two case studies follow that feature ethical issues in benefit administration, one dealing with a county taxpayer-funded tuition refund program and the other with outsourcing state human resource services. The final section concludes with a brief summary and discussion of the utility of the analysis.

3.2   Background

To provide a backdrop to the ethics of benefit administration, this section briefly reviews (1) relevant national trends, (2) the importance of benefits to employers and employees, and (3) the human resource profession as the administrator of benefits. A decision-making matrix, useful in addressing ethical and economic trade-offs in benefit policy and administration is also described. In general, the public sector offers more types of plans, covering a larger portion of its workforce, than the private sector, and it has been less successful than the corporate world in controlling benefit costs.

Employer-provided benefits have increased markedly over the past seven decades and benefit-related costs have risen even more dramatically. In 1935 benefits accounted for less than one percent of total labor costs (Gerhardt and Milkovich, 1994), a figure that increased to 44 percent by 2006 (U.S. Chamber of Commerce, 2007). It is not surprising, therefore, that public and private organizations are cutting back benefit packages. One consequence, according to Lucero and Allen (1994), is a violation of the psychological contract with workers, creating conflict between employer policies and employee needs. Using deprivation theory, they show how a history of benefit provision creates high expectations, which are dashed when curtailed:

> When benefits are reduced, it is likely that employees experience feelings of both procedural and distributive injustice. From a distributive perspective, they can be dissatisfied with reductions in benefits or with having to pay some or all of the costs associated with benefits which, historically, had been provided at employer expense. Employees are also likely to experience procedural injustice if policies and procedures are perceived as unfair or leading to unfair outcomes. (p. 433)

As Hacker (2006) points out, this is one reason why many people believe that the safety net in today's society is unraveling. Risks once managed by employers are increasingly being transferred to their employees, causing hardship and anxiety in the workforce.

The ethics of benefits also requires a sense of their significance as well as their vulnerability to abuse. In general, and as just noted, both employers and employees regard benefits as a prominent part of compensation, although some personnel still mistakenly take them for granted as an automatic entitlement (Berman et al., 2006). More specifically, the benefits function is vulnerable to abuse when compared to some other functions when the frequency and seriousness of misconduct are considered. Although unethical behavior is perceived lower for benefits than for some HR functional areas (employment; health, safety, and security; compensation), it is regarded as higher for others (research, information systems). Ethical issues (e.g., misrepresentation and collusion, misuse of data, manipulation and coercion, technical ineptness, oversight and disclosure, interpretation of benefits, confidentiality, professional care) clearly arise in benefit administration (Danley et al., 1996; Wiley, 1998; Wooten, 2001).

In light of the cost and importance of benefits, professional standards are central to their administration. The ethics codes of five human resource associations and other professional societies include statements on the obligations to: society (e.g., to maintain the highest ethical standards, protecting people's rights to fair and equitable treatment), the employer (e.g., to recognize individual rights and privileges, keep competence in the HR field, allocate resources objectively), clients (e.g., to maintain confidentiality of privileged information, avoid the appearance of personal bias) (Wiley, 2000), and employees (e.g., to provide administrative means for dissent and due process rights) (American Society for Public Administration, 2005). Implementing the values found in the codes and balancing the sometimes conflicting responsibilities, although challenging, define the profession as codes provide an ethical context for the practice of benefit administration.

To weigh ethical principles and economic imperatives, choices can be seen in terms of their ethical right and wrong and their economic good and bad (Bowman, 1995) as shown in Figure 3.1 below. The resulting decision quadrant, then, categorizes different ways to address an issue. The ethical content of cells in the matrix can be assessed by considering the greatest good for the greatest number (consequentialism or teleology) and what is good for one is good for all (the use of universal principles or deontology).

Complementing these two philosophies are the "hard" (utilitarian-instrumental) and "soft" (developmental-humanistic) approaches to managing human resources (Stace and Dunphy, 1991; Truss et al., 1997; Edgar and Geare, 2005). The hard strategy sees employees as costs to be minimized and resources to be used for maximum return; the soft policy regards employees as assets worthy of investment and a source of competitive advantage.[1]

What is striking in thinking about ethical principles and economic imperatives is that affirmative moral obligations are easier (at least in the abstract) for the public sector to undertake than the private sector. The reason is straightforward: the classical theory of the firm posits that business has no responsibility beyond that of making a profit for its shareholders (Greenwood, 2002: 266–278). To argue that it does suggests that there may be no limit to additional obligations, thereby making impossible demands upon a corporation, and raising the question who will select the problems and in what order will they be addressed. In contrast, however, the public

Ethical contribution

		Right	Wrong
Economic contribution	Good	Ethically correct and economically efficient	Ethically deficient but apparently economically efficient
	Bad	Ethically correct but economically inefficient	Ethically incorrect and economically inefficient

Figure 3.1 Decision framework for weighing ethical principles and economic imperatives. (Adapted from Bowman, J., *Quality Management Today*, ed., J. West, International City/County Management Association, Washington DC, 1995.)

sector exists, at least in a democratic society, to serve the commonweal; deciding among responsibilities and duties to citizens is the purpose of government.

To summarize, for many citizens deepening economic insecurity is a consequence of the "great risk shift" from organizations to individuals, impacting psychological contracts at work and making it increasingly clear the key role of benefits to individual and societal well-being. Although code provisions can provide guideposts for ethical action, weighing competing values can be facilitated by a decision-making tool that focuses on ethical and economic concerns, concerns that parallel hard versus soft HRM philosophies. The discussion now turns to issues in benefit policy and administration.

3.3 Benefits Issues

As examined elsewhere in this volume, there are a wide variety of mandatory and discretionary benefit programs. For reasons of space, only an illustrative selection of these programs is examined: healthcare coverage, retirement pensions, employee assistance programs, work/family initiatives, and work break policies. The objective is to explore the nature of each program and then to seek best practice—an ethically correct and economically sound policy.

3.3.1 Health Insurance

3.3.1.1 Scope and Magnitude

Leading concerns include (1) spending trends, (2) load shifting and contingent labor, (3) generational differentials, (4) differing perceptions, and (5) fraud reduction. Spending on benefits has grown more rapidly than wages, due primarily to rising costs for health insurance and retirement programs. Figure 3.2 shows the growth in private employer costs for employee compensation, wages, and benefits for workers from 1991 to 2005 (wages and benefits increased by approximately the same percentages during this period until 2002, after which wages stagnated and benefit costs continued to escalate). Wage stagnation has long been a problem in government to the point the any gains are frequently canceled by increases in healthcare premiums. More generally, healthcare expenditures have risen steadily over the years, and 40 percent of the population lack health coverage. Healthcare coverage, then, is a critical benefit for most people.

Yet there has been a decline in the percentage of employers offering the benefit since 2000, although this is more typical of private than public organizations. Further, it is no longer the norm for business and government employers to absorb the full cost of individual health insurance and family health premiums as organizations are adjusting their plans and transferring the costs to employees through higher premiums, co-pays, and deductibles (Hacker, 2006: 139). There are also employer

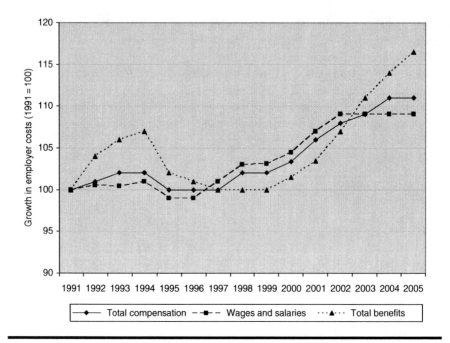

Figure 3.2   Growth in real employer costs for employee total compensation, wages, and total benefits for all workers, 1991–2005. (From U.S. General Accountability Office, February. Employee compensation: Employer spending on benefits has grown faster than wages, due largely to rising costs for health insurance and retirement benefits, U.S. GAO, Washington, DC, 2006.)

initiatives to promote health (wellness programs, smoking cessation, and exercise promotion) by encouraging wholesome lifestyles as well as to deter high-risk behaviors (smoking, excessive weight, high cholesterol, participation in high-risk activities) by increasing premiums or limiting (or eliminating) coverage (Wojcik, 2007).

The most dramatic example of load-shedding occurs with the use of part-time and temporary employees (Thompson and Mastracci, 2005; Klingner and Lynn, 2005), leading to the emergence of a "two-tier labor force" (core and peripheral) with benefits concentrated in the first tier (Clark, 1997). About 15.8 percent of the entire workforce is permanent part-time (Roberts, 2003), many of whom desire full-time work. In the public sphere, although nearly all federal agencies offer part-time work, only a small percentage of personnel, primarily women, is in this category (U.S. Office of Personnel Management, 1998; Daniel, 1999). In local jurisdictions, 15.4 percent of employees are part-time (Roberts, 2003). As much as 20 percent of Florida's state government workforce, for example, is part-time, many of whom work 35 hours per week. Temporary employees also have become more prevalent as organizations economize and downsize. For example, in 1997 Texas experienced a

300 percent increase in temp workers compared to a decade earlier (Berman et al., 2006, Chapter 7); there is every reason to believe that this trend continues.

Some of the tensions caused by such practices may be intergenerational in nature such as (a) employees in the sandwich generation (people with child- and elder-care responsibilities) are more likely to experience the burden of higher costs compared to other groups, (b) cuts of retiree healthcare benefits disproportionately affect older workers, and (c) computer-savvy younger workers, comfortable with obtaining data from the Internet, may find it easier than older employees to become informed of healthcare options as organizations move toward consumer-driven programs (Denker et al., 2007).

Irrespective of generational differences, there is often a gap between the perceptions, with employers' utilitarian, business-based perspective based on benefit spending, and employees' evaluations of what they receive compared to the costs. Richardson (1998) asks "Ethically, which carries more weight? Holding down costs or keeping your employees satisfied and healthy?" As organizations shift from full-time workers with secure jobs to contingent workers holding less secure positions, he continues, "Is it legitimate for employers to require employees to assume an increasing burden of economic risk simply because it is advantageous," or "should organizations, frequently large and well-resourced, accept responsibility for the promotion of employee well-being?"

Last, one way to hold down costs is to reduce fraud and abuse in health benefits. Fraud occurs when someone intentionally provides fake or misleading information for personal financial gain; abuse involves bending if not breaking the rules (Nicholas, 2005; Sekerka and Zolin, 2007). These actions are clearly inconsistent with public service values of honesty, integrity and trustworthiness, and undervalue the role of civil servants as stewards of the commonweal. Examples of unethical behavior might include submission of fraudulent claims or contractors billing for services not performed and/or falsifying invoices. These actions can fuel inflated healthcare expenses, costing employers billions through self-insuring or higher premiums (Kendall, 2005). Nicholas (2005) reports that one insurance company in 2004 recovered over $7 million as a result of its fraud prevention program. Ventriss and Barney (2003) examine the largest scandal in Medicare's history in the 1990s, and how a whistle-blower uncovered fraudulent practices at one of America's largest hospital conglomerates. It is incumbent upon HR managers, then, to assess the fraud prevention plans of insurers and to be looking for "red flag" indicators of potential fraud.

3.3.1.2   *Ethical Analysis*

Using the decision quadrant, a right–good decision—best practice—would be one that keeps personnel healthy and controls expense. This is illustrated by the debate over national health insurance and by examining Canadian, French, British, and the U.S. Veterans Health Administration models—all of which achieve both objectives as ethically right and economically good (Kline, 2007). An ethically right/economically bad policy could, in the name of good health, lead to system bankruptcy. An ethically wrong, but economically good approach would for reasons of cost savings reduce benefits and/or coverage leaving employees vulnerable. A wrong–bad strategy would fail to provide comprehensive care and nevertheless be very expensive, a situation that critics believe describes much of American healthcare today.

Key factors in developing a sustainable policy include the greatest good for the greatest number and what is good for one is good for all. Health policy debates revolve around ways to protect the partially insured and uninsured although simultaneously controlling costs. Until the United States adopts universal coverage with effective cost controls, employers will have to wrestle with their responsibilities to address these issues. What is the employer's obligation to their primary stakeholders, specifically, in this instance, employees and shareholders/taxpayers? Is this a zero-sum game where there are clear winners and losers and, if so, what is the appropriate ethical course of action? Resolving this conundrum depends on which ethical principles are used in thinking through the options. Principles of rights (individual, property), justice (distributive, procedural), utilitarianism (ratio of benefits to costs), and beneficence (serving the good) come into play and must be thoughtfully balanced in establishing an equilibrium that promotes the greatest good and avoids the greatest harm, which advances the good for one without jeopardizing the good for all.

In developing the policy both HRM hard and soft approaches should be considered. Hard strategies look to the bottom line and managerial prerogatives, supporting health benefits so long as they promote business objectives and conserve resources. Proponents of this approach advance shareholder value theory and focus on the expense of obligation to the workforce. Soft plans seek coverage that expresses "caring" by addressing employee needs, respecting individual rights and promoting healthy lifestyles. Although the language used to support health policies is often linked to the soft approach, the reality of what is offered (especially in the private sector) is more closely aligned with the hard perspective of HRM.

To summarize this discussion briefly, issues surrounding healthcare benefits include not only their coverage, but also their changing nature which impacts organizational responsibilities, generations, employee perceptions, fraud strategies, and raises competing ethical and economic concerns in search of best practice.

3.3.2 Retirement Security

3.3.2.1 Scope and Magnitude

Key concerns include the nature and security of pension plans, and their susceptibility to fraud. As with healthcare, individuals are assuming greater responsibility as business and government organizations shift retirement investment risks to workers. Indeed, retirement security itself is increasingly precarious as evidenced by defaults on pension plans and loss of retirement savings at Enron, United Airlines,

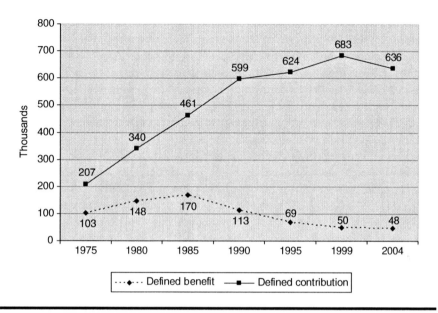

Figure 3.3 **Number of defined benefit and defined contribution plans, 1975–2004. (From Employee Benefit Research Institute, Private pension plan bulleting: Abstract of 2004 Form 550 Annual Reports, Table A1, Retrieved on July 24, 2007 from http://www.ebri.org/publications/facts/1298fact.pdf, 2007; McDonnell, K., Benefit cost comparisons between state and local governments and private-sector employees. EBRI Notes 26(4), 7. 2004 Data: Retrieved on July 25, 2007 from http://www.dol.gov/ebsa/PDF/2004pensionplanbulletin.PDF, 2005. With permission.)**

and U.S. Steel. Over the period from 1975 to 2004 the number of defined benefit plans in the nation decreased from 103,000 to 48,000, although the number of defined contribution plans increased from 207,000 to 636,000 during the same period (Figure 3.3). There is also considerable variety in pension program matching provisions (a match of 50 percent of contributions up to 6 percent of salary, 50 per-cent match up to 4 percent, a match of less than 50 percent, no match; Rauch, 2005); the tendency is to reduce or eliminate the match. Although these trends have affected the public service, most government employees remain in defined benefit plans—although longer life spans and early retirement add pressure on them to offer defined contribution policies.

Governments are not obligated to fully fund pension plans, however, they must have sufficient resources to pay out each year's benefits. Indeed, one of the largest items in the federal budget is civilian and military pensions. At the subnational level, 16 states have overall pension deficits larger than their total yearly budget, and some states do not disclose their condition for fear it will result in benefit cuts. New Jersey will need $58 billion just to provide healthcare to its current and future retirees, an amount twice the state budget and twice its outstanding debt (Walsh, 2007). In Illinois the unfunded pension liability averages $3406 for every resident (Greenblat, 2007). Responding to similar concerns, California Governor Arnold Schwarzenegger attempted, unsuccessfully, to reform the state pension plan in 2005 by shifting from a defined benefit to a defined contribution approach. Cities are not immune to pension problems either. For instance, San Diego officials dipped into the pension fund to pay expenses and used unfunded pension liability to hide municipal debt. As the pension deficit neared a billion dollars in 2004, the mayor resigned and other officials were later indicted for conspiracy and fraud (Greenblat, 2007). Although these problems may be extreme, some of the decisions made in San Deigo are not uncommon. The difference between what is owed and what state and local jurisdictions can afford suggests that a national healthcare plan is the only available long-range remedy.

Fraud and abuse, as noted, are potential problems with pension plans, and HR managers need to be able to prevent, identify, and correct wrongful acts. The United States Department of Labor's "Getting it Right" program supplies guidance in five areas: understanding pension plans and their responsibilities, screening and monitoring service providers, making timely contributions to 401(k) plans, avoiding illegal transactions, and disclosing information to employees and the government on time (Carlson, 2005).

3.3.2.2 Ethical Analysis

In seeking best practice, a right–good policy would preserve security and contain costs, a right–bad approach would maintain security but ignore expense, a wrong–good strategy would erode security for financial reasons, and a wrong–bad solution would neither uphold security nor restrain costs. In recent times, the public sector has found itself in a right–bad situation although the private sector often uses a wrong–good approach. American society as a whole is recognizing that its wrong–bad retirement strategy needs attention if retirement security is to be protected and costs managed.

As the future of government policy (Medicare, Medicaid, Social Security) becomes problematic, and as employers reduce pension funding, the well-being of Americans in their senior years—absent extensive public education on financial planning, and greater discipline in personal savings—is far from assured. Some combination of government support, employer contribution, and employee savings come closest to meeting the "greatest good" criterion as well as the "good for one is good for all" principle.

The resulting policy should attend to both the soft and hard approaches to HRM. From the soft perspective, reneging on promised pensions (or severely cutting them) is theft, robbing employees of their investment; the principle of "fidelity of purpose" is crucial in building enduring, trustworthy relationships with workers. The obligation to pay for "human depreciation" has been likened to the responsibility to pay replacement costs for worn-out equipment. From the hard side, pensions are viewed as a voluntary and expensive obligation of management. Stewardship of stockholder and taxpayer resources requires prudent decision making, especially in an era of rising costs, competitive pressures, and an unpredictable future. If the benefits of pensions (e.g., employee loyalty, recruitment and retention edge) do not outweigh the costs, then the reality of doing business requires moving away from paternalistic policies of the past and insisting that employees assume more personal responsibility for their financial future. Public and private employers need to find a balance between these two competing philosophies.

In sum, risk-shifting, under-funding, and wrongdoing have added to retirement insecurity for many; in response, carefully calibrated actions by decision makers to address ethical and economic dimensions of the problem are required in the name of best practice.

3.3.3   *Employee Assistance Programs*

3.3.3.1   *Scope and Magnitude*

If healthcare and pension plans are seen as essential, employee assistance programs are very desirable to well-being, but perhaps not necessarily vital in comparison. The employee assistance program (EAP) benefit aims to improve health and helps individuals resolve problems that affect performance including difficulties resulting from work and family conflict. It is an educational, treatment, and referral service to aid personnel to recognize and deal with problems such as substance abuse, personal debt, and domestic violence. EAPs seek to enhance employee behavioral skills, on-the-job performance, and personal well-being. Usually the initial intake is free; however, those to whom employees are referred usually charge for their services. Governments at all levels typically have EAPs as nearly eight in ten cities, for instance, have such a program (Roberts, 2004).

EAP professionals must treat all employee contacts and the nature, content, or duration of participation in the program as strictly confidential.[2] Personnel should be informed fully of their rights regarding these limits on confidential communications during the assessment, referral, and treatment process. More specifically, providers who work with impaired professionals confront ethical dilemmas including (1) the obligation to warn clients of the professional's impairment versus the obligation to respect the impaired professional's confidentiality; (2) the obligation to consider voluntary, compulsory, or refusal of, treatment involving the impaired professional; (3) the obligation to oversee the professional's performance versus the obligation to respect his or her autonomy (Mines et al., 1991: 26). Such dilemmas can affect the service quality as well as employee rights, and require thoughtful consideration of legal provisions, professional codes, and organizational values before taking action.

A national survey of EAP administrators highlights potential conflicts between the financial interests of employers, EAP vendors, and clients (Sharar and White, 2001). Alluding to vendor mergers showing that "ten vendors now manage 75 percent of EAP enrollment" (p. 1), respondents indicated they were apprehensive about the knowledge, experience, and technical skills of national subcontractors and lack of understanding of local workplace conditions. Service quality may be compromised due to underpricing (low balling), overpromising, and under-resourcing of services.

Sharar and White (n.d.) also expressed concern about "cowboy capitalism" and asked whether EAP professionals, like others in the helping professions, should be held to a higher moral standard, thereby ensuring practices built on principles of "…fidelity (keeping promises), stewardship (using resources wisely to achieve the greatest good), and honesty (being truthful and factual in making representations)." (p. 3) Too often with subcontracts that is not the case. They identified deceptive marketing practices (misrepresentation, false and inflated claims) by vendors and outsourced services that are in some instances EAPs in name only, providing limited or inferior services. In the case study dealing with outsourcing of state HR services (see below), similar concerns are expressed.[3]

3.3.3.2 Ethical Analysis

Right–good EAP policies provide comprehensive services in recognition of the ethical and economic benefits of such an approach. As noted earlier, a right–bad strategy (at least without an infusion of funds) would be unsustainable, a condition found in some public jurisdictions. A wrong–good strategy would fail to meet legitimate employee (and arguably organizational) needs in the name of saving money, an approach that characterizes some small businesses. A wrong–bad plan, similar to selected benefit programs discussed above, would be a lose–lose strategy that is ineffective ethically, yet economically costly.

In sorting out the best practice for a given location, factors to be examined in developing a sustainable policy include the greatest good for the greatest number and what is good for one is good for all. The utilitarian, consequentialist stance would view such programs as morally justified by the surplus of benefit over harm that most clients are likely to experience. EAPs would be seen positively if they reduce health expenditures, workers compensation and disability costs, and risks of workplace violence, sexual harassment, and other behavior problems. In order for the good for one is good for all principle to be satisfied, EAPs would need to offer a range of educational, treatment, or referral services customized to meet diverse client needs. Fulfilling employee needs would be an end in itself, providing personnel with confidential, 24/7 access to professionals who would assess their needs. Applying the hard versus soft HRM approaches, the former would be more interested in beneficial consequences in terms of employee performance (reduced absenteeism, increased productivity), although the latter would emphasize employee well-being and satisfaction, acknowledging the employers obligation to address employee needs.

Overall, then, EAPs promote both utilitarian and altruistic objectives, but ethical dilemmas and fiscal concerns, especially in an era of widespread outsourcing, require adroit juggling to assure individual well-being and organizational productivity.

3.3.4 Family/Work Programs

3.3.4.1 Scope and Magnitude

Health and retirement plans are essential and EAPs very desirable, however, family/work initiatives are attractive benefits but not necessarily vital. They include (but are not limited to) child care, elder care, flextime and telecommuting, leave sharing and pooling, domestic partner benefits, and adoption assistance. The nature and extent of these programs varies:[4]

- On-site or near-site day care centers are provided by a small percentage of organizations; however a far larger percentage offer financial assistance for off-site child care and information/referral services (Berman et al., 2006).
- Programs with elder care services are found in half of America's cities and one third of private corporations (Mercer, 1996; Berman and West, 1996).
- More than 27 million full-time wage and salaried employees (27.5 percent) had flexible schedules, but about one-tenth of these worked flexible hours as a component of a formal employer-sponsored flextime program (U.S. Bureau of Labor Statistics, 2005).
- About 13–19.6 million business employees in America telecommute and 119,248 federal employees, representing nine percent of civil servants, were teleworking in 2005 (Gupta, 2007); however, the definition of the concept varies substantially, fewer than one in ten eligible federal employees participate, and just 35 percent of federal managers today think their agencies support telecommuting (Bednarz, 2007).
- The national government, two-thirds of state governments, and many municipal jurisdictions and public school districts allow leave sharing and pooling (CSG, 1997; U.S. Office of Personnal Management, 2007a).
- The percentage of private organizations offering adoption assistance ranges from 15 to 32 percent depending on the survey (Mercer, 1996; U.S. Office of Personnal Management, 2007b).
- Domestic partner health benefits were offered by 5805 employers in 2003 (Human Rights Campaign Foundation, 2003).[5]

These initiatives are built on the perspective that an employee is a "whole person," and as such attempt to satisfy competing on- and off-the-job demands.

Administrators' views differ from those of the employees. Miller et al. (1991) found that managers do not believe that job performance is affected by dependent care responsibilities, although employees do think these responsibilities impact performance. The two groups also diverge with regard to employer responsibility to alleviate dependent care burdens; managers perceive little obligation although the rank-and-file think organizations should address such problems.[6]

3.3.4.2 Ethical Analysis

From an ethical perspective, caring for members of the "organizational family," including employees' dependent care needs, is a core organizational value fundamental to the quality of working life and workplaces as "communities of purpose." Thus, an ethically right/economically good approach would be a cafeteria plan that provides a wide variety of selections from which to choose with an overall funding cap. An ethically right, but economically bad, strategy by definition would be unsustainable in the long term. An ethically wrong/economically good policy would focus on saving money irrespective of the consequences on employees—something that in the long term likely would be economically counterproductive. An ethically wrong/economically bad program would include benefits that employees do not want or appreciate and that are nonetheless expensive, a situation that characterizes some plans today.

Factors to be examined in developing a sustainable policy include the greatest good for the greatest number and what is good for one is good for all. Sorting out the competing interests of claimant groups—owners/taxpayers, employees, customer/citizens, and society—is difficult and involves thorny trade-offs. It can be argued that family-friendly policies are a worthwhile investment for organizations, enhance the work life of employees, and thereby benefit society even though they impose costs on public and private employers. When escalating expenses threaten organizational budgets, however, the calculation of the "greater good" can lead to a different result. Similarly, what is beneficial family-friendly policy for one employee (child care, elder care, adoption assistance, or health and life insurance) may be inappropriate and unavailable to others (single employees without dependents, part-time workers); those deprived of the benefit are likely to press for comparable or customized benefit offerings based on "what is good for one is good for all." HR policies and procedures must avoid perceptions of bias and unfairness. Again, cafeteria type plans with an array of options and funding limits seem prudent.

The resulting policy should attempt to accommodate both hard and soft approaches to HRM. Hard approaches lean toward reducing employee friendly benefit costs, especially where they are ill defined or characterized by high expenses and low gains. The certainty of short-term financial advantage to the organization is likely to outweigh the uncertainty of any long-term payoff for the employer. Soft approaches tend to emphasize human capital investment and goals of flexibility and adaptability as justification for continuing with programs that are costly in the short range but that bring long-range advantages in employee morale, loyalty, and commitment.

Summing up, family/work initiatives try to accommodate and enhance the person–organization "fit" by offering programs that demonstrate caring, providing employee choice, and accepting short-term expenses in exchange for long-term performance payoffs.

3.3.5 Work Breaks

3.3.5.1 Scope and Magnitude

Periodic breaks, an important benefit, can aid in coping with the negative effects that stress has on employees' judgment, productivity and working relationships.[7] Stress can cause absenteeism, "presentism" (here in body, but not in mind), anger and resentment, accidents, mistakes, and turnover (*HR Focus*, 2001; Irvine, 2005; Mental Health America, 2007; Page and Tate, 2007).

Break-taking serves three broad purposes. First, it allows workers to stop and think about their work experiences (Gosling and Mintzberg, 2004). For example, 29 percent of employees often or very often felt they "didn't have the time to step back and process or reflect on the work they're doing" (*HR Focus*, 2001: 9). Second, breaks are a way to physically and mentally restore oneself, which impacts effectiveness in several ways: (a) because work may produce emotional as well as physical stress, which can affect judgment, restorative time is needed for better decisions and improved interactions with others and (b) as the mind relaxes or thinks about other things, new thoughts might serendipitously arise which allow a person to see matters in a different light.[8] Third, a pause allows managers to balance work with nonwork obligations, such as taking care of personal or family matters.

Although federal statutes do not require meal or coffee breaks, when employers offer rests, federal law considers them to be work time that must be compensated (U.S. Department of Labor, 2007). Also, several states have legal provisions for workplace breaks, most of which require a rest or meal time (Dearing, 2005). In practice, however, many employees expect two 15 minute work stops per day, which often are part of collective bargaining agreements. In any case, policies and expectations must be clearly communicated.

There is always the possibility, nevertheless, that employees will abuse the rules. They may spend time surfing the Web, looking for jobs, or socializing with colleagues. This is stealing time from the employer and a violation of the "honest day's work for an honest day's pay" psychological contract. Some form of monitoring may be necessary to promptly detect and appropriately correct such abuses.

3.3.5.2 Ethical Analysis

A right–good policy approach would provide adequate breaks because it is ethically and economically the prudent thing to do. A right–bad strategy, as discussed in other topics above, may be ethically laudable but economically unwise. A wrong–good plan would treat employees as commodities to save money, at least in the short run. An ethically wrong/economically bad approach, like the wrong–good strategy, would not recognize the need for breaks and yet would be very expensive in the long run in the form of recruitment, turnover, and training costs. Although few organizations have this as a formal policy, some large retailers are willing to absorb the personnel costs involved because of low wages, high profits, and clever marketing.

Decisions on break-taking can be guided by the "greatest good" and "good for one is good for all" principles. At periodic intervals, all members of the organization experience fatigue, need rest, and require balance between work and nonwork responsibilities. Whether required by law, negotiated by collective agreement, authorized by formal policy, or informally adopted by managerial discretion, individual and organizational needs can be served by well-spaced work breaks. Break-taking can promote the greater good and insure that what is good for one is equitably available to all if the policy is properly designed, free of abuse, and consistently implemented.

Employers adopting appropriate policies encourage reflection, restoration, or balance in work, and nonwork obligations follow a soft HRM approach and apply principles of beneficence (active goodness) and caring (genuine concern for the welfare of others) toward workers. They may see employees as an end in themselves following Kantian ethics. Employers concerned about organizational efficiency and following the hard approach regard employees largely in instrumental, utilitarian terms. They may either support break-taking as a way to reduce mistakes, accidents, and turnover (and thereby advance employer interests), or fail to establish a policy because they believe it minimizes employer prerogatives and employee productivity (Legge, 1996). Best practice would establish a policy on breaks (e.g., 15 minutes after four hours of work) and monitor implementation to avoid abuse.

Linder and Nygaard (1998, Chapter 9) argue for changes in the Fair Labor Standards Act (FLSA), Occupational Health and Safety Act (OSHA), and Americans with Disabilities Act (ADA) provisions, proposing that FLSA establish minimum standards for meal (45 minutes) and rest breaks (6 minutes per hour). OSHA (n.d.) makes break-taking easier with its downloadable program, "Remind Me," which prompts the computer to alert employees to pause. Recognizing the importance of staff being relaxed and fit for work, some organizations provide opportunities for comfortable and convenient breaks (i.e., providing areas to relax) (Simhan and Chandramouli, 2003; Baxter and Kroll-Smith, 2005; Smerd, 2007).

To recap, work breaks can reduce stress, refresh workers, and enhance productivity, but they can also be abused if insufficiently monitored and controlled. Ethical principles of caring, trust, and beneficence, together with economic values of accountability, efficiency, and resource conservation, should inform the practice and policy.

3.4 Case Studies

The studies that follow further illustrate the nexus between ethics and employee benefits. In the first case, personnel abused the privilege of participating in a benefit program with a noble purpose: investing public monies to encourage employees to further their education. By bilking taxpayers, these individuals threaten the existence of a decades-old program built on the premises of the developmental, humanistic-oriented soft HRM that has enabled thousands of employee students to improve their job performance and career prospects. In the second case, the states of Florida and Texas, consistent with the premises of economically oriented hard HRM, outsourced their human resource management function, which led to avoidable problems if the states had properly planned and monitored the initiatives.

3.4.1 Miami-Dade County, Florida Tuition-Reimbursement Program: Lax Oversight and Cheating Taxpayers

The county tuition-reimbursement program was implemented in 1963 as a way for employees to improve their competencies and job effectiveness. Full-time workers, once eligible, can be reimbursed for half of their tuition costs, if they provide documentation. They must agree to remain employed with the county for one year following completion of the coursework. There are no geographical limits on the schools or annual limits on the amount that can be reimbursed; the only restriction on course selection is that it be "related to any of the county's thousands of job titles, whether or not it applies to the worker's job description" (*The Miami Herald*, 2006). The county has dispersed $9.3 million to county employees since 2000.

Benefit administration can grab headlines when inadequate oversight and unethical or illegal conduct are uncovered. This happened with the tuition-refund program. An interim grand jury reported widespread overpayments, grade falsification by employees to collect cash, and use of county time to attend classes (Miami-Dade State Attorney's Office, 2006). The investigation, still underway at the time of this writing, extends to human resource managers and others who oversee the program. The county's employee relations department requested an inspector general's investigation after whistle-blowers reported some irregularities in documentation.

The inspector general found $182,556 of illegal payments based on initial examination of a mere 20 percent of the 275 employees initially under investigation (1500 employees participated in the program in 2005). There were scores of instances in which unscrupulous people misled or cheated the county out of money. One example cited was an employee who attended a three-week class at Harvard University. The person was in class although on county time and, in further violation of guidelines, filed for reimbursement of half the $10,000 tuition. Eighty three of the 275 people investigated thus far were reimbursed amounts exceeding the cost of their tuition; they have been ordered to repay the money with interest and given a ten-day suspension without pay (alternative is termination), and denied future eligibility in the program. Four employees are charged with deliberately changing their grades to qualify for reimbursements. These four had garnered $38,000 in overpayments and an additional $7,563 after illegally tampering with their grades. Ironically, one of the four was a supervisor in the employee relations department responsible for overseeing the program. Felony indictments include grand theft, official misconduct by a public servant, and organized fraud (Mazzella, 2006; Miami-Dade State Attorney's Office, 2006; Pinzur, 2006; Rabin, 2006).

The Miami Herald (2006) editorialized in favor of revamping the program with an eye to reducing waste and abuse, protecting taxpayers, and emphasizing common sense. The inspector general report (Mazzella, 2006) stipulated greater scrutiny and careful verification of documents. The interim grand jury offered 13 recommendations "to stem this tide of mismanagement and fraud," including procedural changes, additional safeguards, and management controls (Miami-Dade State Attorney's Office, 2006).

An ethically right/economically good tuition-refund policy would combine the noble purposes of skill enhancement and fiscal discipline (e.g., expenditure caps, course approval, and reimbursement reporting). An ethically right/economically bad approach, like Miami-Dade's policy, expands opportunity for employee growth, but enables abuse and endangers program viability. Where ethically wrong/economically good policies are adopted, fiscal constraints trump competency-building efforts and freeze skill deficits. Ethically wrong/economically bad programs might refund tuition for courses with little work relevance and lack preapproval or postaudit controls, not unlike some features of Miami-Dade's program.

The "greater good" criterion would weigh taxpayer interests in measured use of fiscal resources with worker interest in skill- and career-enhancement. To achieve this balance is to invest in worker competencies that likely yield improved services to citizen/taxpayers, a win–win approach. The "good for one and all" occurs when there is a convergence among program participants and those overseeing or providing resources. Soft HRM supports human capital investment programs like tuition refund initiatives, which recognize the worth of individuals and show respect for their capabilities. Hard HRM takes a more instrumental approach that seeks a return on the organization's investment in skill development, reflected in such metrics as improved quality and quantity of outputs and outcomes and as institutionally verified by pre- and postreimbursement reporting and evaluation requirements.

Several issues of fairness are raised by this case. For example, fairness requires detecting and responding to violations, which occurred in this instance, if belatedly. Fairness also requires that expectations be reasonably clear (codified) which was partially done, but insufficiently. Fairness further requires that those who violate ethical standards be appropriately disciplined; this has occurred for the most egregious wrongdoers. Fairness to taxpayer requires sufficient safeguards to ensure that the public interest is protected; actions recommended by the press, inspector general, and grand jury, if properly implemented, should provide such protection in the future.

3.4.2 Privatizing Human Resources in Florida and Texas

The outsourcing of specific human resource functions, such as employee assistance programs and salary surveys, is not new or novel. What is different, as

Jerrell Coggburn (2007) points out, is the outsourcing of all human resource activities, a recent trend that began in the private sector and has spread to selected local jurisdictions, state governments, and at least one federal agency. The allure of market forces that promise reduced costs and increased service quality through economies of scale, instant access to state-of-the-art services, and avoidance of capital outlays for technology upgrades can be compelling in the face of aggressive marketing and distaste for government bureaucracy. Benefit programs, in particular, as large and labor-intensive, are an especially attractive component of outsourcing plans.

In 2002, the state of Florida signed a seven-year, $278.6 million contract—the largest such project in the nation—with Convergys to manage the state's human capital. The goal of the Web-based interactive system, dubbed "People First," is to modernize the human resource function, increase service quality; the projected savings were once estimated at $173 million (for further details, see Chapter 13, this volume). The consensus of the participants in a study of People First by Crowell and Guy (forthcoming) is that "it has become more difficult to manage the HR function since it was outsourced."

Widespread problems include improper cancellation of health insurance, over and under charges, incorrect electronic fund transfers and payroll deductions as well as illegal subcontracting, employees hired without background checks, and identity theft. These issues have been compounded by a user-unfriendly online system and a grossly inadequate telephone helpline. High staff turnover both at the Florida Department of Management Services (the entity responsible for contract management) and at Convergys have contributed to a chaotic environment where state legislators complain that their offices have been turned into personnel complaint bureaus. The cost to update the automated system that People First replaced had been estimated at some $75 million.

Like Florida, Texas did not heed the uneven outsourcing experience in the private sector. Nor did it perform due diligence in critically examining outsourcing in the public arena. Coggburn (2007, p. 16) notes that Texas, in its 2004 selection of Convergys as its HR vendor, was "influenced by the firm's previous experience in Florida" (sic). Not surprisingly, like in Florida, official audits later revealed that the decision to outsource was not based on accurate financial data, that there was insufficient contract maintenance, and that it is doubtful that the initiative is cost effective. In both the states, projected savings have been lowered and contract costs increased.

Among the many lessons (Chapter 13) drawn from such experiences, the necessity to conduct a comprehensive needs assessment prior to outsourcing, the establishment of a system to track cost saving once the program is launched, and the provision for an economical exit strategy in case of program failure. The political rhetoric and commercial advertising that entices decision makers to contract out must be weighed against the reality that these initiatives are complex and may not meet expectations.

Applying the decision quadrant used earlier to outsourcing, a right/good strategy would be a one that is ethically sound (thoroughly researched with accurate data) and economically efficient (cost savings can be tracked and documented). A right/bad approach would be ethically robust, but economically unsustainable as unplanned costs escalate. A wrong/good plan would be ethically dubious but economical at least (in the short run) as the Florida and Texas programs initially appeared. A wrong/bad initiative, like those found in the two states, is deficient both ethically and economically. In seeking an optimal decision to outsource, then, some combination of soft and hard HRM strategies may be helpful in formulating a right/good approach.

Policy makers in Florida and Texas sought to modernize human resources by privatizing the entire function and thereby hoped to advance the greater good and the good for one and all. However, these expectations were not grounded in due diligence sufficient to inform prudential judgment. Difficulties were not anticipated and expected gains in improved services have been uneven, although management problems have bedeviled the programs from the outset. The uncritical borrowing by one state (Texas) of an unproven privatization initiative in another (Florida), on the implicit assumption that "business does it best," and the premise that cross-sector transferability of functions is seamless, led to a situation that few would claim advances the "greater good" or the "good for one is good for all" principles. Although it is premature to pronounce a definitive judgment on what took place in these two states, preliminary assessments are mixed at best. Indeed, Florida is currently seeking to identify characteristics of a world-class system with the understanding that the Convergys contract may be revoked.

From a hard HRM perspective outsourcing has immediate appeal: cumbersome government bureaucracy can be circumvented, business efficiencies can yield cost savings, and clients will be better served. Difficulties in managing the HR function by the contractor have shown that there is a downside to privatization that was not thoroughly explored before contracts were let. Ethical issues (cancelled insurance, illegal subcontracts, inaccessible services) as well as economic issues (high contractor costs, lower-than-projected savings) call into question the assumed advantages. Soft HRM also seeks improved services, but supports strategies that encourage employee growth and commitment. Personnel officials of the government-operated HR system in Florida were treated as disposable commodities when the state relinquished control of HR to Convergys, and current employee-users of People First, despite recent improvements, share considerable dissatisfaction with the system. The soft HR approach suggests that such treatment is avoidable, unfortunate, and failed to treat employees with respect.

3.5 Conclusion

Employers are shifting economic risks involved in benefit policy and administration to employees. However, competing ethical and economic values can be addressed in the search for best practice in healthcare, retirement security, EAPs, family/worklife plans, and work break policies. This can be accomplished by using the ethically right/wrong-economically good/bad decision-making quadrant. The content of each of four cells in the matrix can be assessed by posing the "greatest good for the greatest number" and "what is good for one is good for all" principles, and employing hard and soft HRM styles as policy guidelines. This framework, together with professional codes of ethics, can be useful to teasing out the underlying logic by which different ideas are justified; they do not, of course, produce perfect policies. The need for considered judgment is not eliminated, but rather illuminated, as the quadrant enables skilled management of ethical ambiguity. There are no easy answers. The objective is to strive for balance—an ethically right and economically good policy.

Acknowledgments

The authors would like to thank Adrian Buckland and Sonia Desai for their assistance.

Endnotes

[1] This distinction has similarities with McGregor's (1960) Theory X and Theory Y perspectives on human nature and appropriate managerial strategies.

[2] Information may not be released without the employee's written consent. There are some mandatory exceptions to confidentiality, such as, instances where disclosure would indicate imminent threat of serious bodily harm to the employee or others.

[3] However, Bates (2007) provides a counter example with a more positive assessment of outsourcing that includes shared HR services between agencies. Using the example of EquaTerra, a consulting firm with interests in the public sector, Bates describes the company's strategy: to transform public HR; creating considerable improvements in practices, processes, and technology to realize goals of higher productivity; better services; and reduced costs. He cites an EquaTerra survey which shows that 53 percent of public sector HR leaders were satisfied with outsourcing and shared services, a figure that is open to interpretation by outsourcing advocates and skeptics.

[4] Material provided in this subsection on employee friendly policies is updated and adapted, in part, from Berman et al. (2006, Chapter 7).

[5] The rationale for employers providing the latter two benefits above is linked to equity: If birth parents receive benefits why not adoptive parents? If married partners receive benefits why not cohabiting couples or same-sex domestic partners? These two benefits are part of a trend toward little-used, inexpensive benefits that boost morale. Equity issues also arise with other "family-friendly," but "single-hostile" policies. There are some employees (single, childless employees or without dependents) who may resent policies designed for married coworkers.

⁶ It is a matter of speculation whether such views have changed during the intervening years, although to the extent that hard HRM strategies are employed it is likely that employer–employee differences remain.

⁷ The material in the subsection on work breaks is adapted from a forthcoming article by Berman and West (2007).

⁸ This idea is echoed by Mathis (1999) who advocates planning for quiet time: "(it) is a requirement in our world. Personal quiet time involves shutting out pressures and, in a quiet place where you can be alone, asking yourself key questions to help determine the importance of activities and events that demand your time and attention" (p. 8).

References

American Society for Public Administration. *Code of Ethics*. 2005. Retrieved on July 24, 2007 from www.aspanet.org/scriptcontent/index_codeofethics.cfm.

Bates, S. 2007. Outsourcing, shared services transform public sector HR. *Society for Human Resource Management HR News*, July 3. Retrieved on July 5, 2007 from http://www.shrm.org/hrnews_published/articles/CMS_02128.asp.

Baxter, V. and S. Kroll-Smith. 2005. Normalizing the workplace nap: Blurring the boundaries between public and private space and time. *Current Sociology*, 53(1), 33–55.

Bednarz, A. 2007. Fed managers clueless on telework, study says. *Network World*, January 23. Retrieved on July 11, 2007 from http://www.intergovworld.com/article/4f6f2ab00a01040800cd2bfc88d2972a/pg0.htm.

Berman, E., J. Bowman, J. West, and M. Van Wart. 2006. *Human Resource Management in Public Service*. Thousand Oaks, California: Sage.

Berman, E. and J. West. 1996. Managerial responses to an aging municipal workforce: A national survey. *Review of Public Personnel Administration*, 16(3) Summer: 38–58.

Berman, E. and J. West. 2007. The effective manager…takes a break. *Review of Public Personnel Administration,* 27(4): 380–400.

Bowman, J. 1995. Ethics and quality: A "right–good" combination, In *Quality Management Today* (Ed.) J. West. Washington, DC: International City/County Management Association. pp. 64–69.

Carlson, L. 2005, November 1. Smelling a rat: How to catch shady moves in plans. *Employee Benefit News*, 1–2.

Clark, C. 1997. Contingent work force. *CQ Researcher*, 7(40): 937–960.

Coggburn, J. 2007. Outsourcing human resources: The case of the Texas health and Human Services Commission. *Review of Public Personnel Administration*, 27(4): 315–335.

Council of State Governments (CSG). 1997. *The Book of the States*. Lexington, Kentucky: CSG.

Crowell, E. and M. Guy. (forthcoming). Florida's HR reforms: Service first, service worst, and something in between? *Public Personal Management.*

Daniel, L. 1999, April. Feds and families. *Government Executive*, 41–46.

Danley, J., E. Harrick, D. Schaefer, D. Strickland, and G. Sullivan. 1996. HR's view of ethics in the work place: Are the barbarians at the gate? *Journal of Business Ethics*, 15(3): 273–285.

Dearing, J. 2005. Business advisors: Break policies. *SFGate.com*. Retrieved on February 26, 2007 from http://allbusiness.sfgate.com/blog/OfficeManagementBlog/10950/003817.html.

Denker, J., J. Aparna, and J. Martocchio. 2007. Employee benefits as context for intergenerational conflict. *Human Resource Management Review*, 17: 208–220.

Edgar, F. and A. Geare. 2005. HRM practice and employee attitudes: Different measures—different results. *Personnel Review*, 34(5): 534–549.

Employee Benefit Research Institute. 2007. Private pension plan bulleting: Abstract of 2004 Form 550 Annual Reports, Table A1. Retrieved on July 24, 2007 from http://www.ebri.org/publications/facts/1298fact.pdf.

Gerhardt, B. and G. Milkovich. 1994. Employee compensation: Research and practice. In *Handbook of Industrial and Organizational Psychology* 2nd ed., Vol. 3 (Eds.) M. Dunnette and L. Hough. Palo Alto, California: Consulting Psychologists Press. pp. 481–570.

Gosling, J. and H. Mintzberg. 2004. Reflect yourself: Take time out of your busy day to reflect on yourself and where your team is headed. *HR Magazine*, September. Retrieved on June 26, 2007 from http://www.findarticles.com/p/articles/mi_m3495/is_9_49/ai_n6355175.

Greenwood, M. 2002. Ethics and HRM: A review and conceptual analysis. *Journal of Business Ethics*, 36: 261–178.

Greenblat, A. 2007. Pension crisis. In CQ Researcher (Ed.) *Issues for Debate in American Public Policy*. Washington, DC: CQ Press, pp. 261–283.

Gupta, A. 2007, June 18. OPM says telework increased despite appearances. Retrieved on July 20, 2007 from www.govexec.com/story_page.cfm?articleid=37233&dcn=e_gvet.

Hacker, J. 2006. *The Great Risk Shift*. New York: Oxford University Press.

HR Focus. 2001. The negative effects of overwork and related stress. 78(11): 9.

Human Rights Campaign Foundation. 2003. The state of the family. Retrieved on July 10, 2007 from http://www.hrc.org/Content/ContentGroups/Publications1/SoTF.pdf.

Irvine, K.N. 2005. Work breaks and well being: The effect of nature on hospital nurses (Doctoral dissertation). *Dissertation Abstracts International*, 65(10-B): 5445.

Kendall, J. 2005, August. Curbing health fraud. *HR Magazine*, 65–67, 70, 72.

Kline, E. 2007. How Europe, Canada, and our own VA do health care better. *American Prospect*, 18(5): 17–21.

Klingner, D. and D. Lynn. 2005. Beyond civil service: The politics of the emergent paradigms. In *Handbook of Human Resource Management in Government* (Ed.) S.E. Condrey. San Francisco, California: Jossey-Bass. pp. 37–57.

Legge, K. 1996. Morality bound. *People Management*, 25(2): 34–36.

Linder, M. and I. Nygaard. 1998. *Void Where Prohibited: Rest Breaks and the Right to Urinate on Company Time*. Ithaca, New York: ILR/Cornell University Press.

Lucero, M. and R. Allen. 1994. Employee benefits: A growing source of psychological contract violations. *Human Resource Management*, 33(3): 425–446.

Mathis, W. 1999. Reclaiming a balanced life: Reinventing our schedules. *Public Management*, 81(1): 6–8.

Mazzella, C. 2006. *Miami-Dade County-Tuition Refund Program: Interim Report*. Miami-Dade County Office of Inspector General, Ref. IG06–17, August 16.

McDonnell, K. 2005. Benefit cost comparisons between state and local governments and private-sector employees. EBRI Notes 26(4), 7. 2004 Data: Retrieved on July 25, 2007 from http://www.dol.gov/ebsa/PDF/2004pensionplanbulletin.PDF.

McGregor, D. 1960. Theory X and Theory Y. In *Organization Theory: Selected Readings* (Ed.) D. Pugh. London: Penguin.

Mental Health America. 2007. *Finding Your Balance: At Work and Home.* Retrieved on February 19, 2007 from http://www.nmha.org/go/informaiton/get-info/workplace/finding-your-balance-at-work-and-home.

Mercer, W. 1996. *Mercer Work/Life and Diversity Initiatives.* Retrieved on July 30, 2007 from http://www.dcclifecare.com/mercer/mercer-1.html.

Miami-Dade State Attorney's Office. 2006. *Interim Report: Fraud and Neglect in the Miami-Dade County Tuition Refund Program.* Retrieved on July 10, 2007 from www.miamisao.com/publications/grand-jury/2000/gj2006sinterim.pdf.

Miller, J., B. Snead, and A. Pereira. 1991. Dependent care and the workplace: An analysis of management. *Journal of Business Ethics*, 10(11): 863–869.

Mines, R., S. Anderson, and P. Von Stroh. 1991. EAP ethics and the professions. *EAPA Exchange*, December.

Nicholas, R. 2005, December. Health and dental benefits fraud: The bottom line. *Benefits & Compensation Digest*, 18–21. Retrieved on July 10, 2007 from www.ufebo.org.

Norquist, G. 2005, March. Ownership can be revolutionary. *American Enterprise.* Retrieved on July 18, 2007 from www.taemag.com/issues/issueID.169.TOC.asp.

Occupational Safety and Health Administration (OSHA) n.d. *Occupational Health and Safety Information: Work Related Stress—A Guide for Managers.* Washington, DC: OSHA.

Page, M. and A. Tate. 2007. Extra 15 minutes: Work or take a break? *Real Simple*, January. http://www.realsimple.com/realsimple/content/0,21770,1586017,00.html (accessed February 26, 2007).

Pinzur, M. 2006. Accused scammers get two options. *The Miami Herald*, November 22.

Rabin, C. 2006. Four county workers accused of cheating taxpayers. *The Miami Herald*, November 10.

Rauch, M. 2005. 2005 Employee benefits survey. *Incentive*, October 1.

Richardson, C. 1998. Ethics and employee benefits. *Benefits Quarterly*, 14(1): 9–16.

Roberts, G. 2003. Municipal government part-time employee benefit practices. *Public Personnel Management*, 32(3): 435–454.

Roberts, G. 2004. Municipal government benefits practices and personnel outcomes: Results from a national survey. *Public Personnel Management*, 33(1): 1–22.

Sekerka, L. and R. Zolin. 2007. Rule-bending: Can prudential judgment affect rule compliance and values in the workplace? *Public Integrity*, 9(3): 225–244.

Sharar, D. and W. White. 2001. EAP ethics and quality: Does national vs. local service delivery make a difference? *Performance Resource Press*, Fall. Retrieved on July 5, 2007 from http://www.prponline.net/Work/EAP/Articles/eap_ethics_and_quality.htm.

Sharar, D. and W. White. n. d. The pricing of EAPs. Retrieved on July 5, 2007 from http://www.eapage.com/ThePricingofEAPs.doc.

Simhan, R. and A. Chandramouli. 2003, December 8. Time for a break. *Business Line.* Retrieved on February 19, 2007 from www.thehindubusinessline.com/life/2003/12/08/stories/2003120800110200.htm.

Smerd, J. 2007, February 26. Can a nap at work save your life? *Workforce Management.* Retrieved on February 27, 2007 from www.workforce.com/section/00/article/24/77/44.html.

Stace, D. and D. Dunphy. 1991. Beyond traditional paternalistic and developmental approaches to organizational change and human resource strategies. *The International Journal of Human Resource Management*, 2(3): 263–283.

The Miami Herald. 2006. Editorial: Revise employee tuition policies. *The Miami Herald*, December 28.

Thompson, J. and S. Mastracci. 2005. Toward a more flexible public workforce: Issues and implications. In *Handbook of Human Resource Management in Government* (Ed.) S.E. Condrey. San Francisco, California: Jossey-Bass. pp. 125–142.

Truss, C., L. Gratton, V. Hope-Halley, P. McGovern, and P. Stiles. 1997. Soft and hard models of human resource management: A reappraisal. *Journal of Management Studies*, 34(1): 53–73.

U.S. Bureau of Labor Statistics. 2005. Workers on flexible and shift schedules in 2004. *Bureau of Labor Statistics: Economic New Releases*. Retrieved on July 10, 2007 from http://www.bls.gov/bls/newsrels.htm.

U.S. Chamber of Commerce. 2007. Employee benefit costs continue to rise. Retrieved on July 3, 2007 from http://www.uschamber.com/press/releases/2007/febrary/07-33.htm.

U.S. Department of Labor. 2007. Work hours: Breaks and meal periods. Retrieved on February 26, 2007 from http://www.dol.gov/dol/topic/workhours/breaks.htm.

U.S. General Accountability Office. 2006, February. Employee compensation: Employer spending on benefits has grown faster than wages, due largely to rising costs for health insurance and retirement benefits. Washington, DC: U.S. GAO. GAO-06-285.

U.S. Office of Personnel Management. 1998. Guide to recruiting and retaining women in the federal government. Retrieved on July 26, 2007 from www.opm.gov/employ/women/retain.htm.

U.S. Office of Personnel Management. 2007a. Leave bank program. Retrieved on July 17, 2007 from www.opm.gov/local/leave/HTML/lvbank.htm.

U.S. Office of Personnel Management. 2007b. Work life: Adoption benefits guide. Retrieved on July 17, 2007 from www.opm.gov/Employment_and_Benefits/worklife/officialdocuments/handbooksuides/Adoption/index.asp.

Ventriss, C. and S. Barney. 2003. The making of a whistleblower and the importance of ethical autonomy: James F. Alderson. *Public Integrity*, 5(4): 355–368.

Walsh, M. 2007. $58 Billion Shortfall for New Jersey Retiree Care. *New York Times*, July 25, 1ff.

Wiley, C. 1998. Reexamining perceived ethics issues and ethics roles among employment managers. *Journal of Business Ethics*, 17(2): 147–161.

Wiley, C. 2000. Ethical standards for human resource management professionals: A comparative analysis of five major codes. *Journal of Business Ethics*, 25(2): 93–114.

Wojcik, J. 2007. Employer to fine unhealthy workers. *Workforce Management On-line*. Retrieved on July 24, 2007 from http://www.workforce.com/section/02/feature/25/00/78/index.html.

Wooten, K. 2001. Ethical dilemmas in human resource management: An application of a multidimensional framework, a unifying taxonomy, and applicable codes. *Human Resource Management Review*, 11: 159–175.

Chapter 4

Comparing Federal Employee Benefits with Those in the Private Sector

Mark Musell, Cary Elliott, and David Torregrosa

CONTENTS

The views in this chapter are those of the authors and should not be interpreted as those of the Congressional Budget Office.

55

4.1 Introduction

Employers commonly provide their employees with retirement, health, vacation, and other benefits in addition to wages and salaries. Those benefits form an important part of the total compensation package through which firms compete for and retain workers (Box 4.1). For example, retirement packages provide for long run

---

Box 4.1 Economic Properties of an Optimal Compensation Package

The federal government hires workers in competitive labor markets, which determine the level of compensation that must be paid to attract workers with various skills. Total compensation for each employee consists of current wages and benefits and deferred benefits. A higher valued compensation package allows the government to attract and retain more productive workers. If workers place a lower value of the current compensation package than it costs the government, then there exists a different mix of current and deferred compensation that cost taxpayers less but is preferred by workers.

Although deferred and current compensation are substitutes, they are not perfect substitutes. In particular, the marginal valuation that workers place on an additional unit of deferred as opposed to current, compensation depends on the level of total compensation, and most importantly, on the mix of current and deferred compensation. As the share of deferred compensation increases, the value that the worker attaches to another unit of deferred compensation decreases. Yet, given the current tax code and perhaps a demand for forced savings, if all compensation was current, firms could attract better workers at lower total compensation by offering them some (currently untaxed) deferred benefits. Similarly, if all compensation was deferred, firms could provide a higher valued compensation package by offering some current wages.

Under an optimal compensation scheme, workers would value an additional dollar of deferred compensation and an additional dollar of current compensation equally. If the values were not equal, then a different mix can be designed that would save taxpayers money and make the workers better-off. Gains are exhausted and an efficient mix exists when employees place equal relative values on an additional dollar of deferred income and an additional dollar of current compensation.

income security, and are often structured so that the employee has an incentive to remain with one firm for a long period, thus maximizing those benefits. In addition, employer-sponsored health plans allow employees to obtain cheaper group coverage; firms offer a variety of options and coverage levels that can help differentiate their compensation packages from those of other employers.

In determining the benefit package to offer employees, both governments and private firms consider the practices of competing employers. Employers use different approaches when considering those practices. For the public sector, the standard point of reference is the private sector, where market forces discipline practices and costs. Generally, analysts compare either the specific provisions of benefit plans or the average employer costs for providing benefits. However, one major drawback of those approaches is that specific benefit provisions may have different monetary values for different types of employees, the characteristics of whom tend to differ systematically by employer, industry, and sector.

In the late 1990s the Congressional Budget Office (CBO) conducted two studies of federal and nonfederal benefits that illustrate another approach that offers some advantages in assessing the relative generosity of a government's benefits package. A 1998 study, reviewed in this chapter, found that retirement, health insurance, and other benefits the government provides its rank-in-file employees are generally higher than those provided by other employers (Congressional Budget Office 1998). The federal advantage, according to the study, can reach about 7 percent of pay. Because those results were published, there have been developments in both the private sector and in the federal government that may have increased somewhat the size of the federal advantage in benefits. Nevertheless the study still provides a reliable estimate of the overall size of the difference in federal and nonfederal benefits. It also offers a useful illustration of one approach to making benefit comparisons.

4.2   Federal Civilian Employees and Their Benefits

The federal civilian workforce is large and diverse. According to the Office of Management and Budget (OMB), federal civilian employees numbered about 2.7 million in 2006—representing about 2 percent of all civilian nonagricultural workers in the United States (Office of Management and Budget 2006; Council of Economic Advisors 2006, pp. 336–337). Those federal workers hold jobs in just about every major occupation. The Office of Personnel Management (OPM) reports employment in over 850 different occupations (Office of Personnel Management 2000). More than 100 federal agencies direct the efforts of these workers, and more than three dozen pay systems determine their wages and salaries. Federal employees report to work in federal office and facilities located throughout this country and overseas. As of 2006, in fact, only about 8 percent of the federal civilian workforce was employed in Washington, DC (Office of Personnel Management 2006).

The large and diverse federal workforce exhibits certain prominent characteristics that shape and define it. About six out of every ten federal employees, for example, work for one of just three agencies: the Department of Defense (DOD), the Department of Veterans Affairs, and the U.S. Postal Service. DOD remains the largest single employer, accounting for almost three out of every ten federal civilian workers. In addition, the workforce is concentrated in white-collar occupations, particularly higher level professional and administrative positions such as attorney, accountant, and personnel manager (Congressional Budget Office 2007).

Federal civilian employee benefits represent significant budgetary outlays. The Congressional Budget Office projects that pensions for 2.5 million federal civilian retirees will be just over $63 billion in 2007 and that the government's share of premiums for 1.9 million retirees plus their dependents and survivors enrolled in the Federal Employees Health Benefits (FEHB) program will reach $8.5 billion.* Although a standard set of benefits applies to most civilian employees, the government provides slightly different plans to executives and certain other employees, for example those in the Foreign Service (Box 4.2). The major benefits that make up the standard package are described below. Those served as the focus of the CBO benefit comparisons.

Box 4.2   Pay and Benefits for Members of Congress and the President

The salary of the President was set at $400,000 in January of 2001. Besides salary, the president receives use of the White House, and Camp David, an official travel allowance of $100,000 per year, use of limousines and aircraft for travel, and an official expense allowance of $50,000 per year (Congressional Research Service 2006d). (This expense allowance has not changed since 1949.) The president receives special healthcare through the military and may, like other federal employees, elect health insurance coverage for his family through the Federal Employees Health Benefits program. The president may also purchase the same life insurance available to other federal workers. He takes time off from work at his own discretion. The president retires at the salary of a Cabinet member, $186,600 a year in 2007. He also receives mailing privileges, secret service protection, office allowances, and travel expenses in retirement (Congressional Research Service 2006c).

In addition to an annual salary of $165,200 in 2007, Members of Congress receive many of the same benefits as other federal civilian employees. However, the rules that govern some of those benefits, for retirement in particular, are different for Congress. For example, Members of Congress, like other civil servants, may participate in either the Civil Service Retirement System (CSRS)

---

* In addition, the U.S. Postal Service will contribute about $2 billion for annuitant premiums in 2007.

Box 4.2 (continued)   Pay and Benefits for Members of Congress and the President

or the Federal Employees Retirement System (FERS), depending on their date of employment. But the rate at which members earn benefits under both plans is different than for most other federal workers. Under FERS, for example, civilian employees earn 1 percent of their high-three average salary for each year of service. For members, by contrast, the rate is 1.7 percent. Members also have lower age and years-of-service requirements that establish when they can retire and receive a pension but Members of Congress must contribute toward their future benefits at a higher rate than other employees.

Like other top officials in government and the private sector, Members of Congress can hire staff and obtain supplies, office space, and other necessities at no cost to themselves. In the Congress, members receive allowances to cover such expenses. Allowances vary by member depending on a variety of factors including the size of the state represented and its distance from Washington. In the House of Representatives, allowances ranged in 2005 from $1.1 million to $1.5 million per year, per member. In the Senate, allowances for expenses in the same year ranged from $2.5 million to $4.1 million per year per senator. Members may not use those allowances for personal, political, or campaign expenses (Congressional Research Service 2006a).

4.3   Retirement Benefits

Most federal civilian workers, including postal workers, are covered by either the Civil Service Retirement System (CSRS) or the Federal Employees Retirement System (FERS). CSRS, a traditional defined benefit plan, covers those employees hired on or before December 31, 1983, when federal employees were not covered by the social security system. Currently less than 30 percent of federal workers are covered by CSRS. Federal civilian workers hired since 1984 are covered by FERS, a hybrid system that combines a small traditional pension plan with a 401(k) type defined contribution plan, in addition to coverage under Social Security.

Because CSRS was established in 1920 and preceded Social Security, most CSRS covered workers do not accumulate Social Security benefits.* CSRS is a defined benefit plan, in which the employer promises a benefit level at retirement. This benefit is determined by a formula that ties the size of the benefit to the employee's length of service and earnings.

---

* CSRS employees may have contributed to the social security system while employed outside of the government.

Under CSRS, most employees may retire and begin collecting pensions without penalty at age 55 with thirty years of service, at age 60 with twenty years of service, or at age 62 with five years of service. The annuity paid is a percentage of the average salary for the highest three consecutive years of earnings as a federal employee. This percentage is determined by multiplying the number of years of service by an accrual rate. The CSRS accrual rate increases with length of service: 1.5 percent for each of the first five years of service; 1.75 percent for years six through ten; and 2.0 percent for each year after the tenth. So for a worker who retires with thirty years of service the retirement annuity is equal to 56.25 percent multiplied by the high-three average salary. CSRS retirement annuities are inflation adjusted using the annual change in the Consumer Price Index for Wage and Salary Workers (CPI-W).* Employees generally contribute 7 percent of pay toward their future benefit but make no contributions to Social Security.

FERS was established by the Federal Employees' Retirement System Act of 1986 and covers civilian employees hired after January 1984 and others who elected to switch from CSRS. Under FERS, employees receive retirement income from three sources: the Thrift Savings Plan, a defined benefit plan, and Social Security.

The federal Thrift Savings Plan (TSP) is a defined contribution plan under section 401(k) of the Internal Revenue Code. Under such plans, employers generally make periodic contributions to retirement accounts set up for each employee. The level of the employer contribution is commonly set to match employee contributions according to a specific formula. Employers usually guarantee contributions but not a particular benefit level at retirement, as under defined benefit plans.

In TSP, federal agencies automatically contribute 1 percent of individual earnings to the plan on behalf of any worker covered by FERS. In addition, the employing agency matches voluntary employee deposits dollar for dollar for the first 3 percent of pay and 50 cents for each dollar for the next 2 percent. For employees who put 5 percent of their pay into the TSP, the federal government will put in 5 percent. The government does not match TSP contributions above 5 percent of pay. The Internal Revenue Service limits contributions that both federal and private sector employees can make to defined contribution plans. The limit is $15,500 in 2007.† A retiring employee can withdraw funds from the TSP immediately or at a later date. Employees who separate before reaching retirement age may maintain their TSP accounts or can move the funds to a rollover IRA. Federal employees may borrow money from their TSP accounts for the purchase of a house and certain

---

* Under both FERS and CSRS inflation adjustment occurs after a retiree starts receiving an annuity. For those who leave the Government before they become eligible for an immediate annuity, their high-three salaries are not adjusted to reflecte the time gap before they become eligible.

† Employees over the age of 50 may also make additional "catch-up" contributions of $5000 a year.

other expenses. (Employees in CSRS may also contribute $15,500 TSP, but they receive no matching contribution from the government.)

The defined benefit plan under FERS, like CSRS, provides a pension that is a portion of the high-three average salary. However, FERS employees generally earn pension benefits at a lower rate than under CSRS—generally 1 percent of the high-three salary for each year of service.* The age and service requirements for immediate, unreduced annuities are similar to those under CSRS, but the minimum retirement age requirement rises gradually from 55 for anyone born before 1948 to 57 for those born in 1970 and after, under FERS. Cost-of-living adjustments (COLAs) are limited under FERS in two ways. First, the basic annuity is only fully indexed to increases to the CPI-W under 2 percent. If that inflation measure is between 2 and 3 percent the annuity adjustment remains at 2 percent. If inflation is above 3 percent, the adjustment is the percent change in the CPI-W minus 1 percent. Employee contributions toward future retirement benefits under FERS total 7 percent for Social Security and the defined benefit plan together, plus any voluntary contributions to TSP.

4.3.1 Health Insurance Benefits for Employees and Retirees

The Federal Employees Health Benefits (FEHB) program, which began in July 1960, provides health insurance for over 4 million federal employees and annuitants, as well as their dependents and survivors, at an expected cost to the government of almost $25 billion in 2007. Both the government and the participants contribute toward the cost of health insurance coverage according to a complex formula. Overall, the government's share of premiums for employees and annuitants (including for family coverage) is 72 percent of the weighted average premium for all plans.[†] Enrollees pay the balance. One important benefit for federal civilian employees who retire from government when they are eligible for an immediate annuity is that they are able to continue participating in FEHB and pay the same amount in premiums that they did before retirement.[‡]

FEHB has features that compare favorably with those of plans offered by leading firms. Many federal employees have a wide choice of plans and may change plans during annual "open seasons."[§] Also, the program's participating plans offer catastrophic protection that limits employees' out-of-pocket costs for large medical expenditures. Not all private firms provide such coverage.

---

* The accrual rate rises to 1.1 percent a year for all service if an employee retires after age 60 with at least twenty years of service.
† The share is higher for Postal Service employees under the agency's collective bargaining agreement.
‡ Federal retirees generally must also have participated in the FEHB program during their last five years of service. More than 80 percent of new retirees elect to continue health benefits.
§ The choices depend on plan availability in a particular duty location.

4.3.2 Life Insurance

The federal government offers its employees an opportunity to participate in a group life insurance program. Payments to survivors under the basic program equal the annual amount of an employee's pay plus $2000. The minimum benefit is $10,000. (Additional benefits are provided for employees under age 45.) Costs are shared by the government and the employee: employees cover about two-thirds of premiums and the government one-third. Additional insurance may be purchased entirely at the employee's expense.

4.3.3 Sick Leave and Disability Benefits

Sick leave and disability programs replace all or part of an employee's income when illness or on the job injury results in an inability to work. The federal government provides benefits for both long- and short-term disability. Full-time federal employees earn 13 sick days at full pay per year that they can use for temporary problems. For long-term inability to work, federal employees may receive annuities under FERS and CSRS. Employees under FERS may receive benefits from Social Security and the defined benefit portion of FERS, subject to rules that coordinate benefits under the two programs. Generally, annuity levels under FERS and CSRS are set to make up some portion of predisability income.

4.3.4 Holiday and Vacations

The federal government, like many private employers, provides its employees with paid holidays and vacations. Federal employees receive ten paid holidays from work each year. They earn paid vacation according to length of federal service. New employees working full time earn 13 days of vacation leave per year. Employees with longer service, however, can earn up to 26 days of vacation per year.

4.4 Comparing Benefits

Organizations compare the benefits they offer with those of other employers for a number of reasons. They may, for example, wish to ensure their package of benefits is comparable and, thus, does not place them at a disadvantage in competing and keeping capable employees. Often the concern is to ensure that costs for benefits are not excessive in comparison to others. For governments, the standard reference for comparison is the private sector, where market forces discipline costs for benefits.

Organizations adopt a number of different approaches to comparisons. One involves comparing across organizations the individual provisions of each benefit offered, the employer costs of benefits, or some combination of both. Under such an approach, for example, an employer offering the chance to retire earlier or offering more vacation than other employers may be judged to have superior benefits and perhaps excessive costs, assuming all else equal. Such comparisons may also involve an examination across employers of average employer-paid premiums for health insurance. An organization with premiums significantly higher or lower than others may be judged to offer benefits out of line with the competition.

The approach has a number of advantages and disadvantages. On the plus side, it is relatively straight forward and easy to understand. The comparisons also deal with actual costs and benefits of the provisions, about which information is relatively easily obtainable. On the downside, the comparisons often do not control for difference in the characteristics or behavior of workers and so can lead to misleading conclusions about the generosity of benefits. Take the case of an employer offering the chance to retire earlier with a full pension than other employers. If few workers stay at the organization long enough to become eligible for pensions, then the benefit is only generous on paper. It has little impact on the organizations' costs and little meaningful impact on the lives of employees. In the same way, an employer may have higher than average health premiums for reasons that have nothing to do with the generosity of benefits. In fact, an organization can have relatively stingy benefits and high costs; if, all else equal, it has an older, sicker workforce with a higher rate of utilization of covered health benefits.

The approach adopted by CBO controlled for differences in the characteristics and behavior of workers and therefore leads to more reliable conclusions concerning how generous benefits are relative to those offered by other employers. It does so by comparing the employer costs that would occur if the benefit plans of different organizations were all applied to the same workforce with a fixed set of characteristics and patterns of illness, retirements, separation, and other behaviors.

But CBO's approach also has a number of downsides. It is fairly complex, often involving simulations that require special expertise. They require very detailed information on benefit practices, employee characteristics, and behavior that is often expensive to obtain and not always representative. The information used in the CBO comparisons, for example, covers mostly large private firms. The required detailed data on small firms is generally not available. The results, therefore, reflect how federal benefits compare only to those generally more generous benefits offered by larger firms.* Finally, they deal with hypothetical rather than actual costs; that is, they compare the costs that would obtain if benefit plans were applied to a standard hypothetical workforce rather than those that actually occur.

---

* This may not be a significant limitation if the federal government largely competes with large employers for workers.

4.5 The CBO Comparisons and Results

In 1998, CBO compared the present dollar value of benefits earned for a year of work by hypothetical federal and private employees. The results suggested that federal benefits are generally higher than those of private benefits. The differences in federal and private values ranged from a federal disadvantage of about 2 percent of pay to a federal advantage of about 7 percent of pay (see Table 4.1). FERS offered benefits

Table 4.1 Comparison of the Annual Value of Federal and Private Sector Benefits for Five Hypothetical Employees (in Dollars)

Age (Years)	25	35	55	60	50
Service (Years)	2	10	20	20	25
Salary (Dollars)	25,000	45,000	75,000	45,000	50,000
Retirement					
CSRS	a	a	10,770	3,545	8,309
FERS	1,750	5,320	14,435	6,644	8,715
Private firms	1,110	3,516	10,998	5,116	6,227
Health insurance					
CSRS	a	a	4,091	5,097	3,014
FERS	1,711	2,041	4,091	5,097	3,014
Private firms	2,211	2,538	4,617	5,726	3,459
Retiree health insurance					
CSRS	a	a	1,319	1,778	2,059
FERS	493	1,244	1,319	1,788	2,059
Private firms	225	568	648	820	1,002
Life insurance					
CSRS	a	a	397	479	100
FERS	−53	−64	397	479	100
Private firms	46	101	943	916	423
Sick leave					
CSRS	a	a	2,766	1,750	1,371
FERS	409	882	3,352	2,057	1,598
Private firms	367	779	2,793	1,716	1,354

Table 4.1 (continued) Comparison of the Annual Value of Federal and Private Sector Benefits for Five Hypothetical Employees (in Dollars)

Holiday and vacation					
CSRS	a	a	10,385	6,231	6,923
FERS	2,212	5,193	10,385	6,231	6,923
Private firms	2,067	4,780	9,158	5,495	6,338
Total					
CSRS	a	a	29,728	18,880	21,776
FERS	6,522	14,596	33,979	22,286	22,409
Private firms	6,026	12,282	29,157	19,789	18,803
Benefits as a percentage of pay					
CSRS	a	a	39.6	42.0	43.6
FERS	26.1	32.4	45.3	49.5	44.8
Private firms	24.1	27.3	38.9	44.0	37.6
Differences as a percentage of pay					
CSRS	a	a	0.8	−2.0	5.9
FERS	2.0	5.1	6.4	5.5	7.2

Note: Private sector values reflect practices as of 1996. CSRS, Civil Service Retirement System; FERS, Federal Employees Retirement System. "a" denotes the two youngest employees would not be eligible for CSRS because the plan was closed in 1983.

Source: Congressional Budget Office and the Watson Wyatt & Company.

more generous than many private sector plans offered. The federal system also appeared to offer better vacation, holiday, disability, and retiree health benefits than the private sector firms. Retirement benefits under CSRS and federal health and life insurance benefits, however, sometimes lagged behind those in the private sector.

The dollar values compared in the CBO analysis covered only the portion of benefits that employers provided; they excluded the portion that employees paid for directly. The comparisons were designed so that differences in benefit values reflected only differences in the provisions of benefit plans—they differed, therefore, from comparisons of average costs, which can vary among firms for many reasons other than the level of the benefits provided, such as the characteristics of a firm's workers and the patterns of behavior among employees. Two aspects of the comparisons, in particular, helped ensure a focus on variations in benefit provisions.

First, the analysis compared the value of benefits that the same set of five hypothetical employees would have earned in the federal government versus the private sector. Thus, the results were free of differences that may have been caused by variations in the types of workers employed by the federal sector compared to those employed by the private sector at that time. CBO selected the age, salary, and years of service for each hypothetical employee to illustrate a variety of typical circumstances. The hypothetical employees had the following profile:

Age	Salary (Dollars)	Years of Service
25	25,000	2
35	45,000	10
60	45,000	20
55	75,000	20
50	50,000	25

Second, the analysis used a common set of assumptions about interest rates, retirement patterns, use of health benefits, and other factors to compute the dollar values of both federal and private sector benefits. Thus, results were free of differences that one might expect if one assumed that federal and private sector employees behaved differently. The assumptions about behavior that the analysis used generally reflected the federal experience.

Dollar values were calculated by Watson Wyatt & Company, in consultation with CBO, using information from their proprietary database on private sector compensation. The Bethesda, Maryland, firm specializes in analyzing employee benefit programs and has experience comparing federal and private sector benefits. Most benefit values for private firms reflected the 1996 practices of the 800, predominantly large firms the Watson Wyatt database covered at the time. Those firms employed almost 12 million workers. Dollar values calculated for federal employees were based on data from the Office of Personnel Management on federal employment, benefit provisions, and participation in various benefit programs.

Given the uncertainties of preparing benefit comparisons and the age of the data employed, the results should be thought of as indicating only the general direction and approximate order of magnitude of differences in private sector and federal benefits. As described in the next section, developments since the time that the comparisons were conducted likely increased the federal advantage somewhat. The results and specific method of analysis for each benefit are described below to further illustrate the specific approach to benefit comparisons.

4.5.1 Retirement Comparisons

For retirement, the dollar values compared were the present values of benefits each hypothetical employee earned in 1996. Separate values were computed for each of the federal government's two main retirement systems for private defined benefit and defined contribution plans.* Separate values were also shown for Social Security under the assumption that benefits are paid as scheduled.[†] The values calculated for defined benefits plans represented the present value of future benefits divided by the expected length of service. Generally, the values were the amount the employer would have to put aside in a year to have enough on hand at a hypothetical employee's retirement to pay the benefits earned in that year. The dollar values compared for defined contribution plans were simply the employer contribution that the employee earned during the year. The employer contribution was calculated as the amount the employer would match for a given level of employee contribution, plus any automatic contributions. The amounts used in comparisons for Social Security in the private sector and in FERS, consistent with the approach used in assigning values to defined benefit programs, represented the present value of future benefits earned in a year.

Generally speaking, the benefit provisions of FERS and CSRS were more ample than those of private plans in the database. Only 8 percent of the private plans, for example, provided the kind of automatic postretirement cost-of-living adjustments found in FERS and CSRS. Those COLAs prevent the real value of the defined benefit pension from declining over time. That protection is particularly valuable for employees with long retirements and during periods of high inflation. Only about 15 percent of the private plans allowed employees to retire with full pensions at age 55 with thirty years of service, as federal employees are able to do. Finally, only about 28 percent of private plans provided the kind of automatic, unmatched employer contribution that is part of TSP.

Consistent with those differences in provisions, the estimated dollar values of retirement benefits under FERS exceeded private sector values for each of the hypothetical employees. The disadvantage for CSRS in the comparisons for some of the hypothetical employees reflected a number of factors.[‡] First, some of the hypothetical employees would not have the age and service necessary to benefit from some of the more generous aspects of CSRS. For example, the federal values for the employee at age 60 with twenty years of service do not reflect the generosity of early retirement at age 55 with thirty years of service. Second, other employees (such as the employee who is age 25 with two years of service) would be eligible for early retirement and the other generous benefits under federal retirement but would not be likely to stay

---

* Averages for each type of private plan included zeros for those employers that have no plan of that type.
† Under current law, Social Security benefits can only be paid out of the trust funds. Unless changes are made to either benefits or financing, actuaries at the Social Security Administration project that the trust fund will be running deficits beginning in 2040 and that only 74 percent of projected benefits will be payable. Those cuts would not affect how FERS compares to private plans but would affect how FERS compares with CSRS.
‡ The expected cost to the government of FERS benefits exceeds the cost of CSRS benefits for the average employee. Thus, it is not surprising that FERS is generally more generous than CSRS.

in government to receive them. Those results illustrate the importance of considering behavior and employee characteristics in comparisons. Firms might offer retirement benefits that appear generous on paper. But the career patterns, separation rates, and age and service profiles of employees might mean that few qualify for those benefits. The benefits would have little impact on organizations' costs or on the future security of employees. Finally, the advantage CSRS holds when comparing individual benefit provisions, such as COLAs or early retirement, appears to be more than offset, in many cases, by the fact that CSRS employees did not earn Social Security benefits while employed with the federal government and many private sector plans include a defined contribution plan in addition to a defined benefit plan.

4.5.2 Health Insurance Comparisons

The federal and private values for each hypothetical employee in the comparisons were the employee's estimated medical costs covered by insurance in a year, minus any contributions the employee makes. The method for calculating the values involves two steps. First, Watson Wyatt & Company estimated a package of medical costs that each hypothetical employee could be expected to incur in a year. They used their proprietary client database to obtain the medical expenses and the use of medical services by age, sex, type of insurer, employment status, and family status. It then applied the provisions of each insurance plan against those medical costs to determine the portion each plan would have covered. Private sector values for each hypothetical employee represented the average medical costs covered for all firms in the database. The amount for federal employees is the weighted average medical costs covered by four large plans among the many that participated in FEHB.*

The relatively low values for FEHB, despite the program's obvious advantages, reflected the fact that the government required employees to pay a larger share of the cost of health insurance than do many private sector firms. For example, although the government paid, on average, roughly 70 percent of the premiums for active employees and annuitants, only about one-quarter of all firms in the database picked up the entire cost of individual coverage and only about 10 percent picked up the entire cost for family coverage with up to two dependents. This has changed in recent years, however, and the federal advantage may have narrowed some because the comparison was conducted. Also, if the comparisons covered all private sector employees, about one-third of whom have no health insurance, federal insurance would have compared more favorably.† Finally, the method used for comparing employee health

---

* The plans are the Government Employees Hospital Association's standard benefit plan, the Kaiser Foundation's standard health plan for the mid-Atlantic region, Blue Cross and Blue Shield's standard benefit plan, and Mail Handler's high-option plan. Together, those four plans covered about half of the federal civilian workforce at the time of the comparisons.

† Note that because a higher proportion of federal jobs are in management, professional and related occupations (about 45 percent) compared to the private sector (32 percent), comparing federal benefits to the average benefits received by all private sector workers would be misleading.

benefits did not capture the value associated with the high number of health plan options that federal employees have to suit their needs. Therefore, the federal benefits may actually have a higher value to employees than the comparisons suggest.

4.5.3   Retiree Health Insurance Comparisons

The dollar values estimated are the amounts needed to fund the expected future medical benefits of retirees over each employee's career. Estimated future medical costs for private sector firms were based on the experience of selected Watson Wyatt & Company clients. Plan provisions were applied against those expected costs to determine the portion covered by insurance, taking into consideration eligibility requirements, caps on coverage, and other factors. The calculations used to determine the amounts needed to fund those benefits incorporated the same methods and assumptions used to compute amounts under defined benefit retirement plans. The dollar values for the federal government were based on benefits provided under the government employees hospital association insurance plan.*

The favorable showing for federal retirees' health benefits reflected, in part, the fact that such benefits were less common in the private sector. About 65 percent of the firms in the database provided health programs for retirees. The other factor that increases the value of federal retirees' health insurance compared with private benefits is the approach FEHB takes in coordinating benefits with Medicare. Medicare is the government's health insurance program for people age 65 and older and for certain others. The government and private plans usually adopt one of the several standard methods of integrating their benefits with Medicare's. The method adopted by the federal government is relatively generous. Many retirees enjoy a benefit level superior to that received although employed. The FEHB program pays amounts not covered by Medicare (but no more than what it would have paid in the absence of Medicare).

4.5.4   Values for Sick Leave and Disability in the Comparisons

Benefits for each hypothetical employee were the present value of payments employees receive from employers each year as part of the basic sick and disability benefit programs. For each hypothetical employee, those payments take into consideration the benefits available under employer plans for absences of different durations and the probability that those absences will occur. The probabilities and durations of absences were based on data from the Society of Actuaries. Private sector values were the averages for the database. Long-term disability provisions differ under CSRS and FERS, and separate values were computed for each.

---

* The benefits for this plan are fairly typical of those offered by plans in FEHBP.

The values for federal sick leave and disability benefits exceeded those for the private firms. Most private sector employees are eligible for disability benefits under Social Security. Aside from that, many firms offered limited benefits. For example, even for employees with five years of service, 3 percent of firms in the database offered no sick or disability leave at full pay, 25 percent offered ten days or fewer, and another 40 percent offered 60 days or fewer.*

4.5.5 Other Benefits in the Comparisons

For life insurance, the dollar values compared for each hypothetical employee were the expected payouts under federal or private plans, based on the probability of death and adjusted to exclude the portion of benefits employees contribute toward directly. The federal disadvantage in terms of life insurance benefits reflected a number of factors. About 90 percent of the private firms offered insurance entirely at the employer's expense, and many offered higher benefits than the government did. In addition, many firms in the private sector offered lower premiums to younger employees.

In addition, the Federal Employees Group Life Insurance (FEGLI) program suffers from adverse selection because the federal plan varies premiums only by age. Most healthy employees and retirees who do not smoke generally can find better rates outside the program.† Thus, FEGLI attracts a disproportionate share of unhealthy workers, retirees, and smokers and its rates reflect that adverse selection. Consequently, the value of federal life insurance benefits to younger and healthier workers is lower.

For holidays and vacation, the values compared were the employee's daily rate of pay times the number of days off that the employee receives. The calculations assumed that employees take all the leave available to them or receive cash for the current year's time off. The comparisons show that federal employees received more generous holiday and vacation pay than do employees of private firms.

4.6 Recent Developments and How They Might Affect the Reported Results

Developments since the CBO analysis suggest that the federal advantage in benefits has probably grown slightly. This has most to do with reductions in benefits in the

---

* Some private firms may offer more flexible vacation leave as opposed to earmarked sick leave. However, that difference would be offset in the "other" benefit comparisons below.
† For example, Worldwide Assurance for Employees of Public Agencies, a nonprofit insurer, specifically target federal employees but can reject high risk applicants. Its rates are significantly below those of the federal program. For additional information see www.waepa.org.

private sector that makes the federal package look more generous by comparison. In addition, several recent enhancements of the federal employee health benefit program have increased the relative attractiveness of federal employment though those benefits are employee financed and would not likely affect the dollar values in comparisons.

In the private sector, a study by the Government Accountability Office (GAO) concluded that employee's access to benefits has remained stable in recent years but participation rates declined for health benefits as employee premiums rose. The study also showed that fewer workers had access to sick and personal leave (Government Accountability Office, February 2006). More significantly, rising healthcare costs resulted in cutbacks in employer-sponsored retiree health insurance.* According to a study by the Congressional Research Service, 40 percent of large employers offered retiree health insurance for Medicare-eligible retirees in 1993. By 2004, the percentage offering such benefits had fallen to 20 percent (Congressional Research Service, April, 2006b, page 1).

On the federal side, the federal employee health plan has added high-deductible plans, flexible spending accounts, and long-term care insurance since the CBO report. Although those do not involve any significant contributions by the employing agency, they do add to the desirability and benefits derived from federal employment.

In 2003, FEHB began offering high-deductible plans (HDHP) coupled with tax-advantaged accounts that could be used to pay for qualified medical expenses (Box 4.3). Those types of plans are designed to help control costs by exposing enrollees to more risk for their healthcare expenditures. Some employees may benefit from greater flexibility and discretion over their healthcare spending although building savings for future medical expenses tax free.

In 2003, healthcare flexible spending accounts became available to federal employees for the first time. Those employees can now make up to $4000 pretax contributions to flexible spending accounts to cover qualified medical expenses throughout the year similar to employees at many large civilian firms (over 60 percent of firms with 50 or more workers offer them).

In addition, a supplemental dental and vision plan was added to the federal employee benefits offering starting in 2007. However, enrollees are responsible for 100 percent of premiums. This coverage is secondary to any dental or vision services provided through the employees primary FEHB health plan.

---

* A contributing factor to the long-term decline in retiree health coverage in the private sector was an accounting change in 1993 that required most private firms to recognize the accrual cost of retiree health benefits and a liability for those benefits. That change generally had the effect of lowering firms' reported profits and weakening their balance sheets.

Box 4.3 High-Deductible Health Plans

With high-deductible health plans, patients pay a higher portion of their healthcare costs out-of-pocket giving them greater flexibility and discretion over how their healthcare dollar is spent. This feature, advocates say, provides financial incentives that will transform patients into active consumers who exert pressure on healthcare providers to improve the cost, efficiency, and quality of care. In addition accompanying savings accounts allow patients to build savings, tax free, for future medical expenses.

The HDHP features higher annual deductibles (a minimum of $1,100 for self and $2,200 for self and family coverage) than other traditional health plans. The maximum amount out-of-pocket limits for HDHPs participating in the FEHB program in 2007 is $5,250 for self and $10,500 for self and family enrollment. Depending on the specific plan, members may be limited in choosing providers but the use of in-network providers is cheaper than out-of-network providers. With the exception of preventive care, there is an annual deductible to meet before the plan pays benefits. Preventive care services are generally paid as first dollar coverage or after a small deductible, or co-payments. A maximum dollar amount (up to $300, for instance) may apply.

Each month, the HDHP plan automatically credits a portion of the health plan premium into a Health Savings Account (HSA) or a Health Reimbursement Arrangement (HRA), based on eligibility requirements. (Medicare enrollees are not eligible for an HSA.) Deductibles can be paid from HSA or HRA accounts. In an HSA, deductibles can be paid out-of-pocket, allowing the savings account to grow tax free. HRAs for federal employees generally do not have limits on the carry-over amount but must be used for medical expenses only; one federal plan limits balances to $5,000 for individuals and $10,000 for families.[*] All FEHB HRAs are forfeited when an enrollee leaves the plan. In contrast, federal employees' HSA accounts are more flexible: the unused balances may accumulate tax free without limit and withdrawals may be used for nonmedical expenses, subject to income tax, and an additional penalty for those under 65.[†]

References

Congressional Budget Office. 1998. *Comparing Federal Employee Benefits with Those in the Private Sector*. Washington, DC: Congressional Budget Office.

Congressional Budget Office. 2007. *Characteristics and Pay of Federal Civilian Employees*, Washington, DC: Congressional Budget Office.

---

[*] APWU's Consumer-Driven Health Plan.
[†] Withdrawals used for medical expenses are not taxed.

Congressional Research Service. 2006a. *Congressional Salaries and Allowances*. Washington, DC: Congressional Research Service.

Congressional Research Service. 2006b. *Employer-Sponsored Retiree Health Insurance: An Endangered Benefit?* Washington, DC: Congressional Research Service.

Congressional Research Service. 2006c. *Former Presidents: Federal Pension and Retirement Benefits*. Washington, DC: Congressional Research Service.

Congressional Research Service. 2006d. *President of the United States: Compensation*. Washington, DC: Congressional Research Service.

Council of Economic Advisors. 2006. *Economic Report of the President for 2006*. Washington, DC: Unites States Government Printing Office.

Government Accountability Office. 2006. *Employee Compensation: Employer Spending on Benefits Has Grown Faster Than Wages, due Largely to Rising Costs for Health Insurance and Retirement Benefits*. Washington, DC: Government Accountability Office.

Office of Management and Budget. 2006. *Budget of the United States, 2007. Analytical Perspectives*. Washington, DC: Office of Management and Budget. Chapter 24: Federal Employment and Compensation.

Office of Personnel Management. 2000. *Federal Civilian Workforce Statistics: Occupations of Federal White-Collar and Blue-Collar Workers as of 1999*. Washington, DC: Office of Personnel Management.

Office of Personnel Management. 2006. Data from automated online data retrieval system at *http://www.fedscope.opm.gov/employment.asp*

Chapter 5

Employee Support and Development Benefits: Generational Issues

Ilka M. Decker

CONTENTS

5.1   Introduction

Today's labor force is characterized by several generations of workers: matures, baby boomers, Generation X, and Generation Y. Matures have for the most part left the workforce, and members of the baby boomer generation are nearing retirement age. As increasing numbers of baby boomers retire, the American workplace is experiencing a demographic shift as there are fewer younger workers to replace them. In addition to generational shifts, the traditional social contract in which employees exchange long-term tenure with a public organization for generous benefits and pension programs has also shifted towards more transactional, short-term exchanges (Tulgan 2004). As a result of these changes, public human resource managers who wish to attract and retain qualified employees are faced with the challenge of designing and managing employee benefit packages that meet the wide variety of needs of employees at different stages of their lives and careers.

This chapter will begin by briefly describing demographic shifts occurring in the labor force. We will examine each generation in today's workplace, reviewing the research and literature regarding each generation's historical context, work values, motivations, commitment, and attitudes. This review will focus on the three generational groups with the largest representation in the current labor force, the baby boomers, Generation X, and Generation Y.

Given that compensation and benefits are often among the most costly budget items for public sector organizations, examining and understanding employee work motivations, commitment, and values is essential to designing benefit programs that meet employee needs (Jurkiewicz and Brown 1998). We will discuss generational implications for employee benefits, focusing specifically on benefits that offer personal, professional, and work-related support and development. These benefits are a subset of what have been termed life-cycle benefits (Adolf 1993). They reflect a shift in that organizations are increasingly adopting a more holistic view of employees, recognizing that life events that occur outside their roles within the organization impact job performance (Cayer 2005). Finally, we will raise key considerations for public sector human resource managers responsible for designing and maintaining these benefit programs.

Table 5.1   Generations in the American Labor Force

Generation	Birth Years	Other Labels
Matures	1925–1945	Silent generation, veterans, World War IIers
Baby boomers	1943–1964	Boomers
Generation X	1963–1981	Generation Xers, baby busters
Generation Y	1976–2000	Baby boomer echoes, millenials, nexters

5.2   Generational Shifts in the Labor Force

Although scholars concur on the existence of the generational groups, there is little agreement regarding the exact ranges of birth years that define each group. For clarity, this chapter will use the nomenclature and birth year ranges shown in Table 5.1. The ranges of birth years have been purposefully defined broadly and with some overlap, with the understanding that it is difficult to define hard and fast boundaries on the social, historical, and economic events; trends; and experiences that have shaped and influenced each generational cohort.

The American workplace is undergoing a transformation as the number of retiring baby boomer workers outpaces the number of younger Generation X and Y workers to replace them (West 2005). The United States Bureau of Labor Statistics (BLS 2005) projects that the annual growth rate for workers ages 25–54 will increase by 0.1 between 2004 and 2014, although the growth rate for workers over age 65 is expected to increase by 3.2 over the same period. Civilian labor force participation data from the BLS shown in Table 5.2 evidences this demographic trend.

5.3   Generations in the Workplace

5.3.1   Matures

Americans born before World War II ended in 1946 have been called the matures (Jurkiewicz and Brown 1998), silent generation (Southard and Lewis 2004; Tulgan 2004), veterans (Reynolds 2005), or World War IIers (Smola and Sutton 2002). Born during the Depression, many members of this group served the country during World War II either as members of the armed forces or as workers in industries supporting the war effort. Although members of this generation are for the most part no longer in the labor force, the legacy of their Depression childhood and military service continues to shape organizations today, including an emphasis on pragmatism, hierarchy, seniority, rules, and respect for authority (Toossi 2005).

Table 5.2 United States Civilian Labor Force Participation Rates

Group	Participation Rate			Percentage Point Change			Annual Growth Rate		
	1994	2004	2014	1994–2004	2004–2014		1994–2004	2004–2014	
Total, 16 years and older	66.6	66.0	65.6	−0.6	−0.4		−0.1	−0.1	
16–24	66.4	61.1	59.1	−5.3	−2.0		−0.8	−0.3	
16–19	52.7	43.9	39.3	−8.8	−4.6		−1.8	−1.1	
20–24	77.0	75.0	73.8	−2.0	−1.2		−0.3	−0.2	
25–54	83.4	82.8	83.5	−0.6	0.7		−0.1	0.1	
25–34	83.2	82.7	85.4	−0.5	2.7		−0.1	0.3	
35–44	84.8	83.6	83.0	−1.2	−0.6		−0.1	−0.1	
45–54	81.7	81.8	82.3	0.1	0.5		0.0	0.1	
55 and older	30.1	36.2	41.2	6.1	5.0		1.9	1.3	
55–64	56.8	62.3	65.2	5.5	2.9		0.9	0.5	
65 and older	12.4	14.4	19.7	2.0	5.3		1.5	3.2	
65–74	17.2	21.9	26.9	4.7	5.0		2.4	2.1	
75 and older	5.4	6.1	9.6	0.7	3.5		1.2	4.6	

Source: From U.S. Bureau of Labor Statistics, 2005. With permission.

Traditional benefit plans were designed for members of this generation, who expected to spend most of their careers with a single organization that would reward their service with long-term job security and generous defined benefits (Reynolds 2005). Matures favor workplaces with stability, security, friendly and collegial coworkers, and opportunities to work as part of a team (Jurkiewicz and Brown 1998). Other valued rewards include respect for their knowledge and experience and part-time and temporary employment that allows them the flexibility to transition out of the work force on their own terms (Tulgan 2004; Reynolds 2005). Work-related motivational factors for members of this generation include the opportunity to advance and to use their special abilities (Jurkiewicz and Brown 1998).

5.3.1.1 Discretionary Support and Development Benefits That Appeal to Matures

The American Association of Retired Persons' (AARP) *Working in Retirement Study* reports that preretiree and retiree respondents between the ages of 50 and 70 years old cited the desires to stay mentally active and to be productive and useful as major factors in deciding to work in retirement (2003). Employee training programs offer a chance to build on existing knowledge, learn new skills, and stay mentally active. Flexible work arrangements including part-time employment, job sharing, and retiree rehire programs give matures the opportunity to use their knowledge and abilities, stay mentally active, and remain productive although transitioning towards retirement at their own pace. These arrangements are beneficial to public sector organizations in several ways. Flexible work arrangements enable agencies to retain older workers' expertise and organizational memory. Retiree rehire programs allow retirees to return to work within an organization as part-time contractors. Job-sharing programs allow two part-time employees to share the workload, compensation, and benefits of one full-time position (Friedman n.d.).

When paired with other benefits such as training, development, and mentoring programs, flexible work arrangements also create opportunities for older workers to share their experience and abilities with younger workers (Southard and Lewis 2004). Pairing older and younger workers in mentoring programs is one way for an organization to recognize and show respect for matures' experience (Reynolds 2005). Mentoring programs can also foster skill sharing from Generation X and Y employees to older workers, especially skills related to technology.

5.3.2 Baby Boomers

Although some scholars identify baby boomers as those born between 1943 and 1960 (Jurkiewicz and Brown 1998; Yang and Guy 2006), the more commonly used range is 1946–1964 (Doverspike et al. 2000; O'Bannon 2001; Smola and Sutton

2002; Tulgan 2004; Toossi 2005; Wallace 2006). Born in the wake of World War II, this generation grew up during the prosperity and consumerism of the 1950s. Boomers heeded President John F. Kennedy's call to public service, came of age during the Vietnam War, and used their idealism to fuel the civil rights movement, women's liberation, and sexual revolution. The antiestablishment youth culture of the period protested against powerful social and political institutions, effecting tumultuous societal changes. Watergate, the Vietnam War, and the assassinations of Martin Luther King Jr. and John F. Kennedy instilled distrust and a lack of respect for authority (Tulgan 1995; Yang and Guy 2006).

Baby boomer work motivators' commitment and values are often examined in comparison to those of matures and Generation Xers. Some of the literature indicates that generational cohorts may have more overall similarities than differences. Several scholars suggest that differences that do exist may be attributed to each generation's stage in the life cycle rather than to their historical experiences or generational identity (Jurkiewicz and Brown 1998; Yang and Guy 2006). Other researchers acknowledge the influence of the life cycle and age of employees, but assert that generational experiences are more influential (Smola and Sutton 2002).

One study asked local government employees in the midwestern United States to rank 15 work-related motivational factors (Jurkiewicz and Brown 1998; Jurkiewicz 2000). Initial analysis of survey responses revealed very minimal difference between matures, baby boomers, and Generation Xers. Although boomers and matures did not demonstrate any significant difference on any of the 15 work-related motivational factors, boomer respondents ranked freedom from supervision higher than Generation Xers (Jurkiewicz and Brown 1998). Follow-up survey analysis indicated boomer respondents ranked only three of the fifteen factors significantly different than Generation X respondents. Boomers ranked the chance to learn new things and freedom from pressure to conform both on and off the job higher (Jurkiewicz 2000). Additional research on generational work motivation factors utilized a national sample of state, local, and federal government employees (Yang and Guy 2006). The data indicates no statistically significant differences in work motivators between baby boomer and Generation X respondents.

Although baby boomers are often depicted as committed and dependable, their Generation X coworkers are commonly described as lazy slackers who lack work commitment and are unwilling to pay their dues (Tulgan 1995; O'Bannon 2001). The validity of these perceptions has been tested by research investigating determinants of work commitment for boomer and Generation X lawyers (Wallace 2006). Contrary to these popular stereotypes, findings indicate no significant differences in the degree of work commitment between the two cohorts after accounting for demographic control variables, earnings, work effort, work flexibility, and intrinsic rewards (Wallace 2006).

However, the same study found some important differences in the factors related to each generation's work commitment. Data suggests that earnings, an extrinsic reward, are more important for baby boomers. Factors that have significantly strong positive associations with baby boomer work commitment include a heavier workload, engaging in extra professional activities outside of work hours, and higher earnings (Wallace 2006).

Other research has examined whether work values are influenced by each generation's experiences or whether values change as employees age and mature (Smola and Sutton 2002). Responses revealed similarities and differences between baby boomer and Generation X participants. Data analysis indicated no significant differences in survey items related to pride of craftsmanship and doing a good job between the two generational cohorts. However, baby boomer respondents felt more strongly than Generation Xers that work should be one of the most important parts of a person's life. Older employees expressed lower desire than Xers to be promoted more quickly. Researchers assert that generational work values differ and that values change as society changes and employees age (Smola and Sutton 2002).

5.3.2.1 *Discretionary Support and Development Benefits That Appeal to Baby Boomers*

As noted above, preretirees and retirees cited staying mentally active and remaining productive or useful as important factors in their decision to work in retirement (AARP 2003). Flexible work arrangements and training and development opportunities that enable boomers to remain engaged in work as they gradually transition towards retirement are valued benefits. Opportunities to learn and maintain skills allow boomers to expand their knowledge and try new things or embark on second careers (Reynolds 2005). Flexible work arrangements give boomers freedom to take active roles in their children's lives and to care for aging parents (Southard and Lewis 2004). Part-time employment, flexible work schedules, job sharing, paid and unpaid sabbaticals, flextime, compressed work weeks, and telework give boomers the autonomy to manage their schedules and workload (Reynolds 2005).

Paid and unpaid sabbaticals are a benefit that some organizations offer to employees (Reynolds 2005). Sabbaticals provide employees the opportunity to leave their organization for a planned, specified period of time. Some organizations offer social service sabbaticals during which employees expand and hone their skills although serving a nonprofit organization. Other organizations offer sabbaticals as a benefit to employees with long-term tenure. For example, the city of Claremont, California, offers an eighty-hour longevity leave bonus after ten years of service and then every five years after that. The city encourages employees to match the leave bonus with annual leave to create a mini-sabbatical (Southard and Lewis 2004). Sabbaticals offer baby boomers time out to improve their skills, give back to the community, relax and recharge, care for children and aging family members, travel, or focus on hobbies. However, sabbatical programs must be carefully managed and planned to ensure they are administered fairly, cross-training is adequate, and workloads are covered during time off (Larson 2005).

Two options that give baby boomers greater discretion over their work schedules are flextime and compressed work weeks. Organizations with flextime programs usually have a set of core hours around which employees can choose their own beginning and finishing times. Employees can adjust their work schedules as long as they work during the core operating hours (Doverspike et al. 2000). A compressed work week is an arrangement that offers the ability to work longer hours over fewer days. For example, a compressed schedule might entail working ten hours per day for four days a week rather than the traditional schedule of eight hours per day for five days a week (Friedman n.d.).

Telework is a form of flex-place that involves work from the employee's home or another location. Employees may connect to their workplace via computer. In 2001, the United States Department of Transportation and Related Agencies Appropriations Act directed federal executive agencies to establish telecommuting policies. The United States Office of Personnel Management (U.S. OPM) reports that between 2003 and 2004, there was a 37 percent increase in the number of federal teleworkers (U.S. OPM 2005). Although barriers include management resistance, data security, office coverage, and the nature of the work to be performed, benefits such as decreased transportation costs and commute times, reduced environmental impact, and increased productivity and morale suggest that the usage of telework is likely to grow (Cayer 2005; U.S. OPM 2005).

Training and opportunities for professional development are valued by baby boomers. As they plan for retirement, many boomers are interested in not only remaining mentally active, but also in honing their existing skills and learning new things for a second career (AARP 2003; Reynolds 2005). As noted previously, engaging in professional activities outside of work hours has a significantly strong positive association with baby boomer work commitment (Wallace 2006). Providing boomers with memberships in professional organizations and paid time and travel funds to attend professional conferences, workshops, or seminars are ways that organizations can support employee development (Cayer 2005). Encouraging participation in training and career development opportunities and adapting programs to cater to adult learning styles is one way organizations can signal support for investing in and retaining workers as they near retirement (West and Berman 1996). Tuition reimbursement is a benefit that provides financial assistance to students in job-related programs of study.

Employee assistance programs (EAPs) and wellness programs help employees deal with life stressors and health concerns that can impact job performance. Because of their stage in the life cycle, many boomers face issues related to planning for retirement, caring for elderly parents, raising children, and related financial challenges. Eldercare support provided by EAPs is an important support benefit for baby boomers who are caregivers for elderly parents and relatives. EAP referral services connect caregivers with counseling services as well as names of assisted living facilities, senior centers, adult day care programs, hospices, and home nurses (Adolf 1993). Through the use of contracted referral services and providers, EAPs may also help employees with alcohol and substance abuse, mental health issues, financial planning, elder caregiving, counseling, and stress reduction (Cayer 2002). Wellness programs often focus on increasing healthy behaviors, reducing stress, and reducing risk factors that lead to costly chronic illnesses (Daley 1998). Programs may offer on-campus gyms, reduced-cost memberships to local fitness centers, weight-loss programs, or discounted health insurance premiums for employees who fulfill requirements such as annual physicals and fitness levels.

5.3.3   Generation X

Members of Generation X were born between the mid 1960s and the early 1980s, although there is very little agreement on the exact birth year range. Definitions for this generation include 1961–1981 (Jurkiewicz and Brown 1998; O'Bannon 2001), 1963–1981 (Tulgan 1995; Jurkiewicz 2000), 1965–1977 (Tulgan 2004), 1965–1980 (Doverspike et al. 2000), 1965–1981 (Bova and Kroth 2001). A much smaller cohort than the baby boomers, this generation is sometimes called the baby busters (Toossi 2005; West 2005).

Much has been written about Generation X. Popular stereotypes have described Xers as latchkey kids who relied on television as a surrogate babysitter and learned to be independent and entrepreneurial by taking care of themselves after school although their parents were at work (Tulgan 1995). Growing up during a period of rapid change, Xers were influenced by MTV, yuppie materialism, AIDS, the arms race, video games, a divorce rate that doubled between 1965 and 1977, globalism, the fall of the Berlin Wall, the war on drugs, computers, and the rise of Internet (O'Bannon 2001).

Members of this cohort have often been called slackers and labeled as uncommit-ted although research suggests there are no significant differences between Genera-tion Xers and boomers in their degree of work commitment (Wallace 2006). Generation Xers have also been called lazy, although research findings contradict this stereotype. Generation Xers feel more strongly than boomers that working hard is an indication of a person's worth, and they are more likely than boomers to agree that a person should work hard even in the absence of a supervisor (Smola and Sutton 2002).

At the same time, there is evidence that Generation Xers strive to strike a balance between their work and nonwork lives. Although a study found that Xers expressed a greater desire for rapid promotion than older workers, they also felt less strongly than baby boomer respondents that work should be one of the most important parts of a person's life (Smola and Sutton 2002). Other research indicates that Generation X lawyers try to maintain balance by keeping work at the office; Xers reported work-ing longer hours at the office, although boomers reported working longer hours at home and participating in more professional activities outside of work hours (Wallace 2006). Some have recommended that public sector organizations highlight benefits that foster work–life balance in their efforts to attract Generation X workers (O'Bannon 2001).

Opportunities to develop skills are a driving force for members of Generation X. Xers rank the chance to learn new things higher than matures and baby boomers as a work-related motivational factor (Jurkiewicz and Brown 1998). Research on workplace learning suggests that Generation Xers prefer action learning and incidental learning to traditional learning (Bova and Kroth 2001). Action learning refers to learning through finding solutions to real problems, and incidental learning occurs as an unintended result of another process, such as learning from mistakes or experimentation. This generation views training and development as a personal career investment because they tend to have a stronger commitment to self than to organizations and expect to change jobs and organizations multiple times within their lives (Jurkiewicz 2000). Although frequent job changes are common for Xers, many are willing to stay with an organization if training and opportunities for self-building, or skill set development, are available (Tulgan 1995).

5.3.3.1 Discretionary Support and Development Benefits That Appeal to Generation Xers

Like matures and baby boomers, Generation X employees value support and development benefits that give them greater control over their work schedule and hours. As noted, striking a balance between work and life is very important to members of this cohort. Benefits such as telework, compressed work weeks, job sharing, and flextime allow Generation Xers to concentrate on enriching aspects of their lives outside of work: friends, hobbies, children, family, entrepreneurial activities.

Dependent care benefits help Generation X parents with child care. Xer parents can save money by depositing pretax money into flexible dependent care spending accounts to be used for qualifying expenses. Some organizations offer subsidized child care, on-site day care, discounts for nearby day care facilities, or emergency or drop-in care for the children of the employees (Adolf 1993; Cayer 2002). Convenient child care provides the opportunity for parents and children to have contact during breaks from work, and back up emergency child care allows parents to come to work instead of taking leave time in the event that their regular child care arrangements cannot provide care.

Research on workplace learning documents the importance of continuous individual learning to Generation Xers (Bova and Kroth 2001). The term "self-building" refers to the process by which Generation Xers learn and build their skill sets through new experiences, information, and challenging projects (Tulgan 1995). An example of a support and development benefit that offers self-building opportunities is the city of Claremont, California's employee leadership academy. Created in partnership with Claremont McKenna College's Kravis Leadership Institute, the nine-month program features guest speakers, exercises, assessments, and reading materials with the goal of developing participants' leadership skills and exposing them to experiences outside of their regular duties (Southard and Lewis 2004). Job rotation programs are employee benefits that involve a series of periodically rotating assignments that expose employees to a wide variety of roles within an organization. The experience of learning a completely new job and set of skills every year or two is appealing to Xers because of their preference for action learning and incidental learning. Tuition reimbursement is another development-related employee benefit that sponsors more traditional forms of learning.

Mentoring programs are employee benefits that are valued by members of Generation X. Xers believe mentors and leaders in the workplace should lead by example (Bova and Kroth 1999). Receiving feedback, coaching, and insight from managers and mentors helps Xers improve their skills and knowledge inspires their loyalty (Tulgan 1995). Examples of other notable mentoring activities include encouraging employees to discuss their professional goals with managers, including younger employees in high-level meetings, and allowing them to accompany managers to workshops and seminars (Southard and Lewis 2004).

5.3.4 Generation Y

Generation Y, also called baby-boom echoes, nexters, or millenials, have been variously identified as those born between 1976 and 2000 (Toossi 2005), 1978 and 1987 (Tulgan 2004), 1978 and 1988 (Martin 2005), and 1978 and 1989 (Armour 2005). More numerous than Generation Xers, members of this generation are the most recent entrants into the labor force. They grew up during the dot com boom and witnessed downsizing, the dot com bust, September 11, the war on terror, the Enron scandal, and the ongoing debate about the long-term viability of social security (Armour 2005). Generation Y grew up using the Internet, e-mail, and cell phones. They are technologically savvy and accustomed to accessing, exchanging, and processing large amounts of information quickly (Martin and Tulgan 2001).

Groomed for success by their boomer parents, many Generation Yers had heavily programmed childhoods with multiple extracurricular activities. Described as both high performance and high maintenance, Yers need frequent feedback, recognition, and communication from managers (Martin 2005). This generational cohort values diversity, collaboration, and a sense of community. The popularity of instant messaging, text messaging, blogs, and online social networking communities such as MySpace and Facebook evidences the value this generation places on frequent communication and feedback, friendships, and community.

Empirical research on Generation Y work values, commitment, and motivators is currently lacking. This may be because members of this generational cohort are just beginning to enter the full-time workforce. The literature regarding Generation Y includes anecdotal accounts and characterizations based on the group's historical experiences (Armour 2005; Martin 2005; Reynolds 2005; Glass 2007). As Generation Yers continue to join the workforce, there is a need for research to better understand these workers.

5.3.4.1 *Discretionary Support and Development Benefits That Appeal to Generation Yers*

Like baby boomers and Generation X, members of Generation Y want benefits that allow them to balance work with leisure. Flexible work arrangements including flextime, telework, and compressed work schedules appeal to Yers. Many Yers hope to be able to leave the workforce for a short period of time when they have children (Armour 2005).

Generation Yers were raised with constant feedback and coaching from parents, coaches, and teachers. In the workplace, they want mentors and managers who share knowledge and provide them access to needed information and resources (Martin 2005). Mentoring programs pair them with more experienced older workers from whom they can learn (Reynolds 2005). They are also willing to share their skills with older workers. As one Yer explains: "I am computer savvy ... so people come to me for everything" (Armour 2005). Like mentoring relationships, learning and development programs enable Generation Yers to expand their knowledge and skills. Fast-track leadership programs appeal to the Yer, desire to make an impact, and produce results quickly (Glass 2007). Some have observed that this cohort may prioritize opportunities for growth, learning, and innovation more highly than salary (Zemke 2001).

Another type of support and development benefit that appeals to Generation Y workers is the recognition program. Generation Yers expect praise and recognition from managers for outstanding performance (Martin 2005). Members of this cohort became accustomed to receiving constant feedback on their performance during childhood. They prefer short-term over long-term incentives because they are unwilling to sacrifice immediate rewards for long-term rewards which they do not expect to be around to receive (Tulgan 2004). One organization offers short-term rewards such as a gift-certificate recognition program, a program in which coworkers can nominate one another for a cash bonus up to $700, and a City Manager's Award of Excellence that includes a $1000 cash award (Southard and Lewis 2004). Another has a reward program that awards employees with time off (Armour 2005).

Benefit programs related to social awareness and altruism strike a chord with Generation Y employees (Glass 2007). Core values of this generation include civic duty, a sense of morality, and fairness (Zemke 2001). Examples of these types of benefits include subsidized public transportation passes, carpool programs, employee volunteer programs, time off for volunteer activities, and charitable giving.

5.4 Implications and Considerations for Public Human Resource Managers

5.4.1 *Understanding Organizational and Employee Needs*

Identifying the organizational goals and objectives of each benefit program is a good starting point for human resource managers interested in assessing their organization's employee support and development benefit package (Adolf 1993).

Organizational goals might include increasing recruitment and retention of Generation X and Y workers, demonstrating organizational commitment to child-friendly programs, or promoting energy conservation. Compiling a list of benefits available for employees and identifying which ones that most appeal to each generational cohort are other methods of assessment (Reynolds 2005). Both exercises are especially useful when combined with demographic data.

Collecting basic demographic information for employees including age, gender, home zip code, wage, educational level, and tenure is useful for understanding the employee population. Demographics can point to trends such as upcoming retirements or high turnover rates among certain groups of employees. They can also help to identify benefits that may be useful for employees and to estimate actual or predicted usage (Adolf 1993). For example, investigating telework or public transportation subsidies could be facilitated by employee home zip code data that could be used to assess commute distances and proximity to public transportation routes.

Focus groups and employee surveys can be used to clarify trends suggested by demographics and to provide a forum for employees to provide input regarding benefits. Conducting focus groups with small, diverse groups of employees and surveying the entire employee population are two ways to identify key issues and concerns related to benefits (Adolf 1993). Employee support and development benefits serve as a reflection of the organization's commitment to helping employees balance their work with their nonwork responsibilities. Research indicates that employees' perception that the organization understands family duties is a direct predictor of job satisfaction (Saltzstein, Ting, and Saltzstein 2001). Actively soliciting input conveys to employees that their needs and concerns related to support and development benefits are valued.

Benefits surveys provide data regarding the types of support and development benefits offered by similar organizations. This provides a market perspective on what benefits an organization needs to offer to compete for talented employees (Milkovitch and Newman 2005). Human resource managers should consider information collected through benefits surveys through the lens of organizational goals and strategy. What are the characteristics of the employees the organization wants to attract and retain? Does the organization want to be at the leading edge of offering benefits that help provide work–life balance, or in-line with comparable organizations? The latter question is especially important for public sector organizations, which must find ways to compete for talented employees with private sector firms that often offer more generous compensation.

5.4.2 Offering Benefits to Meet Identified Needs

A number of discretionary support and development benefits have already been identified and described in terms of generational life stage needs. The challenge for public human resource managers is deciding which benefits to offer to employees and how to structure corresponding programs and policies to ensure that the benefits meet organizational objectives and are fairly implemented. The following key questions are useful to ask during the decision-making process (Flannery, Hofrichter, and Platten 1996):

- *What messages does the organization want to convey to employees?* Benefit programs should reward the employees for the behaviors the organization wants to encourage. For example, an organization that wants to promote employee development might reward top performers with additional training opportunities.
- *How much variability and flexibility should be allowed within each program?* Diverse, intergenerational workforces need more flexibility and options than those that are not.
- *What is the cost to implement?* Cost containment is an ongoing issue as public sector organizations face decreasing budgets, funding cutbacks, and public scrutiny of expenses. Public agencies should make the most of support and development benefits that meet employee needs and impose minimal cost to the organization, such as mentoring programs or a negotiated discount with a nearby day care center.
- *How can the program be administered?* Keeping track of employee work schedules and arrangements, administering contracts with employee assistance program providers, facilitating mentoring programs, and managing training and development programs require record-keeping systems and coordination.
- *Will support and development benefits be tied to compensation?* Human resource managers must consider the interactions between pay and benefits as rewards. For example, will employees who successfully complete employee training and development programs be rewarded by promotions and pay raises?
- *How will benefit programs and policies be communicated to employees?* This issue will be addressed in the next section.

5.5   Effectively Communicating Benefits Information to Employees and Potential Hires

Human resource managers must work to ensure they communicate effectively with potential hires and existing employees regarding benefits. One survey found that although municipal employees gave greater importance to their fringe benefits than private sector employees, they demonstrated less knowledge of the benefits they were receiving (Bergmann, Bergmann, and Grahn 1994). Other research found that perceptions of benefits did not differ greatly between public and private sector employees, but also observed gaps in employee awareness of benefit availability (Fredrickson and Soden 1998). Effective communication should increase employees' understanding of the variety of benefits offered, make employees aware of the cost of the benefits to the organization, increase employee appreciation of the programs, and promote the company's efforts to communicate with employees about benefits (Milkovitch and Newman 2005). For benefit packages to contribute to improving employee retention, they must not only include desirable programs, but also be perceived as desirable by employees (Bergmann, Bergmann, and Grahn 1994).

The same principle applies to using benefits as a recruiting tool. Human resource managers should highlight benefit programs to potential hires as part of the recruiting process using the objectives for effective communication noted above. Keep in mind that many of the benefits discussed in this chapter appeal to multiple generations, but for different reasons. Design benefits-related recruiting messages to target the specific characteristics of each generation (Yang and Guy 2006). Make sure to present a realistic picture of the benefit programs available to potential hires, especially members of Generation X and Y. E-mail, instant messages, blogs, text messages, and social networking sites make it easy and quick for younger employees to share their disgruntlement with a large audience (Reynolds 2005).

Benefits information should be shared with employees on a regular basis via multiple formats. Because employees of different generations and ages may be more comfortable with receiving information in a variety of formats, human resource managers should communicate via multiple channels (Milkovitch and Newman 2005). For example, mature and baby boomer employees may prefer to receive information about benefits through face-to-face presentations or question and answer sessions, by telephone, at benefits fairs, or printed newsletters and employee benefit handbooks. Generation X and Y employees may appreciate the format of e-mail, electronic newsletters, Web sites, electronic documents, and online forums where they can post questions and read customized responses regarding benefits.

Another method of ensuring employees of all ages are informed of employee benefits is to educate frontline managers so they can share information with their teams. Supervisors are often more aware, than human resource managers, of life events and challenges faced by the employees they supervise, and can inform subordinates of available benefits. Disseminating information and answering employee inquiries in multiple formats increase the level of access and enable employees to better understand and make informed decisions regarding benefits.

5.5.1   Evaluating and Assessing Benefits

Benefit managers should develop an evaluation and assessment process to ensure benefits are appropriate in relation to organizational objectives, demographics, and employee needs. The process should examine whether the benefit is being implemented as it is intended and fulfilling its objectives (Adolf 1993). For example, a tuition reimbursement program intended to support job-related educational programs should be evaluated to verify that reimbursement recipients are pursuing and completing degrees that are relevant to their roles within the organization. Periodically reviewing benefit offerings as they relate to organizational objectives ensures that the organization's messages are consistent with the behaviors it is reinforcing. Assessing employee awareness and utilization levels for each benefit is also helpful to keeping benefit offerings current and ensuring employee needs are met.

Human resource managers can utilize many of the same channels of communication to collect employee feedback as they do to inform employees of benefits. Electronic and paper versions of a benefits newsletter could periodically include a brief survey to solicit employee feedback regarding benefits. Online forums and on-site benefits-related seminars can also be used to gather employee feedback and clarify needs.

Employee needs can be identified and clarified by seeking employee input through small focus groups or by creating an in-house employee benefits advisory committee. Insights into ways that benefits contribute to recruiting and retention issues can be gained by including benefits-related questions in employee exit interviews or discussions with job candidate finalists who choose not to join the organization. Routinely conducting benefits surveys of comparable organizations provides a market perspective on whether benefits offered are competitive.

HR managers can also compare the needs identified by employees as important with program usage statistics collected from various sources. Electronic employee work schedule and leave records, tuition reimbursement requests, training and development program participation records, and recognition program records can provide reports regarding employee usage and participation rates. Depending on the cost to the organization, benefits that are rarely used may not justify the costs associated with providing the benefit. It is also important to assess how benefits align with the goals and mission of the organization. Benefits are reward strategies that send a message to employees about what is important to the organization, and those messages should support the organization's overall goals, culture, and human resource management strategy (Flannery, Hofrichter, and Platten 1996).

5.6 Conclusion

With the aging of the workforce and accompanying demographic shifts, human resource managers face the challenge of designing, implementing, and assessing employee support and development benefits. These benefits are valuable to employees because they reflect the organization's support for employee development and help to balance work and nonwork responsibilities. Understanding employee demographics and generational cohorts is helpful for providing benefit programs that appeal to employees at various stages of their lives and careers. Human resource managers must consider organizational goals and objectives along with employee demographics and input regarding desired benefits.

Effective communication regarding benefits is also critical to ensuring that employees understand the scope of benefits available to them, appreciate the cost of the benefits to the organization, and perceive the benefits as valuable to them. Benefits-related information must be communicated through multiple channels, because employees of different ages may be more comfortable receiving information in certain formats than others. Finally, employee support and development benefit programs need to be periodically evaluated and assessed to ensure they align with current organizational objectives, human resource trends and strategy, and employee needs.

References

AARP. 2003. *Staying Ahead of the Curve 2003: The AARP Working in Retirement Study.* Washington, DC: AARP.

Adolf, B.A. 1993. Life cycle benefits. *Employee Benefits Journal* Mar. 1993: 13–20.

Armour, S. 2005. Generation Y: They've arrived at work with a new attitude. *USA Today*, November 6, Money section.

Bergmann, T.T., M.A. Bergmann, and J.L. Grahn. 1994. How important are employee benefits to public sector employees. *Public Personnel Management* 23(3): 397–406.

Bova, B. and M. Kroth. 1999. Closing the gap: The mentoring of Generation X. *Journal of Adult Education* 27(1): 7–17.

Bova, B. and M. Kroth. 2001. Workplace learning and Generation X. *Journal of Workplace Learning* 13(2): 57–65.

Cayer, N.J. 2002. Public employee benefits and the changing nature of the workforce. In *Public Personnel Administration: Problems and Prospects* (Eds.) S.W. Hays and R.C. Kearney, Upper Saddle River, New Jersey: Prentice Hall. pp. 167–179.

Cayer, N.J. 2005. Employee benefits: From health care to pensions. In *Handbook of Human Resource Management in Government, 2nd ed.* (Ed.) S.E. Condrey, San Francisco: Jossey-Bass. pp. 735–753.

Daley, D.M. 1998. An overview of benefits for the public sector: Not on the fringes anymore. *Review of Public Personnel Administration* 18(3): 5–22.

Doverspike, D., M.A. Taylor, K.S. Shultz, and P.F. McKay. 2000. Responding to the challenge of a changing workforce: Recruiting nontraditional demographic groups. *Public Personnel Management* 29(4): 445–457.

Flannery, T.P., D.A. Hofrichter, and P.E. Platten. 1996. *People, Performance, and Pay: Dynamic Compensation for Changing Organizations.* New York: Free Press.

Federickson, P.J. and D.L. Soden. 1998. Employee attitudes toward benefit packaging: The job sector dilemma. *Review of Public Personnel Administration* 18(3): 23–41.

Friedman, D.E. (n.d). *Workplace Flexibility: A Guide for Companies.* Families and Work Institute. http://familiesandwork.org/3w/tips/downloads/companies.pdf.

Glass, A. 2007. Understanding generational differences for competitive success. *Industrial and Commercial Training* 39(2): 98–103.

Jurkiewicz, C.L. 2000. Generation X and the public employee. *Public Personnel Management* 29(1): 55–74.

Jurkiewicz, C.L. and R.G. Brown. 1998. GenXers vs. boomers vs. matures: Generational comparisons of public employee motivation. *Review of Public Personnel Administration* 18(4): 18–37.

Larson, C. 2005. Many companies are exploring an increasingly attractive benefit for employees: Paid and unpaid sabbaticals. *U.S. News & World Report*, February 28, Money & Business section.

Martin, C.A. 2005. From high maintenance to high productivity: What managers need to know about Generation Y. *Industrial and Commercial Training* 37(1): 39–44.

Martin, C.A. and B. Tulgan. 2001. M*anaging Generation Y.* Amherst, Massachusetts: HRD Press.

Milkovitch, G.T. and J.M. Newman. 2005. *Compensation, 8th ed.* New York: McGraw Hill.

O'Bannon, G. 2001. Managing our future: The Generation X factor. *Public Personnel Management* 30(1): 95–109.

Reynolds, L.A. 2005. Communicating total rewards to the generations. *Benefits Quarterly* 21(2): 13–17.

Saltzstein, A.L., Y. Ting, and G.H. Saltzstein. 2001. Work–family balance and job satisfaction: The impact of family-friendly policies on attitudes of federal government employees. *Public Administration Review* 61(4): 452–467.

Smola, K.W. and C.D. Sutton. 2002. Generational differences: Revisiting generational work values for the new millenium. *Journal of Organizational Behavior* 23: 363–382.

Southard, G. and J. Lewis. 2004. Building a workplace that recognizes generational diversity. *Public Management* 86(3), http://www2.icma.org/pm/8603/southard.htm (accessed December 5, 2006).

Toossi, M. 2005. Labor force projections to 2014: Retiring Boomers. *Monthly Labor Review* Nov. 2005: 25–44.

Tulgan, B. 1995. *Managing Generation X: How to Bring Out the Best in Young Talent.* Santa Monica, California: Merritt Publishing.

Tulgan, B. 2004. Trends point to a dramatic generation shift in the future workforce. *Employment Relations Today* 30(4): 23–31.

U.S. Bureau of Labor Statistics. 2005. Civilian labor force participation rates by sex, age, race, and Hispanic origin, 1984, 1994, 2004, and projected 2014. Bureau of Labor Statistics. http://www.bls.gov/emp/emplab05.htm (Last modified date: December 7, 2005).

U.S. Office of Personnel Management. 2005. *The Status of Telework in the Federal Government.* Washington, DC: U.S. OPM.

Wallace, J.E. 2006. Work commitment in the legal profession: A study of baby boomers and Generation Xers. *International Journal of the Legal Profession* 13(2): 137–151.

West, J.P. 2005. Managing an aging workforce: Trends, issues, and prospects. In *Handbook of Human Resource Management in Government, 2nd ed.* (Ed.) S.E. Condrey, San Francisco: Jossey-Bass. pp. 164–188.

West, J.P. and E.M. Berman. 1996. Managerial responses to an aging municipal workforce. *Review of Public Personnel Administration* 16(3): 38–58.

Yang, S.-B. and M.E. Guy. 2006. GenXers versus Boomers: Work motivators and management implications. *Public Performance and Management Review* 29(3): 267–284.

Zemke, R. 2001. Here come the Millenials. *Training* 38(7): 44–49.

Chapter 6

The Social and Economic Context of Employee Healthcare Benefits

Ann Beck

CONTENTS

6.1   Introduction

To respond effectively to rising public sector employee/retiree health insurance costs, it is critical that elected officials, public managers, human resources specialists, and benefits specialists understand what factors affect the provision and cost of this compensation element. The focus of this chapter is to describe the social, economic, political, and workplace context in which health benefit decisions are made and to develop a richer model of the determinants of public employer health insurance benefit level, cost, and cost-sharing provisions. Factors that appear to affect the cost of health insurance or how much and what type of coverage is offered are outlined.

6.2   Importance of Employer-Provided Health Insurance

The use of employer-sponsored health insurance in the United States as the principal method of healthcare provision for members of the national community is unique among industrialized (OECD) nations (Wong 1997; Beland and Hacker 2004; Inglehart 2004; Haase 2005). Despite a declining percentage of workers in the last years who take up the health insurance benefit when it is offered by an employer, over 60 percent of all workers remain covered by employment-based health plans from their own employer, with another 15 percent receiving coverage through an employer as a dependent (Fronstin 2007, p. 4). In a recent public survey, over three-fourths of the respondents recognized that employer-provided insurance is cheaper than the employee could get on her own and those surveyed preferred obtaining insurance through the employer rather than individually securing it (Kaiser Family Foundation and Harvard School of Public Health 2005). Haase (2005, p. 55), viewing public opinion polls across time, argues that "a critical mass of well-insured people have been satisfied with their care under a private, employer-based system and think that any alternative system will be much worse." Similarly, most employers remain committed to providing health insurance benefits to their employees if insurance premium costs can be controlled and administrative expenses can be reduced (Whitmore et al. 2006).

Under the U.S. employer-sponsored system of health insurance, public employers, like their private sector counterparts, are charged with making a variety of voluntary (and sometimes mandatory) decisions about whether to offer a health insurance benefit and how much of what types of health insurance and related benefits should be provided to their employees and dependents at what cost. Because public jurisdictions employ about 1/6 of all workers in the U.S. civilian workforce (U.S. Census Bureau 2007, Table 618: p. 403), decisions made by public employers about health insurance provision directly affect more than 21 million public workers and their dependents, the taxpayers who pay for these compensation costs, and the healthcare service and insurance providers (and stockholders) who provide healthcare goods and services within a public jurisdiction. In this way, governments as employers play a crucial distributive role within their own communities because of the size, visibility, and potential for reflection of public policy that public employers have (Watts et al. 2003). Likewise, within each community, health insurance coverage for public employees and for private employees is a local public good that affects the overall well-being of the community (Goldstein and Pauly 1976).

As employers, public managers in each jurisdiction or establishment compete with other public and private employers in the appropriate labor market or markets to attract highly qualified applicants and retain high quality employees. These government employees provide valued and often critical health and security services to citizens—education, criminal justice, police, fire, public health, etc. Local, state, and federal employers face a serious challenge in finding sufficiently skilled employees to fill these critical positions, especially in management positions (Hall 2004; Barrett and Greene 2005; Lancaster and Stillman 2005). Because the healthcare benefit remains the most highly valued benefit for public sector applicants and employees (Bergmann, Bergmann, and Gahn 1994; Roberts et al. 2004; OPM 2005), the level of the health insurance benefit may directly affect the quality of applicants and public employees. Despite these impacts, health benefits among public jurisdictions have been relatively understudied (Reddick and Coggburn 2007).

In addition to attracting and retaining employees, the provision of sufficient health benefits is associated with many positive outcomes for employers such as increased employee satisfaction with the employer, reduced turnover, increased retention and productivity, and opportunities for retirement decisions that might benefit employers (Ward and Davis 1995; O'Brien 2003; Fronstin and Werntz 2004; Roberts et al. 2004; GAO 2006; Whitmore et al. 2006; Reddick and Coggburn 2007). Insured workers over the long-term have better health and longevity than those who do not (Stanton 2004, p. 1). Despite these positive outcomes, there has been growing concern among public management officials about the high cost of this particular health insurance benefit. In recent years, local officials have ranked rising health insurance costs among the most pressing issues facing their jurisdictions, with a negative impact on both local government finances and the ability to meet city needs (ICMA 2002b, p. 2; Brennan, Wheel, and Hoene 2005, p. 1). This high level of concern may seem somewhat overstated as health insurance costs are only a small portion of overall employer compensation—about 11 percent. Given the myriad concerns that face government managers, what makes employee health benefit costs standout so starkly and be evaluated so negatively?

6.3 Why Local Government Managers Are Concerned?

A number of trends related to health insurance costs likely account for the high level of concern among local government managers and finance directors. The first trend, the rising rate of overall spending on healthcare in the United States, reduces societal and public choices for other valued services. Increased spending for medical healthcare, in large part, drives healthcare premium costs—the largest component of health benefit costs for employers. Healthcare spending in 2007 was estimated at about 16.2 percent of the Gross Domestic Product (GDP) (Center for Medicare and Medicaid 2005, Table 1) and about 50 percent higher than the proportion of GDP generated by healthcare in the typical OECD country (Reinhardt, Hussey, and Anderson 2004; Anderson et al., 2005). As more dollars in the U.S. economy are spent on healthcare, other desired goods and services must be foregone by employees and employers. This very high level of healthcare spending limits the ability of citizens and their federal, state, and local governments to address other high priority community needs. For example, Sheils and Haught (2004, p. 108) estimated that health insurance costs for 2004 were almost $600 billion and over $200 billion of revenue to the national and state governments was forgone (a tax expenditure) because of the tax treatment of health insurance benefits under the existing tax codes.

A second trend is the above average increases in health premium costs relative to other factors of employee compensation. The rate of increase in premium costs has significantly exceeded the growth for both inflation and real wages in all but three of the last eighteen years (Kaiser Family Foundation 2005a, 2006). The increases are due to both higher payments for healthcare services and goods (medical care providers, hospitals, medical equipment, drugs, etc.) and administrative costs that include profit. Some of the highest health insurance premium growth rates in the last fifteen years have been recorded in recent years. Between 2000 and 2005, the cost of health insurance premiums increased about 73 percent although the Consumer Price Index-Urban inflation rate increased 14 percent and the wage rate increased by fifteen percent (Kaiser Family Foundation 2005a, Summary 1). Health premium cost increases even exceed the Consumer Price Index costs for medical services (Census Bureau 2007, Table 706: p. 469). In part, this is due to soaring administrative costs associated with employer-sponsored health insurance that rose 16.2 percent from 2000 to 2001, 19.6 percent from 2001 to 2002, and 16.9 percent from 2002 to 2003 (Kaiser Family Foundation 2005a, Exhibit 6.11). Although the rate of increase in health insurance costs has been moderating since their high in 2003, annual increases remain about double the inflation rate (Kaiser Family Foundation 2006,

p. 1). By December 2006, the cost of health insurance for state and local government employers was 10.7 percent of total compensation at an average cost of $4.09 per hour (BLS 2007a, Table 3). This was significantly higher than in the private sector where aggregate health insurance costs were $1.79 per hour and 7.0 percent of total compensation costs (BLS 2007a, Table 5). Health insurance costs are now the largest single component of benefit compensation for public employers, significantly exceeding both paid leave and retirement costs. In dollar terms, it is estimated that local governments alone (about 2/3 of all public employees) pay about $68 billion annually for employee health insurance coverage for about 11 million employees (Konde 2005). The estimated aggregate state and local long-term liability for retiree healthcare is about $1 trillion (Walters 2007, p. 1).

Even when similar types of coverage are compared, public sector state and local government employers typically pay about 2–10 percent higher costs for premiums than private sector employers (Kaiser Family Foundation 2005b, Exhibit 1.15; 2006, Exhibit 1.12). In part, these higher rates may be because of a higher level of add-on services offered by state and local government such as wellness programs, injury prevention, smoking cessation, etc. (Kaiser Family Foundation 2006, pp. 140–143). However, the very large rates of increases in health insurance premiums over the last seven years have created the situation where the average health insurance premium for family coverage now exceeds the annual income for a full-time, minimum wage job. The average annual premium cost for work-related coverage in 2006 for a single employee was $4,242–$627 from the worker, $3,615 from the employer; for family coverage, the average premium was $11,480–$2,973 from the worker, $8,508 from the employer (Kaiser Family Foundation 2006, p. 2). Local government officials as employers and agents of the taxpaying public would like to control these costs without harming their ability to provide effective services to the public. However, this is a much more difficult project especially in the labor intensive local government jurisdictions where total compensation costs are about 60–80 percent of operating expenses compared to about 36 percent of private employer operating expenses (Hansen 2004, p. 79).

For both the public and private employer, these premium increases have not been easily passed on to taxpayers, consumers, or producers because of increasing market competitiveness (especially for small businesses) and fiscal stress for state and local governments in the period 2001–2005. As a result, small business employers are reducing or eliminating provision of healthcare benefits (BLS 2005a; Fronstin 2005a; Gabel et al. 2005). The number of all private firms offering health insurance benefits dropped from about 69 percent to 61 percent (Kaiser Family Foundation 2007, p. 32) with the greatest reductions by smaller firms. As private employers eliminate or reduce coverage, overall public expenditures for healthcare increase. For example, local governments must increase expenditures for public hospitals, public clinics, and indigent care that are not covered by Medicaid or medicare programs (Cowan et al. 2002; Matthews 2003; National Association of Counties and National Association of Community Health Centers 2003; Fronstin 2005c). The state and federal government have to increase amounts spent for Medicaid and related programs. Stoll (2005, p. 3) estimates that these additional public health costs paid through state and local taxes amounted to approximately $14 billion for 2005. Others have estimated the total costs to other insurance consumers and all levels of government for caring for the uninsured from $65 billion to $130 billion per year (Institute of Medicine 2004, p. 1). This includes the increases in the costs of healthcare premiums that become cost-shifted onto the employers who continue to offer coverage and to the employees who buy individual insurance (Cowan et al. 2002).

As small businesses eliminate or reduce health insurance benefits for their employees, this sector again begins to question the "richness" of public sector health and related benefits (Byrnes and Palmeri 2005; Revell 2005). In light of these spillover impacts of reduced or eliminated health insurance coverage by small private employers, local government officials face rising health benefit costs as employers, higher expenditures for public health within their jurisdictions, and greater levels of small business opposition to the health benefits that state and local governments provide to their own public employees. Such a mixture dramatically increases salience of the issue for administrators and elected officials at the state and local government level.

Finally, local government administrators note that these sky-rocketing health benefit costs are becoming a larger component of local government operating budgets because there has not been an off-setting reduction in personnel costs or significant increase in revenue. Premium increases far outpaced the rate of growth in revenue for local governments over the period 2000–2004 and healthcare premiums are estimated to have increased from 3.4 percent of total operating expenses of local governments in 2000 to 5.4 percent of total operating expenses in 2004 (Litvak, Doppelt, and Laskey 2004, p. 2). In part, local governments have been unable to reduce total compensation for employees because of low unemployment rates coupled with high levels of demand for more highly educated employees (Ingraham, Selden, and Moynihan 2000; ICMA 2002b; Regopoulos and Trude 2004). Instead, local governments must work much harder to recruit high quality employees as young adults entering the workforce do not consider the public sector as a strong employer and often view government as the employer of last resort (Chetovich 2002; Lewis and Frank 2002). Local government officials are alternately pressured to find and keep high quality employees and to provide a full array of services to residents at a constant or declining cost. Within this setting, appointed and elected officials must make increasingly difficult and contentious decisions regarding expenditure and service trade-offs among competing external interests for fewer local government resources. These trade-offs lead to rising internal labor-management tensions as administrators push public employee unions for concessions on personnel cost elements (Bennett and Masters 2003; Guiler and Shafritz 2004; Litvak, Doppelt, and Laskey 2004). Increasingly, elected officials are looking for ways to shift health premium costs to other jurisdictions. The National League of Cities formed a Working Group on Health Care to recommend action that the League of Cities can take to help control such costs or shift rising municipal healthcare costs to the national government (McGee and Konde 2005; Walters 2007).

6.4 Contemporary Health Insurance Design Decisions in State and Local Governments

Within constraints imposed by state legislatures and local government councils, commissions, and boards, it is the state and local government appointed and elected managers who determine the jurisdiction's principal strategy for providing health benefits. In a highly decentralized and largely autonomous process for most jurisdictions, elected, and appointed local government actors negotiate and approve contracts with health insurance providers or third-party administrators for health benefit services. At the same or different times, these same actors also negotiate and approve labor-management contracts that often contain specific language about health insurance and related health benefits. Finally, these same elected and appointed actors must also consider the impacts that their decisions may have on the healthcare providers within their communities, especially if the jurisdiction is a large employer in the community or there are few major providers in the location. As Christianson and Trude (2003) document, healthcare providers often bring pressure on local elected officials about assuring the continuation of local hospitals and health services. Similarly, other external actors such as insurance providers and taxpayer groups may also try to affect health plan design (Employee Benefit Research Institute 2005).

Most commonly, it is the central Human Resources Department of each local government that creates the management design of health benefit programs (ICMA 2000, p. 2). For the most part, health benefit plans are individually designed and operated by each jurisdiction for its own employees, and few local or state governments cooperatively purchase or provide health insurance (Hurley et al. 2006, W202). Unlike the past when community rating and actuarial rating systems helped localities and employers share risk, the new systems of experience rating, self-insurance, and health savings plans have led to a "world of employment-based insurance is now largely one of every firm on its own, and the advent of health savings accounts (HSAs) reduces cross-subsidization even among employees in the same firm" (Enthoven and Fuchs 2006, p. 1540).

An International City and County Management Association (ICMA) survey (2002, p. 7) disclosed that the top three factors that influenced the local government employer's selection of a health insurance plan were cost (quantity of services and cost-sharing provisions) followed by access to care (quality of coverage and number of plans and providers) along with employee satisfaction with plan in previous year, and customer service/administration of the plan (quality of provider). Similarly, Reddick and Coggburn (2007, p. 13) found that total cost, access to care, and employee cost were the leading influences on plan choice for state public employers. As Bergmann, Bergmann, and Gahn (1994, p. 405) described in their study of public sector benefit satisfaction and understanding, "The benefit level is constrained by product market considerations (so costs are similar to the firm's competitors in the product market); the benefit structure (the composition of benefits at a fixed cost) is constrained by product market considerations (costs) and employee preferences (to get value for dollars spent)." That is, in designing health insurance and related health benefits, employers must make a multitude of benefit design decisions that are affected by employee preferences and local conditions such as availability of various types of insurance coverage within the area and what other employers offer their employees.

Each state or local government makes multiple decisions about who will be made eligible for health benefits, what specific types of plans and programs will be made available to employees, and what cost-sharing arrangements between employer and employee will be applied. Decisions within each jurisdiction on health insurance benefits are often bundled because strategy and decisions about one component—quantity, quality, or cost sharing—often affect simultaneous or subsequent decisions about the other components. As a result of these three sets of health benefit design decisions made in each jurisdiction within unique localities, premium costs vary significantly from one government employer to another, often up to 100 percent for both single employee and family coverage (Litvak, Doplett, and Laskey 2004, p. 2; GAO 2005, p. 1).

6.4.1 Health Insurance Quantity

Some of the most important decision choices that affect the *quantity* of the health insurance benefit include (a) is group health insurance offered to any employees at all? (b) which employees and nonemployees will be offered the benefit—full-time, part-time, seasonal, intermittent and temporary, dependents, retirees? and (c) how many types of medical and related health benefits under insurance will be provided—medical, dental, vision, pharmacy, etc.

Although the provision of medical insurance by state and local governments is close to universal (ICMA 2002; BLS 2004; Roberts 2004; Kaiser Family Foundation 2005b), rates of health insurance coverage and amount paid for that health insurance vary widely among the states (Kaiser Family Foundation 2002; Stumpf 2005). Over time, there has been a slight increase in the number of jurisdictions that have chosen not to offer medical insurance to any of its employees (Hurley et al., 2006). The more common distinction among local governments is the breadth of extent of employees, dependents, and retirees covered. The potential range among jurisdictions offering group medical insurance (or self-insurance) coverage is very broad. For example, a jurisdiction may offer medical insurance coverage to the full-time, regular employee only. Another local or state government may offer coverage to most all employees regardless of type of appointment, and coverage will be extended to the dependents of active employees as well as retirees and their dependents. For example, about 1/3 of municipal employers in a nationwide sample offered health insurance to part-time employees (ICMA 2002a; Roberts 2003); although over 70 percent of states offered part-time employees coverage (Kaiser Family Foundation 2002). There is also variation among local governments on the provision of additional types of health insurance, and the amount of specialty health services offered (ICMA 2002a; Roberts 2004).

When the decision to offer benefits is implemented, government employees also "take-up" offered insurance at higher rates than private sector employees do. That is, a significantly higher proportion of state and local government employees than private sector employees participate in health insurance programs when the program is offered by the public employer and the public employee becomes eligible (BLS 1998, 2005; Kaiser Family Foundation 2002). This higher participation rate accounts for much of the difference in health insurance expenditures between the public and private sectors (Long and Marquis 1999; McDonnell 2005). These higher take-up rates are also associated with higher salary and wage compensation in the public sector, a greater number of health insurance programs offered by public employers, higher unionization rates in public jurisdictions, larger sized public employers, and more metropolitan establishment locations among public employers (BLS 2006). In 2006, about 85 percent of employees in public organizations were covered by employer-provided health insurance compared to 65 percent in the private sector (Kaiser Family Foundation 2006, p. 56).

6.4.2   Health Insurance Quality

Another decision choice for management is the *quality* of the health benefit. This consideration asks (a) what will be the benefit level for each type of coverage provided—maximum lifetime amount of coverage and level and types of services covered? (b) within medical insurance coverage, what choices of providers/plans will an employee have—Indemnity, Preferred Provider Organization (PPO), Point-of-Service (POS), Health Maintenance Organization (HMO)? and (c) what quality levels are required of providers?

These benefit design features affect overall insurance cost less than the quantity considerations, but their impact is more than incidental. In general, administrative and premium expenses increase as employers offer more options to employees (number of different types of plans) and as the maximum lifetime benefit amount under the plan increases, so does the cost of the premium. In general, public employers are more likely to offer multiple plans and have higher rates of employees enrolled in HMOs (BLS 1998; ICMA 2002a; Kaiser Family Foundation 2002, 2006; Hurley et al. 2006, W197).

6.4.3   Health Insurance Cost Sharing

A third set of decision choices affect the *cost-sharing* provisions between the employer and employee. The more that the employees bear the costs of health insurance and out-of-pocket expenses, the less is the expense to the employer. These decision choices include (a) how much of the total premium should the employer or employee/retiree pay? (b) how much of the total administrative cost should the employer or employee/retiree pay? and (c) how much additional out-of-pocket expenses (excluding premium) should the employer or employee/retiree bear—cost of deductibles, co-pays, and co-insurance?

As out-of-pocket costs for any plan design decrease for the employee, plan cost increase. Even when employee out-of-pocket costs increase, the employer may choose to provide additional money or compensation for these employee out-of-pocket expenses through various medical and health savings account instruments. The amount that the employer may contribute is an additional cost and there other costs associated with the administration of these savings account instruments (plan development and implementation). Other administrative support costs are incurred in benefit design, planning, and administration of each type of plan and service program. Some of these costs can be passed to employees (e.g., COBRA administrative costs) although others cannot.

According to the ICMA survey on health benefits in 2002, the "average" local government provides coverage for a range of traditional health insurance programs (medical, dental, vision, prescription drugs), multiple types of medical plans for employees to choose from (HMO, PPO, POS, and traditional indemnity), and some premium costs shared between the employer and employee. In the case of union employees, about 40 percent of the time, no premium contribution is made by employee for employee-only coverage; and only very rarely does a local government base the premium on salary level of the employee (ICMA 2002b). Similarly, Long and Marquis (1999) found that about 70 percent of state and local workers had a choice of plan types, and premiums paid by state and local employers were similar to those paid by private sector employers.

Interestingly, despite premium increase pressure on employers, there has been little or only a slight change in the cost-share proportion for the employer, the average deductible for the employee or the out-of-pocket expenses for employees in the last years (Gabel et al., 2005). Again, it appears that, at least at the aggregate level, changes in the cost-sharing component are not made with great frequency, do not have a rapid impact on cost because of lag factors in health insurance negotiation cycles, or that the changes made by employers do not share the same direction (increases by one employers are canceled by decreases for another employer).

These complex health insurance benefit design considerations are only one part of the decision-making process for the public employer. Public employers must also consider (a) time-consuming competitive bid requirements for third-party administrators and health insurance plan providers that exist in many local governments; (b) the politics, cost, and length of collective bargaining agreement negotiation or employee input processes related to health benefit plan design; and (c) the difficulty of evaluating and comparing various insurance provider proposals on benefit programs. Taken together, all these considerations create very high transactional costs for government employers and limit frequent reexamination or reconsideration of previous decisions about most of the components in the decision bundle. Although almost one half of employers consider changing benefit design components annually, only about one-quarter actually do so in any given year (Kaiser Family Foundation 2005b, p. 29). Similarly, state-level public employers only rebid health insurance packages about every three years compared to annually for Fortune 500 firms

(Maxwell, Temin, and Petigara 2004). However, as health insurance related costs continue to skyrocket, there is more pressure to reconsider previous health insurance decisions more frequently, even though it may take many years for some changes to be implemented because of multiple-year collective bargaining agreements or the need for new statutory authority. Despite these conservative elements, health benefit decisions among state and local public employers are not static. They are constantly being reformed and reshaped by workplace, local, and regional events over time.

6.5 Factors and Forces That Affect Design Decisions

Kearney (2003a) recognized that there had been few public sector studies that tried to explain benefit or total compensation differences across public employers. His study sought to identify factors that might account for different salary and benefit levels among the 50 state government employers. Kearney's model used a variety of state-level political, social, economic, and decision-making factors to explain variation in four separate components of discretionary benefits and compensation—paid leave, salary level, health benefit costs paid by employees, and level of retirement benefit. The specific forces he suggested which accounted for differences in cost of health insurance benefits among the states were union density, labor force quality, percentage of female legislators, density of state employees, per capita personal income, and per capita revenue. Only state average per capita income level for all workers and union density among the state public employees were significantly related to variations in the amount the employee paid for health insurance coverage. His models were able to explain very little of the variation among the states and he pressed for "improved measurement of benefit measures ... [and] better specification of independent variables" (Kearney 2003a, p. 320). He suggested that other possible control variables might include distribution of jobs among professions, urbanization, and extent of responsibility of the jurisdiction relative to other levels of government.

Other related studies have examined provision, cost, and satisfaction with various health benefits. To explain the availability of healthcare benefits in North Carolina, Daley (1993) used municipality size, form of government (professional management) as explanatory variables, and found that each affected the availability of healthcare benefits in the municipalities. To examine municipal Human Resource Managers satisfaction with healthcare plans, Perry and Cayer (1997) used multiple independent variables including level of employee payment for health insurance premium, extent of plan coverage for services, extent of annual premium increases, cost of an individual health plan relative to total government healthcare costs, cost-contracting arrangements, size of municipality, and number of complaints as possible explanatory variables. Among all these factors, the number of plans, the contracting arrangements, the percent of total health benefit, and the size of employer were found to be significantly correlated with satisfaction for Preferred Provider

Organization (PPO) plans—the most common type of healthcare plan now offered by local governments (ICMA 2002a).

Similarly, Streib (1996) used size of jurisdiction, region of country, form of government, number of specialty services offered in health plans, level of employee contribution, purchase arrangement, and retiree coverage to explore both cost of health plans and satisfaction with those plans. Interestingly, he found a relationship between the number of services and the premium costs for PPO plans, but not for HMO plans (Streib 1996, pp. 67–69); he also found size, region, and level of contribution to be associated with cost or level of satisfaction.

Roberts et al. (2004) studied family-friendly benefits adoption (including some healthcare benefits), and used form of government, region, budget size, workforce age and gender, the state of labor relations, the percentage of part-time employees, the number of structural strategies, and number of cost-shifting displacement methods used, level of municipal fiscal stress currently and anticipated, and level of benefits stress currently and anticipated as independent and control variables to explain the perceived important of the benefit. None of the organizational characteristics, benefit cost reduction strategies, fiscal stress levels, or state of labor-management relations was associated with the perceived importance of family-friendly benefits.

Finally, in reporting on health insurance provision, quality, cost, and cost sharing, the U.S. Bureau of Labor Statistics and Census Bureau have developed implicit models of what affects these health insurance characteristics. The models rely on the nature of employment (full- or part-time), industry, occupation, unionization, firm size, region, metropolitan location, race and ethnicity, family type and age to explore differences. Fronstin (2005c) suggests that all of these variables are important in explaining whether a person has health insurance coverage and he calls for the use of multivariate regression analysis to examine "the impact of various job characteristics and unionization on the probability of having employment-based health benefits" (2005b, p. 6).

6.6   Model with Three Levels of Forces and Factors

Three different levels of explanatory variables or forces—state, local area, and jurisdiction-specific—appear to be at work in health insurance decision making. The first level factors are the result of the general political culture in each state. Because local governments are creatures of the states in which they exist, the state political culture can dramatically affect the range of options and discretion that state and local public employers have about employee health insurance benefits. A state's political culture specifically affects the state government's friendliness towards local government collective bargaining and the state government's requirements that local governments (or employers in general) provide various health insurance benefits to its employees. The second level of forces is the specific community factors that impact the public employer. The most important factors within this level are the extent of competition among and health insurance and reinsurance providers and the extent of competition for labor. Finally, unique workplace characteristics affect decision choices and the method of decision making about health insurance within each government jurisdiction. These factors include form of government, density of unions within the jurisdiction, wage level of employees in the jurisdiction, and size of the jurisdiction, occupational distribution and age of the workforce. All three levels of forces (variables) interact to affect decision making on three different components of health insurance provision—the quantity of health insurance provided, the quality of the insurance coverage, and the cost-sharing provisions of insurance coverage between the employer and the employee.

6.6.1   State Political Culture

The political culture of a state continues to affect budgetary and political behavior in American states and communities (Koven and Mausolff 2002; Lieske 2005). A state's political culture may constrain or enhance state and local government employer discretion in decision making about employee health insurance benefits in two important ways. First, state political culture (Elazar 1984) affects expectations about the quality and quantity of government service provision that indirectly affects the willingness of lawmakers and public employers to provide higher levels of health benefits to their public employees. Second, a state's political culture affects the state-level friendliness towards public sector unions in local governments. More specifically, moralistic and individualistic state political cultures tend to have higher levels of public bureaucracies and moralistic cultures tend to see local government (and, therefore, public employees) as a positive force in the community. As a result, moralistic states are more likely to allow public unions to form and bargain collectively and even require the provision of certain levels of health benefits for state and local public employees. Some states have relatively long histories of providing the health insurance benefit at no cost to their employees (Kaiser Family Foundation 2002). Similarly, individualistic states with more focus on partisan rivalry may also allow public unions to form and bargain, although traditionalistic states are less likely to support either public union formation or extension of health insurance benefits to local government units. Differences in costs among political cultures parallel significant regional differences in the cost of health insurance (Kaiser Family Foundation 2006; BLS 2007).

6.6.2   State-Level Public Union Friendliness

Although Kearney (2003b, p. 567) argues that the institutional environment in which public unions are embedded is friendlier to collective bargaining than the institutional environment for private unions, there is still enormous variation in the degree to which state legislatures are supportive of public sector unions. The legal environment varies widely across and within states for different groups of public employees. Kearney has described labor relations in the public sector as "highly irregular and jurisdiction specific" with a "hodgepodge" of federal, state, and local statutes and ordinances and State Attorney General and Court decisions that characterize the policy environment (Kearney 2003b, p. 567). As reported by Bennett and Masters (2003, p. 534) there is a "crazy-quilt arrangement" as about half of states give rights to all municipal employees to collectively bargain, almost two-third give collective bargaining rights to police and fire. About 70 percent give public school teachers the right to collectively bargain, 39 states allow at least one set of public workers to bargain, and 23 states allow all sets to bargain, and over 40 percent of local government workers are unionized. In addition, thirteen states limit bargaining rights, nine states allow public employees no bargaining rights, and thirteen states allow some work stoppage (Kearney and Carnevale 2001, pp. 58–74; Kearney 2003b, pp. 567–568). Evidence from the Community Tracking Survey conducted in 2000 and again in 2005 shows that public employers in large public agencies believe that unions exert a very strong impact on health benefit design and cost across time and these same unions have limited major changes that are occurring in the private sector (Watts et al. 2003; Maxwell, Temin, and Petigara 2004; Hurley et al. 2006).

From the work done by Kadleck (2003) and Guiler and Shafritz (2004), the dimensions that appear important for evaluating public union strength include state statutory or regulatory provisions that cover (1) the range of government employees that may unionize, (2) the range of government employees that may collectively bargain, (3) the range of issues on which government bargaining units may negotiate, (4) the availability of public employee strikes, (5) the availability of automatic or closed-shop membership for the bargaining unit, (6) the availability of dues check-off procedures. States that have more of these provisions are more likely to have higher costs for the employer and a greater range of benefit levels.

6.6.3 Local/Regional Market Competition for Employees

Community tracking study reports by Christianson and Trude (2003) and Hurley et al. (2006) found that labor market consideration was the primary driver of certain health benefits decision making among public and private employers. On the basis of the interviews from these tracking studies conducted among more than 20 public employers in 12 communities both sets of scholars found that all public employers and benefits specialists interviewed (over 100 in each time frame) perceived that health benefits were extremely important in attracting and retaining employees across all skill categories because the respondents viewed their public jurisdictions as less salary competitive than private firms. Employers were hesitant to reduce or eliminate any provisions or cost sharing for fear that they would lose employees or be able to attract high quality applicants. Marquis and Long (2001) also found that small employers' decisions about the provision and amount of health insurance for employees were affected by local market employment conditions. Likewise, City and County Managers continue to express high levels of concern about their ability to find adequate numbers of qualified employees at the local level (ICMA 2002b; Brennan et al. 2005). Although provision of the health insurance benefit is almost universal among governments, other quantity, quality, and cost-sharing provisions differ among the jurisdictions (ICMA 2002b). In local governments where there is greater labor market competition, there should be more types and levels of coverage for a wider range of employees and retirees as well as lower cost to employees for premiums and higher overall costs for employers.

6.6.4 Local Market Competition for Providers of Insurance/Reinsurance and Healthcare

Fully insured health providers are subject to regulation by each of the states in which they operate. About two-thirds of all local governments use fully insured providers (ICMA 2002a), and those that are self-insured almost always use regulated reinsurers to cover excessive claim costs. Recently, there has been a significant increase in the level of concentration of health insurance and reinsurance providers within most of the states. Robinson (2004, 2006) argues that the increased dominance of a few firms in statewide and local markets has likely decreased price competition and allowed for much greater profit taking because of entry barriers for possible providers in other sectors, absence of substitute products, and reduced rivalry among existing providers. He reports that in 38 states, the largest firm has one-third or more control of the market within the state (Robinson 2004, p. 15). Similarly, Scott (2003) reports that the market for health insurance has hardened and the cost of coverage is rising. In the August 2005 report on healthcare provider costs under the Federal Employee Health Benefit Program that operates in all 50 U.S. states, the Government Accountability Organization found that hospital prices varied over 250 percent and physician prices varied by almost 100 percent across metropolitan areas and that these variations were associated with competition among providers, HMO presence, and region (GAO 2005, p. 4).

Taken together, these changes in concentration among insurers and providers create pressure to redesign health benefit packages in response to increased premium costs that are due to market factors rather than employee utilization of the insurance benefit. In a similar vein, risk pooling has decreased the relationship between the cost of insurance utilization by employees in the covered group and the cost of the insurance premium. Pauly (2005) found that total group health insurance premiums only varied slightly with health risk because of practices by providers in "frontloading" risk costs and the existence of various requirements for community rating and guaranteed renewability imposed state governments. This means that premiums are becoming less a reflection of actual healthcare utilization by employees covered by a plan, and more a reflection of community or nationwide health and health-related administrative and profit costs. It is expected that increased concentration limits the quality of health insurance benefit types offered by an employer as well as increases the cost of premium. This in turn places greater pressure on employers to cost-shift more of the premium cost to employees or reduce the extent of coverage for employees and retirees.

6.6.5 Average Salary in the Local Government Unit

Higher levels of salary are positively associated with greater levels of health benefit coverage and a greater range of benefits and lower proportions of co-pay. In general, persons in higher wage jobs are offered and take-up health insurance benefits at much higher levels (BLS 2005b). This is because higher salaried employees can afford higher premium payments and the tighter labor markets for these higher wage managerial and professional positions (Lancaster and Stillman 2005) will make the local government employers more eager to maintain or improve the quality, quantity, and cost-sharing provisions of health benefits to assure sufficiently high total compensation to attract high quality applicants.

6.6.6 Existence and Density of Unionization in the Local Government

The existence of a union (or unions) and its (their) density in a jurisdiction are suggested by many as the most important determinants of quantity, quality, and cost-sharing provisions of health insurance benefits in either the public or private sector. In the private sector, holding other variables constant, union workers are 16.4 percent more likely to have health insurance coverage than nonunion workers are and employers have 25–50 percent higher expenditures on nonmandatory benefit items when there are union members in the workplace (John Budd 2005, p. 1). Budd suggests that both the monopoly power of unionization to capture returns from productivity increases in the form of higher benefits for the workers (the quantity of benefits and the cost-sharing provisions) and the collective voice that impacts the range of benefit mix (the quality of benefits) are still at work in health benefit decision making (Budd 2005). In the private sector, this union power is clear as the union workers' share of health insurance premiums for both self- and family coverage is about one half of that for the nonunion workers and access to all forms of traditional plan types is 30–100 percent higher among unionized workers (BLS, NCS 2006, p. 3). Although the union effect on the provision and cost of health insurance benefits for unionized workers remains strong, about 20–35 percent of the decline in employee health coverage in the period 1980–1997 has been due to the declining strength of unions in the private sector (Buchmueller, DiNardo, and Valleta 2001, p. 23).

Unlike the private sector where only 8 percent of workers are represented by unions, unions represent almost 46 percent of all workers in local government (BLS 2007b).

One of the multiple reasons given for 60 percent higher employer benefit cost in the public sector than in the private sector is the much higher level of unionization in the public sector (McDonnell 2005, p. 5). Paul Fronstin (2005b, pp. 2–3) demonstrates that higher levels of unionization in the public sector are responsible for the 26 percent greater coverage of public employees compared to private employees. Interviews conducted with both state and local public sector managers and benefit specialists confirm these aggregate statistical findings. In those interviews, management officials perceived that unions within their jurisdiction had a strong affect on health benefits design and cost-sharing provisions (Watts et al. 2003; Maxwell, Temin, and Petigara 2004; Hurley et al. 2006). Related research among public sector unions has shown that the mere presence of union has been show likely to affect managerial decision making (Travis 2000) and unions have effects on both the benefits and the policy pursued by the local government (Feuille, Delaney, and Hendricks 1985; Hunter and Rankin 1988; Zhao and Lovrich 1997). At the state level, Maxwell, Temin, and Petigara (2004, pp. 187–188) found that unionized state governments have effects similar to those of unionized private firms on the provision and cost sharing of health insurance benefits.

The union effect in public sector may be even more powerful than in the private sector because management incentives and motives in collective bargaining in the public sector are "mixed" and there are more areas where union and management/elected official interests overlap (Kearney 2003, p. 569). Likewise, union members who are about 18 percent of all voters have about 13 percent higher turnout in non-presidential elections (Freeman 2003), which can significantly affect local election results where turnout among the general population is low in off-year elections. Public unions may be able to sway or help select those elected officials who are more willing to approve higher health benefit levels at lower costs to union members.

6.6.7   Size of Jurisdiction

Size of the municipality or jurisdiction is also considered important as larger jurisdictions may have more slack resources; may be able to exercise more power in purchasing health insurance; may have more resources to buy the expertise necessary to find, evaluate, and negotiate health insurance benefits; and may have more cash available for negotiations with providers (Perry and Cayer 1997). In evaluating private sector jobs, size of firm was associated with the provision of and cost sharing of health insurance even when controlling for unionization (Wunnava and Ewing 1999). Similarly, Perry and Cayer (1997), Streib (1996) and Daley (1993) all found size to be associated with health benefit provision or importance. The larger the size the more likely the jurisdiction is to have more types of plans and greater employer contribution to premium.

6.6.8   Management Form of Jurisdiction

There is empirical support for higher levels of fringe benefits in cities without professional managers. Edwards and Edwards (1982) found that in mayor council cities there were higher levels of fringe benefits because political bargaining and pressure is more accepted in these jurisdictions and there is greater possibility for employees and elected officials to engage in political action that results in higher health benefit levels.

6.6.9 Age and Level of Professionalization of the Workforce

Two characteristics of an employee/retiree group, the age structure of the insured group and the occupational distribution of the workforce, affect insurance utilization rates, which can drive a part of the total insurance premium. As worker age increases, the use of benefits typically increases (Rappaport 2000) so that as the average age of a workforce increases, so does utilization of the insurance benefit. As reported in the Bureau of Labor Statistics Employee Tenure report (2006b), public sector workers have, on average, a higher age and greater job tenure than private employees (6.9 years versus 3.6 years of tenure). This greater tenure and higher age is very likely to affect various elements of health benefit design. In particular, retiree healthcare coverage likely becomes more critical as employees age. The age difference between the sectors, coupled with strong and dense unions in the public sector likely explains why the public sector retains retiree health benefit coverage at higher levels than in the private sector.

Inversely, as professionalization levels increase in a workforce, insurance utilization often decreases. However, at the same time, the level of professionalization of a jurisdiction may also drive up coverage, quality, and cost-sharing components because employers must offer much higher levels of benefits to attract and retain these more "valuable" employees. Within the private and public sectors, BLS data (2006 and 1998) consistently demonstrate that professional employees have higher levels of coverage and better cost-sharing provisions than other occupational groups.

6.7 Conclusion

If appointed and elected officials want to find ways to try to manipulate, modify, or cost-shift the health benefit portion of total compensation, they must understand what specific economic, social, political, and workplace factors may affect the extent, quality, and cost sharing of health insurance for public employees. The public sector has higher levels of well-educated and college-educated workers in highly competitive professional occupations, greater levels of unionization, older and more tenured workers in larger public establishments, and a higher proportion of its workforce in metropolitan areas. Many of these factors, alone or together have been shown to affect the provision, cost, and types of health benefits. These factors make it unlikely that the current mix of health insurance benefit quantity, quality, and cost-sharing provisions will change soon or quickly. Public employers are largely unable to "outsource" critical functions performed within public jurisdictions and many of these functions cannot be easily performed or monitored using contingent or temporary workers. All of the factors that promote high levels of health insurance benefits and high employer cost sharing will only be changed slowly. As described by McKethan et al. (2006, p. 1527) after they interviewed 12 large state public employer health benefit executive directors about the types of changes they are pursuing,

> In the long run, public employees' and retirees' benefits are likely to undergo a gradual transformation, mirroring the private sector's changes over the past few decades. The pace and form of this evolution will vary from state to state, for at least two reasons. The first is the enduring public employee benefits philosophy, more politically embedded in some states, of placing greater emphasis on benefit security and retirement than on wages, relative to the private sector. The second is the varied presence and role of unions. Policymakers in states with a stronger public employee union presence might be slower to modify (heretofore generous) PEHP benefits and cost sharing.

The next step in developing our understanding of what affects design health insurance benefit design strategies is to collect the type of data that will allow for both cross-sectional and longitudinal analysis of variation and changes in the provision, cost, and quality of the health insurance benefit. These analyses, supplemented with interviews among decision-makers, may give us an opportunity to explore in greater detail similarities and differences between the public and private sectors in providing health benefits although controlling for such factors as size, level of unionization, age, professionalization, and local conditions of the labor and insurance markets.

References

Anderson, G., P.S. Hussey, B. Frogner, and H. Waters. 2005. Health care spending in the United States and the rest of the industrialized world. *Health Affairs* 24(4):903–914.

Barrett, K. and R. Greene. 2005. Grading the states: A management report card. *Governing: Special Issue.* February:24–95.

Beland, D. and J.S. Hacker. 2004. Ideas, private institutions and American Welfare State 'Exceptionalism': The case of health and old-age insurance, 1915–1965. *International Journal of Social Welfare* 13(1):42–54.

Bennett, J.T. and M.F. Masters. 2003. The future of public sector labor-management relations? *Journal of Labor Research* 24(4):533–545.

Bergmann, T.J., M.A. Bergmann, and J.L. Gahn. 1994. How important are employee benefits to public sector employees? *Public Personnel Management* 23(3):397–406.

Brennan, C., E. Wheel, and C. Hoene. 2005. The State of America's Cities 2005: The annual opinion survey of municipal elected officials. Washington, DC, National

League of Cities www.nlc.org/ASSETS/5C8EBE817F604AE093F6072BD398F7E0/rmpsoacrpt05.pdf (May 9, 2007).

Buchmueller, T., J.D. Nardo, and R. Valletta. 2001. *Union Effects on Health Insurance Provision and Coverage in the United States,* National Bureau of Economic Research, U.S. Department of Labor. Working Paper 8238. http://www.nber.org/papers/w8238 (October 31, 2005).

Budd, J. 2005. The effect of unions on employee benefits: Recent results from the employer cost for employee compensation data June 29, 2005 Bureau of Labor Statistics. http://www.bls.gov/opub/cwc/cm20050616ar01p1.htm (November 28, 2005).

Byrnes, N. and C. Palmeri. 2005. Sinkhole: How public pension promises are draining state and city budgets. *Business Week* June 13:3937.

Chetovich, C. 2002. Winning the best and the brightest: Increasing the attraction of public service. In M. Abramson and N. Gardner Eds. *Human Capital.* Lanham: Rowan and Littlefield.

Christianson, J.B. and S. Trude. 2003. Managing costs, managing benefits: Employer decisions in local health care markets. *Health Services Research* 38(1):3573–73.

Cowan, C.A., P.A. McDonnell, K.R. Levit, and M.A. Zezza. 2002. Burden of health care costs: Businesses, households, and governments, 1987–2000. *Health Care Financing Review* 23(3):131–141.

Daley, D. 1993. Health care benefits in the public sector: An examination of availability, size, and managerial effects among North Carolina municipalities. *International Journal of Public Administration* 16(10):1519–1539.

Edwards, L.N. and F.R. Edwards. 1982. Wellington-winter revisited: The case of municipal sanitation workers. *Industrial and Labor Relations Review* 35 (April):307–318.

Elazar, D.J. (1984). American federalism: A view from the states, 3rd ed. New York: Harper & Row.

Employee Benefit Research Institute. 2005. *Fundamentals of Employee Benefit Programs, Part Five Public Sector.* Washington, DC: Employee Benefit Research Institute. http://www.ebri.org/pdf/publications/books/fundamentals/Fnd05.Prt05.Chp39.pdf (October 15, 2005).

Enthoven, A.C. and V.R. Fuchs. 2006. Employment-based health insurance: Past, present and future. *Health Affairs* 25(6):1538–1547.

Feuille, P.J., T. Delaney, and W. Hendricks. 1985. Police bargaining, arbitration, and fringe benefits. *Journal of Labor Research* 6(4):1–20.

Freeman, R. 2003. What do unions do… to voting? Working paper 9992. National Bureau of Economic Research, Cambridge: Massachusetts. www.nber.org/papers/29992.

Fronstin, P. 2005a. Uninsured unchanged in 2004, but employment-based health coverage declined employee benefit research institute notes, October 2005 26(10):1–12. http://www.ebri.org/pdf/EBRI_IB_11-2005.pdf (November 28, 2005).

Fronstin, P. 2005b. Union status and employment-based health benefits, facts from EBRI: The basics of social security, new publications and internet sites. *Employee Benefit Research Institute Notes* May 25(5):2–6. http://www.ebri.org/publications/notes/index.cfm?fa=notesDisp&content_id=3327 (November 28, 2005).

Fronstin, P. 2005c. Sources of health insurance and characteristics of the uninsured: Analysis of the March 2005 current population survey. *Employee Benefit Research Institute Issue Brief Number 287,* November. http://www.ebri.org/pdf/EBRI_IB_11-2005.pdf (November 28, 2005).

Fronstin, P. 2007. Employment-based health benefits: Access and coverage, 1988–2005. *Employee Benefit Research Institute Issue Brief No. 303,* March.

Fronstin, P. and R. Werntz. 2004. The 'business case' for investing in employee health: A review of the literature and employer self-assessments. *Employee Benefit Research Institute Issue Brief #267,* March. http://www.ebri.org/pdf/briefspdf/0304ib.pdf (November 30, 2005).

Gabel, J., G. Claxton, I. Gil, J. Pickreign, H. Whitmore, B. Finder, S. Hawkins, and D. Rowland. 2005. Health benefits in 2005: Premium increases slow to single digit but coverage continues to erode, *Health Affairs* 24(5):1273–1280.

Goldstein, G.S. and M.V. Pauly. 1976. Group health insurance as a local public good. In R. Rosett, Ed., *The Role of Health Insurance in the Health Services Sector*. Cambridge, MA: National Bureau of Economic Research.

Guiler, J.K. and J. Shafritz. 2004. Dual personnel systems—organized labor and civil service: Side by side in the public sector. *Journal of Labor Research* 25(2):199–209.

Hall, M. 2004. Police, fire departments see shortages across USA. *USA Today*. 11/29/04. www.usatoday.com/news/nation/2004-11-28-police-shortages-cover_x.htm (November 30, 2005).

Haase, L.W. 2005. A new deal for health: how to cover everyone and get medical costs under control. *Century Foundation*. www.tcf.org/Publications/HealthCare/newdealhealth.pdf (March 22, 2007).

Hansen, F. 2004. Kill or be killed. *Workforce Management* 83(8):79–80.

Hunter, W.J. and C.H. Rankin. 1988. The composition of public sector compensation: The effects of unionization and bureaucratic size. *Journal of Labor Research* 9(1):29–42.

Hurley, R.E., L. Felland, A. Gerland, and J. Pickreign. 2006. Public employees' health benefits survive major threats, so far. *Health Affairs*, 2006 Web exclusives supplement 25:W195–W203 (April 18).

Inglehart, J. 2004. The challenges facing private health insurance. *Health Affairs* 23(6):9–10.

Ingraham, P.W., S.C. Selden, and D.P. Moynihan. 2000. People and performance: challenges for the future public service—the report from the Wye river conference. *Public Administration Review* 60(1):54–60.

International City/County Managers Association. 2000. Local Government Human Resource Functions 2000. Washington, DC: ICMA. http://www.icma.org/upload/bc/attach/{91512095-241F-457C-B85C-BA97F04C6207}hr2000web.pdf (November 22, 2005).

International City/County Management Association. 2002a. Health Care Plans for Local Government Employees, 2002. Washington, DC: ICMA. http://www.icma.org/upload/bc/attach/{17DEA897-90B8-4D6E-BA8D-7751E59D27B8}hcare2002web.pdf (November 22, 2005).

International City/County Managers Association. 2002b. State of the Profession-Fringe Benefits, 2002 Washington, DC: ICMA http://www.icma.org/upload/bc/attach/{5B707AA6-0132-47F8-94FE-C42B4404990B}sop02web.pdf (November 22, 2005).

Institute of Medicine, Board on Health Care Services, Committee on the Consequences of Uninsurance. 2004. Hidden Costs, Values Lost: Uninsurance in America. Washington, DC: The National Academies Press. www.nap.edu. (April 23, 2007).

Kadleck, C. 2003. Police Employee Organizations. *Policing* 26(2):341–351.

Kaiser Family Foundation and Health Research and Educational Trust. 2002. State Employee Health Plans. http://www.kff.org/insurance/upload/Kaiser-HRET-Survey-2002-State- Employee-Health-Plans-Report.pdf (April 10, 2007).

Kaiser Family Foundation and Health Research and Educational Trust. 2005. Employer Health Benefits 2005. *Annual Survey.* http://www.kff.org/insurance/7315/sections/ehbs05-3-2.cfm (November 22, 2005).

Kaiser Family Foundation and Harvard School of Public Health. 2005. Health Care Agenda for the New Congress. News Release: Americans Favor Malpractice Reform and Drug Importation, but Rank Them Low on Health Priority List for the Congress and President. January 11, 2005. http://www.kff.org/kaiserpolls/pomr011105nr.cfm (November 22, 2005).

Kaiser Family Foundation. 2005a. Trends and Indicators in the Changing Health Care Marketplace. Publication Number 7031. http://www.kff.org/insurance/7031/index.cfm (November 22, 2005).

Kaiser Family Foundation and Health Research and Educational Trust. 2005b. Employer Health Benefits 2005. *Annual Survey.* September 14, 2005. http://www.kff.org/insurance/7148/sections/ehbs04-1-15.cfm (November 30, 2005).

Kaiser Family Foundation and Health Research and Educational Trust. 2006. Employer Health Benefits 2006. *Annual Survey.* http://www.kff.org/insurance/7527/upload/7527.pdf (April 26, 2007).

Kaiser Family Foundation and Health Research and Educational Trust. 2006. Employer Health Benefits: 2006. *Annual Survey.* (www.kff.org/insurance/7527/upload/7527.pdf) (May 13, 2007).

Kaiser Family Foundation. 2007. Insurance Premium Cost-Sharing and Coverage Take-up. February. http://www.kff.org/insurance/snapshot/chcm020707oth.cfm (May 8, 2007).

Kearney, R.C. 2003a. The determinants of state employee compensation. *Review of Public Personnel Administration* 23(4):305–322.

Kearney, R.C. 2003b. Patterns of union decline and growth: An organizational ecology perspective. *Journal of Labor Research* 24(4):561–578.

Kearney, R.C. and D.G. Carnevale. 2001. *Labor Relations in the Public Sector,* 3rd ed. New York: Marcel Dekker.

Konde, P.S. 2005. NLC creates working group on health care to tackle rising municipal health care costs. *Nation's Cities Weekly.* April 4, 2005. http://www.nlc.org/Newsroom/Nation_s_Cities_Weekly/Weekly_NCW/2005/04/ 04/3446.cfm (November 22, 2005).

Koven, S. and C. Mausolff. 2002. The influence of political culture on state budgets: Another look at Elazar's formulation. *American Review of Public Administration* 32(1):66–77.

Lancaster, L.C. and D. Stillman. 2005. If I Pass the Baton, Who Will Grab It? Creating Bench Strength in Public Management. *Public Management* 87(8):8–15.

Lieske, J. 2005. Subcultural Effects on Voting Turnout in U.S. Presidential Elections Paper presented at the annual meeting of the American Political Science Association Marriott Wardman Park, Omni Shoreham, Washington Hilton, Washington, DC, September 1, 2005 http://convention2.allacademic.com/getfile.php?file=apsa05_proceeding/2005-08-30/42128/apsa05_proceeding_42128.pdf&PHPSESSID= fcee6e831956be85f33ca4aeb344e78e (April 29, 2007).

Litvak, D., A. Doppelt, and A. Laskey. 2004. Local Government Pressured by Rising Employee Health Care Costs. Fitch Special Report dated December 13, 2004.

http://www.fitchratings.com/corporate/reports/report_frame.cfm?rpt_id=228936& sector_flag=&marketsector=3&detail= (May 13, 2007).

Lewis, G. and S.A. Frank. 2002. Who wants to work for the government? *Public Administration Review* 62(4):395–404.

Long, S.H. and M.S. Marquis. 1999. Comparing employee health benefits in the public and private sectors, 1997. *Health Affairs* 18(6):183–193.

Marquis, M.S. and S.H. Long. 2001. Employer health insurance and local labor market conditions. *International Journal of Health Care Finance and Economics* 1(3–4): 273–292.

Matthews, T. 2003. Health care's perfect storm. *State Government News* 46(2):19–22.

Maxwell, J., P. Temin, and T. Petigara. 2004. Private health purchasing practices in the public sector: A comparison of state employers and the fortune 500. *Health Affairs* 23(2):182–190.

McDonnell, K. 2005. Benefit cost comparisons between state and local governments and private-sector employers. *Employee Benefit Research Institute Notes* April 2005 26(4):2–11. http://www.ebri.org/pdf/notespdf/0405notes.pdf (May 13, 2007).

McGee, J. and P.S. Konde. 2005. Working group examines health care costs. *Nation's Cities Weekly*. June 13, 2005. http://www.nlc.org/Newsroom/Nation_s_Cities_Weekly/Weekly_NCW/2005/06/13/5146.cfm (November 22, 2005).

McKethan, A., D. Gitterman, A. Feezor, and A. Enthoven. 2006. New directions for public health care purchasers? Responses to looming challenges. *Health Affairs* 25(6):1518–1528.

National Association of Counties and National Association of Community Health Centers. 2003. Community health centers and public health services: Where are counties devoting their resources for health care? July 30, 2003. Washington, DC http://www.naco.org/ContentManagement/ContentDisplay.cfm?ContentID=9454 (May 13, 2007).

O'Brien, E. 2003. Employers' benefits from workers' health insurance. *The Milbank Quarterly* 81(1):2003:5–43.

Pauly, M. 2005. How Private Health Insurance Pools Risk National Bureau of Economic Research Reporter Research Summary, Summer 2005. http://www.nber.org/reporter/summer05/pauly.html (May 13, 2007).

Perry, R.W. and N.J. Cayer. 1997. Factors affecting municipal satisfaction with health care plans. *Review of Public Personnel Administration* 17(2):5–19.

Rappaport, A. 2000. Variation of employee benefit costs by age. *Social Security Bulletin* 63(4):47–56.

Reddick, C.G. and J. Coggburn. 2007. State government employee health benefits in the United States. *Review of Public Personnel Administration* 27(1):5–20.

Regopoulos, L. and S. Trude. 2004. Employers shift rising health care costs to workers: No long-term solution in sight *Issue Brief No. 83*, May 2004. Center for Studying Health System Change. http://www.hschange.com/CONTENT/677/677.pdf (May 13, 2007).

Reinhardt, U.E., P.S. Hussey, and G.F. Anderson. 2004. U.S. health care spending in an international context: Why is U.S. spending so high, and can we afford it? *Health Affairs* 23(3):10–25.

Revell, J. 2005. The great state health-care giveaway. *Fortune* May 2, 2005 151:9.

Roberts, G.E. 2001. An examination of employee benefits cost control strategies in New Jersey local governments. *Public Personnel Management* 30(3):303–321.

Roberts, G.E. 2003. Municipal government part-time employee benefits practices. *Public Personnel Management* 32(3):435–454.

Roberts, G.E., J.A. Gianakis, C. McCue, and X. Wang. 2004. Traditional and family-friendly benefits practices in local governments: Results from a national survey. *Public Personnel Management* 33(3):291–306.

Robinson, J.C. 2004. Consolidation and the transformation of competition in health insurance. *Health Affairs* November–December 23(6):11–24.

Robinson, J.C. 2006. The commercial health insurance industry in an era of eroding employer coverage. *Health Affairs* 25(6):1475–1486.

Scott, L. 2003. Employee health coverage crisis. *State Government News* 46(2):28–29.

Sheils, J. and R. Haught. 2004. The cost of tax-exempt health benefits in 2004. *Health Affairs* 23:106–112 Supp Web Exclusives.

Stanton, M.W. 2004. Employer-sponsored health insurance: Trends in cost and access. *Research in Action Issue* 17, September. Agency for Healthcare Research and Quality. http://www.ahrq.gov/research/empspria/empspria.pdf (April 25, 2007).

Stoll, K. 2005. Paying a premium: The added cost of care for the uninsured. Publication number 05-101 of Families USA. http://www.familiesusa.org/assets/pdfs/Paying_a_Premium_rev_July_13731e.pdf (May 13, 2007).

Streib, G. 1996. Specialty health care services in municipal government. *Review of Public Personnel Administration* 16(2):57–72.

Stumpf, E.C. 2005. Issues related to state and employer innovation in insurance coverage. The Commonwealth Fund. Issue Brief, July. http://www.cmwf.org/usr_doc/835_Strumpf_state.pdf (May 13, 2007).

Travis, L.F. 2000. Managerial Freedom and Collective Bargaining in Ohio Municipal Police Agencies: The current State of the Art. Law Enforcement Foundation: Dublin, Ohio.

U.S. Department of Commerce. Bureau of the Census. 2007. *Statistical Abstract of the United States.* http://www.census.gov/prod/www/statistical-abstract.html (May 8, 2007).

United States Department of Health and Human Services. Center for Medicare and Medicaid Services. 2005. Office of the Actuary NHE Projections 2006–2016, Forecast Summary and Selected Tables. http://www.cms.hhs.gov/NationalHealthExpendData/downloads/proj2006.pdf (April 23, 2007).

United States Department of Labor. Bureau of Labor Statistics. 1998. Employee Benefits in State and Local Government, 1998. http://www.bls.gov/ncs/ebs/sp/ebbl0018.pdf (March 19, 2007).

United States Department of Labor. Bureau of Labor Statistics. 2005. News: Employer Costs for Employee Compensation. September 21, 2005.

United States Department of Labor. Bureau of Labor Statistics. 2005a. National Compensation Survey: Employee Benefits in Private Industry in the United States, March 2005 Summary 05-01.

United States Department of Labor. Bureau of Labor Statistics. 2005b. Union Membership in 2004 dated January 27, 2005. Table 3: Union affiliation of employed wage and salary workers by occupation and industry. http://www.bls.gov/news.release/union2.nr0.htm (November 28, 2005).

United States Department of Labor. Bureau of Labor Statistics. 2006. National Compensation Survey: Employee Benefits in Private Industry in the United States, March 2006. August. http://www.bls.gov/ncs/ebs/sp/ebsm0004.pdf. (April 30, 2007).

United States Department of Labor. Bureau of Labor Statistics. 2006b. Employee Tenure in 2006. USDL 06-1563, September. http://www.bls.gov/news.release/tenure.t05.htm (May 1, 2007).

United States Department of Labor. Bureau of Labor Statistics. 2007a. Employer Cost for Employee Compensation—December 2006. USDL 07-0453, March. http://www.bls.gov/news.release/pdf/ecec.pdf (May 1, 2007).

United States Department of Labor. Bureau of Labor Statistics. 2007b. Union Members Summary dated January 25. http://stats.bls.gov/news/release/pdf/union2.htm. (March 20, 2007).

United States Government Accountability Office. 2005. Federal Employees Health Benefits Program: Competition and Other Factors Linked to Wide Variation in Health Care Prices. Report Number GAO-05-856. http://www.gao.gov/new.items/d05856.pdf (December 5, 2005).

United States Government Accountability Office. 2006. Employer Spending on Benefits has Grown Faster than Wages, Due Largely to Rising Costs for Health Insurance and Retirement Benefits. Report Number GAO-06-285.

United States Office of Personnel Management. 2005. 2004 Employee Benefits Survey http://www.opm.gov/employment_and_benefits/survey/benefitssurveyresults.asp (May 13, 2007).

Walters, J. 2007. Paying for promises. *Governing.Com.* February. http://governing.com/articles/2retire.htm (May 13, 2007).

Ward, E.D. and E. Davis. 1995. Health benefit satisfaction in the public and private sectors: The role of distributive and procedural justice. *Public Personnel Management* 24(3):255–271.

Watts, C., J.B. Christianson, L. Heineccius, and S. Trude. 2003. The role of public employers in a changing health care market. *Health Affairs* 22(1):173–180.

Whitmore, H., S.R. Collins, J. Gabel, and J. Pickreign. 2006. Employers' views on incremental measures to expand health coverage. *Health Affairs* 25(6):1668–1678.

Wong, J. 1997. Health care finance in the United States: Past, present, and future. *International Journal of Public Administration* 20(6):1297–1315.

Wunnava, P.V. and B.T Ewing. 1999. Union-nonunion differentials and establishment size: Evidence from the NLSY. *Journal of Labor Research* 20(2):177–183.

Zhao, J. and N.P Lovrich. 1997. Collective bargaining and the police: The consequences for supplemental compensation policies in large agencies. *Policing* 20(3):508–518.

HEALTH AND RETIREMENT BENEFITS

Chapter 7

An Overview of Federal Retirement Benefits

David Torregrosa, Cary Elliott, and Mark Musell

CONTENTS

7.1   An Overview of Federal Retirement Benefits

Retirement benefits are an important part of the total compensation offered by the government to attract and retain a skilled workforce. Federal civilian retirement programs cover about 2,670,000 active government employees, including those of

---

The views expressed in this chapter are those of the authors and should not be interpreted as those of the Congressional Budget Office.

the U.S. Postal Service. The Congressional Budget Office (CBO) expects federal pension and annuitant health payments to 2,450,000 civilian annuitants and survivors to reach $72 billion in 2007 (CBO 2007a).

Several attributes of federal pensions are especially noteworthy. Unlike most private employers, the federal government still provides traditional defined benefit plans, which are based on years of service and salary. Moreover, the federal plans offer inflation-protected annuities, various early retirement options, and disability coverage. Inflation protection is particularly valuable as longevity increases and is rarely found in private pension plans. In addition to the traditional pension benefits, the federal government offers a 401(k) plan—the Thrift Savings Plan (TSP), which offers several indexed stock and bond funds, as well as life-cycle funds. As a result, investment returns match market returns, opportunities for political interference are limited, and management fees are minimal.

Federal retirees may also receive retiree health benefits, subject to eligibility requirements, through the Federal Employees' Health Benefits (FEHB) program. Participants and the government share the cost of premiums, which vary according to plan. FEHB offers participants a range of insurance options, including fee-for-service providers, Health Maintenance Organizations, and high deductible plans. Thus, participants can enroll in the plan that best suits their needs. Most FEHB plans provide prescription drug benefits, and thus most retirees do not enroll in Medicare's optional drug coverage.

The federal budget reports retirement costs on both a cash basis and on a partial accrual basis. The federal budget reports outlays for pension and health benefits to retired federal workers when those payments are made—a cash basis of accounting. Civilian pension payments totaled $60 billion in 2006 and the government paid $8.3 billion toward annuitants' health insurance (Table 7.1). In addition, agencies make payments to on-budget retirement funds to cover some of the cost of benefits as they are earned—an accrual basis of accounting. However, those payments are intragovernmental and thus do not affect the budget totals or the budget deficit or surplus. Instead, those payments are reported as agency outlays and receipts to the retirement funds.

The budgetary treatment of federal retirement programs has important implications for workers and annuitants that affect the budget savings options available to congress for dealing with retirement programs. In particular, cutting benefits as they are earned would generate only limited savings in the short run. But immediate savings can be realized by reducing benefits paid to current retirees.

In contrast, the federal financial statements report an operating expense for the estimated cost of all retirement benefits when those benefits are earned. Estimates of expenses accrued for federal pensions were about $136 billion in 2006 and another $16 billion for retiree health benefits. In 2006, total federal liabilities were $1349 billion for civilian pensions and $295 billion for retiree health (Department of the Treasury 2006).

Federal retirement plans, other than TSP, hold only Treasury securities and are "underfunded" from an actuarial standpoint. If private plans were funded like federal

Table 7.1   Federal Civilian Employees' Benefits (Billions of Dollars)

	1997	1998	1999	2000	2001	2002	2003	2004	2005	2006
Estimates of liabilities										
Pensions	977.2	996.4	1025.2	1071.9	1112.9	1129.8	1190.4	1230.2	1273.0	1349.0
Retirement health benefits	158.9	181.8	179.7	198.1	205.2	221.4	244.4	266.1	290.7	295.2
Estimates of accrual expenses										
Pensions	72.2	68.8	81.0	92.0	89.9	65.9	106.9	94.7	100.5	135.5
Retirement health benefits	16.0	24.0	4.3	24.7	14.6	24.4	41.5	31.3	35.3	15.8
Benefits Paid										
Pensions	41.6	42.9	43.8	45.1	47.2	48.8	50.2	52.1	54.6	60.3
Retiree health premiums[a]	3.9	4.1	4.6	5.0	5.5	6.1	6.7	7.3	7.8	8.3

[a] Excludes contributions from the U.S. Postal Service for their annuitants. Those payments were $1.6 billion in 2006.

Sources: From Department of the Treasury, in *Financial Report of the United States Government,* Department of the Treasury, Washington, D.C., 2006; Budget of the U.S. Government: Historical Tables (Fiscal Year 2007), Table 11-3; Office of Personnel Management, 2006a, *Federal Civilian Workforce Statistics: The Fact Book* (2005 edition).

ones, they would be considered completely unfunded. However, the degree of underfunding has few implications for federal retirees because the government relies on current tax revenues and borrowing from the public to pay for all of its spending.

7.2 The Federal Employees' Retirement System

The Federal Employees' Retirement System (FERS) covers most civilian employees hired since January 1984. FERS supplements Social Security coverage, which workers who are covered under FERS also receive. FERS provides both a traditional pension based on years of service and final salary and a 401(k) plan. Most civilian employees not in FERS are covered by the Civil Service Retirement System (CSRS), which is a closed system that is new employees are not eligible to join. It covers most workers hired before 1984. Participants in CSRS are covered only by a traditional pension plan and do not generally receive Social Security benefits as a result of federal employment. (CSRS was established before there was Social Security.) When the FERS was created, employees covered by CSRS had the option to join FERS.

When the Social Security Amendments of 1983 extended Social Security coverage to new federal workers and Members of Congress, policy makers recognized that a new retirement system was needed. Social Security benefits overlapped with some of the benefits covered under the CSRS. In addition, employee contributions to CSRS were 7 percent of salary, and adding Social Security contributions on top of CSRS contributions would have then brought the combined contributions to over 13 percent of pay (CRS 1986).

In designing the new system, policy makers had several goals. First, the expected cost to the government of providing benefits, including Social Security, under the two systems was to be about the same. Second, the new system should be modeled on the best attributes of the private sector plans. Third, the new system should increase the portability of benefits. By effectively tying all retirement benefits to final salary, CSRS provided workers with strong incentives to remain with the government until they were eligible for retirement.

Retirement income for workers covered under FERS consists of three parts: Social Security benefits; a traditional defined benefit pension plan; and the Thrift Savings Plan (TSP), which is similar to the 401(k) plans offered by many private employers. Policy makers considered, but ultimately rejected, eliminating the defined benefit plan and substituting a larger defined contribution plan.

The FERS defined benefit component bases retirement benefits on an employee's years of service and the highest three consecutive years of salary, which are generally an employees' final three years. Replacement rates though are lower under FERS than CSRS, because participants also will accumulate balances in their TSP accounts and receive Social Security (Box 7.1). On an accrual basis, the cost of CSRS benefits is 25.2 percent of salary versus 12 percent for FERS (excluding Social Security and

Box 7.1 Defined Benefit Pension, Benefit Formulas, and Eligibility Requirements

Both the Civil Service Retirement System (CSRS) and the Federal Employees Retirement System (FERS) provide a defined benefit pension based on an employee's length of service and salary, subject to certain eligibility requirements. Under both systems, most employees are eligible for retirement benefits, that is, they are "vested," after five years of service (18 months for survivor and disability benefits). In addition, both systems generally base initial benefits on an average of the employee's three highest-salaried years. However, other provisions differ significantly. Although not discussed below, both systems also provide survivor and disability benefits. The benefits and eligibility requirements also differ for federal law enforcement officers, firefighters, air traffic controllers, and Congressional employees.

Civil Service Retirement System

CSRS provides a large defined benefit pension with full inflation protection.

Eligibility requirements. Most employees are eligible for an immediate pension at

- 55 and 30 years of service
- 60 and 20 years of service
- 62 and 5 years of service

Benefit formula. The initial benefit is 1.5 percent of an employee's high-three salary for the first five years of employment, 1.75 percent for the next five, and 2 percent thereon. Thus, a CSRS-covered employee who retires at age 60 with twenty-five years of service would receive an initial pension of 46.25 percent of his high-three salary. (Benefits are reduced for those electing survivor benefits.)

COLAs. Retirees receive cost-of-living adjustments that provide complete protection against inflation.

Federal Employees' Retirement System

FERS provides a smaller initial defined benefit and less complete inflation protection than CSRS.

Eligibility requirements. Most employees are eligible for an immediate pension if they meet one of three basic requirements:

(continued)

Box 7.1 (continued)   Defined Benefit Pension, Benefit Formulas, and Eligibility Requirements

1. Minimum retirement age and 30 years of service. The minimum retirement age is 55 for those born before 1948 and gradually rises to 57 for those born after 1970.
2. 60 and 20 years of service.
3. 62 and 5 years of service.

Under certain circumstances, employees may be able to retire earlier and receive reduced benefits, an option not available under CSRS. Reduced benefits are payable to those with at least ten years of service and of minimum retirement age. Benefits are reduced 5 percent a year for those under age 62. This is another example of FERS increasing the portability of benefits relative to CSRS. Deferred benefits are generally payable at age 62 to those who leave before retirement with at least five years of service.

Benefit formula. The initial benefit is 1 percent of your high-three average pay times the years of service. (The benefit factor rises to 1.1 percent for those retiring at age 62 or later.) Thus, an FERS participant who retires after 25 years of service at age 60 would initially receive 25 percent of his high-three salary in retirement. In addition, this employee might receive a retirement supplement until the age of 62 when Social Security benefits would start. The amount of the supplement, which is subject to an earnings test, would cover the portion of his expected Social Security benefits attributable to the employee's federal employment. (Benefits are reduced for participants who want survivor benefits.)

COLAs. FERS pensions are fully protected only when the rate of inflation is less than 2 percent a year. If inflation is between 2 and 3 percent, FERS annuitants receive a COLA of 2 percent. If inflation exceeds 3 percent, their COLA is the rate of inflation minus 1 percentage point. Most retirees are not eligible to receive a COLA until age 62. (Survivors and those retiring on a disability usually receive a COLA regardless of their ages.)

TSP). Most federal employees covered under CSRS contribute 7 percent of pay toward their benefits although most FERS workers contribute 0.8 percent of pay (plus 6.25 percent to Social Security).

As of September 30, 2006, the average annual annuity to an FERS retiree was about $9200 although the average annuity for a CSRS retiree was about $31,800, according to the Office of Personnel Management. On the basis of the accrual cost of the benefit plans, one would have expected that the CSRS benefit would be just over twice the size of the FERS defined pension benefit, not more than three times as big. Some of the disparity reflects different characteristics of the average retiree under the two systems. Retirees who have already retired under FERS must have some combination of lower salaries and fewer years of service than CSRS retirees. In particular, current retirees in FERS would not have the opportunity to accumulate many years of service—at most, 22 years of service. Thus, the comparison may be too early to reveal much useful information about the relative generosity of the programs.

Both FERS and CSRS provide enhanced benefits for special groups of employees, such as law enforcement officers, firefighters, air traffic controllers, and members of congress and their staffs. In some cases, those additional benefits may be justified by the specific personnel needs of an employer. For example, Box 7.2 provides details on the benefits provided to law enforcement officers.

Box 7.2 Special Retirement Provisions for Federal Law Enforcement Officers

Federal law enforcement officers receive special retirement provisions under both CSRS and FERS.* Those provisions include voluntary early retirement with an enhanced annuity formula and a mandatory retirement age. Those retirement enhancements, coupled with maximum entry age requirements— officers who are at least 57 years old with 20 years of service generally must retire—help to ensure that the government maintains a young and vigorous law enforcement workforce (OPM 2004). However in recent years, with the increased demand for law enforcement since 9/11 and increases in life expectancy, there is concern that experienced officers are retiring when they may still be effective. According to the U.S. Office of Personnel Management, a significant percentage of retired law enforcement officers are still able to work, and many who have retired from federal service may go to work for state and local or private law enforcement employers (OPM 2004).

(continued)

---

* For purposes of retirement eligibility, the definition of law enforcement officer in federal statute has a more restrictive meaning than any commonly understood notion. The statutory definition is that the employee's duties must be primarily the "investigation, apprehension, or detention of individuals suspected or convicted of offenses against the criminal laws of the United States." Although piecemeal legislation has extended coverage to some uniformed police officers, some groups of employees—such as police officers, guards, and inspectors (including customs inspectors and immigration inspectors)—do not generally meet this definition because they prevent or detect violations instead of investigating them. The FERS definition (5 U.S.C. 8401(17)(A)(i)(II)) of a law enforcement officer is more inclusive—adding officers who protect government officials—than the CSRS definition (5 U.S.C. 8331(20)).

Box 7.2 (continued)   Special Retirement Provisions for Federal Law Enforcement Officers

CSRS Law Enforcement Retirement Provisions

- *Employee contributions.* Under CSRS, law enforcement officers pay retirement contributions at 7.5 percent of basic pay.
- *Eligibility requirements.* Law enforcement officers are eligible for immediate pension at age 50 with a minimum of 20 years of qualifying service.
- *Benefit formula.* The benefit is 2.5 percent of high-three average pay times years of qualifying service up to 20 years, plus 2.0 percent of high-three average pay times for each year of service over 20 years.

FERS Law Enforcement Retirement Provisions

- *Employee contributions.* Under FERS, law enforcement officers contribute 1.3 percent of basic pay to retirement.
- *Eligibility requirements.* FERS employee may retire at age 50 with a minimum of 20 years service as a law enforcement officer, or at any age with at least 25 years of such service.
- *Benefit formula.* The FERS formula for law enforcement officers is 1.7 percent times high-three average pay times eligible service up to 20 years, plus 1.0 percent times high-three average pay times any eligible service over 20 years.

Some uncertainty surrounds the security of the promise of a federal defined benefit pension because congress may cut federal retirement benefits after they have been earned. For example, COLAs have been delayed or reduced during periods of budgetary stress. To date, the courts have not recognized any property rights for federal workers and retirees to defined benefit pensions.* (In contrast, the Pension Benefit Guaranty Corporation protects most private employees' pensions should their firm go bankrupt and have an underfunded plan.)

7.2.1 The Thrift Savings Plan

The Thrift Savings Plan (TSP) has proven to be very popular with employees for several reasons. (See Box 7.3 for an analysis of the trade-offs between defined benefit and defined contribution pensions.) First, the benefits are portable, that is, vested

---

* For example, see *National Association for Retired Federal Employees v. Horner*, 633 F. Suppl. 511 (D.D.C. 1986) which upheld a reduction in cost-of-living adjustments in 1985.

Box 7.3 The Trade-Offs between Defined Benefit and Defined Contribution Plans

The role of pensions may be viewed from multiple perspectives (Bodie 1990; Gustman, Mitchell, and Steinmeier 1994). Pensions are a form of insurance that provide retirement income security. Pensions affect labor market incentives through their vesting and retirement eligibility rules, which affect employee turnover, effort, and the timing of retirement. Pensions also have tax effects. For example, federal workers can defer taxes on a large portion of their compensation. Those perspectives inform the trade-offs between defined benefit and defined contribution plans (Bodie, Marcus, and Merton 1988). As policy makers determined when FERS was structured, there is probably a beneficial role for both types of plans to play in the federal government.

Defined benefit plans offer some advantages to workers. They shield them from the investment risk inherent in defined contribution plans, and are easy to integrate with survivor and disability benefits. They provide retirement income security because they replace a specified share of average salary during an employee's peak earning years. CSRS and FERS provide more security than private pensions because they are indexed to inflation. Because they provide annuities, they reduce longevity risk—the risk that a retiree lives longer than expected and runs out of savings.

However, defined benefit plans may be difficult for most employees to value, and they are less likely than defined contribution plans to help attract young workers. Their lack of portability is perhaps the greatest disadvantage—employees who leave government service before qualifying for retirement suffer a loss of pension wealth for two reasons. First, the accumulation of pension benefits is backloaded—most benefits are earned in the last ten years of employment due to the time value of money and increases in salary. Second, although workers who leave service before retirement age may be entitled to a deferred annuity, the purchasing power of the deferred annuity is eroded by inflation in the period between an employee's departure from the government and the start of the annuity.

From an employer's perspective, defined benefit plans help retain experienced workers, but may encourage some to stay too long and others to leave too soon—as soon as they become eligible for retirement. Because benefits depend on final average salary, workers have an additional incentive to sustain their productivity over the entire career to achieve a higher final salary.

Defined contribution plans are tax-deferred savings accounts that are held in trust for the individual employee. Thus, the benefits are secure and portable. Moreover, they are easily understood by workers. Defined contribution plans

(continued)

Box 7.3 (continued)   The Trade-Offs between Defined Benefit and Defined Contribution Plans

generally do not affect labor market incentives. Although employers could alter the pattern of contribution rates over an employee's career to rise with age and tenure—effectively backloading benefit accruals, changing retention incentives—most, including the federal government, do not.

A major disadvantage of defined contribution plans is that the participants bear the entire investment risk under a defined contribution plan, although employers bear the investment risk in a defined benefit plan. Those with limited information and understanding about investments may make poor decisions. However, TSP's government security fund is very low risk, and the life-cycle funds are designed to appeal to workers who are willing to accept more risk but need help allocating their portfolio. But there is no guarantee that benefits will keep pace with wages or inflation.* Defined contribution plans do not provide annuities—though they can be purchased—and thus offer less retirement income insurance against longevity risk than a defined benefit plan. Because FERS participants are also covered by a defined benefit plan, they have less need to purchase an annuity at retirement with their TSP funds. Because annuity markets suffer from adverse selection—those in poor health opt out—they frequently offer below market returns.

---

individuals who switch jobs suffer no loss of pension wealth. Second, the accounts are safe from political tampering. Third, individuals who are willing to assume greater risks have the potential to earn high returns. (On the other hand, TSP does shift the investment risk to the individual participant.) Fourth, employees may borrow from their TSP accounts. At the end of 2006, over $200 billion was in the Thrift Savings Plan making it the nation's largest defined contribution plan (Federal Retirement Thrift Investment Board 2007b).

In 2007, most federal workers can direct up to $15,500 of their salary to the TSP, which is similar to a 401(k) plan. (Employees who are 50 and older are able to make additional catchup contributions up to $5000). Contributions to the plan are tax deferred; the Internal Revenue Service sets the contribution limit and adjusts it annually.

The federal government matches contributions made by FERS employees but not those made by CSRS-covered employees. Under FERS, federal agencies automatically contribute an amount equal to 1 percent of an employee's salary to the

---

* If the Thrift Savings Plan added an indexed bond fund, participants would have the option of investing in a fund that provided returns higher the rate of inflation. The trade-off would be lower real returns.

TSP; agencies also match the first 3 percent of workers' voluntary contributions to the TSP dollar for dollar and match the next 2 percent of contributions at 50 cents on the dollar. Thus, although those employees can save higher shares of their earnings in TSP, they receive the maximum government match by contributing just 5 percent. There is immediate vesting of the agency's matching contributions and the automatic 1 percent contributions vests for most employees after three years. Federal practice is more generous than those of the private sector, which usually provides lower matches and no automatic contributions to defined contribution plans.

The budgetary treatment of TSP is simple. The agencies' contributions to the plan are reported as budget outlays as the benefits are earned and paid. The government's responsibility ends with the contributions to the accounts, and by definition, the plans are fully funded.

Most employees contribute to TSP. Over 85 percent of FERS-covered employees are contributing and nearly 70 percent of CSRS-covered employees participate even though they receive no matching contributions (Federal Retirement Thrift Investment Board 2007a). Those rates have risen sharply over time; however, participation by FERS-covered employees appears to have leveled off. By comparison, depending upon the size of the employer, between two-thirds and three-quarters of employees who can contribute to a defined contribution plan do so (Watson Wyatt Worldwide 2007).

The federal employees who contribute to TSP do so at higher rates than employees in the private sector, who typically contribute about 7.3 percent of pay (Watson Wyatt Worldwide 2007). The salary deferral rate was 8.6 percent for FERS contributors in 2005 and 7.5 percent for CSRS contributors (Federal Retirement Thrift Investment Board 2007b). As shown in Table 7.2, employees' contributions typically rise with both age and salary. (Employees in higher-tax brackets receive bigger tax benefits from their contributions.) Not surprisingly, FERS's employees contribute somewhat more than CSRS employees, who expect larger pension annuities. Contribution rates have increased every year, in part due to higher statutory limits and the maturation of the system. During the plan's first full year of operations, 1988, the average contribution rate for FERS was 4.4 percent (Federal Retirement Thrift Investment Board 2007b).

Under a defined contribution approach like TSP, the participants rather than the government would own the assets and direct the investments. The future value of benefits depends on the amount of contributions and the performance of the assets in which contributions are invested (Box 7.3). The federal government's TSP now offers participants multiple investment options. All the options follow passive investment strategies and most match broad market indexes.* That strategy provides participants investment options with extremely low fees—recently between $3 and $5 per $10,000 invested—for each of the funds. The options offer different degrees and types of risk and returns. New options have been added over time allowing participants more diversification. The current choices are:

---

* Information about the funds and their returns is available at the Thrift Savings Plan's Web site: www.tsp.gov/rates/index.html.

Table 7.2 Average Contribution Rates to the Thrift Savings Plan, 2005 (as a Percentage of Salary)

	Age					
	Under 30	*30–39*	*40–49*	*50–59*	*60–69*	*70±*
FERS participants	6.4	7.6	8.4	9.9	11.1	11.5
CSRS participants	N.A.	5.7	6.3	7.9	8.4	8.3
	Salary Quintiles					
	Lowest	*Mid-low*	*Middle*	*Mid-High*	*Highest*	
FERS participants	6.4	7.9	8.4	9.5	10.5	
CSRS participants	6.2	6.9	7.4	8.3	8.9	

Note: N.A., not applicable.

Source: Authors, based on data from the Thrift Savings Investment Board, "Thrift Savings Plan: Participant Behavior and Demographics: Analysis for 2000–2005" (2007).

■ A government bond fund (G Fund) offers participants an opportunity not available in the marketplace. This fund holds only special Treasury securities issued to the TSP, which allows investments in short-term securities that earn long-term interest rates—the average market yield on outstanding marketable U.S. Treasuries with four or more years to maturity. The value of an investment in the G Fund grows with the interest rate rather the market value of the underlying long-term securities. This means the G Fund can never lose value. In contrast, rising interest rates can cause returns on other bond funds to be negative when the market value of the bonds falls. For example, when rates were rising in 1999, the G Fund returned 5.99 percent although the fixed-income indexed investment fund replicating the U.S. bond market lost 0.85 percent. Only federal government employees have direct access to this investment opportunity, which averaged about 1.8 percentage points higher than three-month Treasury-bill rate between January 1988 and December 2005.* Since its inception on April 1, 1987, the fund has averaged 6.6 percent annual returns. As of January 2007, the fund had $69 billion in assets.

---

* The G Fund essentially gives federal employees a free swap—they hold the rough equivalent of three-month T-Bills but receive the interest rate payments of funds that have a weighted average maturity of about eleven years.

- A fixed-income index investment fund represents the U.S. bond market, including Treasuries and corporate debt with maturities of more than one year. It is broadly diversified and includes only investment-grade securities, so no "junk bonds" are held. Since its inception on January 29, 1988, through December 31, 2005, the fund has averaged annual returns of 7.4 percent after expenses. As of January 2007, the fund had $10 billion in assets.
- A stock-indexed fund tracks the Standard & Poor's 500 Index, which is a market-weighted portfolio of 500 large- to medium-size companies that account for over 70 percent of the value of the U.S. stock markets. Investors are exposed to stock market volatility but not the greater idiosyncratic risk of an individual stock. Since inception on January 29, 1988, the fund has averaged 11.6 percent annual returns after expenses. As of January 2007, the fund had assets of $74 billion.
- A small capitalization stock-indexed fund tracks the performance of a broad index made up of companies not included in the S&P 500. Over time, its returns are likely to be more volatile than the S&P 500 index but potentially higher on average. Since its inception on May 1, 2001, the fund has averaged annual returns of 8.9 percent. As of January 2007, the fund had $17 billion in net assets.
- An international stock-indexed fund tracks the performance of more than 1000 companies in over 20 foreign countries. Although international funds have market and currency risk (changes in the value of the U.S. dollar will affect returns), adding international funds to a portfolio can reduce its risk and increase its expected return. Since its inception on May 1, 2001, the fund has averaged annual returns of 6.42 percent after expenses. As of January 2007, the fund had $22 billion in assets.
- In August 2005, a new option was added, life-cycle funds, which diversify account holdings by blending the funds above according to professionally determined allocations set to various retirement dates for participants. As retirement approaches, life-cycle funds become more conservatively invested. The objective of each life-cycle fund is to provide the highest return for the amount of risk taken. Currently, TSP offers four life-cycle funds for participants with retirement dates around 2010, 2020, 2030, and 2040. An "income" life-cycle fund is available for those in retirement or very close to retirement. That fund is predominately allocated to the G fund but does hold some of the various stock funds. As of January 2007, the life-cycle funds held about $18 billion.

Congress structured TSP to preclude political interference and to diversify investors' risk (Hustead and Hustead 2001). The funds are passively managed, which limits the opportunities for congress to direct investment into or away from targeted areas. At retirement, participants can convert all or part of their TSP holdings into an annuity or transfer the funds into another tax-deferred retirement plan. TSP purchases annuities from Metropolitan Life Insurance Company. A standard annuity provides a fixed monthly payment for as long as the retiree lives. Other options are available including annuities with survivor benefits, annuities whose payments rise over time, and annuities with special payouts in the case of early deaths.

7.2.2 Federal Retiree Health Benefits

Although large employers in the private sector have been paring back retiree health benefits and tightening eligibility requirements for new hires, the federal government continues to provide nearly identical coverage to current employees and retirees (GAO 2007). Moreover, premiums are the same for both groups (though current employees pay their premiums out of pretax income). The FEHB program is unique in that it allows participants a great deal of choice. About 300 health insurance plans participate, including fee-for-service plans (with options of preferred provider plans), Health Maintenance Organizations, and high deductible plans (OPM 2006b). However, not all plans are available to all employees. Some plans are available nation-wide, although others are open only to certain groups or are available in only certain areas. For example, HMOs generally operate on a regional basis. Consequently, most participants are choosing from less than 15 different plans (Chaikind 2007). According to estimates from the Office of Personnel Management, the accrual cost of postretirement health benefits was roughly $5200 a year per employee enrolled in FEHB in 2006. The accrual cost is a good measure of the value of retiree health benefits that the average employee earns during the year.

The FEHB program provides health insurance coverage to 1.9 million federal annuitants, as well as their dependents and survivors, at an expected cost to the government of almost $8.5 billion in 2007. Federal retirees are generally allowed to continue receiving benefits from the FEHB if they have participated in the program during each of their last five years of service and are eligible to receive an immediate annuity. More than 80 percent of new retirees elect to continue health benefits. For those over age 65, FEHB benefits are coordinated with Medicare benefits; the FEHB program pays amounts not covered by Medicare (but no more than what it would have paid in the absence of Medicare. This is the most generous approach among several used by employers to coordinate benefits with Medicare).* Because the FEHB plans cover prescription drugs, few federal retirees enroll in Medicare Part D, which charges a separate premium for drug coverage.

Benefits vary across plans, but all offer coverage for hospital, surgical, physician, and emergency care. Plans also must offer prescription drug benefits, mental health benefits, child immunizations, and limits on an enrollee's total out-of-pocket costs. In most cases, once that catastrophic limit is reached, the plan pays all the remaining covered cost for the rest of the year (Chaikind 2007).

Participants in the FEHB program and the government share the cost of premiums. The cost-sharing provision sets the government's share for all enrollees at 72

---

* In contrast to private employers offering retiree health coverage, the federal government does not require retirees to sign up and pay premiums for benefits under Medicare Part B, Supplementary Medical Insurance, which covers physician services and hospital out-patient services. In fact, the Office of Personnel Management estimates that about 15 percent of Medicare-eligible retirees do not pay Part B premiums. Opting out of Part B coverage is significantly more attractive to retirees who are members of HMOs than fee-for-service plans.

percent of the weighted average premium of all participating plans (up to a cap of 75 percent of the premium for any individual plan). The cost-sharing structure encourages participants to switch from higher- to lower-cost plans to blunt the effects of rising premiums; it also intensifies competitive pressures on all participating plans to hold down premiums. In 2007, the Congressional Budget Office expects that the government's share of premiums will be about $3600 for individual coverage and $8400 for family coverage. CBO also estimates that FEHB premiums will grow three times as fast as inflation over the next ten years (CBO 2007b).

Participants have the option of switching plans during the annual open season, which is particularly valuable to those whose health or financial status has changed. The Office of Personnel Management provides participants with information about all the plans, including reports on participants' level of satisfaction for the larger plans. Because plans offer different benefits, participants who anticipate specific claims may be able to find plans that lower their total costs—premiums plus out-of-pocket expenses.

Most plans have different deductibles and co-payments. For example, high deductible and consumer-driven health plans combine health savings accounts—tax-advantaged savings accounts—with insurance plans offering significantly higher deductibles and catastrophic coverage in exchange for lower premiums. Because those plans provide stronger financial incentives for patients to monitor costs and utilization, they may help keep costs low. High deductible plans have been available since 2003 in some form. The majority of federal retirees, however, opt for coverage under the Blue Cross/Blue Shield plans, which are fee-for-service plans. Blue Cross/Blue Shield plans, however, typically impose higher out-of-pocket charges on participants if they do not use preferred providers. (Under the Blue Cross/Blue Shield basic plan, which has lower premiums than the standard plan, in most cases participants pick up all the costs of using services outside a plan's network of preferred providers.) The FEHB program started offering separate supplemental vision and dental plans in 2007; however, participants pay the full premium. Even though those plans are not subsidized by the government, they do provide access to coverage at group rates.

FEHB does not provide long-term care coverage for custodial care. For example, it does not cover long stays in nursing homes. Long-term care insurance may be separately purchased. Participants pay all the premiums and must pass a medical screening test. Premiums depend on your age, and are lower if you apply at a younger age (CBO 2004).

7.3   Funding Retirement Benefits

The funding of federal pension plans is very different from private and state and local government plans (Blum 1997). Those differences, however, may be more important to taxpayers than to federal employees and retirees. Federal plans hold no corporate stocks or bonds; but rather hold only nonmarketable debt securities issued by the government itself. Instead, pension obligations are backed by the power of the national government to raise money through taxes and borrow when payments fall due. (For a discussion of whether the government could prefund pension benefits, see Box 7.4.) Holding nonmarketable Treasury debt securities creates the appearance of funding without providing the independent capacity to make future payments.

The federal civilian defined benefit pension systems held about $666 billion in Treasury securities and owe about $1242 billion in benefits as of September 30, 2005, the date of the most recent actuarial valuation. Accordingly, about 46 percent of federal liabilities appear to have been unfunded (Table 7.3). Some people have described the unfunded liability incorrectly as the cost of federal retirement that future taxpayers must bear. In fact, unless the federal government renegotiates its pension promises, future taxpayers must pay the entire earned

---

Box 7.4   Could the Government Prefund Retirement Benefits?

State and local governments generally prefund pension benefits to provide beneficiaries some assurance that their annuities will be paid and to have current taxpayers pay the cost of current services. In a sense, prefunding protects future taxpayers. The federal government could turn the civil service retirement fund into a plan that holds private securities and thus would be more comparable to other pension plans, but doing so might provide little additional protection to beneficiaries or to future taxpayers. A substantial increase in federal debt—over $1.3 trillion—would be required in the near term to finance the new pension fund.

The federal government's power to tax is what protects retirees. Even if a federal plan were fully funded with marketable assets, benefits might not be secure. If the total tax burden shifted to future citizens is so heavy as to be intolerable, it will not be borne, and the government will not be able to meet all its promises. When a government is subject to severe fiscal pressures, assets in its defined benefit pension plans might be used to cover other public spending and promised payments to retirees reduced (CBO 2003).

Some analysts believe that making retirement costs more visible in the budget or alternatively moving the funds out of the budget might also help. However, changing the budgetary treatment of federal retirement benefits so that the accrual cost of the benefits was reported in the budget totals rather than the cash costs would require a major accounting change that might also increase the scope for budget gimmickry (Blum 1995, 1997). The federal government's financial statements show that such an accounting change for civilian pension funds would have increased the budget deficit by about $75 billion in 2006, as measured by the difference between the accrued expense and the benefits paid (Department of the Treasury 2006).

Table 7.3 Status of the Civil Service Retirement and Disability Fund on September 30, 2005 (Billions of Dollars)

	CSRS	FERS	Total
Actuarial accrued liability	1019.1	222.9	1242.0
Less: Assets	437.8	228.1	665.9
Unfunded liability	581.3	−5.2	576.1

Note: CSRS, Civil Service Retirement System; FERS, Federal Employees' Retirement System.

Source: Office of Personnel Management, "Civil Service Retirement & Disability Fund" (Annual Report 2005).

benefit of $1242 billion funded or not. Those federal securities are merely the promise of the federal government to itself. The federal government could "fully fund" its retirement system through an intragovernmental transfer of more securities from Treasury to the plans. Such funding would cost the current taxpayers nothing and do nothing to reduce the burden on future taxpayers (Blum 1995). (It would, however, require that the federal debt ceiling be raised by that amount.) From the perspective of the federal government as a whole, none of the $1242 billion in promised pensions is funded.

To "fund" a federal pension plan is to recognize the cost of benefits in the budget as those benefits are being earned. This recognition takes place as the employing agency makes periodic payments to the plan to cover either part or all of the cost of benefits as they are earned. Those payments are for the purposes of internal bookkeeping—they provide agency managers and policy makers with information about the cost of the federal workforce. They have no effect on the federal outlays or the deficit because the federal pension funds are also part of government. Only payments that flow from or to entities outside the government affect the deficit. Employees' contributions to defined benefit plans are also credited to the pension plan funds. For employees covered by FERS, agency transfers of credit cover the present value of the normal cost of earned benefits. For employees covered by CSRS, the agency transfer payments of 7 percent of pay cover only part of the 18.2 percent of pay cost to the government. Another source of income to the civil service retirement fund is interest from the Treasury on its holdings of Treasury securities. In contrast, agencies make no transfers to the trust funds for the cost of FEHB retiree healthcare benefits. Those costs are paid out of the general fund of the Treasury.

Funding the federal pension liability with private assets is not necessary to ensure that retirees receive their benefits. Private pension funds in contrast, are required to set aside resources to protect workers' pension benefits in case the employer goes out of business. The federal government does not risk business failure, because it has the sovereign power to tax. However, policy makers can reduce retiree benefits to achieve budget savings.

There have been several budget proposals in the past—most recently the 2003 budget—for federal agencies to pay the full cost of their employees' pension and retiree benefits as those benefits are earned (CBO 2002). The main reason for reporting the full costs would be to provide policy makers and agency managers with a more complete measure of the cost of providing current services. Because the payments federal agencies make for accrual costs are counted as receipts to the on-budget retirement accounts, the proposed changes would not have increased total outlays, nor would they have affected the budget surplus or deficit.

The budget proposal would have expanded the accrual accounting system now in place for certain retirement programs, including FERS, treating the cost of current pay and all deferred compensation equivalently in each agency's budget. Federal agencies already recognize the full cost of pensions and postretirement healthcare in their financial statements, and must consider the full cost when deciding whether to contract out services. The payments that agencies make for CSRS benefits would have more than doubled from 7 to 18.2 percent of salary. Agencies collectively would have paid over $11 billion to cover the cost of retiree health benefits in 2006 (Department of the Treasury 2006). They are currently paying nothing.

The distinction between cash and accrual accounting affects what types of budget options policy makers consider when they need to come up with savings (CBO 2007b). In general, reducing benefits as they are earned would lead to relatively modest short-run budgetary savings even if the long-run savings would be considerable. An example of cutting benefits as they are earned would be to modify the formula used to set federal pensions. In contrast, immediate and substantial savings could be attained by reducing benefits paid to current retirees. An example would be reducing the cost-of-living adjustments paid to workers.

The insecurity of retirement benefits is a disadvantage to beneficiaries. The uncertainty of benefits can reduce the value that current employees assign to future benefits. If federal employees do discount for risk, then the federal government might have to raise the total compensation that must be offered to attract employees to government. Many private employees face a similar problem with retiree health benefits, which often are not contractual and thus can be reduced. In fact, cuts in retiree health benefits have been substantial. To date, cuts in federal retirement benefits have not been significant.

7.4 The Federal Compensation Mix

The federal government competes with other prospective employers by paying compensation sufficient to attract workers with various skills. Total compensation consists of current wages and benefits and deferred benefits. The attractiveness of a compensation package that includes current and deferred benefits depends heavily on the value that workers attach to deferred benefits. A higher valued compensation package allows employers to attract and retain more productive workers. If the government can revise the mix of current and deferred compensation to better match the preferences of workers, it may reduce the cost of compensation that taxpayers must bear although adding value for workers.

Private employers have strong incentives to offer efficient compensation packages to attract and retain workers. In addition, they must recognize the accrual costs of retirement as current expenses just as wages and salaries are current expenses. The compensation mix that private employers offer differs from that provided by the federal government. An analysis by the Congressional Budget Office found that most large private employers deferred less compensation than the federal government did (CBO 1998). The federal government also relies more heavily on defined benefit pension plans than the private sector, which is increasingly relying on 401(k) plans (GAO 2007). One study found that more than 80 percent of private retirement plan contributions were due to 401(k) plans and other personal accounts in 2000 and 2001 (Poterba, Venti, and Wise 2007).

Those findings raise the question of whether the federal government is providing the right compensation mix. One possibility is that the budgetary treatment of federal retirement creates an incentive for the government to defer compensation (Leonard 1986). With the exception of the government's TSP contributions, no retirement accrual costs are reflected in the budget's outlays and deficit. Deferring increases in compensation initially makes the reported deficit smaller and thus could encourage the government to back-load compensation. However, the federal government rarely changes the deferred compensation mix, although annual salary increases are reported in the budget. Moreover, when FERS was created, the addition of TSP meant that more of the retirement costs were recognized as earned. Thus, the budgetary treatment is just one of the many factors influencing the design of retirement programs.

No uniquely optimal compensation mix exists for all employers. To the extent that the federal government offers greater employment stability than most private sector employers, greater reliance on deferred compensation may be optimal. For example, defined benefit pensions are most attractive to employees with long tenures who expect to remain until reaching retirement age. Where private sector employees face a higher degree of uncertainty about job tenure, they might apply higher discount rates to promises of deferred compensation that are contingent on long tenure.

Defined benefit plans are less portable than defined contribution plans, so defined benefit plans reduce employee turnover. Federal employee turnover is lower than that of the private sector. Low turnover and an older work force can mean that experience and expensively trained personnel are retained. The federal work force is considerable older and more educated than the national work force (CBO 2007c). Alternatively, this could point to a compensation package that defers too much compensation. CSRS imposed a disproportionately large pension penalty on those who leave the government before retirement benefits start. One study found that the pension penalty imposed on federal workers covered by CSRS who quit was almost four times larger in relation to cash wages than pension penalties found in the private sector (Ippolito 1987). Some analysts believed that the "golden handcuffs" of CSRS contributed to a stagnant federal workforce. However, Congress created FERS with a Thrift Savings Plan to address this concern. The high participation rates and growing contribution rates in the TSP by employees covered by both FERS and CSRS provide some evidence suggesting that the government is not deferring more income than employees would desire. CSRS employees are contributing even in the absence of a government match, and most FERS employees are contributing more than 5 percent of their salaries, which is the amount that would maximize the government's matching contribution.

References

Blum, J.M. 1995. *Financing Retirement for Federal Civilian Employees*. Washington, D.C.: Congressional Budget Office. Statement to the House Subcommittee on Civil Service of the Committee on Government Reform and Oversight, June 28.

Blum, J.M. 1997. *Financing Government Employee Retirement Systems*. Washington, D.C.: Congressional Budget Office. Statement to the House Subcommittee on Civil Service of the Committee on Government Reform and Oversight, April 29.

Bodie, Z., A.J. Marcus, and R.C. Merton. 1988. Defined benefit versus defined contribution pension plans: What are the real trade-offs? In *Pensions in the U.S. Economy* (Eds.) Z. Bodie, J.B. Shoven, and D. Wise. National Bureau of Economic Research, Chicago: University of Chicago Press, pp. 139–162.

Bodie, Z. 1990. Pensions as retirement income insurance. *Journal of Economic Literature*, 28(March): 28–49.

Chaikind, H. 2007. Federal employees health benefits program: Available health insurance options. *CRS Report for Congress RS21974*. Washington, D.C.: Congressional Research Service, January 5.

Congressional Budget Office (CBO). 1998. *Comparing Federal Employee Benefits with Those in the Private Sector*. Washington, D.C.: Congressional Budget Office, August.

Congressional Budget Office. 2002. *The President's Proposal to Accrue Retirement Costs for Federal Employees*. Washington, D.C.: Congressional Budget Office, June.

Congressional Budget Office. 2003. *Acquiring Financial Assets to Fund Future Entitlements*. Long-Range Fiscal Policy Brief No. 8. Washington, D.C.: Congressional Budget Office, June 16.

Congressional Budget Office. 2004. *Financing Long-Term Care for the Elderly*. Washington, D.C.: Congressional Budget Office, April.

Congressional Budget Office. 2007a. *The Budget and Economic Outlook: Fiscal Years 2008 to 2017*. Washington, D.C.: Congressional Budget Office, January.

Congressional Budget Office. 2007b. *Budget Options*. Washington, D.C.: Congressional Budget Office, February.

Congressional Budget Office. 2007c. *Characteristics and Pay of Federal Civilian Employees*. Washington, D.C.: Congressional Budget Office, March.

Congressional Research Service (CRS), Civil Service Retirement Team. 1986. A Retirement Plan for Federal Workers Covered by Social Security: An Analysis of the Federal Employees Retirement System (P.L. 99–335), CRS Report for Congress 86–137 EPW. Washington, D.C.: Congressional Research Service, July 21.

Department of the Treasury. 2006. *Financial Report of the United States Government.* Washington, D.C.: Department of the Treasury, December.

Federal Retirement Thrift Investment Board. 2007a. *Thrift Savings Fund Statistics.* Washington, D.C.: Federal Retirement Thrift Investment Board, March. www.frtib. gov/FOIA/MM-2007MAR_Att1.pdf.

Federal Retirement Thrift Investment Board. 2007b. *Thrift Savings Plan: Participant Behavior and Demographics: Analysis for 2000–2005.* Washington, D.C.: Federal Retirement Thrift Investment Board, March 9. www.frtib.gov/FOIA/MM-2007MAR_Att6.pdf.

Government Accountability Office (GAO). 2007. *Employer-Sponsored Health and Retirement Benefits: Efforts to Control Employer Costs and the Implications for Workers.* Washington, D.C.: Government Accountability Office, GAO-07-355, March.

Gustman, A.L., O.S. Mitchell, and T. Steinmeier. 1994. The role of pensions in the labor market: A survey of the literature. *Industrial and Labor Relations Review* 47, 3(April): 417–438.

Hustead, E. and T. Hustead. 2001. Federal civilian and military retirement systems. In *Pensions in the Public Sector* (Eds.) O.S. Mitchell and E.C. Hustead. Philadelphia, Pennsylvania.: University of Pennsylvania Press, pp. 66–104.

Ippolito, R.A. 1987. Why federal workers don't quit. *The Journal of Human Resources* 22(Spring): 281–299.

Leonard, H. 1986. *Checks Unbalanced.* New York: Basic Books.

Office of Personnel Management (OPM). 2004. *Federal Law Enforcement Pay and Benefits.* Washington, D.C.: Office of Personnel Management, July. http://www.opm.gov/oca/ LEO_Report04.pdf.

Office of Personnel Management. 2006a. *Federal Civilian Workforce Statistics.* 2005 ed. Washington, D.C.: Office of Personnel Management, February.

Office of Personnel Management. 2006b. *Guide to Federal Employees Health Benefits Plans.* Washington, D.C.: Office of Personnel Management, November. www.opm. gov/insure/health.

Poterba, J., S. Venti, and D. Wise. 2007. The decline of defined benefit retirement plans and asset flows. National Bureau of Economic Research Working Paper No. 12834, January.

Watson Wyatt Worldwide. 2007. *Thrift Savings Plan Participant Survey Results 2006* (paper presented to the Federal Retirement Thrift Investment Board). Washington, D.C., January. www.frtib.gov/FOIA/2006-TSP-Survey-Results.pdf.

Chapter 8

The Changing Environment of State and Local Government Public Pensions

Albert C. Hyde

CONTENTS

Pensions are an integral part of the compensation system for public sector employees. Conceptually the model for pensions for government employment fits the traditional ideal of public service long-term protected employment with conservative salary increases tied to seniority and tenure. This concept for pensions is termed "defined benefit" as a specific annual payment is determined based on an employee's years of service and salary levels and paid to the employee as a retiree for the remainder of his or her life. In terms of incentives, public workers are financially motivated to stay in the same system because their postretirement compensation would usually be based in large part on the average salary they obtained in the last several years of employment. This has been especially true at state and local government levels where compensation levels are negotiated through collective bargaining arrangements that have generally precluded strikes and work stoppages.

Ironically, traditional state and local government convention now stands in strong contrast to the American private sector and the federal government (and increasingly other countries). Since the 1980s, corporate and federal systems in and outside the U.S. have moved to a "defined contribution" model where organizational and employee contributions are set aside into an investment account and interest is not taxed until payment after retirement. Defined contribution is the dominant mode over 90 percent of private sector employees in retirement plans (Gale et al. 2005). There are of course numerous "hybrid plans" that blend defined contribution and defined benefit. The most prevalent is called cash balance in which the defined benefit payment is calculated and tied to a fixed rate of return. Retirees generally cash out of these organizational accounts and take their balance as a lump sum distribution. A fourth benefit model used extensively in the private sector is a stock ownership plan in which employees are given stock options or awards in the corporation. These plans are rather more controversial these days. The poster child model—Microsoft which at one point in its early days had the largest number of millionaires among its workforce based on their stock plan accumulations (and stock value)—being replaced by Enron where employees lost everything in the bankruptcy and resulting valueless stock.

Although each pension system has its plus and minuses, defined benefit has one bottom-line requirement—that the organization (governmental or private) has invested adequate reserves to pay the pension benefits for its retirees. Budget requirements are annually determined (and reported) that assess the difference between current reserves and what will be needed for the future payouts as "unfunded pension liabilities." So current estimates show the following anomaly (Spiotto 2006). Pension systems for public sector workers which are less than 10 percent of the U.S. workforce have an estimated $750 billion of unfunded pension liabilities. Private sector unfunded pension liabilities covering over 80 percent of the workforce have only estimated $450 billion. Although there are serious pension funding issues in some private sector industries, most notably automotive and telecom companies (Ford and General Motors alone have over 60 billion in unfunded pension liabilities alone [Matton 2006]), the movement toward defined contribution systems for most of the private sector is the real causal factor for the statistic noted above.

This overview of state and local public pension issues is more an advance than a review. It will largely focus on two core issues. First, can state and local governments cope with the unfunded pension liability issues that have emerged in the twenty-first century and somewhat related to that—the even more contentious issue of other post employment benefits (OPEB) mainly providing healthcare insurance for retirees. The second core issue is whether state and local public pensions will remain as the last bastion of defined benefit systems or migrate to defined contribution. Closely linked to that issue is the effect on the future workforce in state and local government in terms of mobility and retention.

This advance will not provide any form of comprehensive assessment about state and local pension systems—their governance, system mechanics, funding structures, and plan designs. There is a fair amount of existing work that covers trends and infrastructure numbers for public pension systems (Hustead and Mitchell 2001; Cayer 2003; Kearney 2003; Reddick and Coggburn 2007). Likewise, there are numerous periodic surveys that well illustrate the current state of public pensions (Wilshire 2004; U.S. Census Reports 2005). The primary contention here is that state and local pensions will strategically move over the next decade further along the defined benefit-contribution continuum towards the private sector and the federal government. This movement will have significant political and economic consequences, but it will come.

It is also important to note from the outset that even the idea of drawing any general conclusion about state and local public pensions is statistically daunting. This is because there are over 2500 state and local retirement systems in the U.S. covering 18 million plus members with about a third currently receiving periodic benefit payments. Table 8.1, using current census data available shows the diversity of retirement systems that constitute the whole.

8.1 A Haunting Prophecy

Our review of the public pension arena at the threshold of the 21st century finds a generally robust, well-funded, and reasonably well managed pension environment. Notwithstanding this positive assessment, many challenges remain for the future. The ageing and more mobile workforce will exacerbate pressures to make changes such as replacing defined benefit plans with hybrid or defined contribution plans. It would also be painful if there were a substantial and long-term economic downturn. Pension funding ratios are quite healthy at present—but this is partly a result of strong stock returns—which may not persist in the future.

Edwin C Hustead and Olivia S Mitchell
Pension Research Council—The Wharton School (2001)

Table 8.1 Number and Membership of State and Local Government Employment Retirement Systems Fiscal Year 2004–2005

State and Type of Local Government	Number of Systems	Membership (Total)	Membership (Active)	Membership (Inactive)	Total Beneficiaries Receiving Periodic Payments
United States (all)	2,656	18,012,078	14,193,043	3,819,035	6,946,309
State	222	16,207,122	12,569,872	3,637,250	5,846,393
Local (total)	2434	1,804,956	1,623,171	181,785	1,099,916
County	161	527,196	464,832	62,364	249,727
Municipality	1749	1,100,725	1,002,889	97,836	754,523
Township	401	36,998	34,632	2,366	21,248
Special district	110	53,430	48,266	5,164	29,861
School district	13	86,607	72,552	14,055	44,557

Source: U.S. Census. 2005. State and Local Government-Employee Retirement Systems (Table 5a) http://www.census.gov/retire/2005retosa.html (last referenced December 1, 2007).

Seldom has an assessment covered with seemingly only a few caveats so quickly come to pass. As the above quote in 2001 by the Pension Research Council warns, the average 100 percent full funding of pension liability for state and local government quickly evaporated. Three years later, the Wilshire Report on state retirement systems would find that of the more than 125 separate state retirement systems it surveyed, 93 percent would be under funded, up from 79 percent in 2002 and 51 percent in 2001. Average under funding of all plans would have a ratio of assets to liabilities equal to 77 percent (Spiotto 2006). More troubling still 14 states— Colorado, Connecticut, Delaware, Hawaii, Illinois, Indiana, Louisiana, Maine, Massachusetts, Mississippi, New Hampshire, Oklahoma, Rhode Island, and West Virginia—had pension plan under funding ratios fall below 70 percent (West Virginia the lowest at 40 percent). The magnitude of unfounded pension liabilities can be daunting. As Wilshire reported in 2004, 16 states had unfunded liabilities that exceeded the state's total budget (Wilshire Research 2004).

Before discussing how this rapid turnabout occurred, it is important to note that levels of unfunded pension liability at state and local levels have fluctuated greatly over the past 30 years. According to a recent Standard & Poor's report average funding ratio has grown and declined over time, as reflected in the figures noted below:

Funding Percentage of Total Pension

Period	Liabilities (Percent)
Mid-1970s	50
1990	80
2000	100
2003	77

Source: Standard & Poor's, Research: Managing State Pension Liabilities: A Growing Credit Concern, Jan 2006.

The astute business reader will note that the most probable cause for this variation is the performance of the U.S. stock market. That is basically what occurred at the state and local level in the last decade. Following the recession in 1991–1993, state and local governments were able to expand their workforces, keep public salaries and budgets (even reduce tax levels) in line, and limit—in some cases even reduce—their funding contributions to pension funds because of stock market boom. When the stock market crashed after 2001 followed by recession, the entire strategy came down like a house of cards.

One other factor should be included for context—changes in state and local employment numbers. Using the annual employment numbers from Governing,

Table 8.2   Change in State and Local Government Employment (1997–2006)

	1997–2002 (Percent)	*2002–2007 (Percent)*
State government employees	+7.0	+2.5
Local government employees	+12.5	+4.8
Selected states with below 70 percent pension funding liability		
Colorado	+13.5	+2.7
Connecticut	+4.1	−5.8
Delaware	+9.6	+8.6
Hawaii	+23.4	+2.9
Illinois	+2.7	−9.4
Indiana	−2.0	+3.8
Louisiana	+0.5	−0.7
Maine	+10.4	−0.7
Massachusetts	+8.3	+0.6
Mississippi	+18.5	−2.1
New Hampshire	+3.8	+3.8
Oklahoma	+6.4	+3.0
Rhode Island	+1.2	−4.4
West Virginia	+6.0	−1.7

Source: Change in Number if State Government Employees. Source book at http://sourcebook:governing.com/topicresults.jsp?ind=682. (last referenced: December 1, 2007).

Table 8.2 shows average rates of growth of state and local employees over the last decade and for comparison purposes—how the 14 states with the highest levels of unfunded pension liability coped, or rather dramatically shifted, for the most part—their employment strategies over the decade.

The issue to be decided here is whether the current state of affairs is a simple stock market adjustment or a real situation where public pension and healthcare liabilities have morphed into a full blown budget insolvency epidemic. Put in its simplest terms—is it merely an "incident" likened to a hangover due to the stock market decline in 2000–2001 wrecking some poorly timed financial strategies of expecting over performing investment yields to make up for under funding public pensions? Or is it something much more serious—potentially a "situation" where state and local governments are facing the cumulative consequences of past compensation bargaining policies of providing large future pension and healthcare benefits in exchange for smaller salary increases and the demographics of the workforce is really what is pushing governments into potential fiscal insolvency, or what some analysts call, "pension deficit disorder" (O'Grady 2007).

Further complicating the situation, potentially on an exponential scale are new requirements that state and local governments now account for other post employment benefits (OPEB) primarily healthcare insurance. As of December 2006, new Government Accounting Standards Board standards (Nos. 43 and 45) went into effect which require that all state and local governments must show in their annual (audited) fiscal statements healthcare expenses and future liabilities. In addition, GASB stipulates that governments must shift from a pay as you go system for healthcare to one that estimates and funds future costs. The Government Accounting Standards Board issued these new requirements for two reasons. First, these types of benefits which GASB defines as health insurance coverage for retirees and their families, dental insurance, life insurance and term care coverage (note the requirements don't include one time termination benefits such as accrued sick leave and vacation) have been increasing in cost as healthcare costs have dramatically escalated in the United States. And because most government entities fund OPEB on a pay as you go basis, the real cost burden is shifted to the future as life spans increase. Unlike pension fund obligations, most government entities do not make OPEB investments on some form of prefunding basis.

Little wonder, analysts like Rick Matton of the Chicago Federal Reserve Bank call OPEB the "800 pound gorilla in the room." Matton aptly sums up the predicament to be faced by state and local governments when they square up to the brave new world of GASB 43 and 45."

Estimating the total OPEB liability is an accounting nightmare. Unlike pensions where actuarial estimates can be at least somewhat understood, OPEB requires making guesses about things like health care and prescription drug inflation and utilization. One estimate suggests the unfunded liability is around $700 billion, but this is a back of the envelope guess. Other estimates suggest that OPEB exposure could range from five to ten times current outlays for retiree health care.

Managing OPEB costs is tricky. In most cases, retiree health care is not a contractual responsibility like pensions. It is a voluntary benefit offered by the employer. However where it is a contractual responsibility, the ability to require retiree contributions, increase co-pays or cut benefit coverage is limited. Where retiree health insurance can be modified, a concern is

> *that when these liabilities are reported, some governments may choose to abandon or significantly reduce coverage, forcing the federal government to serve as the health care insurer of last resort. (Matton 2007)*

Although this assessment focuses primarily on pension systems, the future effect of the potential cost of pensions and healthcare liability for public employees is a significant factor. When headline media stories report how healthcare liabilities are critical challenges affecting corporate competitiveness in the U.S. auto industry, there is a fall-out effect on public sector systems. Increasingly, what is becoming apparent to government pension managers and union leaders is a potential shift in public sentiment about benefits for public sector workers.

At a Chicago Federal Reserve Board Forum (Chicago Fed Letter, May 2006) this was cast in very stark terms. As Michael Moskow, the President and CEO of the Chicago Federal Reserve Bank has pointed out—not only are public pensions not subject to ERISA (Employment Retirement Income Security Act) which has allowed governments to offer increased pension benefits without setting aside commensurate funding, "but 90 percent of public pensions are still defined benefit plans, and many of them include cost of living increases that increase liabilities even further." The contrast becomes very marked when compared to the private sector where only 11 percent of corporations offer defined benefit.

8.2   Pension Deficit Disorder—Four Scenarios for the Future

How will state and local governments cope? As a means to a selective assessment that can show different paths, four scenarios are outlined here based on an actual state or city's recent response. Each of these scenarios is developed briefly, using media reporting. Space precludes developing any type of real case study, but because the objective is to illustrate a range of scenarios, they do show actual examples of political and fiscal response to pension reform.

8.2.1   Legislative Absolution—The Oregon Scenario

One political scenario is to terminate a defined benefit system and convert it to a defined contribution system through state legislation. This legislated change of a system crafts a financial rescue plan to clear fiscal liability issues and bypasses collective bargaining entirely. Oregon in 2003 is the classic example of how this conversion can be done (O'Keefe 2006). After changing benefit calculations and demographic assumptions for current employees, legislation was passed that prevented new employees from going into the defined benefit system. The state then issued $2 billion in pension obligation bonds to cover the funding for the system for old employees. Basically, over time, of course, defined benefit pensions in Oregon will be phased out in favor of a hybrid defined benefit-contribution system. Pension bonds effectively convert a potential liability to a current one, although it should be pointed out that the state still is factoring into its financing strategy investing bond proceeds. Another difference with this type of pension bond is that these are not tax exempt bonds and thus not quite the attractive investment that most state and local government bonds are.

Another variation of legislative absolution is through voter proposition. California governor Schwarzenegger tried this in 2004 at considerable risk with a voter referendum that would have moved California state employees to defined contribution. Facing heavy opposition by the public unions, the voters rejected the effort. There were a number of political factors involved that complicated the vote, including the fact that a real nexus between California's budget crises (then) and state pension liabilities was never firmly established. It is unfortunately the case that significant change politically is hard to achieve without a visible crises or burning platform to compel action.

8.2.2 Fiscal Meltdown—The San Diego Scenario

Although states can not declare bankruptcy, many municipal governments can (of course governments can repudiate debt). At the far end of the political spectrum here, but not alone, is the City of San Diego which faced a 1.4 billion dollar budget deficit for funding of its pension fund (Walsh 2006, Spiotto). San Diego had criminal charges levied at its officials for not only deliberately under funding pensions, but also illegally concealing the fact that it had two billion in unfunded pension liabilities. Although San Diego must figure out how to raise the funding it needs to meet its pension liabilities, it must do so without having access to the public bond markets, which it can't do until it has a certified audited financial statement. But fiscal meltdown is a solution— the taxpayers of San Diego, just those of Orange County a decade ago, will have to solve first its fiscal deficit, either by cuts in expenditures (decreasing city services and employees) or raising taxes. The second part will then be a mixture of reducing or containing retirement liabilities and then issuing bonds (once their financial credibility is restored) to close the gap between required assets and future obligations.

8.2.3 Workforce Compartmentalization—The Chicago Scenario

The first two scenarios involve changing retirement assets and liabilities within the system. Another model is to change the mix of the workforce. Chicago is the classic example—it is buying, rather selling its way, out of its projected eight billion pension deficit. First up was the sale of a city toll road (privatization) to a multinational infrastructure management corporation of 1.8 billion (Financial Times, July 11, 2006). Chicago also is intending to sell Midway airport, several waste disposal plants, parking garages, among others. A portion of the proceeds go to cover the pension deficit and of course, by getting out of "businesses"—defined as any city enterprise that generates cash flow, current, and future city employees are shed. Chicago's compartmentalization scenario assumes that governments will only carry employees that are part of core, essential, inherently government services, ensure that their pension and benefits are fully funded and while still relying on a defined benefit system—be totally transparent in the city budget.

Workforce compartmentalization does not preclude any of the other strategies for reducing or containing retirement liabilities or issuing bonds to lock in assets to meet future obligations. It also makes clear to public unions and taxpayers its commitment to a smaller core workforce even if it means foreswearing more entrepreneurial government activities and shedding employees.

8.2.4 Labor Management "Smackdown"—The New York City Scenario

New York City represents a fourth scenario, where pension and healthcare benefits are increasingly a part of the city's strategy for union negotiations (Cooper 2006; Walsh 2006). The front end of the strategy is for the city to ask for concessions on health insurance and pensions in the form of increased contributions from employees. At the back end are more structural reforms to include raising the retirement age to qualify for a full pension among current employees and limiting benefits for new employees. The city for its part will move the funding issues from simply one of showing percentage of pension funds that are fully funded to one that shows the city's pension contribution as a percentage of workers salaries.

Such a strategy will surely lead to increased tension and confrontation between city officials and unions. Unions will claim betrayal and insist that all past settlements are off the table. The 2005 short transit strike before the holidays in New York City (Greenhouse 2005) was supposedly triggered by attempts to include that even in the talks. Efforts by city officials to lower retirement liabilities and provide less generous benefits will be labeled "cramdowns." Whether city officials in New York or in any city or state will want to continue pursue this type of confrontation strategy will also hinge on levels of political support by unions and party affiliations.

Two other factors should be mentioned in closing this section on government scenarios. The first is a significant change in media attention and attitude. Although public sector employees and their unions talk about their commitment to defined benefit systems and pension obligations, they see solutions centering on simply raising taxes and modernizing tax bases. As Hank Scheff of AFSCME notes, the larger issue is how to pay public employees, and pay for public services. Tax structures are antiquated, tax bases are too narrow and rates too flat. From the union perspective, it's not just pension systems that aren't getting funded, but public services as a whole (Scheff 2006).

But attempting to dismiss current pension issues as a series of "exceptions" would miss the fact that the media attention devoted to this issue has increasingly changed the tone of the debate about a $700 billion future liability problem to one about the need for much broader public sector pension reform. Thus far the media have had some interesting stories to focus on in New York, San Diego, Illinois, New Jersey, and others. But the tone is that states and cities have made deals that they cannot pay for and some form of radical reform is essential. As an example, *The New York Times* covered pension reform in a three story series in August of 2006 but handled the coverage more like investigative reporting of back room political deals (Cooper and Walsh 2006). When this type of media attention rolls over into front page stories in U.S. Today (Cauchon 2007) that report how much more favorable public sector benefits are than what typical workers receive, there are implications for future support. This type of article is also starting to appear on healthcare coverage for public sector employees (Walsh 2007).

A second factor is a legal development that may also offer a different track for change. In the summer of 2006, a federal appellate panel reversed a 2003 court ruling that IBM's major change of its pension system discriminated against older workers (Walsh 2006). The essence of IBM's solution was to switch employees from a length of service pension based plan to a "cash-balance" system. Although workers keep their defined benefit system, the pension is earned in equal amounts over their tenure at IBM, rather than the number of years of seniority and their "high three" i.e., the average of the three final years of service. Obviously, this type of change would take dead aim at the seniority advantage and neutralize the attraction of staying in only one system. Although the cash-balance approach covered here has been primarily a legal issue involving age discrimination complaints, the debate may now shift to more economic and political grounds.

This IBM factor, for want of a better term, also aligns with a major shift in how employment benefits have evolved over the past two decades. Table 8.3 illustrates this development.

The basic categories of what organizations offer employees to support recruitment and retention are as listed above—retirement, healthcare, and more intangible benefits revolving around work–life issues. The traditional benefits package of a pension, healthcare coverage, and paid sick leave and vacation has become both more diverse and elaborate. Benefits packages today offer a myriad of options and choices. But what is more significant is that many of the options—such as deferred compensation, health savings accounts, thrift savings plans, and now training and education accounts—are based on an individual ownership model. The organization no longer simply pays a benefit or offers a service at a group cost. Many of the benefits are tied to accounts which are "owned" by the employee, reported on periodically, and are portable in that they go with the employee should they chose to leave the organization. In short, increasingly benefits in organizations are moving further along the defined contributions continuum.

Table 8.3   The Evolution of Employee Benefits

Category	Traditional	Modern-Range of Choices
Retirement income	Defined benefit pension Payroll savings plan	Defined benefit Hybrid (cash balance) Defined contribution Deferred compensation Employee savings plans
Medical and insurance	Healthcare and life insurance Disability/workers compensation	Health insurance (medical, dental, long term disability) Health savings accounts E.A.P. (Employee Assistance Programs) Fitness programs
Quality of work life	Sick leave Paid vacation	Subsidized transit and parking Flexi-place (work from home) Subsidized meals Frequent flyer accounts Web site accounts Concierge services Training and education accounts
Other		Flexible benefit plans

8.3   New Workers in Old Systems–Old Workers in New Systems

This fits the new ideal of the modern worker portable benefits to match a portable career. That being said, it is too soon to tell what the public sector workforce of the future will value. Partly this is because public workforces since 1985 have become more white-collar, older, and more concentrated in highly skilled occupations. Using the federal government as the example, MSPB has reported that in 1985, about 25 percent of the federal workforce was over age 50. By 2001, the comparable figure was almost 40 percent. In comparison nearly three-quarters of the federal workforce is over age 40 while only about half of all employed workers in the United States are.

More importantly, federal workforce surveys continually show the significance of benefits programs to workforce retention. In the 2000 USMP Merit Principles survey—easily the most trusted and comprehensive survey of the federal workforce—employees were asked to rank the top factors for leaving or staying.

Factors to Leave	Factors to Stay
Better use of skills and abilities	Federal benefit programs
Increased opportunities to advance	Job security
Desire to earn more money	Current job duties
Lack of recognition	Pay compared to private sector
Improve opportunities for training	Current working schedule

Source: U.S. MSPB, 2000 Merit Principles Survey.

Although there are some age difference, the rankings hold up remarkably well across all age brackets.

	Top Factors for Retention	All	Under 40	40–49	Over 50
1	Federal benefit programs	90.5	88.7	88.9	91.0
2	Job security	85.2	81.5	87.2	91.5

Source: U.S. MSPB, 2000 Merit Principles Survey.

Whether these numbers would apply to state and local government employees is another issue, but the point remains that the new model of worker touted in the private sector has yet to reach critical mass in the public sector. Everyone accepts that the baby boomers will retire (although predictions of the mass exodus forecast annually over the past decade and a half have not yet been realized) and that the next generation of workforce will have different ideals and motivations. How this will affect the movement towards defined contribution systems is still unclear, much less government human resource management strategies for recruitment, development, and retention.

Perhaps a better way of forecasting the prospects for change over the next decade in the state and local pension arena is to create a stakeholders diagram. Table 8.4 attempts this. It highlights five principal stakeholders and their designated agents or representatives. For example, in the case of state and local employees, their viewpoints are important but they are represented by their unions which negotiate benefit goals and pursue specific retirement strategies.

Less obvious is the operating strategy for each of the stakeholders as expressed in the actions and reaction of their agents. The most obvious conflicts are between unions and elected officials and pension fund managers and creditors. In the past, compromises that worked traded off short-term concessions from unions that kept budgets in balance without resorting to tax increases in exchange for long-term gains in benefits that might be realized by successful investments or at least would be payable in someone else's term of office or management. Furthermore, less transparency about future obligations aided this process.

Table 8.4   Public Pension Arena: The Stakeholders

Stakeholder	Agent/Representative	Preferred Strategy (Political/Economic)
Employee	Union/employee professional association	Maximize payments-PCT of salary paid in retirement
Elected executive officials	Appointed budget and HRM managers	Optimal public support for current budget-trade off long-term for short-term stability
Legislative representatives	Committee chairs and party leaders	Optimal government spending and revenue solutions—for re-election and constituency approval
Pension fund board trustees	Pension fund investment managers	Maximize long-term investment capability and sometimes use weight of fund for social ends
Taxpayers	Key business and interest groups auditors	Accountability—highest services for taxes paid—fair wage for employees
Creditors (bond holders)	Credit agencies and financial	Highest credit rating for government minimize credit risk minimize credit risk

And that is precisely why current reporting on pension funding liability and soon OPEB via GASB 43 and 45 is so significant. State and local governments will first report their numbers and in the process of getting audited financial statements have to reveal their assumptions and projection methods. As Matton rightly points out, it is (especially for healthcare liabilities) a potential mess of contradictions and adjustments. However, transparency will over time create consistency, if not rationality. The auditing community will complete this task, since as past financial disasters have show, they are just as liable as fund managers and city officials.

This is not to say that it will come easy. Several states are resisting the GASB requirements on the grounds that the financial consequences are too severe for an area like healthcare liability which is not all that understood. The Texas legislature passed a bill (HB 2365) basically exempting its major cities from GASB 43 and 45 if they deemed it appropriate (Walsh 2007), which Governor Rick Perry signed into law on June 15. The state of Connecticut was also considering even harsher legislation.

Perhaps that's the real benefit of a stakeholder's diagram. Reform, as opposed to simple refinancing initiatives will come, sooner than later, because the old routes for bargaining and negotiation without considering the long-term consequences will be cut off. In all likelihood, many state and local systems will be able to maintain their defined benefit systems if they choose or move towards a hybrid system such as cash balance. But keeping a defined benefit system will require a much higher level of fiscal discipline than what was practiced in the twentieth century. As state and local governments watch their older workforces depart, the pressures (fiscal competitiveness, at best unsympathetic media and public reaction, and increasing awareness public sector benefits are at odds with private and nonprofit benefit programs) will mount.

As governments and workers and unions try to reconcile appropriate reward systems with tough fiscal choices, they will have to recognize that what is at stake is the real future of the public service. For all the talk about pay for performance in the modern public service, pension and health benefits are its real soul. Nowhere is this more relevant than the states and local governments in the United States.

Bibliography

Advisory Commission on Intergovernmental Relations. 1980. *State and Local Pension Systems: Federal Regulatory Issues.* Washington DC Report A-71.

Antos, J.R. and A.M. Rivlin. 2007. Overview & rising health care spending-federal and national. In Antos, J.R. and Rivlin, A.M. (Eds.) *Restoring Fiscal Sanity 2007 The Health Spending Challenge.* Washington DC: The Brookings Institution Press, pp. 1–28.

Cayer, N.J. 2003. Public employee benefits and the changing nature of the workforce. In Hayes, S.W. and Kearney, R.C. (Eds.) *Public Personnel Management: Problems and Prospects.* Englewood Cliffs, New Jersey: Prentice-Hall, pp. 167–179.

EBRI Notes, April 2005, Vol. 26, No.4 www.ebri.org Benefit Cost Comparisons Between State and Local Governments and Private-Sector Employers Ken McDonnell, EBRI.

Eitelberg, C. Public pension design and responses to a changing workforce. In Mitchell, O.S. and Hustead, E.C. *Pensions in the Public Sector.* Philadelphia: University of Pennsylvania Press, pp. 363–373.

Federal Reserve Bank of Chicago. 2006. State and Local Government Public Pension Forum: Conference Summary. *Chicago Fed Letter.* Number, 226a.

Gale, W.G., J.B. Shoven, and M. Warshawskey (Eds.). 2005. *The Evolving Pension System: Trends, Effects, and Proposals for Reform.* Washington DC: The Brookings Institution Press.

Hustead, E.C. and O.S. Mitchell. 2001. Public sector pension plans: Lessons and challenges for the twenty-first century In Mitchell, O.S. and Hustead, E.C. *Pensions in the Public Sector.* Philadelphia: University of Pennsylvania Press, pp. 5–10.

Kearney, R.C. 2003. The determinants of state employment compensation. *Review of Public Personnel Administration.* Vol. 23, 4, 305–322.

Mitchell, O.S, D. McCarthy, S.C. Wisniewski, and P. Zorn. Development in State and Local Pension Plans In Mitchell, O.S. and Hustead, E.C. *Pensions in the Public Sector.* Philadelphia: University of Pennsylvania Press, pp. 11–37.

Reddick, C.G. and J.D. Coggburn. 2007. State government employee health benefits in the United States. *Review of Public Personnel Administration.* Vol. 27, 1, 5–20.

Reilly, T., S. Schoener, and A. Bolin. Public sector compensation in local governments. *Review of Public Personnel Administration.* Vol. 27, 1, 39–58.

Standard & Poor's Research: Managing state pension liabilities: A growing credit concern Jan 2006.

U.S. Census Bureau. 2005. State and Local Government Employee Retirement Statistics. http://www.census.gov/retire.html.

U.S. Merits Systems Protection Board: 2000. Merit Principles Survey: Office of Policy Evaluation. Washington DC. 2001.

Wilshire Research 2004: 2004. Wilshire Report on State Retirement Systems: Funding Levels and Asset Allocation.

Print Media

Barr, S. Mounting retirement worries, *The Washington Post*, July 31, 2006, D-4.

Cauchon, Dennis. Pension tension: More and more retirees finding that it pays to have worked for the Government instead of the private sector, *USA Today*, February 21, 2007, 1.

Cooper, M., Retirees get Albany attention and New York City gets the bill: Costly promises-sweetening pensions, *The New York Times*, August 22, 2006, A-1.

Cooper, M. and Williams Walsh M. New York gets sobering look at its pensions: New Calculations find big shortfall possible, *New York Times*, August 20, 2006, A-1.

Dvorak, P., Group Turns Governance Spotlight on Pension Plans, *The Wall Street Journal*, June 4, 2007, b-3.

Financial Times, Chicago Trims its Portfolio to focus on core businesses: Officials looking at assets to privatize as city seeks to close its pension deficit, July 11, 2006.

Greenhouse, S., In Look Back on Talks, Questions on M.T.A.'s Final Pension Demand, *New York Times*, December 21, 2005, A-29.

Karmin, C., Missouri Treasurer's Demand: 'Terror-Free' Pension Funds, *The Wall Street Journal*, June 14, 2007, c-1.

MuniNet Guide, Strike in Philly Brings Focus on Health Care, Retirement Costs, July 12, 2006, 1–2.

O'Grady, M., Anasatia Pension Deficit Disorder, *The Wall Street Journal*, March 26, 2007, A-14.

Walsh, M.W., Court Rules for I.B.M. on Pension, *The New York Times*, August 8, 2006, C-1.

Walsh, M.W., Public Pension Plans Face Billions in Shortages, *The New York Times*, August 8, 2006, A-25.

Walsh, M.W., San Diego Broke Laws in Pension Crises, Panel Says, *The New York Times*, August 9, 2006, C-3.

Walsh, M.W., Auditing Rule is put at risk by Texas Bill, *The New York Times*, May 18, 2007, C-1.

Walsh, M.W., Pension Fund in New Jersey Faces Scrutiny from S.E.C., *The New York Times*, June 1, 2007, A-25.

Walsh, M.W., A 58$ Billion Shortfall for New Jersey's Retiree Health Coverage, *The New York Times*, July 25, 2007, A-14.

Web References

Conference on Public Pensions. Civic Federation of Chicago and Federal Reserve Bank of Chicago, February 28, 2006

These presentations are currently on the Chicago Federal Bank's Web site—http://pension conference.chicagofedblogs.org. In the event that these presentations are no longer available, the author may be contacted for copies.

An Independent View of the Credit Risks of Pension Under funding

Richard Ciccarone, Managing Director & Chief Research Officer

McDonnell Investment Management LLC

Are Public Pensions Able to Break from the Path of Social Security and the Private Sector?

J. Fred Giertz, Institute of Government and Public Affairs, University of Illinois

The Credit Risks of Underfunded Pension Liabilities for State & Local Governments

John Kenward

Standard & Poors Chicago

Credit Risks of Under funding Pensions

Joseph O'Keefe

Senior Director, Fitch

Notional Pensions: Does Sweden Have the Answer?

Rick Mattoon, Senior Economist and Economic Advisor

U.S. Federal Reserve Bank of Chicago

OPEB—The 800 Pound Gorilla in the Room

Rick Mattoon, Senior Economist and Economic Advisor

U.S. Federal Reserve Bank of Chicago

The Impending Pension and Health Plan Crisis and the Impact of the Aging Workforce and Talent Management

Tim Phoenix and Lance Weiss

Deloitte Consulting LLP

Public Pension Funding: The Organized Labor Perspective

Hank Scheff

Director of Employee Benefits

AFSCME Council 31

If the Pension Bomb Stops Ticking, What Happens Next?

James E. Spiotto

Chapman and Cutler LLP

Recommendations to Reform Public Pension Boards of Trustees in Illinois

Lise Valentine

Research Director, The Civic Federation

Chapter 9

Retirement Planning in the United Kingdom

Orla Gough and Rod Hick

CONTENTS

9.1 Introduction

This chapter will provide an overview of retirement planning in the United Kingdom. In order to analyze retirement planning in the United Kingdom, it is essential to look not just at the system of state retirement pensions, but also at occupational and personal pensions, which, as we will see, perform a significant role in providing retirement income. Thus, the focus of this chapter will be on the whole spectrum of pension savings schemes in the United Kingdom.

The chapter is divided into six sections and will begin with (1) an outline of pension provision in the United Kingdom and (2) a brief discussion of the recent Pensions Commission. This will be followed by (3) an analysis of current pensioner income among those who are retired and (4) levels of retirement saving among those of working age. We will highlight (5) the variety of factors that affect the age at which people retire and (6) discuss recent legislative changes in this area that have been introduced in the United Kingdom.

Pension systems across the world have come under greater scrutiny in recent decades due to increasing awareness of the challenges of population aging, and with the publication of controversial work in this area by the World Bank (1994, 2005) which has stimulated significant debate. Population aging is caused by, inter alia, increasing life expectancy and falling fertility levels, which increase the ratio of retirees to workers, or the age dependency ratio, and thus puts pressure on the sustainability of pay-as-you-go pension systems.

In the United Kingdom, the issue of retirement planning has received greater attention following the reports of the government-appointed Pensions Commission (2004, 2005, 2006), which was charged with analyzing the adequacy of private retirement saving in the United Kingdom (2005: p. v). The United Kingdom differs from many other European countries in the emphasis it places on private pensions for providing retirement income. The state pension system in the United Kingdom does not attempt to provide individuals with an income that is related to their salary from employment. Rather, individuals who wish to receive an income which maintains some continuity with that received during their working life are expected to contribute to one of a variety of voluntary supplementary pensions available. The 1998 green paper, published by the Blair government that had assumed office the previous year set out the aim of intensifying the role of private provision in retirement income. It noted that approximately 60 percent of retirement income was received from state sources and 40 percent from private sources, and set out the aim of reversing this balance by 2050 (DSS, 1998).

9.2 Policy Background

9.2.1 State Benefits

This section will provide an overview of the United Kingdom's public pension system. An understanding of how this system works is essential to analyze retirement planning in the United Kingdom and the recent debates regarding retirement saving. The state pension system in the United Kingdom is comprised of the basic state pension, the state second pension, and the pension credit.

9.2.1.1 Basic State Pension

The basic state pension is a contributory, pay-as-you-go, flat-rate pension scheme payable to men at 65 and women at 60, where sufficient National Insurance (NI) contributions have been paid. NI contributions are either paid by individuals themselves or can be credited on behalf of certain categories of individuals, such as those who have spent time either caring in the home for children or ill relatives, or for those who have had periods claiming benefits such as jobseeker's allowance or incapacity benefit. In order to receive a full basic state pension it is necessary to have contributed for 90 percent of one's working life, but a reduced rate of state pension is available for those who have an insufficient number of contributions.

In 2007, the weekly value of the basic state pension was £87.30 ($174.04).* Women who have not contributed in their own right but claim on their husband's NI contributions and individuals who claim the over-80s noncontributory pension receive £52.30 ($104.27), although those over 80 receive an additional 25 pence on the basic state pension amount (DWP Web site) (Table 9.1).

Table 9.1　Value of Basic State Pension

Based on your own or your late husband's, wife's, or civil partner's National Insurance contributions	£87.30 ($174.04)
Based on your husband's National Insurance contributions	£52.30 ($104.27)
Noncontributory over 80 pension	£52.30 ($104.27)
Age addition	£0.25 ($0.50)

Note:　2007 values, per week.

Source: Department of Work and Pensions Web site, http://www.dwp.gov.uk/. With permission.

---

* All dollar amounts based on conversion rate of 1 GBP = 1.99375 USD taken from http://www.xe.com/ucc/convert.cgi on 30th April 2007.

Table 9.2   Income from State Pension for Men and Women above Retirement Age

	Men (Percent)	Women (Percent)
Yes	98.5	95.7
No	1.5	4.3

Source: Family Resources Survey (2004/2005). Data provided by the UK Data Archive.

Data from the Family Resources Survey shows that 98.5 percent of men and 95.7 percent of women in 2004/5 over the retirement age received the basic state pension (Table 9.2).

9.2.1.2   State Second Pension

The state second pension is a contributory, earnings-related pension, introduced in 2002 to reform the State Earnings Related Pensions Scheme (SERPS) that preceded it. Like the basic state pension, the state second pension is a public pay-as-you-go scheme which is paid through NI contributions. However, it differs from the basic state pension in that it is related to earnings.

The replacement of the SERPS with the state second pension in 2002 shifted its focus so that it provided more generous benefits for those on low and moderate incomes. Individuals pay into the state second pension through their NI contributions, but can "contract out" if they have an occupational pension or personal pension. In practice "contracting out" is a popular response from workers who may receive more generous benefits from an occupational scheme (Tanner, 1998: p. 186). Like the basic state pension, contributions are credited for certain individuals who are unable to pay them themselves, namely certain categories of carers and those with long-term illnesses and disabilities (The Pensions Service Web site).

9.2.1.3   Pension Credit

The pension credit operates on a different basis to the two other state pension schemes. It is comprised of the guarantee credit and the savings credit, and is a means-tested top-up payment reserved for low-income pensioners. The guarantee element is paid to those over 60, and acts as an income floor by supplementing the income of low-income elderly people to a proscribed minimum level. The credit pays individuals the difference between their current income level and the guarantee amount, which in 2007 was £119.05 ($237.34) for a single person and £181.70 ($362.22) for a couple.

The savings credit is available to pensioners over the age of 65 for those who have some retirement saving over and above the state pension. Despite its name, both income and savings are assessed in deciding whether to make the payment. The savings credit pays pensioners 60 pence for every £1 that they have saved for their retirement over the basic state pension amount up to a maximum of £19.05 ($37.98) per week for a single person and £25.26 ($50.36) per week for those who have a partner. Thus, the savings credit tapers the withdrawal of the guarantee credit and improves incentives to save. As such, the pension credit attempts to ensure that no older person is forced to live on an inadequate income, although also rewarding those who have made some savings.

9.2.1.4   Discussion

The United Kingdom's public pension system is considerably less successful at replacing preretirement income than many other European Union (EU) nations. Even with complete basic state pension and state second pension records, the United Kingdom's public pension system provides a gross replacement rate for the average United Kingdom earner of 37 percent of earnings, compared with 70 percent in the Netherlands, 76 percent in Sweden, 71 percent in France, and 45 percent in the United States of America (Pensions Commission, 2004: p. 58). This is reflected in the fact that the United Kingdom's public pension expenditure stood at 5.5 percent of GDP in 2000 which, with the exception of Ireland, was a substantially lower figure than any other country in the EU-15 (Pensions Commission, 2004: p. 61).

9.2.2   Voluntary Provision

In addition to the State schemes, there are a variety of occupational and personal pension schemes available in the United Kingdom which form an important part of pension provision. The fact the basic state pension is paid at a lower rate than the guarantee element of the pension credit clearly shows that it is not intended that individuals rely on the basic state pension alone; rather, it is intended that they will top this up with income from other sources. These voluntary pensions may be run on either a defined benefit or defined contribution basis, can be connected with employment, or might be a personal pension held by an individual who is currently outside the workforce. Throughout this chapter, they are collectively referred to as supplementary pensions. In all cases they are voluntary, and are subsidized by the state in the form of tax relief on contributions, which is paid at the marginal tax rate. Although it has been illegal for employers to make membership of a company pension scheme a condition of employment since 1988, they may automatically enroll employees provided that the employee can opt out of the scheme should they desire to do so (GAD, 2005: p. 56).

9.2.2.1   Stakeholder Pensions

A new portable defined contribution product, the stakeholder pension, was introduced in 2001 to improve supplementary pension coverage among low-income earners who have no access to an occupational pension. To attract potential savers, charges are fixed at a low level, and the scheme facilitates low and intermittent contributions. The scheme is intended for those who earned between £10,000 and £20,000 (in 2001 amounts) and who had no access to an occupational scheme, and for those who are

**Table 9.3 Income from Supplementary Pension
for Men and Women above Retirement Age**

	Men (Percent)	Women (Percent)
Yes	75.8	44.4
No	24.2	55.6

Source: Family Resources Survey (2004/2005). Data provided
by the UK Data Archive.

self-employed or outside the workforce. Companies with five or more workers are compelled to provide access to a stakeholder pension to their employees where they do not run an occupational scheme, but neither they, nor the employees themselves, are required to make contributions. When it reported, the Pensions Commission (2006: p. 16) judged that stakeholders had made a minimal impact on pension coverage rates. They declared that the vast majority of stakeholder schemes were "empty shells," with no contributing members (Pensions Commission, 2004: p. 92). Overall, among current pensioners, three-quarters of men were receiving a supplementary pension of some sort in 2004/2005, in comparison to 44 percent of women (Table 9.3).

9.3   Pensions Commission

The Pensions Commission was established by the government in 2002 and published a number of reports culminating in its final report and recommendations in 2006. Their remit was to analyze the extent of the private pension savings in the United Kingdom and to assess whether these levels justified moving beyond the current voluntary approach to supplementary pensions (Pensions Commission, 2004: p. ix).

The Pensions Commission noted that in dealing with the problem of population aging, there are only four possible choices that the government can choose from, but emphasized that any solution could, and most probably would, be a combination of these. These were (1) pensioners getting poorer relative to other groups in society, (2) increasing taxes, (3) more saving for retirement, and (4) retiring later (Pensions Commission, 2004: p. 12). Although difficult choices will have to be made, research shows that there is little support for the prospect of pensioners getting poorer compared to other groups (DWP, 2006a: p. 72, 84–86; ABI, 2006: p. 26). The Commission proposed significant changes to the pension's landscape and their recommendations have been influential among government and policy makers. We will discuss the impact of their recommendations on government policy in the section on recent legislative changes.

9.4   Current Pensioner Income

This section will detail the levels of income received in retirement by current pensioners in the United Kingdom, and will show the variations in these amounts by

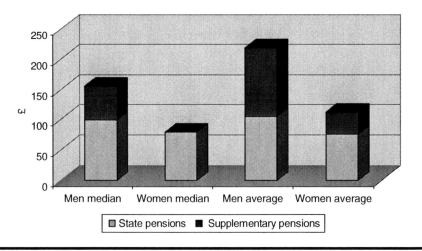

Figure 9.1 Pension income for men and women by source. (From Family Resources Survey [2004/2005]. Data provided by the UK Data Archive. With permission.)

both gender and ethnicity. Figure 9.1 illustrates the pension income amounts for both men and women by breaking it down into state and supplementary pension income. The median and mean figures are both included as they provide different, but important, illustrations of the disparity in pension incomes.

It shows that the median pension income for men from state sources was £100 and from supplementary pensions was £55. In contrast, these figures for women were £79 and zero respectively. This latter figure does not suggest that there are no women who receive supplementary pension income. Rather, it is zero because less than half of women of pensionable age receive income from a supplementary pension.

When the mean (or average) amount received by both men and women is analyzed, we see that men received £105 from state and £114 from supplementary pension sources, in comparison to £75 and £36, respectively, for women. The reason that the mean supplementary pension income for men is greater than the amount received from the state, although when we calculate the median value it is not, is because of the fact that a relatively small number of individuals receive a very large income from supplementary pension sources, thus boosting the average figure. Thus, we find that regardless of whether we use the mean or median figure, men receive substantially more pension income than women from both state and supplementary sources.

We can also see that there are clear differences in the pension amounts received by different ethnic groups. The mean amount from state pension sources for white British, those from other white backgrounds, black or black British, and mixed race respondents was between £82 and £88. Among these, mixed race respondents received the highest amount. In contrast, Asian or Asian British respondents received an average of £68, although those from other ethnic groups received just £65.

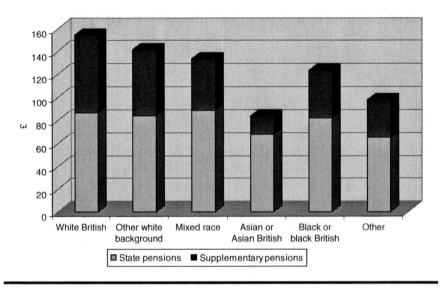

Figure 9.2 Pension income by ethnicity by source. (From Family Resources Survey [2004/2005]. Data provided by the UK Data Archive. With permission.)

In terms of supplementary pensions, the average amount received by white British respondent was £68, higher than any other ethnic group. Respondents from other white backgrounds received £58, with mixed race and black or black British receiving an average of £45 and £41, respectively. Pensioners from the category of other ethnic groups received £33, although Asian or Asian British respondents received an average of just £16 from supplementary pensions. For each group, the average amount received from supplementary pensions was lower that that from state sources (Figure 9.2).

The combination of state and supplementary sources means white British respondents had higher levels of retirement pension income than respondents from any other ethnic group, and although these differences were not all particularly substantial, considerable disparities do exist between white British respondents and those from either other ethnic groups or those who are Asian or Asian British. One trend stands out when looking at pension income breakdown either by gender or by ethnicity, which is that the level of retirement income from state sources is clearly less variable than is the income received from supplementary pensions.

9.5 Current Retirement Saving

9.5.1 Supplementary Pension Coverage Rates

In a system where private saving is considered necessary to guarantee an adequate income in old age, whether individuals of working age are currently saving for

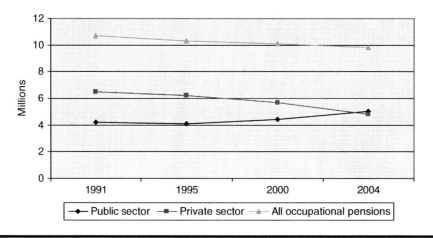

Figure 9.3   Trends in occupational pension scheme membership. (From Government Actuary Department, *Occupational Pensions Schemes 2004: The Twelfth Survey by the Government Actuary,* **HMSO, London, 2005. With permission.)**

retirement is of considerable political importance. In 2004, there were almost ten million individuals paying into an occupational pension scheme in the United Kingdom (GAD, 2005). Figure 9.3 shows the trend whereby membership of an occupational pension has fallen from 10.7 million in 1991 to 9.8 million in 2004. Within this overall figure, membership of occupational pension schemes has declined in the private sector from 6.5 million in 1991 to 4.8 million in 2004, although membership in the public sector has risen from 4.2 to 5 million during the same period.

However, coverage of supplementary pension schemes is not equal across all groups in the society. Women have been identified as being particularly vulnerable to retirement undersaving (ABI, 2004). Table 9.4 draws on previous analysis conducted elsewhere (DWP, 2005), but uses the most up-to-date figures from the Family Resources Survey. When we look at those of working age, we see that young women are marginally more likely to be contributing to a supplementary pension than men. However, a disparity in pension coverage exists among older age groups. This gap appears among those who are between 30 and 39 and is even more pronounced among those between 40 and 49, with men contributing to supplementary pensions at a greater rate than women. Coverage rates for both men and women between 50 and the state pension age (SPA) are lower than for the two preceding age groups, but the rate for men remains higher then that of women.

As Table 9.4 shows, pension coverage rates are related to age to a considerable extent, but the gender disparity that can be seen with older groups is not evident among those between 18 and 29. In fact, women in this age group who are in employment and, in particular, in full-time employment are actually more likely to contribute to a supplementary pension than men.

Table 9.4   Supplementary Pension Rates for Men and Women by Employment Status (Percent)

	18–29	30–39	40–49	50–State Pension Age
All men of working age	24.9	53.9	60.4	43.1
All women of working age	25.9	44.5	47.5	38.7
All employed men	28.9	62.6	72.4	66.6
All employed women	33	59.1	60.6	59.7
All full-time employed men	31.8	63.2	73.5	70.1
All full-time employed women	40.5	66.8	68.8	69.1

Source: Family Resources Survey (2004/2005). Data provided by the UK Data Archive.

Among older groups, however, we can see the impact of women's different career trajectories on their pension coverage rates. Amongst those who work full-time, men and women exhibit differential coverage rates, but these are not in a uniform direction. However, the fact that a substantial proportion of women in the United Kingdom who are employed work part-time and do not contribute means that for all those in employment, women exhibit considerably lower coverage rates among those between the age of 30 and the SPA.

The disparity in coverage rates is not restricted to matters of gender, however. When we look at the rates of different ethnic groups, shown in Table 9.5, we find that white British individuals of working age are more likely to be contributing to a supplementary pension than any ethnic minority group. Forty-five percent of white

Table 9.5   Percentage of Individuals Contributing to a Supplementary Pension by Ethnicity

	Coverage Rates (Percent)
White British	44.5
Any other white background	33.6
Mixed background	32.4
Asian or Asian British	29.3
Black or black British	33.1
Other ethnic groups	27.2

Source: Family Resources Survey (2004/2005). Data provided by the UK Data Archive.

British respondents were contributing to a supplementary pension in comparison to 34 percent for other white groups and 33 percent of black or black British individuals. Thirty-two percent of those from a mixed race background and just 30 percent of Asian of all Asian or Asian British adults of working age were contributing to a supplementary pension. The lowest observed rate is for members of other ethnic groups, of whom just 27 percent are currently contributing. Despite the difficulty in analyzing these relationships between ethnic minorities in detail due to low case numbers, we can see that a significant challenge exists in encouraging sufficient pension savings are made, in particular by women and among ethnic minorities.

9.5.2 Scheme Changes: The Shift from DB to DC

For those who have been contributing to a supplementary pension one of the major trends in recent years has been the replacement of defined benefit schemes with defined contribution ones in the private sector, whether for the whole of a company's workforce, or for new members. A defined benefit (DB) scheme is one where the amount received in retirement is calculated by a proscribed formula, often based on an individual's final salary. As such it offers a reasonably predictable income in retirement. In contrast, the value of a pension in defined contribution (DC) schemes is the amount contributed plus the investment accrued. The value of the fund at retirement is then used to purchase an annuity. The invested income is exposed to market fluctuations and thus, it can fall in value as well as rise. A shift to DC schemes therefore exposes the individual to an investment risk that is not present in DB schemes.

Data from 2004 indicates that almost 88 percent of occupational scheme members are contributing to DB schemes, with 12 percent contributing to schemes run on a DC basis (Figure 9.4). Although current workers may be allowed to continue

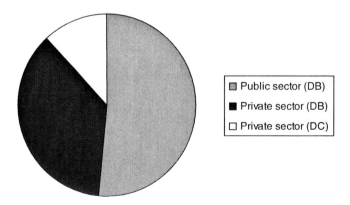

Figure 9.4 Occupational scheme membership by type of scheme. (From Government Actuary Department, *Occupational Pensions Schemes 2004: The Twelfth Survey by the Government Actuary*, HMSO, London, 2005. With permission.)

within a DB scheme, access to such schemes is often denied to new members. Within the public sector, all schemes (DB) continue to remain open to new members. Of the 3.59 million DB schemes in the private sector in 2004, however, 53 percent are closed to new members (GAD, 2005). The Government Actuary Department called the closure of DB schemes to new members "the most common single change made to private sector Defined Benefit schemes" (GAD, 2005: p. 15).

The reason that this shift is important is not just because of its impact on risk bearing for current workers but also due to the likely impact on contribution rates. As data from the Government Actuary Department indicates, there is a clear distinction between contribution rates for DC and DB schemes (Table 9.6).

Sixty-seven percent of active pension members surveyed contributed 4 percent or more to their private sector DB scheme, with 10 percent saying that they contributed less than 4 percent. In comparison, half of private sector DC scheme members surveyed claimed that they contributed less than 4 percent of their income to their pension scheme, with a little over a quarter indicating that they saved more than 4 percent of their salary.

This trend is mirrored when we look at employer contribution rates for these schemes also, where employer contributions to DC schemes are lower than those to DB schemes. The data shows that the shift from DB to DC schemes not only results in a transfer of risk from employers to employees, but is also likely to result in lower pension contribution levels. This is clearly of concern due to its likely negative effect on income in retirement. However, this shift raises a wider issue: coverage rates for private pensions are only a proxy for adequate pension saving. It is important that the contribution levels that individuals place in their pensions are sufficient to match their aspirations for the living standard that they desire in retirement.

Thus, retirement undersaving can be subclassified further, between those who are making no additional saving for their retirement and those who are currently

Table 9.6 Comparison between Defined Benefit (DB) and Defined Contribution (DC) Employee Contribution Rates in Private Sector Schemes (Percent), 2004

	Defined Benefit	Defined Contribution
Noncontributory or other basis	20	16
Under 4 percent	10	50
4 percent and over	67	26
No response	3	8

Source: Government Actuary Department, *Occupational Pensions Schemes 2004: The Twelfth Survey by the Government Actuary*, HMSO, London, 2005. With permission.

saving, but at rates considered too low to guarantee an adequate income in old age. Research by the Association of British Insurers found that there are more individuals in employment who are either not saving at all or saving too little than are considered to be saving enough. They find that 7.9 million workers are not saving anything for their retirement, with a further 4.3 million who are currently under-saving, in comparison to 11.1 million who they deem to be saving at an adequate level (ABI, 2006).

However, there are a number of difficulties in determining what constitute under-saving. These include the fact that future rates of return on invested contributions and changes in annuity rates are unknown, the arbitrary decision of what constitutes an "adequate" income, and the erroneous assumption that individuals do not save for their retirement outside pensions savings products. For example, Mayhew (2003) found 17 percent of those who had nonpension savings indicated that some of this money was being saved specifically for retirement. Furthermore, research by the Association of British Insurers (ABI, 2006: p. 9) shows that 29 percent of nonsavers were confident that they would have enough money to live comfortably on in their retirement while 44 percent of ABI-defined adequate savers worry they will not have enough money for comfortable living in their old age.

A number of significant challenges exist in promoting retirement saving. Often, individuals have unrealistic expectations of the future. This is with regard to many variables. Analysis by the Pensions Commission shows that the perceived probability among both men and women of living to the age of 75 is lower than that which is currently projected (Pensions Commission, 2004: p. 19). Research has shown that the barriers to voluntary retirement provision include a difficulty and reluctance to think about the future, the fear of tempting fate, and inaffordability (Rowlingson, 2002). Other barriers include the inherent complexity of the United Kingdom's pension system, a lack of trust in pension schemes, lack of incentives due to means-testing of state pension benefits (Pensions Commission, 2004: p. 214). One further difficulty is that although people may consider pensions to be an important issue, it is one that they often do not know a great deal about (DWP, 2006a: pp. 16–18).

The challenge of retirement saving is particularly great for women. Not only do they fare worse in terms of their pension outcomes, but even among working age women, there is evidence that pension literacy is lower than among men. Using data from 2002, Mayhew (2003) finds that women were more likely than men to claim to know little or nothing about pensions, and were more likely to have given little or no thought to their retirement arrangements than men.

Retirement planning is also hindered by a lack of trust in pension schemes. This has been fuelled by a number of pension scandals in recent decades including the mis-selling of personal pensions, and the Equitable Life affair, where a prominent life insurer had to cut the levels of pension benefits promised to its members to keep the company afloat. Interestingly, this lack of trust appears to be particularly directed to the government, with more people saying that they would trust their employer or a pension provider when it came to pensions ahead of the government (ABI, 2006: p. 22). Only 24 percent of people surveyed by the Association of British Insurers felt that they could trust the government in relation to state pensions (ABI, 2006).

9.6 Age of Retirement

Another aspect of retirement planning is the age at which individuals retire. This has received much attention recently, as there is an awareness that one key way to deal with the problem of population aging is to attempt to reduce the age dependency ratio by encouraging older workers to remain in employment. One such method to achieve this is by raising the SPA. This is already due to begin in 2010, when the SPA for women will increase over a ten-year period to the age of 65, thus equalizing it with that of men (Blake, 2003: p. 333). However, it is important to note that actual retirement ages are not entirely sensitive to changes in the SPA and that exit from the labor market may occur before the SPA.

Data from the United Kingdom Retirement Survey 1996 shows that although the modal age of retirement for both men and women was the SPA, a significant proportion of males retired in the years before the SPA and approximately 15 percent of women waited until the age of 65 to retire (Gough, 2003). As might be expected in a country where women can receive the state pension five years younger than their male counterparts, women do retire earlier than men, but the gap between their average retirement ages, although statistically significant, is not particularly large. The author's estimate of the average retirement ages from data from the December 2005–February 2006 release of the Quarterly Labour Force Survey indicates that the average male retirement age was 63.3 although the average female retirement age was 62.1 years ($p < .05$).

Disney et al. (1997: p. 55) classified the reasons for early retirement as being firm instigated, due to health reasons, or for individual reasons. Data from the final 1994 wave of the United Kingdom Retirement Survey shows that 35 percent of those who retired early were either made redundant or dismissed. Thirty percent retired early due to the ill health either of themselves or of their partner, although individual, voluntary reasons, such as spending more time with their family accounted for 35 percent (Gough, 2003: p. 254).

Thus, withdrawal from the labor market is not always a voluntary process (Vickerstaff, 2006). In particular, withdrawal due to ill health is an important feature in the United Kingdom: comparative data from the late 1990s has indicated that illness and disability is a more significant factor in early labor-market exit among males than in many other European countries (Blondall and Scarpetta, 1999: p. 55).

Almost 16 percent of men aged between 50 and 64 were in receipt of incapacity related benefits in 2003, a reduction from a high of almost 18 percent in the mid-1990s, although almost 12 percent of women were claiming, which was a twenty-year high for them (Pensions Commission, 2004: pp. 39–40). Thus, although increasing the SPA will undoubtedly affect the age at which people retire, it is important to appreciate that people retire for reasons other than reaching the SPA, and that their actual retirement age will not be entirely sensitive to changes in the SPA.

9.7 Recent Legislative Changes

9.7.1 White Paper Reforms 2006

9.7.1.1 Pensions Commission Conclusions

The Pensions Commission's final report, which was published in 2006, concluded that voluntarism had ultimately failed in encouraging sufficient pension saving (2006: p. 16), and that a greater degree of compulsion with regard to supplementary pension saving needed to be considered. Furthermore, it argued that significant reform of the United Kingdom's pensions system should occur in order to meet the challenges of population aging. They proposed three main reforms of its existing structure. These were (1) to increase the SPA, (2) to reform the state pensions system, and (3) to introduce a new National Pensions Savings Scheme (NPSS).

9.7.1.2 2006 White Papers

In response to the Pensions Commission's recommendations, the government published two white papers on pension reform in 2006. The impact of the Commission's work is clearly evident in these papers as they include each of the Commission's three major recommendations.

The first of these recommendations is to increase the SPA from 65 to 66 from 2024 to 2026, and then from 66 to 67 from 2034 to 2036 and from 67 to 68 from 2044 to 2046 (DWP, 2006b: p. 18). The government argued that such a move would ensure the sustainability of the scheme by sharing "the growth in life expectancy between time spent in work and time spent in retirement" (DWP, 2006b: p. 18).

The second recommendation is to reform the public pension system by making it entirely flat rate and by expanding coverage. It proposes to make the basic state pension available to more people and that, within the next parliament, its value will be indexed in line with earnings instead of the current system of price indexation (DWP, 2006b: p. 19). Furthermore, it aims to transform the state second pension into a flat-rate payment to be paid in addition to the basic state pension. This process would begin at the same time as linking the basic state pension to earnings and it would become a completely flat-rate payment by about 2030.

Finally, the white papers pave the way for a new NPSS. If implemented, this will be a personal, DC pension scheme, into which all individuals who do not currently save for retirement will automatically be enrolled. As per the recommendations of the Pensions Commission, individuals will retain the ability to opt out, should they desire to do so. The Commission had argued that by harnessing "the power of inertia,"

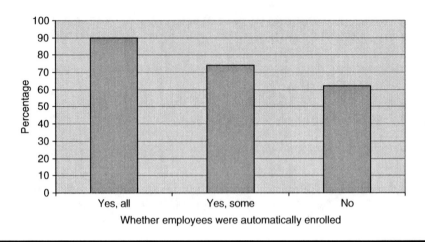

Figure 9.5 Percentage employees who were active members of private sector occupational schemes by method of enrollment. (From Government Actuary Department, *Occupational Pensions Schemes 2004: The Twelfth Survey by the Government Actuary*, HMSO, London, 2005. With permission.)

auto-enrollment would "overcome the behavioral barriers to long-term saving, although leaving people ultimately free to make their own decisions" (2006: p. 16).

As Figure 9.5 indicates, there is evidence that automatic enrollment can have a significant effect on subsequent pension scheme membership. In the United Kingdom, 90 percent of employees in organizations where all workers were automatically enrolled in an occupational pension scheme remained active members. This compares with 74 percent of employees where automatic enrollment exists for some of the workforce and 62 percent where there was no automatic enrollment and employees were free to choose whether to join the scheme or not (2005: p. 58). In addition, research from the United States of America also suggests that automatic enrollment is an effective tool, in particular among groups who typically have low coverage rates (Madrian and Shea, 2002, cited in Pensions Commission, 2004: p. 207; DWP, 2006c: p. 51).

It is proposed that employee contributions be set at 4 percent of earnings between £5,000 and £33,000 a year although employers will contribute 3 percent with an additional 1 percent from the state in the form of tax relief (DWP, 2006c: p. 50). The default contribution rates are set at a level that will achieve an estimated 45 percent replacement rate for median earners who start saving by age 30. They are thus still likely to produce lower replacement rate of preretirement income than is typical in many other countries, and those who wish to achieve a higher standard of living will need to save more than the default amount. If introduced, the scheme will set a new precedent in pensions policy in the United Kingdom that employers will be compelled to make contributions for their workers (who are over 22), where workers choose to remain in the scheme.

One key factor that will determine the success, or otherwise, of the NPSS will be whether sufficient numbers of people remain in the scheme and whether they will contribute to it in sufficient amounts. During the National Pensions Debate, held in early 2006, a quarter of people said that they personally would opt out of the scheme (DWP, 2006a: p. 56). Interestingly, the lack of trust in government when it comes to pension matters was highlighted when research by the Association of British Insurers (2006) indicated that only 30 percent of people believed that the government would actually implement their proposals on personal accounts and auto-enrollment. There was, however, another legislative change enacted in 2006 that will impact on individuals' retirement planning decisions, to which we will now turn.

9.7.2 *Employment Equality Age Regulations*

The Employment Equality (Age) Regulations 2006 were introduced in response to a directive from the EU (Directive 2000/78 EC) which establishes a general framework for equal treatment in employment and vocational training. The Regulations make it unlawful to discriminate against a worker on the grounds of her or his age. For the purposes of this chapter, the regulations are of interest as they prohibit companies from implementing a mandatory retirement age below 65 in most cases. Employers can still retire employees before the age of 65 where they can provide "objective justification" of the need to do so. The regulations provide employees with a right to request to work beyond 65 or the normal retirement age, and her or his employer will have a "duty to consider" such a request. Under the Act, employers retain the right to compulsorily retire staff once they reach the age of 65. The regulations give additional protection to older workers who wish to remain in employment, and thus may help ameliorate the demographic burden of population aging.

9.8   Conclusion

The debate about retirement saving is, at present, an extremely active one. The reports of the Pensions Commission offered a stark critique of the current system and a radical blueprint for future reform, and have generated significant debate in policy circles and the wider media. As has been shown, retirement undersaving is clearly a significant problem in the United Kingdom, and the success, or otherwise, of the proposals will rest to a considerable extent on whether "the power of inertia" is successful in ensuring sufficient numbers of people remain within the proposed NPSS.

For the individual, retirement planning remains a difficult issue, and although added debate may heighten awareness, it may also serve to confuse. However, although the prospect of retirement may seem rather abstract for those who are currently young, the reality of facing into old age relying solely on the state pensions would, for many, undoubtedly prove extremely difficult. Only time will tell whether the proposed reforms will successfully encourage retirement saving in the United Kingdom.

References

Association of British Insurers. 2004. *The Gender Pay Gap: Encouraging Women to Save for Retirement.* https://www.abi.org.uk/Display/File/364/The_Gender_Pensions_Gap_FINAL.pdf

Association of British Insurers. 2006. *The State of the Nation's Savings, 2006/7.* London: Association of British Insurers.

Blake, D. 2003. The UK pension system: Key issues, *Pensions*, 8(4), 330–375.

Blondall, S. and Scarpetta, S. 1999. "The Retirement Decision in OECD Countries," OECD Economics Department Working Papers, No. 202, Paris, OECD.

Department of Social Security. 1998. *A New Contract for Welfare: Partnership in Pensions.* London: DSS.

Department of Work and Pensions. 2005. *Women and Pensions: The Evidence.* http://www.dwp.gov.uk/publications/dwp/2005/wp/women-pensions.pdf.

Department of Work and Pensions. 2006a. *National Pensions Debate: Final Report.* London: HMSO.

Department of Work and Pensions. 2006b. *Security in Retirement: Towards a New Pensions System.* London: HMSO.

Department of Work and Pensions. 2006c. *Personal Accounts: A New Way to Save.* London: HMSO.

Department of Work and Pensions. Website, http://www.dwp.gov.uk/.

Disney, R., Grundy, E., and Johnson, P. (Eds.) 1997. *The Dynamics of Retirement*, Department of Social Security Report No. 72, London: HMSO.

Gough, O. 2003. Factors that influence voluntary and involuntary retirement, *Pensions*, 8(3), 252–264.

Government Actuary Department. 2005. *Occupational Pensions Schemes 2004: The Twelfth Survey by the Government Actuary.* London: HMSO.

Mayhew, V. 2003. *Pensions 2002: Public Attitudes to Pensions and Saving For Retirement.* DWP Research Report 193. London: HMSO.

The Pensions Service. Website, http://www.thepensionservice.gov.uk/.

Pensions Commission. 2004. *Pensions: Challenges and Choices: The First Report of the Pensions Commission.* London: HMSO.

Pensions Commission. 2005. *A New Pension Settlement for the Twenty-First Century: The Second Report of the Pensions Commission.* London: HMSO.

Pensions Commission. 2006. *Implementing an Integrated Package of Pension Reforms: The Final Report of the Pensions Commission.* London: HMSO.

Rowlingson, K. 2002. Private pension planning: The rhetoric of responsibility, the reality of insecurity, *Journal of Social Policy*, 31(4), 623–642.

Tanner, S. 1998. The dynamics of male retirement behaviour, *Fiscal Studies*, 19(2), 175–196.

Vickerstaff, S. 2006. I'd rather keep running to the end and then jump off the cliff: Retirement decisions: Who decides? *Journal of Social Policy*, 35(3), 455–472.

World Bank. 1994. *Averting the Old Age Crisis: Policies to Protect the Old and Promote Growth.* New York: Oxford University Press.

World Bank. 2005. *Old Age Income Support in the 21st Century: An International Perspective on Pension Systems and Reform.* Washington, DC: World Bank.

Chapter 10

Comparing Public and Private Sector Wage and Health Benefit Compensation

Ann Beck

CONTENTS

10.1 Introduction

Over 30 years ago, Rosow (1976, p. 543), writing about criticism of federal government pay and benefits, argued that "Government employees are caught in a cross-current of public criticism of government as an institution. In a period of cynicism, the harassed taxpayers find the public workers as likely scapegoats for their own frustrations." A few years later, research by Porter and Keller (1981) found that many jobs in federal, state, and local governments were underpaid relative to those in the private sector. About 15 years later, after the recession of 1990–1991, *Business Week* and similar publications began criticizing "excessive" government employee compensation, especially benefits. Miller (1993), writing in *Public Budgeting and Finance*, asked whether the changes in the levels of employment and compensation of state and local government workers could be considered profligacy or prudent. Miller used Bureau of Labor Statistics and Census Bureau data to attempt to find the answer. He concluded that although the data was not conclusive, state and local government spending on wages and benefits could not be considered profligate. In the same year, Belman and Heywood (1993) also argued that public sector and private sector wages and total compensation (wages plus benefits) were very similar when controlling for firm size and sector occupational differences.

Little has changed since then. After the recession of 2002–2004, small and large business magazine writers were again criticizing the level of benefits for public workers as excessive (profligate). Revell (2005), writing for *Fortune* magazine, referred to the provision of postemployment retirement benefits to various public employees as "the great state healthcare giveaway." In her article, she noted that 48 of 50 states and more than half of all cities "still" provided health benefits for their workers after retirement. She indirectly argues that because only about 1/5 of all large private companies in the United States still cover retirees with health benefits, there should be a significant reduction in the number of public employers who offer such a benefit to their retirees.

In a companion article by Byrnes and Palmeri in *Business Week* (2005), the authors referred to public employer provision of high levels of defined benefit pension plans and health insurance benefits as a "Sinkhole!" that are an extreme "drain" on state and city budgets. Again, the authors assert that public employees are paid better than private employees and public employees should not receive as much salary and, especially, employee benefits as they do. The authors used aggregate data from the Bureau of Labor Statistics to compare public and private compensation costs to demonstrate that public employees are paid too much. As with Revell, these authors indirectly suggested that unions and state constitutional guarantees related to equal protection are the major barriers to reducing health and pension benefits for employees and retirees.

In this chapter, I use a variety of federal and other data sources to describe existing aggregate wage and benefit level information for both public and private employers. A variety of national government sources of information about compensation are used (Employment Cost Index and Employer Cost of Employee Compensation of the National Compensation Survey, the Current Employment Statistics Survey, the Quarterly Census of Employment and Wages, the Current Population Survey, and the Medical Expenditure Panel Survey). Differences in the compensation trends shown among them are a result of differences in the definitions of terms, the size and inclusiveness of the samples, and the source of information provided—individuals or administrative records (Meisenheimer, 2005).

To understand the employer costs of health benefits, one must first understand wage compensation because most employer health benefit cost is indirectly tied to the employee's wage. That is, better paid workers are better able to pay for health benefits. Although compensation systems are designed and implemented primarily to attract and retain high quality employees, other factors also affect an employer's level of wage and health benefits in both sectors. These factors need to be taken into account to compare "apples to apples." I describe these factors and demonstrate how both wages and health benefits compare when we consider these factors. I explain Baumol's proposition about compensation convergence between the sectors and then evaluate the soundness of the proposition using these various data. I also address the current thinking about the future of employer-provided health benefits for both public and private employees.

10.2   Theory of Convergence in Compensation

Economists argue that any increases in real (controlling for inflation) compensation (wages and benefits) must be principally and generally based on increases in productivity or profitability. However, increases in compensation often do not reflect fully increases in productivity or economic growth. The Baumol hypothesis argues that when there is a significant increase in productivity in the private sector, compensation increases in both sectors. As described by Fisher (1988), the economist Baumol argues that both the labor-intensiveness of many government operations and methods as well as the monopoly or near-monopoly of public provision of such services (national defense, immigration, schools, fire protection, police) make it very difficult for government to make the types of productivity gains made in the private sector where labor is more easily replaced by technology. Although there may not be as much "productivity" gain in the public sector, there is greater inelasticity of demand for public services. This inelasticity of demands means that even if costs for services increase (because wages go up) the public does not decrease its consumption of those services. For Baumol, these forces create, over time, a convergence between compensation in the public and private sectors. The evidence from the national databases suggests that his hypothesis is supported.

Over the last decade and a half, aggregate total employee compensation for all civilian employees (public and private, nonmilitary employees) has not increased as much as the gross domestic product (GDP) or nonfarm business productivity. From 1991 to 2006, the real GDP of the United States increased more than 60 percent.* During the last recession of 2001–2004, private employers recorded substantial jumps in profitability (hence productivity) per employee. For example, revenue per employee in the private sector in 2003 was reported as $312,738, up 18 percent just since 2001 (Hansen, 2004, p. 79). Similarly, during the period 1991–2006, the index for nonfarm business output per hour per person (productivity) increased 42 percent.† Although productivity increased about 42 percent and real GDP increased more than 60 percent, the real hourly nonfarm business total compensation (wages and benefits) increased only 24 percent.‡ However, the constant dollar Employment Cost Index (ECI) for total compensation for all civilian workers, which includes both public and private employees, grew only 13.3 percent.§ This growth in aggregate real compensation has been less than productivity gains for many years, and recent year gains in compensation have been unequally distributed among workers with more of the gains going to the more highly compensated workers (United States Congressional Budget Office, 2007a, p. 1).

10.3 Comparing Total, Wage, and Benefit Compensation across Employers and Sectors

Table 10.1 demonstrates the real (constant dollar) growth of employer costs for compensation for three groups of employers—those in state and local government establishments, those in all private establishments, and those in private establishments with any union presence.

The comparison of data for state and local government employers and private employers with union presence is particularly appropriate as there is compelling

---

* The increase across this time period was from 7,100.5 in 1991 to 11,415.3 in 2006. U.S. Bureau of Economic Analysis, compiled from Current-Dollar and "Real" Gross Domestic Product (Seasonally adjusted annual rates) dated 03/29/07 at http://www.bea.gov/national/nipaweb/TableView.asp#Mid accessed 04/1/07.
† The increase across this time period was from 96.1 in 1991 to 136.7 in 2006. U.S. Bureau of Labor Statistics, compiled from Series PRS85006093 Output per Hour, Nonfarm Business 1991 through 2006 from http://data.bls.gov/PDQ/servlet/SurveyOutputServlet accessed April 19, 2007.
‡ The increase across this time period was from 97.4 in 1991 to 120.8 in 2006. U.S. Bureau of Labor Statistics, compiled from Series PRS85006153 Real Hourly Compensation 1991 through 2006 from http://data.bls.gov/cgi-bin/srgate accessed March 19, 2007.
§ The increase across this time period was from 88.9 in 1991 to 100.8 in 2006. U.S. Bureau of Labor Statistics, compiled from Employment Cost Index Historical Listing Constant-dollar March 2001–December 2006 (December 2005=100) at http://www.bls.gov/web/ecconstnaics.pdf and Employment Cost Index Historical Listing Constant-dollar 1975 at http://www.bls.gov/web/ecconst.pdf accessed March 19, 2007.

Table 10.1 Change in Employment Cost Index in Constant Dollars for State and Local, All Private, and Private with Union Presence Employers between 1991 and 2005

	State and Local	*Private*	*Private Union*
Total ECI June 1991	101.6	100.2	99.3
Total ECI June 2005	116.8	113.9	114.2
Percent change 1991–2005	15.0	13.7	15.0
Wage component June 1991	101.2	98.9	97.7
Wage component June 2005	106.4	107.4	103.4
Percent change 1991–2005	5.1	8.6	5.8
Benefits component June 1991	104.4	103.6	103.6
Benefits component June 2005	123.8	130.7	135.1
Percent change 1991–2005	18.6	26.2	30.4

Source: U.S. Bureau of Labor Statistics, compiled from the Employment Cost Index Constant Dollar Historical Listing (June 1989=100), dated July 29, 2005 and found at http://www.bls.gov/web/econst.pdf accessed December 3, 2005.

evidence that unionization increases compensation in both the private and public sectors (Freeman and Medoff, 1984; Freeman and Ichniowski, 1988; Hunter and Rankin, 1988; Fronstin, 2005; BLS National Compensation Survey, 2006). Today, about half of all union members in the United States work in the public sector. The overall rate of union membership in the public sector is about 36 percent although the private sector rate is 7.4 percent and the percent of total public sector employees represented by unions is about 40 percent compared to only 8.1 percent of employees in the private sector.* Unionization in the public sector overlaps with sector-specific occupational groups as well. For example, almost 37 percent of all protective service (police and fire) employees; about 42 percent of education, training, and library employees; and 20 percent of professional employees are represented by unions,† and these occupational groups of quasi-professional and professional employees exist predominantly in the public sector. Among larger-size local and county units of government, most have one or more unions. According to a 1999 International City/County Management Association survey, almost 75 percent of the jurisdictions responding had employees currently organized into multiple bargaining unions or associations that represented about half of all employees in the jurisdiction, and 90 percent of these local governments engaged in collective bargaining that had been on-going for almost 30 years (ICMA, 1999). This history of bargaining (especially at the local level) affects all aspects of compensation. The pervasiveness of unionization in the public sector across a wide range of public sector establishments suggests that one of the proper comparisons of wages and benefits across sectors must be between public sector employers and private employers with union presence.

The data from Table 10.1 suggest that growth in compensation level from the base period was not remarkably different for one sector or group. Neither sector's gains in compensation fully reflected increases in either productivity or the GDP during the same period. The cost index for state and local government employers increased only slightly more than for private establishments but almost exactly the same amount as for private establishments with union presence. During that same period, the wage cost index increased more, on average, for private firm employers with and without union presence than for state and local employers. The benefit component of the index increased substantially more than wages for all three groups of employers and the least dramatic change in the benefit cost index over the time period occurred for public sector employers.

There is real growth in the cost of total compensation for all three groups, but no one group of employers stands out as facing more excessive increases in total compensation cost relative to the other groups of employers. This suggests that the rate of public sector compensation cost increases for total compensation has been consistent with or less than those experienced in the private sector. In both the public and

---

* U.S. Department of Labor, Bureau of Labor Statistics, "Union Members Summary" dated January 25, 2007 Table 1 "Union affiliation of employed wage and salary workers by selected characteristics," found at http://stats.bls.gov/news/release/pdf/union2.htm accessed March 20, 2007.

† U.S. Department of Labor, Bureau of Labor Statistics, "Union Members Summary" dated January 25, 2007 Table 3 "Union affiliation of employed wage and salary workers by occupation and industry," found at http://stats.bls.gov/news/release/pdf/union2.htm accessed March 20, 2007.

private sector, the rate of increase in benefit costs to the employer is about three times greater than the rate of increase in wage cost. For private employers and those with union presence, the rate of increase in the costs of benefits has been higher than the rate of increase for public sector employers. On the basis of this measure, there is no profligacy in the rate of growth of wage or benefit cost relative to private sector employers. When the real growth in the total, wage, or benefits component is compared to productivity and GDP increases over the same period, it does not appear that any compensation elements are "growing" faster than increases in productivity for any group of employers.

Part of the reason for the smaller rates of increase in total costs for public employers is that public employers started the period with significantly higher levels of compensation costs than all private employers (but not substantially higher levels than private employers with union presence). In Table 10.2, actual, dollar cost to the employer for employee compensation (ECEC) is shown for the periods 1991 and 2006. The average total compensation cost is higher for public sector employers than for all private sector employers in both time periods (1991 and 2006). The total compensation level for state and local governments in 1991 is about 45 percent higher—$22.31 versus $15.40—than for all private employers and about 13 percent higher—$22.31 versus $19.76—than for private employers with a union presence. Similar to the disparity between the sectors in 1991, by 2006, total compensation costs for public employers are 47 percent higher—$37.91 versus $25.52—than for all private employers. However, the gap between public employers and private employers with union presence has been reduced to 7 percent—$37.91 versus $35.08. There is no evidence that the rate of public sector compensation increase is significantly greater than that experienced in the private sector; and there is some sign of convergence as the gap is closing between the highly unionized public sector and the unionized private sector employers.

In addition to productivity growth and unionization, other factors influence compensation decisions as employers design and implement such systems to attract and retain high quality employees. Forces and factors external to the employer include occupational compensation practices, labor market and benefit-provider market competitiveness, the location of the jobs (metropolitan or rural), the political culture of a community as expressed in various statutes about wages and benefits (e.g., minimum and leave laws, worker compensation practices, tax treatment of benefits, etc.), and the willingness of customers and citizens to pay for goods and services desired (elasticity of demand) to name a few. Internal forces and factors include size of establishment, level and intensity of unionization, the history of compensation practices at the specific workplace, the number of employees who "take-up" an offered benefit, and the age distribution, education, skill and length of service (experience) of the workers. Compensation differences between establishments and between sectors may well be the result of the difference and interactions among many of these factors within and between each sector.

Table 10.2 Employer Costs for Employee Compensation for State and Local, Private, and Private with Union Presence Employers in Current Dollars, March 1991 to September 2006

1991	State and Local	Private	Union
Private/union			
Total compensation	$22.31	$15.40	$19.76
Wage (percent)	15.40 (70)	11.14 (72)	13.02 (66)
Benefits (percent)	6.79 (30)	4.27 (28)	6.75 (34)
Paid leave	1.75	1.05	1.43
Health insurance (percent)	1.54 (6.9)	0.92 (6.0)	1.63 (8.2)
Retirement	1.85	0.44	0.87
Legally mandated	1.34	1.40	1.93
2006	State and Local	Private	Union
Private/union			
Total compensation	$37.91	$25.52	$35.08
Wage (percent)	25.53 (67)	18.04 (71)	21.73 (62)
Benefits (percent)	12.38 (33)	7.02 (29)	13.35 (38)
Paid leave	2.98	1.73	2.65
Health insurance (percent)	4.05 (10.7)	1.76 (6.9)	3.69 (10.5)
Retirement	2.68	0.93	2.47
Legally mandated	2.22	2.18	3.10

Source: U.S. Bureau of Labor Statistics, complied from the Employer Costs for Employee Compensation, 1986–1999 at http://www.bls.gov/ncs/ect/sp/ecbl0013.pdf and the Employer Costs for Employee Compensation, Historical Listing (Quarterly), 2004–2006 at http://www.bls.gov/ncs/ect/sp/ececqrtn.pdf accessed March 19, 2007.

10.4 Wage Differences and Similarities between the Sectors

The pattern for wage differences between the three types of employers—state and local public sector, all private, and private with union presence—is similar to that for total compensation. On the basis of information provided in Table 10.2, the actual dollar changes in cost for wages across the two time periods are almost identical for the public sector and unionized private employers. The current dollar change in the cost of wages between the sectors increased about 66 percent in the entire public sector ($15.40–$25.53), about 62 percent in the private sector ($11.04–18.04), and 67 percent in the private unionized sector ($13.02–$21.73). Again, the actual dollar wage gap between the sectors remains almost the same between the time period 1991 and 2006.

However, when we examine the benefit cost component, the rate of increase pattern is much higher for all three types of employers. As shown in both Table 10.1 and Table 10.2, the proportion benefits compensation relative to total compensation became larger over time for all three types of employers. On the basis of Table 10.2, the current dollar increase in the benefit cost factor for public employers over the time period has been 82 percent ($6.79–$12.38), for all private employers the increase was 64 percent ($4.27–7.02), and for private employers with unions, there was a 98 percent increase ($6.75–$13.35) in benefit costs. By 2006, private union employers are paying more for benefits per hour than employers in the public sector and those benefit costs are an even higher percentage of total compensation than in the public sector. Unionized private and all public sector state and local establishment employers appear to have almost identical benefit compensation amounts and proportions of total compensation in 1991. By 2006, private sector establishments with a union presence have exceeded state and local governments in both actual cost of benefits and proportion of total benefits. Again, when unionized settings are compared, there are few if any overall benefit compensation differences between the sectors.

Some of the difference in aggregate wage levels between the public and private sector may be because of differences in the educational and occupational mix of workers in each sector. Belman and Heywood (1993) partly accounted for the difference by the much higher concentration of professional and related jobs in the public sector, and, therefore, a much greater proportion of college educated persons working in the public sector. Using data from the 1989 Annual Earnings File, they found that twice as many state and local government employees had college degrees as in the private sector and the proportion of professionals in state and local governments was three or four times greater than in the private sector (Belman and Heywood, 1993, p. 4). Braden and Hyland (1993, p. 17) found that about one-quarter of the private sector jobs are professional and technical, although over one-half of all public sector jobs can be considered professional or technical. The distribution of professional and related jobs in both the public and private sectors remains quite similar today.* The most recent analysis of the federal workforce distribution (MSPB, 2007a, p. 3) found twice as many jobs in official and

---

* For specific information about the distribution of occupational groups in the public sector, the best source is the U.S. Department of Commerce, Bureau of the Census, Census of Governments, Compendium of Public Employment: 2002, Volume III, Public Employment, issued September 2004. Table 8 "Percent Distribution of Full-Time Equivalent Public Employment by Type of Government and Function: March 2002" at http://www.census. gov/prod/2004pubs/gc023x2.pdf accessed March 20, 2007.

managerial ranks and about 80 percent more professional jobs in the federal sector than in the private sector. Recent work by the United States Congressional Budget Office (2007, p. 5) shows that white collar federal employees are more likely to be in management, professional, and related categories compared to the private sector and that 43 percent of federal employees have a college degree although about 28 percent of private employees have college degrees.

The difference in educational level and proportion of managers and professionals should support an even higher average salary for the public sector than is actually observed. However, despite the higher proportion of college educated persons who work for government, Poterba and Rueben (1994), using Current Population Survey data at the individual level for years 1979–1992, found that men with college degrees (but not women) in state and local government were paid much lower than their counterparts in the private sector. Similarly, Miller (1996) and Buckley (1996) using data from the Occupational Compensation Survey program found that high-level professional and administrative personnel in state and local governments earned less when compared to private sector occupants of similar levels of similar occupational jobs. In a recent study of private, nonprofit, and government hospitals and universities (Shahpoori and Smith, 2005), wages were slightly lower or converged for government facilities compared with private and nonprofit.

Still other authors have indicated that when higher total compensation does occur in the public sector, it is likely the result of the higher proportions of professional and white collar employees who are able to command both higher wages and greater benefits (Schumann, 1987; Miller, 1993). Similarly, McDonnell (2005) argues that greater education, skills, level of physical risk, and compelling interest in public employment increases the wage levels in the public sector service jobs, principally protective service jobs—police, firefighters, and corrections officers—relative to the very different types of service jobs found in the private sector. Also, a higher proportion of public sector jobs are located in metropolitan environments where wages are typically higher by about three dollars per hour than for the 20 percent of employees who live in nonmetropolitan areas (Cover, 2005, p. 1).

Current evidence about compensation differences between major occupational groups and occupations in each sector can be found in latest National Compensation Survey of 2005. The survey documents that the range of wages within the private sector is greater than those within state and local government across many occupations, that is, many occupations in the private sector start at a lower wage, but those same occupations in the private sector have higher upper-end wages or salaries than in the public sector. The public sector has more wage compression as lower level employees earn higher salaries in the public sector than in the private sector and higher level employees in the public sector earn less than those in the private sector. After comparing average wage levels among hundreds of white collar, professional, blue collar, and service occupations in the public and private sector, no clear pattern emerges, except that relatively incomparable service jobs in the public sector have much higher wages than in the private sector and there are high rates of standard error in the average pay

Table 10.3 Comparison of Private Industry and State and Local Government Mean Hourly Earnings by Occupational group, June 2005 National Compensation Survey

	Private	*State and Local*
All	$17.82	$23.31
White collar	22.21	26.32
Professional	29.80	31.25
Executive	34.21	31.04
Administrative support	14.44	14.98
Blue collar	15.75	17.96
Service	9.38	17.55

Source: Table 1-1 "Summary, United States: Mean hourly earnings and weekly hours by selected characteristics, private industry and State and local government, National Compensation Survey, June 2005c" at http://www.bls.gov/ncs/ocs/sp/ncbl0832.pdf accessed on March 19, 2007.

levels for many specific occupations in government in the survey because of the low number of sampled jobs in each occupation in the survey.*

Table 10.3 compares average wage across various broad occupational groupings in the public and private sectors. The table indicates that public employees continue to earn higher hourly earnings across almost all occupational groups. The average wage for administrative support group occupations in the public and private sectors appears to have converged. There are minor differences between the sectors in both professional and executive groups, with executives in the private sector earning more than those in the public sector. The wage difference between the service occupations is the result of the difference in the specific occupations that make up the category in each sector. Most service occupation comparisons between the two sectors are considered inappropriate by the Bureau of Labor Statistics, the agency that collects the data. Direct comparison is inappropriate because there are few private police or firefighters although there are almost a million of such public sector employees who are categorized as service workers in the National Compensation Survey.

---

* U.S. Bureau of Labor Statistics, National Compensation Survey Occupational Wage data from the June 2006, National Compensation Survey available at http://www.bls.gov/ncs/ocs/sp/ncbl0832.pdf Tables 2-2 "Private industry: Mean hourly earnings and weekly hours by full-time and part-time workers for selected occupations, National Compensation Survey, June 2005" and Table 2-3 "State and local government: mean hourly earnings and weekly hours by full-time and part-time workers for selected occupations, National Compensation Survey, June 2005" on pp. 12–30.

Another useful source for wage comparison between the sectors is available from the Bureau of Labor Statistics in the Quarterly Census of Employment and Wages (QCEW). The QCEW data source includes every business and government establishment in the United States that has employees covered by the unemployment insurance programs and files a quarterly unemployment tax report. It includes the federal government as an employer. Data is produced by quarterly counts of establishments.

The December 2005 data from the QCEW presented in Table 10.4 suggests even stronger wage convergence between the public and private sectors. The QCEW data shows that the average weekly wage in December 2005 for government employees in 265,000 government establishments representing 21 million employees was $800; and it was $779 for about 8 million private business establishments and 108 million private sector employees.* Of course, the government averages mask large differences in average weekly wage across levels of government. For example, in 2005, private industry employee average weekly wage was $779; for state government employees, the average wage was $812; for local government employees, the wage was $725; and for federal government employees it was $1,151. Because local public sector employment dwarfs both state and federal public sector employment, the average wage for all government employees is dominated by local public sector employees. The average weekly wage for these local government employees is about 7 percent below the wage for the average wage of the private sector employee. The

Table 10.4 Average Weekly Salaries for Public Sector Workers by Level of Government and for All Private Workers, December 2005

	Public ($)	Private ($)
Average weekly wage (all)	800	779
Local	725	
State	812	
Federal	1151	

Source: Bureau of Labor Statistics Employment and Wages, Annual Averages 2005b Table 2: Private industry by six-digit NAICS industry and government by level of government, 2005 annual averages: Establishments, employment, and wages, change from 2004 at http://www.bls.gov/cew/ew05table2.pdf accessed March 19, 2007.

---

* Source: Bureau of Labor Statistics Employment and Wages, Annual Averages 2005b Table 2: Private industry by six-digit NAICS industry and government by level of government, 2005 annual averages: Establishments, employment, and wages, change from 2004 at http://www.bls.gov/cew/ew05table2.pdf accessed March 19, 2007.

average government employee weekly wage of $800 is about three percent above the private sector average weekly wage. Overall, it appears that the typical public employee at the local level of government is earning slightly less in weekly wage than the typical private industry employee. Again, it appears that Baumol's hypothesis is supported by the Quarterly Census of Employment and Wages data.

In addition to occupational, location, and unionization differences between the sectors, a fourth influence on compensation is size of establishment. Larger employers normally provide both higher wages and higher levels of benefits for their workers. Size also interacts with occupation and the distribution of various occupation changes with increasing or decreasing size of establishment. Occupations like sales and food preparation (large proportions of private sector occupations) are found in smaller establishments although occupations such a protective services, education and training, community service, and health (large proportions of public sector occupations) are found in larger establishments (Hajiha, 2003). In the National Compensation Survey (NCS) of Occupational Wages, the Bureau of Labor Statistics computes the average wage by size of establishment for both private and state and local government participants in the sample. The data for the latest survey in 2005 related to size of establishment and unionization is summarized for private and public employers in Table 10.5.

In each sector as size of establishment increases so does the wage, but the amount of wage increase across different sizes of establishment is smaller (more compressed) in the public sector—$18.86–$24.06 for the public sector and $15.73–$25.44 for

Table 10.5   Effect of Size and Unionization on Average Hourly Wage in Current Dollars by Sector, June 2005 National Compensation Study

Size of Establishment	Total	Private	Public
1–99 workers	$15.73	$15.69	$18.86
100–499 workers	18.13	17.72	21.79
500–999 workers	20.79	19.94	23.83
1000–2499 workers	21.65	21.07	23.37
2500 workers or more	25.44	27.05	24.06
Union	22.18	20.67	25.49
Nonunion	17.21	17.43	21.22

Source: Bureau of Labor Statistics, National Compensation Survey: Occupational Wages in the United States, June 2005c Table 1-1. "Summary, United States: Mean hourly earnings and weekly hours by selected characteristics, private industry and State and local government" found at http://www.bls.gov/ncs/ocs/sp/ncbl0832.pdf

the private sector. Within the largest sized establishments (2500+), the average hourly wage of the private sector employees is higher than those in the public sector. Again, unionization appears to have a positive effect on wage in both sectors as there is a 17–18 percent greater wage for unionized establishments in both the public and the private sectors.

The QCEW tracks about 265,000 government establishments with 21 million public employees and eight million private business establishments with 108 million private sector employees.* The single national government employs about 2.5 million employees although the 50 state governments are employers for another five million public employees. For 2002, the number of state government employees varied from more than 471,000 in California to about 13,000 in Wyom-ing (Census, 2004, p. 12). We consider most all state public sector establishments to be more than 1,000 in employee size and many will be 10,000 or more. The local governments—counties, municipalities, townships, school districts, and other special districts—employ about 13 million public employees in more than 50,000 units of government. However, about three-fourths of the U.S. population lives in just 473 counties with population of 100,000 or more so that the local governments in those jurisdictions employ the bulk of all local public employees.

Table 10.6 compares size of the private establishment and public government units that employ public and private employees in the United States. From this table we can locate in what size establishment the median public or private employee works. Table 10.6 suggests that the "average" or median private and public employee work in very different sized units. The QCEW data for the 1st quarter of 2005 is used for size of establishment. About 57 percent of all "private" employees are in establishments of less than 100 employees in size, another 32 percent are in establishments between 100 and 999 workers, and the remaining 11 percent of private employees are in establishments of 1000 or more workers. Almost the opposite distribution occurs for "public" employees. About 5 percent of public employees work in units smaller than 100 employees, and about 60 percent work in places of 1000 or more employees. So the typical private worker is in an establishment of less than 100 persons, although the typical public worker is in a unit with 1000 or more workers. On the basis of the "typical" public employee, the appropriate comparison between the sectors should be between public employees and private employees in establishments of 1000 or more employees. As previously reported, when average wage compensation is compared between these two groups, the wages for the average public and private sector employee converge.

---

* Monthly Labor Review, 2006, Volume 191, issue 1, Table 22, "Quarterly Census of Employment: 10 Largest Counties, fourth quarter 2003," page 86 and found at http://www.bls.gov/opub/mlr/2006/01/cls0601.pdf

Table 10.6   Private Establishment and Local Public Unit of Government Size and Percent of all Public and Private Employees within Establishments or Units of that Size

Percentage of Establishments			Percentage of Employees		
Size All	*Private*	*Public Local*	*Private*	*Public Local*	*Public*
0–99	98	76	57.0	6.7	4.3
100–999	1	21	33.0	35.1	33.3
1000+	1	2	11.0	58.2	62.4
100	100	100.0	100.0	100.0	
Total number	8.2 M	55.4 K	108.5 M	11.4 M	17.5 M

Source: Computed from information contained in Quarterly Census of Employment and Wages, Table 4 "Private industry by supersector and size of establishment: Establishments and employment, first quarter 2005d" at http://www.bls.gov/cew/ew05table4.pdf accessed March 21, 2007 and tabulation from U.S. Department of Commerce, Bureau of the Census, Volume III, Compendium of Public Employment Table 20. Distribution of Local Governments and Full-Time Equivalent Employment by Employment-Size Group, Type of Government, and State: March 2002 published September 2004a, pp. 248–49 at http://www.census.gov/prod/2004pubs/gc023x2.pdf accessed March 20, 2007.

10.5   Health Benefit Cost Differences between the Sectors

As shown in Table 10.2, one of the areas of greatest difference between the public and private sectors is the higher cost of health benefits for the public sector employer. Health benefit costs for the average public employer and the average private employer with a union presence are now the most expensive element of all benefit costs for employers. Employer-provided health insurance benefits are the cornerstone of healthcare provision in the United States as about 60 percent of all persons, about 160 million Americans under age 65, are covered by health insurance plans related to employment (DeNavas-Walt et al., 2004; Gabel et al., 2005). This reliance on voluntary, private provision of health insurance through employers as the primary method of addressing healthcare is deeply embedded in our culture and is unique among industrialized nations (Wong, 1997; Beland and Hacker, 2004; Inglehart, 2004). It is the risk-pooling through employer-provided health insurance that obtains insurance for employees at a lower cost than they could get in the individual insurance market.

As previously shown in Tabe 10.2, healthcare insurance costs for public sector employers in 1991 were about 67 percent higher than for all private sector employers, but slightly lower than for private sector employers with union presence. By 2006, healthcare insurance costs for public sector employers were about 130 percent higher than for all private sector employers, but only slightly higher (10 percent) than for private sector employers with union presence. The increased costs of health benefits for all employers are driven by many factors. A recent report by the U.S. Government Accountability Office (2006, p. 15) argued that "… in addition to increases in the cost of providing medical services, several factors were noted to drive trends in employer costs. These include the health insurance underwriting cycle, the emergence of managed care, competition, and consolidation in the healthcare industry." One of the principal reasons that the cost of health benefits is higher for government employers is much greater rates of participation (take-up) by public employees in offered health benefit programs (Long and Marquis, 1999; McDonnell, 2005). This means a significantly higher proportion of state and local government employees participate in insurance programs when eligible and offered than do private sector employees. The greater rate of participation drives up the cost of the health benefit for the public employer especially where the public employer contributes to premium payments.

Again, the National Compensation Survey conducted by the U.S. Bureau of Labor Statistics collects and reports information on many aspects of the health insurance benefit. Table 10.7 supplies information about the differences in participation rates among the three groups of employers. As shown, unionization in the private sector significantly increases the likelihood of access, participation and take-up of health insurance benefits by workers. The participation rates by private establishments with union presence are quite similar to the state and local government participation rates even though the data for the public sector is seven years old. More recent studies of government establishment participation and take-up rates show only slight changes from the 1998 NCS study of the public sector (Kaiser Family Foundation, 2005).

Rates of participation of private union workers in health insurance plans are very similar to that found for union workers in state and local governments. Fronstin (2005) demonstrates a strong and consistent correlation between union presence and health benefit provision. Fronstin used data from the 2003 Current Population Survey to demonstrate that higher levels of unionization in the public sector are responsible for the 26 percent greater coverage of public employees; and he found that the positive effect of unionization on health insurance benefit provision in the private sector holds across firm size, industry, occupation, hours of work, and annual earnings (Fronstin, 2005, pp. 2–5). Although the union effect on the provision and cost of health benefits for private sector unionized workers remains strong, Buchmueller et al. (2001, p. 23) estimated that about 20–35 percent of the decline in private employee health coverage in the period 1980–1997 has been due to the declining strength of unions in the private sector. Most importantly, union employees often pay less of the

Table 10.7   Percent of Workers with Access, Participating, and Taking-Up
Health Insurance in Private Industry by Union Presence

Percent with Access to Plan	Medical	Dental	Vision	Drug
All private	71	46	29	67
Union private	89	69	54	86
Nonunion private	68	43	26	64
Percent participating				
All private	52	36	22	49
Union private	80	63	48	77
Nonunion private	49	33	19	46
State and local[a]	86	60	43	84
Union public	86	74	57	85
Nonunion public	86	47	29	83
Take-up rates (percent with access who participate)				
All private	74	78	75	74
Union private	90	91	90	90
Nonunion private	72	75	72	71

[a] Data for public sector from Bureau of Labor Statistics: Employee Benefits in State and Local Government, 1998; remainder of table from Bureau of Labor Statistics: Summary National Compensation: Employee Benefits in Private Industry in the United States, March 2006c.

Source: Bureau of Labor Statistics: Summary National Compensation: Employee Benefits in Private Industry in the United States, March 2006c. Tables 1, 2, and 6, pp. 6, 7, and 11 Table 1: "Percent of workers with access to retirement and healthcare benefits, by selected characteristics, private industry, National Compensation Survey, March 2006"; Table 2: Percent of workers participating in retirement and healthcare benefits, by selected characteristics, private industry, National Compensation Survey, March 2006; Table 6: Take-up rates for retirement, healthcare, life insurance, and disability benefits, by selected characteristics, private industry, National Compensation Survey, March 2006 accessed at http://www.bls.gov/ncs/ebs/sp/ebsm0004.pdf; State and Local: Bureau of Labor Statistics: Employee Benefits in State and Local Government, 1998; Table 1: Summary: Participation in selected employee benefit programs, full-time employees, state and local governments, 1998 (in percent), p. 4 accessed at http://www.bls.gov/ncs/ebs/sp/ebbl0018.pdf

premium payment for health insurance coverage than nonunion employees. The data from the 2006 National Compensation Survey shows that union employees pay about 9 percent of premium costs for single coverage although nonunion employees pay more than twice that much, 20 percent, and union employees pay 14 percent of family coverage compared to 33 percent for nonunion.* Almost one-half of union employees make no contribution for single health coverage although only 20 percent nonunion employees make no contribution, and 92 percent of nonunion employees contribute to family coverage compared to only 60 percent of union employees.† The rates of noncontribution for state and local public employers are very similar to those for private sector union members. In 1998, about 49 percent of public employees did not have to make any contribution for self-only coverage and 25 percent made no contribution for family coverage.‡ A more recent study of local governments (ICMA, 2002) found that (a) over 98 percent offered a healthcare plan in medical, dental, vision, and prescription drugs; (b) about 88 percent of offered employees enrolled in one or more plans; (c) almost 45 percent of union employees paid no premium contribution; and (d) the "average" local government offered multiple types of plans (HMO, PPO, POS, and traditional indemnity).

As with unionization, the difference in size of establishment between the public and private sectors affects the employer offer rate for health insurance, the employee participation rates in the benefit, and the cost-sharing arrangements between employer and employee. Larger sized establishments have more slack resources; are able to exercise more power in purchasing health insurance; have more resources to buy the expertise necessary to find, evaluate, and negotiate health insurance benefits; and have more cash available for negotiations with providers (Perry and Cayer, 1997). Perry and Cayer (1997), Streib (1996), and Daley (1993) all found size to be associated with greater levels of health benefit provision and employer cost share in the public sector. Table 10.8 below outlines the impact of difference in size of establishment on various elements related to health insurance benefits in private industry.

---

* Source: Bureau of Labor Statistics: Summary National Compensation: Employee Benefits in Private Industry in the United State, March 2006c. Table 11: Percent of medical insurance premiums paid by employer and employee, by selected characteristics, private industry, National Compensation Survey, March 2006, p. 14 at http://www.bls.gov/ncs/ebs/sp/ebsm0004.pdf accessed March 20, 2007.

† Source: Bureau of Labor Statistics: Summary National Compensation: Employee Benefits in Private Industry in the United State, March 2006c. Tables 12 and 13: Percent of medical plan participants and employer premiums per participant by requirements for employee contribution for single coverage (family coverage), private industry, National Compensation Survey, March 2005, pp. 16, 17 at http://www.bls.gov/ncs/ebs/sp/ebsm0004.pdf accessed March 20, 2007.

‡ Source: Bureau of Labor Statistics: Employee Benefits in State and Local Government, 1998; Table 36: Medical care benefits: Requirements for employee contributions, by fee arrangement, full-time employees, State and Local Government, 1998, p. 43 accessed at http://www.bls.gov/ncs/ebs/sp/ebbl0018.pdf

Table 10.8   Effect of Size of Establishment on Access, Participation, Payment, and Share of Employee Contribution for Health Insurance, Private Industry

Establishment Size of Characteristic	<100 Workers	>100 Workers
Percent workers		
With access to medical plan	59	84
With access to dental plan	31	64
With access to vision plan	20	40
With access to drug plan	56	80
Participating in medical plan	43	63
Participating in dental plan	24	50
Participating in vision plan	14	31
Participating in drug plan	40	60
Percent of establishments		
Offering health benefits	60	96
With no contribution for single	32	18
With no contribution for family	15	11
Percent of health premium cost paid by employee: single coverage	19	18
Percent of health premium cost paid by employee: family coverage	35	26

Source: Bureau of Labor Statistics: Summary National Compensation: Employee Benefits in Private Industry in the United State, March 2006c. Tables 1, 2, and 10, 11, and 12, pp. 5, 6, 14, 15, and 16; Table 1: "Percent of workers with access to retirement and healthcare benefits, by selected characteristics, private industry, National Compensation Survey, March 2006"; Table 2: Percent of workers participating in retirement and healthcare benefits, by selected characteristics, private industry, National Compensation Survey, March 2006; Table 10: Percent of medical insurance premiums paid by employer and employee, by selected characteristics, private industry, National Compensation Survey, March 2006; Tables 11 and 12: Percent of medical plan participants and employer premiums per participant by requirements for employee contribution for single coverage (family coverage), private industry, National Compensation Survey, March 2005, pp. 15, 16 at http://www.bls.gov/ncs/ebs/sp/ebsm0004.pdf accessed March 20, 2007.

198 ■ *Handbook of Employee Benefits and Administration*

In almost all instances, larger private establishments have much higher levels of access and participation for all four types of health benefits—medical, dental, vision, and prescription drug plans. Private establishments with 100 or more employees, like the public sector counterparts, almost universally (96 percent) offer health insurance for employees. When we compare large private and public sector employers we find more similar levels of take-up, participation, and percentage of cost covered by the employer.

A fourth reason for higher health benefit costs in the public sector is related to higher wages. As wages increase, an employee's ability to pay for health premiums, especially for family coverage, increases. If they are able to pay for the benefits, then the take-up rate increases. And when participation increases, employer cost usually increases. The Summary National Compensation Employee Benefits data confirms that where the average wage is $15 per hour or higher, access and participation are considerably higher than when wages are below $15.*

Size, unionization, and wage each appear to be associated with higher health benefit costs for employer, and many of these variables interact with one another. For example, higher salaries are also associated with greater levels of unionization and size of the jurisdiction.† Some preliminary work done by Fronstin (2005), using data from the 2001 Survey of Income and Program Participation, Wave 9, found that even across establishment size, industry, occupation, hours of work and annual earnings, union membership for both the public and private sectors appeared to have an independent effect on health benefit coverage. Likewise, Mishel and Walters (2003) report that six previous studies using Current Population Survey data, Survey of Income and Program Participation data, National Compensation Survey data, and ECI data clearly support a consistent pattern that unionization has a powerful influence on increasing both wage and benefit levels although reducing employee cost sharing on health insurance premiums.

Another source of data also supports the findings of the NCS. The Medical Expenditure Panel-Insurance Component data is collected by the Agency for Healthcare Research and Quality (AHRQ) within the U.S. Department of Health and Human Services. The data from the Insurance Component is based on data from over 42,000 establishments as well as surveys of individuals. Crimmel (2004) analyzed the MEPS-IC 2000 MEPS Full Year Population Characteristics Public Use File (HC-039) data and found results similar to those portrayed in the National Compensation Survey. Persons who belong to unions are about 40 percent more

---

* Source: Bureau of Labor Statistics: Summary National Compensation: Employee Benefits in Private Industry in the United State, March 2005a. Tables 1 and 2, pp. 5, 6. Table 1: "Percent of workers with access to retirement and healthcare benefits, by selected characteristics, private industry, National Compensation Survey, March 2005"; Table 2: Percent of workers participating in retirement and healthcare benefits, by selected characteristics, private industry, National Compensation Survey, March 2005; 16 accessed at http://www. bls.gov/ncs/ebs/sp/ebsm0003.pdf
† ibid.

likely to have coverage; public employees were almost 30 percent more likely to have health insurance coverage through their work; employees in large establishments of 500 or more were twice as likely to have health insurance through their jobs as those employees in the smallest establishments; higher paid employees (above $21/hour) were more than twice as likely as those making minimum wage to have employer-provided health insurance; full-time workers were seven times more likely to have health insurance than part time employees; people working in different industry groups had very different likelihood's of coverage—highest in public administration and manufacturing and lowest in personal service and agricultural; and persons in managerial and administrative occupations had more than twice the likelihood of coverage compared to farm workers. Also, in recent work based on the Current Population Survey, 2001–2005, Gould (2005, p. 4) demonstrates that coverage of employer-provided health insurance varies markedly based on both education and income. Similarly, the Kaiser Family Foundation, Employer Health Benefits 2006 Annual Survey (2006) of both public and private establishments also found the same relationships between health insurance provision and size of establishment, level of salary, unionization, and hours of work. Again, larger firms, settings where there are higher wage employees, and establishments with more full-time and union workers have higher offer rates. At the largest firm size, about 98 percent of establishments continue to offer health benefits.

Stanton and Rutherford (2004, p. 3) use historical MEPS data to show that from 1996 to 2002, offer rates by employers for health insurance increased although eligibility and enrollment rates by employees dropped most likely because the cost of enrollment had risen substantially, and, secondarily, as a result of enrollment in an employee's spouse's employer-sponsored plan. They found (2004, p. 4) that males, full-time employees, union members, workers in public administration or the public sector, workers in larger establishments, and workers with lower or no premiums are much more likely to enroll in health insurance programs offered by their employer.

In addition to higher rates of participation in health insurance benefit programs in the public sector, the average cost of the premium for health insurance for both single employee coverage and family coverage is higher in the public sector. Table 10.9 presents MEPS-IC data for premium costs and employee contribution to premium for all private employers, private employers with union presence, and all public employers.

Premium costs for both single and family coverage are highest in the public sector, and the employee contribution to premium in the public sector is lowest of the three groups. However, the premium cost difference between private firms with a union and the public entities is minimal (averaging about 3 percent difference across both plans). Again, the public sector employer covers a much greater portion of the cost of the premium—91 percent for public employers versus 83 percent private for single premium cost and 82 percent versus 25 percent for family premium cost. Also, the cost of the total premium is about 13 percent higher in the public sector for single coverage and about 2 percent higher for family coverage.

Table 10.9 Difference between Public and Private Sectors in Cost of Insurance Premium and Employee Contribution to Premium, by Type of Coverage: Self or Family, 2005

	Private	*Union Private*	*Public*
Total premium cost single	$3991	$4081	$4595
Total contribution by employee (percent)	723 (18)	681 (17)	409 (9)
Total premium cost family	10,728	10,539	11,308
Total contribution by employee (percent)	2584 (24)	1908 (18)	2059 (18)

Note: Percent of employee (EE) contribution in parenthesis.

Source: MEPS-IC data tabulated from query provided at www.meps.ahrq.gov/ mepsweb/data_stats/ from Tables III.C.1, III.C.2, III.C.3, III.D.2, III.D.3, I.C.1, I.C.2, I.C.3, I.D.2, I.D.3.

Similarly, there is an impact because of size. In 2002, the Kaiser Family Foundation (KFF) issued a report on State Employee Health Plans (2002). The KFF report compared state employee plans with a sample of national firms. The findings from that study demonstrate jumbo-sized public and private employers pay almost identical healthcare premiums, but the public employer pays a larger portion of the total cost than jumbo private employers.

Any difference in price of premiums between the two sectors is likely the result of many factors. In the highly unionized public sector, there are usually much higher transaction costs for negotiating and bidding health benefits. Similarly, the difference in cost may reflect differences in the types and quality of benefits offered under the medical plan or the range of plans offered because of larger-size establishments and higher levels of unionization. Regional or local market considerations may skew premium cost-setting practices of insurance or service providers. Different levels of risk and age distribution for many public sector jobs may result in more expensive claims and, therefore, higher premium costs.

Another reason that health insurance benefit costs might be higher in the public sector is that public managers strongly believe and perceive that high levels of health benefits are crucial for recruiting and retaining public employees. As employers, public establishments compete with other public and private employers in the local, regional, and national labor markets to attract high quality applicants and retain highly skilled employees. All levels of government face a serious challenge in finding sufficiently skilled employees to fill these critical positions, especially in management positions (Hall, 2004; Lancaster and Stillman, 2005; MSPB, 2007). Because the healthcare benefit remains the most highly valued benefit for public sector applicants and employees (Bergmann, et al., 1994; Roberts et al., 2004; OPM, 2005), elected officials and managers may perceive a need to be strategically sensitive to the mix of benefits that will keep and attract highly skilled employees.

Christianson and Trude (2003) in their multi-year study found that labor market consideration was the primary driver of health benefits decision making among both public and private employers during the entire period of the study. On the basis of interviews from this same tracking study conducted among twenty-one public employers in twelve communities across six years, Watts et al. (2003) found that all public employers and benefits specialists interviewed (over 100) perceived that health benefits were extremely important in attracting and retaining employees across all skill categories because the respondents viewed their jurisdictions as less salary competitive than private firms. Marquis and Long (2001) also found that small employers' decisions about the provision and amount of health insurance for employees were affected by local market employment conditions. Similarly, city and county managers continue to express high levels of concern about their ability to find adequate numbers of qualified employees at the local level (ICMA, 2002; Brennan et al., 2005). These same concerns about recruitment and retention by private sector managers were again echoed in a report issued by the U.S. Government Accountability Office (2006) about private employers and their rising benefit costs.

Because public employers want to minimize the high transactional costs of creating many different types of plans for different employee groups, the health benefit level (and therefore cost) is set at a higher level than necessary to retain most employees, but sufficiently high to retain those employees most in demand—high level performers in hard-to-fill, highly specialized, or undesirable occupations. Similarly, many state or local laws may preclude establishing different sets of benefits for different employee groups, and, therefore, the highest level of benefit is set for most or all employees of the government unit or multi-occupational bargaining unit. As any local government negotiator knows, most teachers, police, and fire unions are very aware of what other similar public unions are being paid and they bargain for the highest possible health benefits within their area of labor market competition. From the standpoint of public managers and elected officials facing very high levels of retirements of public employees in the next few years or high levels of turnover for critical employees such as police officers and teachers, reducing or significantly altering the mix of health benefits could have disastrous consequences. Keeping health benefit may be the most prudent course to assure that critical public services are maintained.

10.6 Conclusion

The analysis of wage and salary data from a variety of sources suggests that "average" wages and benefits between the sectors appear to be converging when we control for such factors as size of establishment, level of unionization, and occupational differences between the sectors. When changes in the constant ECI are evaluated, increases in state and local public sector wage compensation costs have kept pace with (but not exceeded), overall private sector real wage compensation cost increases and private union real wage compensation costs during the same period. Both sectors' employer compensation cost increases are below increases in nonfarm productivity and the real growth of the U.S. economy.

The evaluation of the ECEC data shows that although public sector wages are higher than private sector wages, the wage differences are much closer when we compare the highly unionized public sector with private establishments with a union presence. Wages also tend to converge when we compare wages in the public sector that is mostly composed of large-sized establishments with large-sized private sector establishments. When we use the largest federal data source, the Quarterly Census of Employee Wages, we find wage convergence between the sectors. Other survey analyses show a consistent relationship between sizes of establishment, unionization, hours of work, and occupation with wage level. A preliminary analysis of the median public sector worker indicates that they are more likely college educated, working full-time, unionized, and working in very large establishments than the median private sector worker. When we compare public sector wages with these same set of conditions in the private sector, most, if not all wage disparity, disappears.

The disparity in employer costs for health benefits between the sectors is growing greater over time. In part, much of the disparity can be explained by the typically larger size, and higher level of unionization and higher wages in the public sector. All of these factors are strongly associated with higher rates of offering, participating in, and taking-up health benefits.

Higher ratios of employer contribution to health insurance premiums in the public sector than in the private sector are the likely result of higher levels of unionization in the public sector and historical traditions of public employer payment of the entire premium cost in a number of state governments (NCSL, 2005). Slightly higher premium costs in the public sector may be associated with locality differences where a greater number of public employees live in those communities with higher health service and health insurance costs. Finally, the disparity also reflects public managers' desires to compete effectively in a seller's labor market during periods when public service is not highly valued by job applicants, and high turnover and retirement levels may only increase problems of recruitment and retention. Public officials are very concerned about their ability to provide high quality services critically needed by the citizens.

The data and the empirically based findings about intention and behavior of public managers suggest that the median public sector employee has very similar wages and health benefits when compared to similarly situated private employees in unionized, large-sized, white-collared, highly educated, and well-paid (for health benefit compensation purposes) employment settings. Currently, our ability to fully evaluate wage and salary differences between the public and private sectors is hampered by the lack of a uniform, large public and private establishment sample data set that contains information about most of the critical variables that are theoretically or empirically associated with wage and benefit level determination. This work must come next if we are to understand more fully the relationship among these variables within and across the public and private sectors and how these variables affects change in the major components of employee compensation.

Data sets based on these surveys and censuses are accessible through the Internet and are excellent resources for compensation and benefits specialists and analysts. For an excellent analysis of the data available at the national level, see Buckley and Van Glezen (2004). Most of these sources have public query ports where the analyst can individualize the data and years accessed. Instructions and transparent drop-down menus are relatively easy to use. The analyst can use the information to compare wages and benefits at the local, state, regional, national, occupational, and sector levels.

References

Beland, D. and J.S. Hacker. 2004. Ideas, private institutions and American welfare state exceptionalism: The case of health and old-age insurance, 1915–1965. *International Journal of Social Welfare* 13(1):42–54.

Belman, D. and J. Heywood. 1993. The truth about public employees: Underpaid or overpaid? Briefing paper #40, Economic Policy Institute, Washington, DC: April. http://www.epinet.org/briefingpapers/1993_bp_truth.pdf (accessed April 19, 2007).

Bergmann, T.J., M.A. Bergmann, and J.L. Gahn. 1994. How important are employee benefits to public sector employees? *Public Personnel Management* 23(3):397–406.

Braden, B.R. and S.L. Hyland. 1993. Cost of employee compensation in public and private sectors. *Monthly Labor Review* 116(5):14–21.

Brennan, C., E. Wheel, and C. Hoene. 2005. The State of America's Cities 2005: The annual opinion survey of municipal elected officials. Washington, DC: National League of Cities. http://www.nlc.org/ASSETS/5C8EBE817F604AE093F6072BD398F7E0/rmpsoacrpt05.pdf (April 21, 2007).

Buchmueller, T., J.D. Nardo, and R. Valletta. 2001. *Union Effects on Health Insurance Provision and Coverage in the United States.* Washington DC: National Bureau of Economic Research, U.S. Department of Labor. Working Paper 8238, April 2001. http://www.nber.org/papers/w8238 (October 31, 2005).

Buckley, J. 1996. Pay in private industry and state and local governments, 1994. *Compensation and Working Conditions* September:22–26.

Buckley, J. and R.W. Van Glezen. 2004. Federal statistics on healthcare benefits and cost trends: An overview. *Monthly Labor Review* 127(11):43–56. http://www.bls.gov/opub/mlr/2004/11/art5full.pdf (October 28, 2005).

Byrnes, N. and C. Palmeri. 2005. Sinkhole: How public pension promises are draining state and city budgets. *Business Week* June 13, 2005, 3937.

Christianson, J.B. and S. Trude. 2003. Managing costs, managing benefits: Employer decisions in local health care markets. *Health Services Research* 38(1):357–373.

Cover, B. 2005. A comparison of occupational employment and wages in metropolitan areas and nonmetropolitan areas. Publication of the Division of Occupational Employment Statistics, Bureau of Labor Statistics, U.S. Department of Labor. http://www.bls.gov/oes/2004/may/met.pdf (March 21, 2007).

Crimmel, B.L. 2004. Differentials in employment-related health insurance coverage–2000. Statistical Brief #10: June 2004. Agency for Healthcare Research and Quality, Rockville, Maryland. Accessed at http://www.meps.ahrq.gov/papers/st10/stat10.htm. (December 20, 2005).

Daley, D. 1993. Health care benefits in the public sector: An examination of availability, size, and managerial effects among North Carolina municipalities. *International Journal of Public Administration* 16(10):1519–1539.

DeNavas-Walt, C., B.D. Proctor, and R.J. Mills. 2004. U.S. Department of Commerce, Census Bureau, Current Population Reports. 2004. "Income, Poverty, and Health Insurance Coverage in the United States: 2003." P60–P226, issued August 2004.

Fisher, R.C. 1988. *State and Local Public Finance.* Glenview, Illinois: Scott, Foresman.

Fronstin, P. 2005. Union status and employment-based health benefits, facts from EBRI: The basics of social security, new publications and Internet sites. *Employee Benefit Research Institute Notes* May 26(5):2–6. http://www.ebri.org/publications/notes/index.cfm?fa=notesDisp&content_id=3327 (November 28, 2005).

Fronstin, P. 2005a. Employment-based health benefits: Trends in access and coverage. *Employee Benefit Research Institute Issue Brief* August:284. http://www.ebri.org/pdf/briefspdf/EBRI_IB_08-20051.pdf (March 2, 2007).

Freeman, R.B. and J.L. Medoff. 1984. *What do unions do?* New York: Basic Books.

Freeman, R.B. and C. Ichniowski. 1988. *When public sector workers unionize.* A National Bureau of Economic Research project report. Chicago: University of Chicago Press.

Gabel, J., G. Claxton, I. Gil, J. Pickreign, H. Whitmore, B. Finder, S. Hawkins, and D. Rowland. 2005. Health benefits in 2005: Premium increases slow to single digit but coverage continues to Erode. *Health Affairs* 24(5):1273–1280.

Gould, E. 2005. Prognosis worsens for workers' health care: Fourth consecutive year of decline in employer-provided insurance coverage. Briefing Paper #167. Economic Policy Institute, Washington, DC: October. http://www.epi.org/content.cfm/bp167 (January 30, 2006).

Hall, M. 2004. Police, fire departments see shortages across USA. USA Today. Updated 11/29/04. http://www.usatoday.com/news/nation/2004-11-28-police-shortages-cover_x.htm (November 30, 2005).

Hajiha, F. 2003. Employment by occupational group and establishment size. Division of Occupational and Administrative Statistics, Bureau of Labor Statistics, U.S. Department of Labor. http://www.bls.gov/oes/2003/may/employment.pdf (March 21, 2007).

Hansen, F. 2004. Kill or be killed. *Workforce Management* 83(8):79–80.

Hunter, W.J. and C.H. Rankin. 1988. The composition of public sector compensation: The effects of unionization and bureaucratic size. *Journal of Labor Research* 9(1):29–42.

Inglehart, J. 2004. The challenges facing private health insurance. *Health Affairs* 23(6):9–10.

International City/County Management Association. 1999. Labor management relations 1999. Washington, DC: ICMA. http://www.icma.org/upload/bc/attach/{4EA4F29B-3850-4E7C-9DE1-1866EE5AF646}lmr1999web.pdf (November 22, 2005).

International City/County Management Association. 2002. Health care plans for local government employees, 2002. Washington, DC: ICMA. http://www.icma.org/upload/bc/attach/{17DEA897-90B8-4D6E-BA8D-7751E59D27B8}hcare2002web.pdf (November 22, 2005).

Kaiser Family Foundation and Health Research and Educational Trust. 2002. State Employee Health Plans. http://www.kff.org/insurance/upload/Kaiser-HRET-Survey-2002-State-Employee-Health-Plans-Report.pdf (April 10, 2007).

Kaiser Family Foundation. 2005. Trends and indicators in the changing health care marketplace. Publication Number 7031. http://www.kff.org/insurance/7031/index.cfm (November 22, 2005).

Kaiser Family Foundation and Health Research and Educational Trust. 2006. Employer Health Benefits 2006 Annual Survey. September 2006. http://www.kff.org/insurance/7315/sections/ehbs05-3-2.cfm. (November 15, 2006).

Lancaster, L.C. and D. Stillman. 2005. If I pass the Baton, who will grab it? Creating bench strength in public management. *Public Management* 87(8):8–15.

Long, S.H. and M.S. Marquis. 1999. Comparing employee health benefits in the public and private sectors, 1997. *Health Affairs* 18(6):183–193.

Marquis, M.S. and S.H. Long. 2001. Employer health insurance and local labor market conditions. *International Journal of Health Care Finance and Economics* 1(3–4): 273–292.

McDonnell, K. 2005. Benefit cost comparisons between state and local governments and private-sector employers. *Employee Benefit Research Institute Notes* April, 26(4):2–11. http://www.ebri.org/pdf/notespdf/0405notes.pdf (November 28, 2005).

Meisenheimer, J.R. 2005. Real compensation, 1979–2003: Analysis from several data sources. *Monthly Labor Review* 128(5):3–22. http://www.bls.gov/opub/mlr/2005/05/art1full.pdf (September 11, 2006).

Miller, G.H. Jr. 1993. Profligacy or prudence? Changes in employment and compensation of state and local government workers. *Public Budgeting and Finance*, Spring: 95–106.

Miller, M. 1996. The public-private pay debate: What do the data show? *Monthly Labor Review* 119(5):18–29. http://www.bls.gov/opub/mlr/1996/05/art2full.pdf (April 23, 2007).

Mishel, L. and M. Walters. 2003. How Unions help all workers. Briefing Paper #143 Economic Policy Institute, Washington DC. August. http://www.epinet.org/content.cfm/briefingpapers_bp143 (November 15, 2005).

Monthly Labor Review. 2006. Table 22 Quarterly Census of Employment: 10 Largest Counties, fourth quarter 2003, 191(1):86. http://www.bls.gov/opub/mlr/2006/01/cls0601.pdf (September 5, 2006).

National Council of State Legislatures. 2005. Chart of State Employee Health Premiums. Updated May 2005 at http://64.82.65.67/health/StateEmpl-healthpremiums04.xls (March 20, 2007).

Perry, R.W. and N.J. Cayer. 1997. Factors affecting municipal satisfaction with health care plans. *Review of Public Personnel Administration* 17(2):5–19.

Porter, F. and R. Keller. 1981. Public and private pay levels: A comparison in large labor markets. *Monthly Labor Review*. 104(7):22–26. http://www.bls.gov/opub/mlr/1981/07/art3full.pdf (April 20, 2007).

Poterba, J. and K. Rueben. 1994. The Distribution of Public Sector Wage Premia: New Evidence Using Quantile Regression Methods. NBER Working Paper Series. Working Paper 4734, May.

Revell, J. 2005. The great state health-care giveaway. *Fortune*, May 2, 2005 151:9.

Roberts, G.E., J.A. Gianakis, C. McCue, and X. Wang. 2004. Traditional and family-friendly benefits practices in local governments: Results from a national survey. *Public Personnel Management* 33(3):291–306.

Rosow, J.M. 1976. Public sector pay and benefits. *Public Administration Review*. 365(Sep-Oct):538–543.

Schumann, R.E. 1987. State and local government pay increases outpace five-year rise in private industry. *Monthly Labor Review*. 110(2):18–20. http://www.bls.gov/opub/mlr/1987/02/art3full.pdf (October 31, 2005).

Shahpoori, K.P. and J. Smith. 2005. Wages in Profit and Nonprofit Hospitals and Universities. Compensation and Working Conditions Online. U.S. Department of Labor, Bureau of Labor Statistics. Posted June 29, 2005 at http://www.bls.gov/opub/cwc/cm20050624ar01p1.htm (March 19, 2007).

Stanton, M.W. and M. Rutherford. 2004. Employer-sponsored health insurance: Trends in cost and access. Agency for Healthcare Research and Quality Publication No. 04-0085. Research in Action Issue 17. http://www.ahrq.gov/research/empspria/empspria.pdf (April 16, 2006).

Streib, G. 1996. Specialty health care services in municipal government. *Review of Public Personnel Administration* 16(2):57–72.

United States Congressional Budget Office. 2007. Characteristics and Pay of Federal Civilian Employees. CBO Paper 7874, March. http://www.cbo.gov/ftpdocs/78xx/doc7874/03-15-Federal_Personnel.pdf (April 9, 2007).

United States Congressional Budget Office. 2007a. Labor Productivity: Developments since 1995. CBO Paper, March. http://www.cbo.gov/ftpdocs/79xx/doc7910/03-26-Labor.pdf (April 9, 2007).

United States Department of Commerce. Bureau of the Census. 2004. Census of Governments Compendium of Public Employment, 2002, Volume III, issued September 2004 at http://www.census.gov/prod/2004pubs/gc023x2.pdf (February 3, 2006).

U.S. Department of Commerce, Bureau of the Census. 2004a. Compendium of Public Employment Table 20. Distribution of Local Governments and Full-Time Equivalent Employment by Employment-Size Group, Type of Government, and State: March 2002, Volume III published September 2004, 248–49 at http://www.census.gov/prod/2004pubs/gc023x2.pdf accessed March 20, 2007.

United States Department of Labor. Bureau of Labor Statistics. 1998. Employee Benefits in State and Local Government, 1998. http://www.bls.gov/ncs/ebs/sp/ebbl0018.pdf (March 19, 2007).

United States Department of Labor. Bureau of Labor Statistics. 2005. Employment Cost Index Constant Dollar Historical Listing (June 1989=100), dated July 29, 2005. http://www.bls.gov/web/econst.pdf (December 3, 2005).

United States Department of Labor. Bureau of Labor Statistics. 2005a. Summary National Compensation: Employee Benefits in Private Industry in the United State, March 2005, dated August 2005. http://www.bls.gov/ncs/ocs/sp/ncbl0832.pdf (April 23, 2007).

United States Department of Bureau of Labor Statistics. 2005b. Employment and Wages, Annual Averages. http://www.bls.gov/cew/ew05table2.pdf accessed March 19, 2007.

United States Department of Bureau of Labor Statistics. 2005c. Summary, United States: Mean hourly earnings and weekly hours by selected characteristics, private industry and State and local government, National Compensation Survey, June 2005" at http://www.bls.gov/ncs/ocs/sp/ncbl0832.pdf accessed on March 19, 2007.

United States Department of Labor. Bureau of Labor Statistics. 2005d. Computed from information contained in Quarterly Census of Employment and Wages at http://www.bls.gov/cew/ew05table4.pdf accessed March 21, 2007.

United States Department of Labor. Bureau of Labor Statistics. 2006. National Compensation Survey: Occupational Wages in the United States, June 2006. http://www.bls.gov/ncs/ocs/sp/ncbl0832.pdf (April 23, 2007).

United States Department of Labor. Bureau of Labor Statistics. 2006a. National Compensation Survey: Employee Benefits in Private Industry in the United States, March 2006. http://www.bls.gov/ncs/ebs/sp/ebsm0004.pdf (April 23, 2007).

United States Department of Labor. Bureau of Labor Statistics. 2006b. National Compensation Survey: Occupational Wages in the United States, June 2005. http://www.bls.gov/ncs/ocs/sp/ncbl0832.pdf (April 23, 2007).

United States Department of Bureau of Labor Statistics. 2006c. Summary National Compensation: Employee Benefits in Private Industry in the United State March 2006.

United States Department of Labor. Bureau of Labor Statistics. 2007. Union Members Summary dated January 25. http://stats.bls.gov/news/release/pdf/union2.htm. (March 20, 2007).

United States Department of Labor. Bureau of Labor Statistics. 2007a. Public access database. Series PRS85006093: Output per Hour, Nonfarm Business 1991 through 2006." http://data.bls.gov/PDQ/servlet/SurveyOutputServlet (April 19, 2007).

United States Department of Labor. Bureau of Labor Statistics. 2007b. Employment Cost Index Historical Listing Constant-dollar March 2001–December 2006 (December 2005=100). http://www.bls.gov/web/ecconstnaics.pdf (March 19, 2007).

United States Department of Labor. Bureau of Labor Statistics. 2007c. Employment Cost Index Historical Listing Constant-dollar 1975. http://www.bls.gov/web/ecconst.pdf (March 19, 2007).

United States Department of Labor. Bureau of Labor Statistics. 2007d. Employer Costs for Employee Compensation, Historical Listing, (Quarterly) 2004–2006. http://www.bls.gov/ncs/ect/sp/ececqrtn.pdf (March 19, 2007).

U.S. Government Accountability Office. 2006. Report Number GAO-06-285 Employer Spending on Benefits Has Grown Faster Than Wages, Due Largely to Rising Costs for Health Insurance and Retirement Benefits. Washington, DC.

United States Merit System Protection Board. 2007. Accomplishing Our Mission: Results of the Merit Principles Survey 2005. February 2007. http://www.mspb.gov/studies/mspbstudiespage.html (April 10, 2007).

U.S. Merit System Protection Board. 2007a. Understanding the Federal Workforce: Compare with Care *Issues of Merit* January 2007. http://www.mspb.gov/studies/newsletters/07jannws/07jannws.pdf (April 10, 2007).

United States Office of Personnel Management. 2005. 2004 Employee Benefits Survey. http://www.opm.gov/employment_and_benefits/survey/benefitssurveyresults.asp (November 22, 2005).

Watts, C., J.B. Christianson, L. Heineccius, and S. Trude. 2003. The role of public employers in a changing health care market. *Health Affairs* 22(1):173–180.

Wong, J. 1997. Health care finance in the United States: Past, present, and future. *International Journal of Public Administration* 20(6):1297–1315.

Bibliography

United States Department of Health and Human Services. Agency for Healthcare Research and Quality. Insurance Component of the Medical Expenditure Panel Survey, 2003. http://www.meps.ahcpr.gov/Data_Pub/IC_Tables.htm (April 20, 2007).

United States. Department of Commerce. Bureau of the Census. 2005. *Statistical Abstract of the United States.* p. 463 Table #698 Consumer Price Indexes (CPI-U) by Major Groups: 1980 to 2003. http://www.census.gov/prod/2004pubs/04statab/prices.pdf (September 30, 2005).

United States Department of Labor. Bureau of Labor Statistics. 2005a. News: Employer Costs for Employee Compensation. September 21, 2005. http://www.bls.gov/news.release/pdf/ecec.pdf (November 30, 2005).

United States Department of Labor. Bureau of Labor Statistics. 2005b. National Compensation Survey: Employee Benefits in Private Industry in the United States, March 2005, Summary 05–01. ftp://ftp.bls.gov/pub/news.release/ebs2.txt (November 29, 2005).

United States Department of Labor. Bureau of Labor Statistics. 2005c. Consumer Price Index All Urban Consumer–(CPI-U) U.S. city average 1982–84=100, dated October 14, 2005. ftp://ftp.bls.gov/pub/special.requests/cpi/cpiai.txt (October 21, 2005).

United States Department of Labor. Bureau of Labor Statistics. 2005d. National Compensation Survey, July 2004, National Compensation Survey: Occupational Wages in the United States, dated September 2005 at http://www.bls.gov/ncs/ocs/sp/ncbl0757.pdf (April 23, 2007).

United States Government Accountability Office. 2005e. Report Number GAO-05-856 Federal Employees Health Benefits Program: Competition and Other Factors Linked to Wide Variation in Health Care Prices. http://www.gao.gov/new.items/d05856.pdf (December 5, 2005).

United States Department of Labor. Bureau of Labor Statistics. 2006. Quarterly Census of Employment and Wages. December 2005. http://www.bls.gov/cew/cewbultn05.htm#Charts%20and%20Maps (March 19, 2007).

United States Department of Labor. Bureau of Economic Analysis, Current-Dollar and "Real" Gross Domestic Product (seasonally adjusted annual rates) http://www.bea.gov/national/nipaweb/TableView.asp#Mid (April 23, 2007).

United States Department of Labor. Bureau of Labor Statistics. 2007a. Current Employment Statistics, Quarterly Census of Employment and Wages. http://data.bls.gov/cgi-bin/surveymost?ce (March 23, 2007).

United States Department of Labor. Bureau of Labor Statistics. 2007b. Employer Costs for Employee Compensation, 1986–1999. http://www.bls.gov/ncs/ect/sp/ecbl0013.pdf (March 31, 2007).

FINANCIAL MANAGEMENT AND EMPLOYEE BENEFITS

Chapter 11

Financial Management Challenges of Other Postemployment Benefits

Justin Marlowe

CONTENTS

11.1   Introduction

The Governmental Accounting Standards Board (GASB) recently adopted rules that require state and local governments to report their long-term costs for retiree healthcare and other (i.e., nonpension) postemployment benefits (OPEB).* Most jurisdictions provide these benefits on a pay-as-you-go basis, meaning they simply pay employee healthcare costs when those costs come due. But under these new accounting rules, they will estimate and report how much it will cost in today's dollars to provide those benefits to both current and future retirees. These rules are motivated in part by a widely shared concern that the impending baby boom retirement, consistent healthcare cost inflation, and other trends will increase OPEB costs beyond what most jurisdictions can handle on a pay-as-you-go basis (Borger et al. 2006; Follette and Scheiner 2005; Burns 2007). Providing information today about future OPEB costs, the logic suggests, is an important first step toward helping citizens and policy makers understand and anticipate the long-term financial implications of providing these benefits.[†]

Early indications suggest those implications are substantial. For instance, some estimates show the subnational[‡] government OPEB liability for all current and future retirees could exceed $2 trillion (Edwards and Gokhale 2006; Hume 2006). Actuarial estimates for certain jurisdictions reinforce the accuracy of those projections. For example, recent financial audits report OPEB liabilities attributable to the city of Los Angeles of $48 billion, $20 billion, $15 billion, and $10 billion for state, county, city, and school district employees, respectively. Together, these liabilities equate to $8000 for each of Los Angeles' approximately 4 million residents. Large and small jurisdictions alike have reported proportionately large liabilities.

These costs are expected to present a formidable financial management challenge for many jurisdictions. In fact, some have likened OPEB liabilities to a doomsday scenario that could lead to everything from reductions of retiree benefits to drastic cutbacks in basic government services. That realignment strategies put forth by General Motors, Northwest Airlines, and other blue chip American corporations have called for draconian cuts in retiree benefits, has exacerbated hese concerns. Regardless of why these liabilities became so large, there is certainly evidence that many jurisdictions are simply unable to meet them and will have no choice but to renege on OPEB promises.

---

* For more on OPEB accounting and reporting see Chapter 14, this volume, Wisniewski (2005), and Voorhees (2005).
† OPEB technically includes health insurance, life insurance, disability and unemployment coverage, and any benefits other than pensions. This analysis looks exclusively at health insurance costs, as these costs are clearly the most expensive and sought-after of OPEB's many components.
‡ Subnational includes state governments, local governments, school districts, and special districts like utilities and transit districts.

But by contrast, consider that the Texas state legislature recently passed legislation allowing its governments to simply opt out of reporting OPEB liabilities. This legislation follows from the claim that OPEB costs are, in fact, not liabilities because they are not based on long-term contractual agreements between jurisdictions and employees. By implication, these benefits are subject to annual legislative appropriation, so there is technically no such thing as an OPEB liability. Several large Texas cities and school districts have publicly stated their intention to report their OPEB liabilities despite this legislation, but the message is clear—OPEB do not warrant unique financial disclosures because they are not directly connected to a jurisdiction's long-term financial condition.

These two perspectives are at the opposite ends of what has emerged as a central issue in the OPEB debate: To what extent are jurisdictions unable, rather than unwilling to pay these liabilities? The prevailing wisdom seems to be that several, perhaps the majority of subnational governments fall in the inability to pay category. But to date there has been no systematic empirical analysis of these trends. This chapter provides that analysis by presenting a variety of OPEB-related information for several hundred local governments, including estimates of OPEB liabilities, the relationship between those liabilities and fiscal capacity available to address them, and the relationship between these liabilities and other "hard" liabilities like debt and pension obligations.

The results suggest there is little evidence of inability to pay among most of the jurisdictions examined here. To be sure, many have large and potentially daunting liabilities. But for most jurisdictions, particularly small- to mid-sized organizations, OPEB liabilities are not nearly the same magnitude as larger agencies that have been heretofore singled out as unable to pay. Moreover, the distribution of OPEB liabilities does not appear to follow any clear pattern relative to other liabilities, fiscal capacity, or even demographic and institutional characteristics.

This is not to suggest that unwillingness to pay is not its own substantial challenge. For this reason the second half of this chapter explores what strategies are available to address OPEB liabilities, and whether those strategies have been employed. The findings on that issue indicate most jurisdictions do not yet employ many of the potentially useful strategies for OPEB cost savings and cost control. This lends additional support to the claim that most jurisdictions have at least some flexibility and latitude to address these issues, and to overcome any potential unwillingness to pay.

This chapter proceeds in four parts. The first section outlines the scope of the OPEB challenge by presenting the previously mentioned OPEB estimates. The second section describes the key financial management challenges of OPEB. It draws upon financial information and survey data to illustrate the financial management options available to jurisdictions, and the implications of those different options. The third section discusses potential OPEB management strategies and which among those strategies have been used thus far. The final section summarizes these findings and their implications for public employee benefits management.

11.2 OPEB Liability Estimates

11.2.1 Background

The new OPEB reporting rules are outlined in two GASB statements: statement 43—"Financial Reporting for Postemployment Benefits Other than Pensions" (i.e., GASB 43) and statement 45—"Accounting and Financial Reporting by Employers for Postemployment Benefits Other than Pensions" (i.e., GASB 45). Agencies that wish to remain compliant with generally accepted accounting principles by implementing these standards are required to do two basic things. First, they must estimate the size of their OPEB liability for all current retirees and all employees who are expected to retire. This estimate, which for most jurisdictions will be conducted by a professional actuary, will then be compared to the assets the jurisdiction has designated to cover that liability. The difference between the designated plan assets and the estimated plan liability is the jurisdiction's unfunded OPEB liability, and will be reported in the footnotes to the jurisdiction's financial statements. Two recent surveys, one a nationwide survey of 321 local government finance officers co-conducted by the author, and one by AllianceBernstein (2006) revealed that approximately 20 percent of local governments have designated assets for OPEB plan funding, and of that 20 percent, less than 5 percent have funded their OPEB liability in full. Those findings allow us to safely conclude that for most jurisdictions the actuarial estimate of the OPEB liability is, in fact, the OPEB liability that will be disclosed in the financial statements.

With the total OPEB liability established, agencies must then report how, if at all, they plan to address that liability. The standards do not require a jurisdiction to address the liability, although most agree ignoring it is not prudent. Most jurisdictions will amortize their liability over several years, with the annual amount identified in that amortization plan designated as the annual required contribution. Those annual contributions will eventually draw the OPEB liability down to zero. If those contributions are not made in full, the difference between required and actual contributions is reported as a liability.

Actuarial estimates of total OPEB liabilities can be derived from a model that requires two basic pieces of information—the number of employees who participate in its healthcare plan and its per employee healthcare costs. This model's structure and simplifying assumptions are described in further detail in the appendix. It was implemented here using data from the International City/County Management Association's "Healthcare Benefits Survey" (Moulder 2004) which was mailed in 2001–2002 to 7856 city and county governments with populations of 2500 or greater. Usable responses were received from 3101 jurisdictions, for an overall response rate of just under 40 percent. The survey asked each jurisdiction to identify what types of healthcare benefits it offered employees, the number of employees who receive those benefits, approximate benefit costs, and how the jurisdiction had addressed or planned to address increases in those costs.

A necessary first step in understanding the contours of OPEB is to simply compare a jurisdiction's OPEB liability to its key demographic and institutional characteristics. This analysis examines four such characteristics. Population is included because larger jurisdictions with more employees are expected to leverage greater buying power in the healthcare market and have subsequently lower per employee costs and OPEB liabilities. Location is included because conventional wisdom suggests the costs of identical healthcare products vary a great deal across regions due to the demand for services, concentration of specialists, and other factors. Whether the jurisdiction is a central city, a suburb, or an independent (i.e., smaller, regional center) city is included for the same reason. By contrast, because council-manager governments have been shown to be more efficient in certain spending areas (Hays and Chang 1990; Stumm and Corrigan 1998; Campbell and Turnbull 2003; Jung 2006) these estimates are also broken out by whether the jurisdiction is a council-manager (or county administrator) or mayor-council format.

This survey data was also combined with data from the comprehensive annual financial reports of several hundred local governments to facilitate a comparison of each jurisdiction's estimated OPEB liability to three key aspects of its financial condition. The first is a modification of the "current ratio" defined here as the jurisdiction's general fund revenues to its general fund expenditures. Higher values on this ratio suggest more year to year budget flexibility. The second is the jurisdiction's per capita pension obligation, which was calculated by subtracting its pension plan liabilities from its plan assets* and dividing the difference by its population. Most jurisdictions are contractually obligated to pay their pension liabilities, so contrasting them against OPEB provides some indication of whether OPEB are competing with other retiree benefits for scare financial resources. The third indicator is the jurisdiction's per capita outstanding debt obligations.† Like pensions, debt is a "hard" obligation that could crowd out OPEB payments. Descriptive statistics for the continuous variables are reported in Table 11.1.

11.2.2 Results and Trends

Table 11.2 presents the OPEB liability estimates for a national sample of 457 jurisdictions. Each column presents estimates derived from different assumptions about three key factors, annual healthcare cost growth, the discount rate (i.e., the

---

* This measure is prone to error because jurisdictions use different methods to calculate pension obligations. Nonetheless, those errors are not believed to have led to improper conclusions about the OPEB/pension relationship.

† There were no noticeable differences between direct and overlapping debt.

Table 11.1 Descriptive Statistics for Continuous Variables

	Population	Current Ratio	Pension ($)	Debt ($)
Mean	70,032	1.05	4,276.00	8,350.00
Minimum	2,558	0.26	4,150.00	—
First quartile	10,881	0.94	115.00	1.00
Second quartile	22,053	0.99	9.00	136.00
Third quartile	37,200	1.05	1.00	503.00
Fourth quartile	77,753	1.13	76.00	1,116.00
Maximum	1,682,585	2.69	54,831.00	392,678.00

pace at which money loses value over time due to inflation and other factors), and the rate at which Medicare and other healthcare subsidies offset an employer's cost for retiree healthcare. This table presents three different scenarios. The "Low" scenario is based on 8 percent annual healthcare cost growth, a discount rate of 5 percent, and a 30 percent subsidy in retiree healthcare costs. The "Medium" scenario assumes 12 percent annual healthcare cost growth, a discount rate of 3 percent, and a 30 percent subsidy. The "High" scenario assumes 15 percent annual cost growth, a 3 percent discount rate, and no subsidy. The reported estimates are the mean for each category of the sorting variables listed above. The difference statistics report whether the mean estimate for any category is significantly different from the mean estimate in the other categories of that same variable.* These tests allow us to examine whether higher OPEB estimates cluster in any discernible way.

This analysis identifies three key trends. First, different assumptions bring about nontrivial differences in the estimated OPEB liabilities. The difference between the mean low and medium estimates was more than 150 percent the value of the former. Differences between the medium and high estimates are even more pronounced.

Second, most OPEB liabilities are manageably sized. To determine that size some additional ratios were calculated by comparing each jurisdiction's total

---

* For the form of government variable that difference was tested with a two-tailed t test assuming unequal variance. For the other variables it was tested with a one way analysis of variance test.

Table 11.2 Estimated OPEB Liabilities by Demographic Characteristics

	N	Low		Medium		High	
		Mean ($)	Difference	Mean ($)	Difference	Mean ($)	Difference
All jurisdictions	457	53.27		135.91		281.08	
Form of government			-1.34		-2.48[a]		-2.95[a]
Council-Manager	362	48.65		117.48		236.10	
Mayor-Council	99	54.52		140.95		293.39	
Population			3.51[a]		2.15		4.18[a]
First quintile	92	59.69		153.45		318.56	
Second quintile	92	57.91		152.25		319.48	
Third quintile	93	47.38		121.12		250.76	
Fourth quintile	92	52.70		135.68		281.85	
Fifth quintile	92	48.71		117.19		235.09	
Type of jurisdiction			0.99		0.63		1.34
Central city	132	54.70		135.24		275.24	
Suburban	223	51.69		131.52		272.47	
Independent	106	55.49		146.00		306.45	

(continued)

Table 11.2 (continued)   Estimated OPEB Liabilities by Demographic Characteristics

	N	Low		Medium		High	
		Mean ($)	Difference	Mean ($)	Difference	Mean ($)	Difference
Location			1.51		2.54[a]		1.17
Mountain	101	49.82		133.11		281.45	
Midwest	118	57.76		142.34		289.22	
Northeast	20	68.74		159.51		313.61	
Southeast	155	53.64		138.66		288.61	
West coast	67	45.07		115.40		239.07	
Current ratio			3.95[a]		2.88[a]		4.42[a]
First quintile	89	167.58		63.46		352.38	
Second quintile	90	117.09		50.86		262.86	
Third quintile	90	129.85		51.80		266.17	
Fourth quintile	96	123.48		48.03		256.29	
Fifth quintile	84	129.46		50.34		268.78	

			2.27		2.03		2.33
Pension obligation							
First quintile	92	58.69		145.68		297.09	
Second quintile	169	50.14		127.91		264.53	
Third quintile	15	34.36		84.62		171.88	
Fourth quintile	92	54.72		140.39		291.03	
Fifth quintile	92	55.41		145.28		304.49	
Direct debt			1.74		1.67		1.77
First quintile	129	57.88		143.83		293.47	
Second quintile	55	45.18		112.70		230.43	
Third quintile	90	49.25		127.66		266.04	
Fourth quintile	92	53.79		139.17		289.80	
Fifth quintile	92	55.85		145.47		303.87	

Note: Difference in mean costs for each category is an F ratio for all variables except Form of Government, which is a t test. All figures in constant 2006 dollars.

[a] $p < .05$.

"Medium" OPEB liability estimate to three different common size indicators from the 2002 financial data: general fund revenue collections, outstanding debt obligations, and outstanding pension obligations. The 75th percentile for the OPEB/revenue ratio was .77, meaning three-quarters of the jurisdictions have OPEB obligations equal to or less than 77 percent of a single year's general fund revenue collections. Because most OPEB obligations will be amortized over several years, the budget impact of those liabilities for any given year will be minimal. A similar conclusion can be drawn from comparing OPEB to other liabilities. For outstanding debt, the 75th percentile is .45, which indicates that three-quarters of the jurisdictions have OPEB liabilities less than one-half their total outstanding debt. And for pensions, the 75th percentile is .60, which suggests OPEB liabilities are equal to no more than 60 percent of the outstanding pension obligations for three-quarters of the jurisdictions. In short, in most cases total OPEB liabilities are comparably sized relative to both the current resources available to pay them, and to other liabilities that will demand current year resources.

A third finding is that OPEB liabilities are only loosely related to demographic, institutional, and fiscal characteristics. Mayor-council governments appear to carry higher liabilities, although that finding is not consistent across the full range of estimation assumptions. Northeast jurisdictions in this sample have slightly higher liabilities, although this difference is not statistically significant and cannot be generalized to the broader population. As expected, liabilities among independent cities are slightly higher than other cities, but the difference is not substantial.

The relationship between OPEB liabilities and other long-term obligations is both expected and unexpected. In general this relationship is curvilinear—the highest liabilities are found among jurisdictions with both the highest and lowest levels of other outstanding debt, and the lowest OPEB liabilities are found in-between.* The far right end of this curve is consistent with the claim noted elsewhere (Marlo we 2007a) that high per capita liabilities are part and parcel to more severe forms of financial stress, including high levels of other outstanding debt. But high OPEB obligations are equally likely at the far left end of this curve, particularly among jurisdictions with little or no other outstanding liabilities. Consider also that jurisdictions with the smallest current ratio, or comparatively lower levels of available general fund revenues, also have significantly higher OPEB liabilities.†

---

* Spearman rank order correlations were calculated to check for linear relationships between OPEB liabilities and these variables. No correlations over .2 were observed.

† Additional analysis not reported in a table indicates jurisdictions in the lowest quintile for the current ratio and for other long-term obligations tend to be "independent" (i.e., not central cities or suburbs) jurisdictions. Form of government, population, and geography are unrelated to a jurisdiction's levels on these variables.

11.2.3 Implications

Taken together these findings suggest for certain local governments OPEB is part of an important fiscal policy trade-off. Presumably, these jurisdictions have kept their long-term obligations in check by financing capital projects with a pay-as-you-go strategy rather than debt. This strategy is advantageous because it limits long-term debt obligations, but disadvantageous because it earmarks nearly every available dollar of general fund revenue. OPEB are apparently not among the liabilities kept in check by that strategy. Incorporating them into the mix of annual pay-as-you-go obligations that compete for scarce annual revenues might present a notable challenge for some jurisdictions. It is also worth noting that previous studies have shown that the corollary of this finding is true: higher unfunded OPEB liabilities associate with higher current year general fund spending for both state (Sneed and Sneed 1997) and local (Marlowe 2007b) governments.

The claim that jurisdictions have neglected OPEB in favor of managing other liabilities characterizes only a small group of jurisdictions, and the notion that high OPEB liabilities are part and parcel larger financial management problems indicated by high obligations in other areas is characteristic of a separate category of municipalities. For the majority of the jurisdictions examined here, OPEB liabilities are generally unrelated to other fiscal, demographic, or institutional characteristics. In other words, there is little evidence of large scale inability to pay.

11.3 Managing OPEB Costs

Inability to pay is also determined in part by the availability of strategies to contain OPEB costs or share those costs with employees, and evidence that jurisdictions have explored or exhausted these options supports inability to pay assertions. Availability of options is a critical concern for management because effectively identifying and exercising (or not exercising) those options are likely to be the main criteria by which credit raters, property owners, and others evaluate efforts to manage the OPEB challenge. More importantly, availability and use of cost management strategies will define the political rules of the OPEB game because of a widespread perception that these benefits are an "exceptionally cushy deal" (McMahon 2007) for government employees. Attempts to fund OPEB costs by reallocating resources away from current programs and services are likely to meet with stiff resistance if citizens perceive OPEB benefits as lavish or government employees as not paying their fare share.

This issue is examined here by analyzing data collected through the previously mentioned ICMA Health Care Benefits Survey. That survey contained a battery of questions about how jurisdictions manage their employee healthcare programs. Several of those items illuminate the availability of options for controlling OPEB costs.

An important consideration is how much employees contribute to their health insurance costs. Jurisdictions where employees contribute little or nothing will presumably have the ability to control future OPEB liabilities by requiring or raising those contributions. Of the 907 municipalities that provided usable responses on these survey items, 42 percent do not require a premium from unionized employees, and 24 percent do not require a premium from retired employees. A comparison of these findings to results of a similar survey conducted in 1993–1994 (Streib 1996) showed that roughly 15 percent of jurisdictions had begun requiring employee premium contributions from 1993 to 2001. These findings seem to indicate premium contributions are a popular, albeit essentially one time cost containment method that will not be available for many jurisdictions.

The survey results also provide information about employee co-payments and deductibles for particular services, which are another means for reducing OPEB liabilities. Use of these methods is mixed. On the one hand, roughly half the jurisdictions require deductibles from retired or unionized employees, and roughly half require co-pays for more specialized services like specialist visits and emergency room care. At the same time, more than 80 percent require co-payments for widely used services like primary care and prescription drugs. Like the trend for premiums, use of co-payments has expanded by about 15 percent since the 1993–1994 iteration of this same survey.

The survey data also provides insights into the feasibility of these options going forward. In short, many jurisdictions are exploring these options. Only 40 percent said employee premiums would not or were unlikely to change in the near future, 51 percent said deductibles would not or were unlikely to change, and roughly half said employee co-pays for primary care, specialist visits, and emergency room visits would not change.

Table 11.3 presents comparisons of the mean OPEB liability estimates for jurisdictions that have and have not employed these various cost-sharing mechanisms. In almost all cases, the mean liability for those that have employed a strategy is nearly identical to the mean for those that have not employed the strategy. In other words, there is no evidence that cost containment strategies have yet to impact OPEB liabilities on any broad scale. This finding, coupled with the fact that many jurisdictions have yet to employ key employee cost-sharing methods, supports the basic claim that municipalities have noteworthy opportunities to reduce OPEB costs by sharing those costs with employees.

Cost containment strategies are another potentially effective tactic for driving down OPEB liabilities. These tactics range from partnering with other jurisdictions to increase the pool of covered employees and negotiate lower prices with providers, to preventative healthcare programs, to incentivizing claims minimization. These methods are a burgeoning area of healthcare management, and have been widely noted throughout the public financial management literature as a source of potential partnerships with third party health management organizations, Medicare, and other major health policy stakeholders. But according to the survey only 29 percent

Table 11.3 Estimated OPEB Liabilities by Potential Benefit Changes

	N	Low		Medium		High	
		Mean ($)	Difference	Mean ($)	Difference	Mean ($)	Difference
Premium			0.62		1.07		1.27
No	145	49.74		129.10		269.24	
Yes	299	49.70		120.52		248.01	
Primary care co-pay			-1.49		-0.93		-0.63
No	183	45.75		119.60		250.26	
Yes	240	50.57		127.01		260.61	
Specialist co-pay			-0.51		0.02		0.3
No	220	47.79		124.29		259.46	
Yes	204	47.50		124.13		254.63	
Prescription co-pay			-0.03		0.59		0.89
No	138	48.40		126.97		266.16	
Yes	297	48.50		122.16		250.99	
ER co-pay			-0.23		0.34		0.62
No	220	48.09		125.06		261.04	
Yes	204	48.80		122.42		250.92	
Deductible			-0.38		0.04		0.25
No	180	48.03		124.52		259.53	
Yes	256	49.25		124.24		255.47	

Note: Difference in mean costs for each category is a t test. All figures in constant 2006 dollars.

of jurisdictions participate in some cost-sharing plan. Clearly, many jurisdictions have only begun to explore the full menu of potential cost containment strategies.* This is not to suggest these strategies are easy to implement. In fact, those requiring cross-jurisdictional cooperation might encounter political and institutional challenges that trump those of managing OPEB.

In the aggregate, the data suggests many municipalities have the ability, at least in the near term, to reduce their OPEB liabilities by sharing costs with employees and deploying various cost containment strategies. Whether these tactics can effectively limit long-term cost growth is a separate but related question that cannot be answered with these data. Caution should also be exercised as these data are is now more than five-years-old. But assuming they are a fair representation of the current OPEB landscape, there is little evidence of inability to pay.

11.4   Financial Management Challenges

The results presented above suggest few jurisdictions can reasonably claim an inability to pay OPEB liabilities. It then follows that the central challenge facing most is how to overcome or at least mitigate unwillingness to pay. This section presents some of the key financial management concerns to that effect, and the advantages and disadvantages of different strategies proposed to address those challenges.

11.5   Estimating and Communicating Costs

Critics of the new accounting standards have argued OPEB should not be reported as a financial liability because healthcare costs are not amenable to reliable estimation. This is an indisputable point. Consider the figures presented in Table 11.1, which indicate that a small change in the assumed annual rate of healthcare cost inflation or the annual discount rate can drastically alter the estimate. This sensitivity is echoed in liability estimates prepared for some of the early GASB 45 implementers. The Los Angeles Unified School district, for instance, has conducted two different actuarial assessments in the course of implementing these new standards. The first study produced a total OPEB liability estimate of $4.9 billion, and the second, using essentially the same data with only minor changes in assumptions, produced an estimate of $10 billion. Staff in Travis County, TX (who spearheaded the previously mentioned state legislation allowing agencies to opt out of the new standards), highlight a similar disparity between an early estimate of $89 million, and a more recent estimate of $320 million.

This sensitivity is the focal point for two ongoing debates regarding OPEB reporting and management. The first is whether estimation sensitivity should preclude a jurisdiction from reporting OPEB liabilities at all. Many, including the GASB, feel

---

* This is generally consistent with findings put forth in Roberts (2001).

they should be reported, and point to the precedent set with pension obligations as evidence supporting that position. In fact, much of the language in GASB 43/45 draws parallels between pension and OPEB estimation processes. But others dispute this point. Pension estimates, in their view, are subject to only two main types of uncertainty—how long each employee will live to draw a pension after retirement, and how future market conditions will affect the pension plan's assets—both of which can be forecasted with surprising accuracy. But OPEB estimation requires additional assumptions, including what sort of healthcare retirees will need, how quickly healthcare costs will increase, how the availability of insurance coverage affects retirees' demand for healthcare, whether Medicare and other subsidies will support retiree healthcare at present levels going forward, and other variables not amenable to accurate forecasting. Supporters of the previously mentioned Texas legislation and others who oppose the new standards say these liabilities are simply too uncertain to be considered a fair presentation of the jurisdiction's financial condition, especially because those estimates could prompt changes in OPEB provision.

Key stakeholders have taken the stance that some estimate, even one subject to substantial uncertainty, is better than nothing. Each of the major credit-rating agencies has stated publicly that not disclosing an OPEB liability does not equate to the absence of a liability. Some analysts have even suggested that not disclosing an OPEB liability could lead to a credit downgrade, as the markets will view that withholding as reason to believe the jurisdiction is either ignoring or hiding that liability. Several high profile taxpayer advocate organizations and other good government groups have made comments to that same effect. Their advice to jurisdictions is simple: get the best available estimate, provide appropriate caveats about that estimate, and then disclose it. Several large jurisdictions, including the state of Texas, have speculated that if enough large and influential jurisdictions opt out of GASB 45 the credit-rating agencies could be forced to issue ratings even without the requisite disclosures. But this seems unlikely, particularly because the city of Houston and others have already stated their intention to comply with GASB. Therefore, disclosure is the prudent course of action.

A second question is how to identify an appropriate estimate. A cynical perspective is that policy makers have strong incentives to minimize their stated liability and will therefore adopt the most aggressive assumptions possible. Anecdotal evidence from jurisdictions that have implemented these standards suggests that communication with stakeholders is key to finding that most appropriate estimate. Most professional actuaries will clearly explicate the assumptions that produced the estimate, and how changing those assumptions impact the estimate. Disclosing some or all of that sensitivity analysis will increase the congruence between taxpayer preferences and the jurisdiction's OPEB management strategy.

11.5.1 Managing Sticker Shock

Critics have also raised concerns about "sticker shock," or the possibility that the sudden disclosure of a large, unfunded OPEB liability will prompt policy makers to take drastic action, including eliminating OPEB altogether, to reduce that liability and protect their financial position. Many OPEB supporters share this concern, but for different reasons. Some are concerned not that OPEB might be scaled back to reduce that liability, but rather that politically savvy antigovernment actors like antitax groups and labor opponents will portray OPEB liabilities, regardless of their size, as evidence of government waste and abuse. Consider, for instance, that survey data has shown that an average private sector employer pays approximately 70 percent of its employee healthcare costs, where an average public sector employer pays approximately 83 percent (Long and Marquis 1999; Chiappetta 2005; AllianceBernstein 2006). This trend toward employee "self-funding" and "risk shifting" is evident elsewhere (Cowan and Hartman 2005; Hacker 2006). These and other figures can be easily be portrayed to support the notion that public employees enjoy unnecessarily generous benefits at taxpayer expense. A related concern is shared by public sector human resource professionals, who feel OPEB is one of the few sources of competitive advantage in certain labor markets. Reducing these benefits places diminishes the public sector's ability to procure top talent, and knee-jerk reactions to these new disclosures, they believe, could have implications far beyond financial reporting. Ironically, some governmental accountants and others within the public financial management community have decried GASB 43/45 because, in their view, new accounting standards should not be the catalyst for such a potentially contentious and intrinsically political discussion. This begs the question of whether sticker shock is a real problem, and if so, what can be done about it?

At this point the landscape is unclear. Several large urban county governments, especially those with questionable past retiree benefits practices like San Diego (California), Orange (California), Milwaukee (Wisconsin), have seen elected officials make largely unopposed calls for sweeping changes in OPEB provision. A similar dynamic has played out in Pittsburgh, Pennsylvania, Duluth, Minnesota and a few other mid to large, mainly Rustbelt cities. But whether this is characteristic of jurisdictions with less noteworthy retiree benefits and stronger financial condition remains uncertain.

However, it is clear that many jurisdictions began taking action to scale back retiree health benefits or shift OPEB funding responsibilities toward employees long before promulgation of the new GASB standards. A study by the Minnesota Office of the State Legislator, for instance, reported that within the past few years more than half of Minnesota local governments had reduced, eliminated, or changed the funding structure of their employee healthcare plans (Shields 2007). Similar studies have, albeit tentatively, reached similar conclusions about local governments elsewhere. These sorts of actions are likely to have mitigated potential sticker shock. And as previously mentioned, the fact that most OPEB liabilities are of manageable size mitigates concerns about fiscal policy changes inconsistent with the scope of the OPEB challenge. Nonetheless, at the present our understanding of sticker shock and its dynamics is evolving.

The experience from early GASB 43 and 45 implementers suggests the best strategy for mitigating potential sticker shock is to simultaneously disclose the OPEB liability and the strategy for addressing that liability. To that end, jurisdictions are encouraged to complete the actuarial valuation as soon as possible. Taking more time to review OPEB-related information before that information must be disclosed in financial statements, the logic suggests, will allow policy makers the opportunity review the full array of potential solutions. In the few cases where OPEB liabilities have been the subject of one-sided criticism, those liabilities were disclosed with apparent management strategy.

11.5.2 Funding the Liability

As shown above, most jurisdictions face multi-period OPEB management challenges. Moving from a single period to a multi-period strategy requires attention to how and when should current year resources be set aside to pay future OPEB liabilities.

Jurisdictions that choose to amortize their OPEB liability have two basic options for funding the annual required contribution toward that liability. The first is to make the contribution out of current year operating funds. In this case the annual liability becomes a budget line item subject to policy maker discretion. As shown above, this strategy might be the most appropriate in many cases where estimated OPEB liabilities appear manageable.

The second option is to establish and finance a formal OPEB trust fund. Like pension trust funds, an OPEB trust is a formal trust designed to segregate and grow the assets required for future OPEB payments. To satisfy the GASB requirements a trust must be irrevocable, meaning that once it is established its terms cannot be changed without the consent of both the jurisdiction and its employees. These trusts can take many forms, the parameters of which are determined mostly by the federal tax code. They vary in terms of their governing structures, whether they are established by a single jurisdiction or a group of jurisdictions, whether they require federal government approval and oversight, and whether limits exist on the amount that can be contributed to the fund.

The obvious disadvantage of establishing a trust is that doing so constrains a jurisdiction's ability to adjust its OPEB management strategy in response to changing circumstances. Once the trust and its contribution schedules are established, agencies face the threat of a substantial new liability if those annual contributions are not made according to schedule. And that liability stands in addition to the political or even legal ramifications of that decision.

This said, all present indications are that trust funds are for most jurisdictions the most appropriate method for addressing OPEB liabilities for two main reasons. First, assets placed in trust have the potential to appreciate at a much faster rate than assets managed in a pay-as-you-go strategy, and faster asset appreciation corresponds to a lower long-term OPEB liability and annual payments. This faster appreciation is in part because a trust allows investments in a wide array of instruments including stocks and other equities that tend to provide higher returns than less risky investments. Jurisdictions are certainly permitted to invest OPEB-designed resources as part of a pay-as-you-go strategy, but those investments are limited to the United States. Treasury securities, money market funds, and other instruments do not provide the same return on investment. Moreover, many of the trust funds available to local governments are managed by leagues of cities, municipal associations, and other multi-jurisdictional organizations that combine contributions into a single asset pool. This allows the trust to leverage larger investments that generate even greater return on each jurisdiction's contribution.

Trusts are also advantageous because their assets offset the jurisdiction's total OPEB liability. The intuition behind this accounting treatment is simple—the trust assets constitute a discernible commitment to address the OPEB liability and therefore reduce that liability. This commitment is immediately reflected on the jurisdiction's balance sheet, which describes its overall, long-term financial condition. Resources dedicated for OPEB payment as part of a pay-as-you-go strategy improve the jurisdiction's budget or financial position for a particular year, but because they can be redirected for other purposes and in turn do not offset the OPEB liability on the balance sheet. This said, irrevocable trusts have a wide variety of governing rules, tax implications, management fees, service options, and other considerations, all of which should be carefully scrutinized before joining.

Jurisdictions that choose to establish a trust must also decide whether to "prepay," or make payments in excess of the annual required contribution. The principal advantage of prepaying is that it reduces the jurisdiction's long-term OPEB liability, and subsequently lowers its future annual required contributions. But the real value of prepayment is that it paves the way toward political compromise on OPEB funding. For instance, jurisdictions that seek to reduce their liability by reducing the scope of OPEB have made prepayments as a goodwill showing. By demonstrating their commitment to funding the liability, they can expect employees to reciprocate by considering subsequent benefit reductions. Prefunding is also a useful tool for promoting intergenerational equity if the funding strategy requires redirecting resources or generating new resources. The most widely noted example of this occurred in New York City, where the Mayor Michael Bloomberg pledged a one-time $1 billion prepayment toward its $50 billion estimated liability, calling it a "down payment" on the city's commitment to fully funding that liability.

Prepayment is disadvantageous because it runs contrary to the basic logic of time value of money. Because "a dollar spent today is more than a dollar spent tomorrow," the cost of prepayment in today's dollars is greater than that same payment in a future period. To that end, jurisdictions should consider the near-term and long-term impact of any prefunding scenario in present value terms.

One aggressive prefunding strategy is to issue OPEB bonds. This strategy calls for the jurisdiction to borrow money in the public capital markets at the prevailing taxable rate, place that money in its irrevocable OPEB trust, and assume the trust's investment proceeds will exceed the required debt service on those bonds. If successful, this strategy has two enormous benefits; it effectively wipes out the jurisdiction's OPEB liability, and the annual payments required to repay the OPEB bonds will be much lower than the annual required OPEB contribution laid out in the amortization plan. But the downside risks are substantial. If the fund does not generate the requisite investment proceeds the debt service payments will exceed the previous liability, resulting in a net loss. Jurisdictions also take on high compliance and monitoring costs to navigate the complex tax rules that govern how money borrowed in the public capital markets can and cannot be invested in other markets.

Most municipal securities experts agree this strategy should be approached with great caution. Like any "arbitrage play," these bonds are highly sensitive to several factors including the business cycle, the amount of outstanding debt in the public capital markets, and future changes to state and local tax policy. Unexpected changes in any of these variables can drastically alter the plan assets available to meet OPEB liabilities. Moreover, issuing bonds convert OPEB from a "soft" liability subject to policy maker discretion to a "hard" liability where annual debt service payments are not subject to discretion. Nonetheless, this strategy has been employed by a few jurisdictions including the city of Gainesville, Florida, and Oakland county, Michigan, and is said to be under consideration by several other jurisdictions. Jurisdictions considering it should carefully monitor the market response to these and any forthcoming OPEB bonds, and carefully consult with municipal market experts to ensure that any such bond issues hit the market at the optimal time (Miller 2007).

11.6 Conclusions and Implications

This chapter described trends in municipal OPEB liabilities, the financial management challenges inherent to addressing those liabilities, and some of the strategies available to meet those challenges. In doing so it has both challenged and confirmed the conventional wisdom about OPEB. It has confirmed that OPEB are a multifaceted financial management issue that involve numerous stakeholders, complex and abstract concepts, and deeply held convictions about past and future promises to government personnel. It has also shown that unmanageably large liabilities—those large enough where the jurisdiction might be considered "unable" to pay—are the exception, rather than the norm among municipal governments, and that OPEB liabilities are generally unrelated to demographic, geographic, institutional, or fiscal characteristics. There is also evidence that many jurisdictions have at least some latitude to either change how they provide or fund benefits or to redirect financial resources to fund OPEB liabilities in the near term. The simple point is that most jurisdictions have the capacity and options to manage their OPEB challenge, but the nature of that challenge varies across jurisdictions.

What all jurisdictions have in common is that financial management decisions about OPEB are made in a political environment. Within that environment decision makers will likely be presented many "quick fixes," including eliminating or scaling back benefits, engaging in risk-laden and potentially costly borrowing strategies, adopting aggressive assumptions to minimize stated OPEB costs, or simply not reporting those cost at all. And the temptation to take those quick fixes and "wallpaper over" (Miller 2007) these liabilities will be even stronger in jurisdictions with strong antilabor or antigovernment sentiment or fiscal stress. The opposite holds true for jurisdictions that have the fiscal or policy flexibility to manage these liabilities, but cannot cut through the din of antigovernment rhetoric likely to surround OPEB liability disclosures. The real risk, then, is not that OPEB will bring on new financial problems, but rather that the response will be incongruent with the problem itself. It then follows that the most important assets for overcoming an OPEB financial management challenge, no matter what the scope or nature of that challenge, are patience, clear and honest communication, and thoughtful deliberation among elected officials, citizens, and professional staff.

References

AllianceBernstein. 2006. A new financial reporting challenge raises a troubling question. *Bernstein Journal: Perspectives on Investing and Wealth Management* (Summer): 19–23.

Amir, E. 1993. The market valuation of accounting information: The case of postretirement benefits other than pensions. *The Accounting Review* 68(4): 703–724.

Borger, C., S. Smith, S. Keehan, C. Truffer, S. Keehan, A. Sisko, J. Poisal, and M.K. Clemens. 2006. U.S. health spending projections through 2015: Changes on the horizon. *Health Affairs* (Web Exclusive, January–June): w61–w73.

Burns, D. 2007. Review of financial audits shows rise in major cities' pension liabilities. New York: Moody's Investors Service.

Campbell, R.J. and G. Turnbull. 2003. On government structure and spending: The effects of management form and separation of powers. *Urban Studies* 40(1): 23–34.

Centers for Disease Control and Prevention. 2004. United States life tables, 2002. *National Vital Statistics Reports* 53(6): (November 10): 140.

Chiappetta, T.O. 2005. Managing healthcare costs. *Public Personnel Management* 34(4): 313–320.

Cowan, C.A. and M.B. Hartman. 2005. Financing health care: Businesses, households, and governments, 1987–2003. *Health Care Financing Review* 1(2): 1–26.

Edwards, C. and J. Gokhale. 2006. The $2 trillion Fiscal hole. *Wall Street Journal* (October 12).

Follette, G. and L. Scheiner. 2005. The sustainability of health spending growth. *National Tax Journal* 58(3): 391–408.

Hacker, J. 2006. *The Great Risk Shift.* New York: Oxford University Press.

Hays, K. and S. Chang. 1990. The relative efficiency of city Manager and Mayor-Council forms of government. *Southern Economic Journal* 57(1): 167–177.

Hume, L. 2006. Panelists warn of OPEB Tsunami, urge early liability disclosure. *The Bond Buyer* (May 5).

Jung, C. 2006. Forms of government and spending on common municipal functions: A longitudinal approach. *International Review of Administrative Sciences* 72(3): 363–376.

Long, S.H. and M.S. Marquis. 1999. Comparing employee health benefits in the public and private sectors, 1997. *Health Affairs* 18(6): 183–193.

Marlowe, J. 2007a. Much Ado about nothing? The size and credit quality implications of municipal other postemployment benefit liabilities. *Public Budgeting & Finance* 27(2): 104–131.

Marlowe, J. 2007b. Intergenerational equity in practice: Evidence from public employee pensions and health care. Working Paper, Department of Public Administration, University of Kansas.

McMahon, E.J. 2007. Accounting, Texas style. *Wall Street Journal* (May 29).

Miller, G. 2007. Bonding with OPEB: Look before you leap. *The Governing Management Letter* (April 1).

Moulder, E.R. 2004. Local government health care plans: Customers, costs, and options for the future. In *The Municipal Yearbook* (Ed.) International City/County Management Association. Washington, DC: International City/County Management Association.

Roberts, G.E. 2001. Employee benefits cost control strategies in municipal government. *Public Performance & Management Review* 24(4): 389–402.

Shields, Y. 2007. Report urges Minnesota to tackle OPEB, pension liabilities. *The Bond Buyer* (January 25).

Sneed, C. and J. Sneed. 1997. The intergenerational consequences of retiree healthcare premiums: What is the evidence? *Journal of Public Budgeting, Accounting, and Financial Management* 9(2): 285–304.

Streib, G. 1996. Municipal health benefits: A first step toward a useful knowledge base. *American Review of Public Administration* 26(3): 345–360.

Stumm, T.J. and M.T. Corrigan 1998. City managers: Do they promote Fiscal efficiency? *Journal of Urban Affairs* 20(3): 343–351.

Voorhees, W.R. 2005. Counting your retirement eggs before they hatch: GASB and the new reporting requirements for OPEB. *Public Budgeting & Finance* 25(4): 59–71.

Warshawsky, M.J. 1992. *The Uncertain Promise of Retiree Health Care Benefits*. Washington, DC: American Enterprise Institute Press.

Wisniewski, S.C. 2005. Potential state government practices impact of the new GASB accounting standard for retiree benefits. *Public Budgeting & Finance* 25(1): 104–118.

Appendix: OPEB Liability Estimation Methods

The estimates presented here were derived from a model developed by Amir (1993) to determine OPEB liabilities for publicly traded corporations. This model is as follows:

$$PV = S\left[\left[\left[n_1 + \left[n_2\left(\frac{1+g}{1+r}\right)^3 P(62,65)\right] + \left[n_3\left(\frac{1+g}{1+r}\right)^8 P(57,65)\right] + \left[n_4\left(\frac{1+g}{1+r}\right)^{13} P(52,65)\right] + \right.\right.\right.$$
$$\left.\left.\left. + \left[n_5\left(\frac{1+g}{1+r}\right)^{18} P(47,65)\right] + \left[n_6\left(\frac{1+g}{1+r}\right)^{23} P(42,65)\right]\right]\right]\right]$$

where

$$S = \sum_{j=1}^{100} C_{65} + (1+g)^j + (1+r)^{-j} P(65+j)$$

In this expression S is the present value of the cost of providing OPEB to each retiree from the current period until the retiree dies, g is an assumed rate of annual healthcare cost growth, r is the assumed rate of annual inflation, n is the number of employees in each of six age cohorts, P is the assumed probability of living to age 65 for employees within a particular age cohort, and C_{65} is the per beneficiary OPEB cost for each current retiree.

The model's basic structure is as follows. In the first stage we estimate the present value of the jurisdiction's future OPEB cost for each current retiree, S, by applying a discounted annual healthcare cost growth rate from the current year until a future year j. $P(65 + j)$ is the probability a retiree will live from age 65 until a number of years, j, beyond retirement. It was derived from life expectancy tables provided by the Centers for Disease Control and Prevention (2004). The model was calculated for a maximum total age (i.e., $65 + j$) of 100.

With S established, the second stage combines estimated OPEB costs for retirees with the present value of the cost of providing OPEB benefits for all active employees who will presumably retire from the jurisdiction and draw those or similar benefits. Those figures are calculated by grouping employees into one of the six age cohorts, and then calculating the probability an employee in that cohort will live until retirement. Expected cost growth is discounted differently for each age cohort, consistent with that cohort's years to expected retirement at age 65. Because demographic data on local government employees is not readily available, the model follows Sneed and Sneed's (1997) analysis of state government employees, which assumed a mean age of 42. Employees were allocated into each group by simply dividing the total number of employees active in the jurisdiction's healthcare plan by five, which resulted in an equal allocation of active employees in each cohort. As a result of this assumption, liabilities will be underforecasted to the extent that, as conventional wisdom suggests, a disproportionate number of local government employees fall in the older age cohorts. The number of current retirees is denoted by n_1.

Because detailed data on OPEB plan provisions and participants was not available, several assumptions were made. First, it is assumed that all employees retire at age 65, current employees leave municipal employment only through death, retired employees leave the retirement system only through death, and the jurisdiction does not restrict the amount of time a retiree can draw benefits. If large numbers of employees retire early, which is common in police and fire services, the model will underestimate a jurisdiction's OPEB liability because early retirees take longer to reach Medicare age and access the subsidy. The model also assumes a zero withdrawal rate, which is not entirely consistent with actuarial practice. In public safety, for instance, first year withdrawal rates of 13 percent are not uncommon. An artificially low withdrawal rate will inflate the OPEB estimates by assuming a higher number of employees will require coverage.

Additional assumptions were required because data on per employee healthcare costs was not readily available. First, per employee healthcare costs were calculated by simply dividing the jurisdiction's self-reported total healthcare costs for fiscal year 2001 by the number of employees, both current and retired, who were active members in its healthcare plan(s). This figure was not adjusted to account for differences in costs, premiums, or plan benefits between active employees and retirees, or between single, spousal, and family insurance plans. These differences are assumed to be reflected in the jurisdiction's average, per employee healthcare cost. With that per employee figure established, it was assumed the jurisdiction's cost of providing healthcare for retirees is substantially less than for current employees because retirees are able to access Medicare and other health insurance subsidies. The precise cost reduction is unknown, so two sets of estimates were conducted. One was based on the full per employee healthcare cost identified by each jurisdiction, and one was based on a 30 percent reduction of that per employee cost. These subsidies follow Warshawsky's (1992) analysis. The model also assumes the inflation rate and healthcare cost growth rate are constant over time, that the jurisdiction has not prepaid any of its OPEB obligations, and that it makes all healthcare payments at the end of the year.

Chapter 12

Benefits and Costs to the Public Sector of Service in the National Guard and Reserves

Anthony G. White

CONTENTS

12.1 Background

Defense or war departments exist for the purpose of bringing physical force to bear—either in reality or in potential—to resolve the policy needs of the governments that created them. In practicality, this means acquiring, training, paying for, maintaining, and controlling soldiers, sailors, marines, and air personnel ultimately for a combat setting; and, providing healthcare, pensions, and other benefits for the survivors or their dependents.

For human relations professionals to adequately provide service both to their organizations and to the employees, it is necessary to understand the environment of National Guardsmen and women, and reservists, and the range of demands and costs and benefits available to them.

Because of its form of government, history, and location, the United States (U.S.) of America has historically maintained a small (relative to its total population) standing military force, backed-up layers of reserve military personnel (National Guard Association, 1954). The United States has seven federal "uniformed" services: Army, Navy, Air Force, Marine Corps, Coast Guard, Public Health Service, and the National Oceanographic and Atmospheric Administration Commissioned Corps (Congress, 2005a). The first six have reserve components—personnel individually or in organizations qualified to such a level that a short refresher or intensive training could quickly create more job-ready military personnel. The first five are considered the "Armed Forces" of the United States. The strength level of these five authorized by Congress in fiscal year 2007 is 1.36 million (Secretary of Defense, 2006).

In addition to these purely federal Armed services, there exist in every state joint federal–state Army and Air National Guards, under the control of state governors in peacetime under U.S. Code Title 32 (Congress, 2005b), but callable to federal service in time of war, widespread natural disaster, civil unrest, or to protect the country's borders and critical infrastructure under Title ten status (NGUS) (Congress, 2005a). The strength level of the NG and reserve authorized by Congress in fiscal year 2007 is 826,000 (Secretary of Defense, 2006).

Yet another layer below the reserve and Guard are quasi-military organizations consisting of veterans, retirees, and other people who might volunteer their time without pay for supporting the role of the Guard or reserves—the federal Coast Guard Auxiliary and Civil Air Patrol, and state-created Defense Forces or NG-reserves.*

In time of peace, reserves and Guard are part-time military personnel, usually training one weekend each month and two to four weeks each year away from their civilian settings. For most, military service is a combination of patriotic duty, second job, and social network. For others, in a weak economy with high unemployment, it may be their sole source of income. As with the Armed Forces, the authorized strength levels of the Guard and reserves are set annually by Congress in appropriations bills (Congress, 2005b).

By 2000–2001, the federal Armed Forces strength had been drawn down to its lowest level (a little under 1.4 million) since the pre-Korean War period. In the period following the September 11, 2001 attacks on the United States, the policy of utilizing Guard and reserves as a strategic reinforcement for the Armed Forces began to change. Although Department of Defense recruiting and stop-loss policies briefly swelled federal ranks to almost 1.5 million in 2003, individual and unit call-ups from Guard and reserve units to active duty rose from 5,000 active duty in 2001 to a peak of 194,000 in 2004 (Department of Defense 2001–2007). At the end of 2006, the activated Guard and reserve numbered about 93,000; somewhat over half were stationed in Iraq or Afghanistan, with the balance serving in the United States or other posts to free up federal Armed Forces to serve in combat zones (Department of Defense 2001–2007).

Because of the way in which Guard and reserve units and individuals are activated ("mobilized") it is difficult to calculate precisely how many citizen–soldiers (as opposed to the professional, active-duty soldiers of the Armed Forces) have served in Afghanistan and Iraq. Approximately 500,000 Guard and reserve personnel have called, individually or in units, to active duty since 2001, of which about 300,000 have served in Iraq or Afghanistan. As of 2006, about 50,000 of the 135,000 troops stationed in Iraq are Guard or reserves (Department of Defense 2001–2007; Figure 12.1).

Almost all of the Guard and reserve personnel activated to federal service have served sufficiently long enough to qualify as veterans, opening them to a range of federally-backed benefits (Congress, 2005c). And although public employees as a whole represent about 20 percent of the U.S. total workforce, almost 40 percent of Guard and reserve members report their primary civilian employment to be in the public sector (Hollingsworth, 2006).

---

* See, for example, http://www.sgaus.org, a national association of most State Defense Forces.

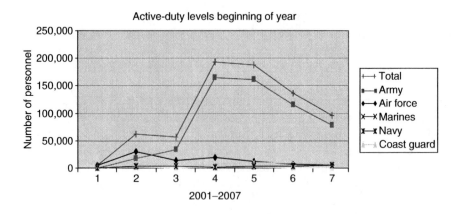

Figure 12.1   Activated National Guard and Reserve.

12.2   Societal Costs and Benefits

For the purposes of this discussion, "society" is defined as the people, politics, economy, institutions, and governments of the United States. The Guard and reserves are drawn mostly from that society, and are intended to fulfill the goals and objectives of that society. Such goals and objectives can be constitutional, military, social, or economic.

12.2.1   Costs: Constitutional

On-going federal–state tensions revolving around control of NG and reserve assets sometimes strain relationships. Clearly, the constitution allows the president to call those assets into national service and direct the use of personnel and material for federal purposes, even if a state or states may be experiencing their own crises (Constitution, 1787). On the other hand, governors who want to direct active-duty troops' activities relative to state or regional efforts in the wake of Hurricane Katrina have been unsuccessful. The department has reportedly been willing, however, to allow Adjutants General (who hold federal commissions) more leeway to integrate their assets with homeland security agencies.

12.2.2   Costs: Military

Integrating citizen–soldiers into active-duty service presents a variety of challenges from a military standpoint. NG and reserve units traditionally have trained for the last war, not the next, resulting in mixed readiness status, obsolete equipment, delays in deployment, and a reduced level of effectiveness from a military standpoint (GAO, 2006).

Delays in deployment can result in increased casualties among active-duty forces. Even when modern equipment is available from NG or reserve assets, because it is almost entirely federally-funded it can be moved away from a state to a combat thea-ter. Defense department strategy may require federal equipment to be left in the theater of operations for future units to utilize, or if destroyed not to be immediately replaced—the priority of replacement being with active-duty organizations. This can leave a state short of necessary equipment (Larabee, 2007).

Strategy can also disrupt NG or reserve unit cohesion if individuals are used piecemeal to replace or reinforce active-duty units. Individual NG or reserve mem-bers can find themselves doing work for which they were not trained, or required to rapidly integrate into a new unit as a temporary replacement, thus increasing the time and stresses necessary to effectively accomplish a mission (Amos, 2006).

12.2.3   Costs: Social

NG or reserve units and individuals often represent a vital core of a community, individuals being employed as police, firefighters, emergency medical technicians, and government officials (Hollingsworth, 2006). States' abilities to respond to emer-gencies are reduced when those trained to do the responding are unavailable due to federal service (Loven, 2007).

A call-up for state service is usually short-term, to respond to a specific disaster such as a flood, storm, or forest fire. Longer-term call-ups for federal service, ranging from six to twenty-four months (Burns, 2007), or multiple call-ups, are more dis-ruptive to the communities from which they are drawn, and reintegration following demobilization can be equally as disruptive. Reclaiming one's job can be challenging (Congress, 1994), and divorce and separation rates among returning service mem-bers may be higher than the general population's (Lake, 2007).

Some NG and reserve will die, removing them from the societal matrix permanently, and depriving society of their skills and abilities. Others will return as casualties, and represent short- and long-term medical and rehabilitation costs borne by society as a whole.

12.2.4   Costs: Economic

States and local agencies incur monetary costs for NG and reserve, usually in the form of facilities, salaries for NG and reserve members who when not deployed are state or local government employees, and certain materials and supplies designed for state ser-vice. Such expenditures are usually incorporated in Adjutant Generals' or state military department budgets. Land devoted to armories and NG bases and reserve centers are public, and not subject to the property taxation that permits governments to recover costs of services. Facilities deemed no longer needed for military use often require extensive rehabilitation before being put to other uses (Phillippe, 2000).

When NG and reserve units and individuals are mobilized, they temporarily leave their civilian jobs. If their employers—private or public—want or need to maintain corporate service and output at a constant level, the workload of those mobilized must be taken on by temporary replacements or spread among remaining workers. In the private sector, some small or one-person firms go out of business because the principal is gone, which is damaging to the social economy as a whole. Even in the public sector, although the federal USERRA statute (Congress, 1994) seems to guarantee NG and reservist job rights, they are often rights that have to be hard-won (Mortenson, 2007; Hollingsworth, 2006).

12.2.5 Benefits: Constitutional

Founders of the United States envisioned that each of the states of the new Union would have and control militias, which could be called into national service by the president (Constitution, 1787). To raise such militias, states would have to recruit their troops and pay part their expenses until and unless called into federal service. The NG fulfills that constitutional goal (National Guard Bureau, 2005).

12.2.6 Benefits: Military

The primary purpose of any military organization is to be an organized force that can be brought to bear to resolve problems and issues either by its mere presence or by the application of controlled violence. A trained, disciplined and competent militia provides such a force to the states, for public safety issues such as crowd and riot control, responding to natural and man-made natural disasters, and search-and-rescue missions (Brown, 2007; Commission, 2007). The organizational structure, based on active military institutions, provides a framework to effectively utilize personal and equipment to resolve problems.

12.2.7 Benefits: Social

The concept of the citizen–soldier has been in part a way to maintain integration of military force with civilian society, wherein the ultimate authority to use such forces resides with civilian officials. Such a system tends to prevent a form of tunnel vision that makes military objectives all-important, maintains contact with the grass-roots level of social order, and prevents undue influence by the military on civilian affairs (Preiss, n.d.).

For many NG and reserve personnel, such service is also a way to gain civilian skills (heavy equipment operation, security principles, planning, teamwork, leadership, and self-discipline) that readily transfer over to civilian life to the general benefit of society.

12.2.8 Benefits: Economic

NG and reserve organizations serve as a conduit for federal dollars to be channeled to state and local levels. Federal monies pay for 100 percent of NG and reserve personnel, equipment, and operations through direct Congressional funding, and lesser amounts for community outreach programs, at the fiscal year 2007 level of $34.1 billion (White House Communications, 2006). Bill-back systems wherein NG operations at the state level that protect federal assets such as national forests are billed back to responsible federal departments such as the Federal Emergency Management Agency (FEMA), Department of the Interior, or the Department of Agriculture. It currently costs about $126,000 a year to keep one NG member on active duty, inclusive of salaries, benefits, food, quarters, weapons and ammunition, and other support (White House Communications, 2006).

12.3 Individual Costs and Benefits

Individual soldiers, sailors, and air personnel in military service cycle through several phases during their time in service, each of which have their own personal costs and benefits. These phases are recruitment, training, duty, and separation—regardless of whether the individual is active-duty, NG, or reserve.

Costs can exist in a variety of forms: money, time, foregone opportunities, and personal relationships. NG and reserves, being usually under their military employers on a part-time basis, nonetheless experience these costs.

12.3.1 Costs: Recruitment

NG and reserve personnel pay no fees to be recruited, although during times when the United States has instituted conscription, the competition to join NG or reserves has been fierce. The time component during recruitment usually consists of several days of pursuit and persuasion, batteries of physical and mental examinations, waiting for completion of background security checks, and orientations. At this point, however, the commitment being made for the all-volunteer U.S. services, NG and reserves is eight years.*

During this time, the recruit is limited in the ability to make other commitments, either personal or professional, until it is known whether the recruitment is successful, so that, for example, job offers in another state or country may have to be foregone. Similarly, some aspects of personal life and relationships must be suspended until the outcome is known.

12.3.2 Costs: Training

Once past the recruiting stage, the individual moves to basic soldier training and advanced vocational skill development. The individual normally pays none of

---

* The usual total time commitment is 8 years, while the enlistee can often elect the number of years of Individual Ready Reserve (IRR) from 2 to 4 years.

these costs, if he or she lives within the allowances for uniforms and incidentals prior to training, which can be considerable: $6–56,000 for an enlisted soldier, $10,000 for a sailor, $340,000 for an officer from a service academy or $32–86,000 from other sources, and up to $1.4 million for jet fighter pilots (Blue Ribbon Commission, 2006). To be accepted in some occupational specialties (medical or legal, for instance) the individual might have to make a commitment of additional years of service.

The time involved in this training regimen ranges from eight to twenty weeks— time away from the civilian community.

The same types of lost opportunity costs and personal relationship costs apply as during the recruitment period. Additionally, the trainee may be limited in residence locations: a California NG person who wishes to move to New York State and is in the middle of the contractual enlistment with no available NG position in New York to transfer to can face substantial costs in the legal arena.

12.3.3 Costs: Duty

NG and reserves, like their active-duty brothers and sisters, are provided with equipment, supplies, transport, food, quarters, and support deemed necessary to do their jobs at the military's cost. In times of peace, most NG and reserves serve eleven to twelve weekends and two weeks in a training mode each year, maintaining old and gaining new skills. Except for Individual Ready Reserve (IRR) and Retired Reserve (RR), NG and reservists are paid for the time they train and time spent on active duty.

Upon call-up, a normal tour of duty for NGUS and reserves is twelve months, although it can be as little as one to two months or as long as eighteen months—and during a full-scale conflict, "for the duration." During this period, once various sorts of available leave or vacation time from a civilian employer are exhausted, the military salary becomes the members' sole source of revenue, whereas during training periods it was a supplemental source of revenue.

Foregone opportunity costs are the same as during training; changing an NG or reserve's civilian position or even occupation may be constrained by military obligations.

There is no way to sugar-coat the fact that NG and reservists in an combat deployment can pay the ultimate cost through death, in either a full-combat or lower-intensity-level conflict, or accidents associated with hostile environments. Today's armored equipment and personal protective gear make that far less likely than just 60 years ago, but the outcome can be injury rather than death. The current ratio of wounded to dead U.S. military personnel in current conflicts is about 8:1 (Department of Defense, 2001–2007). After leaving current combat zones, about 25 percent of veterans have made injury claims (Goldstein, 2007).

The costs to the NGUS or reservist who survives being wounded or injured are measured in pain, limb or organ loss, rehabilitation time and effort, and perhaps loss of a prior civilian occupation that imposes physical requirements that can no longer be met.

Longer-term costs can and do also include wound recovery, loss of hearing or tinnitus from being in a loud environment (Durch and Humes, 2005; Hicks, 2007), post-traumatic stress disorder (PTSD) (Pelofsky, 2007), and exposure to battlefield hazards both identifiable (Agent Orange exposure) and unidentified (Gulf War Syndrome) (Reuters, 2007). Ultimately, these costs may be expressed in the workplace once the NG or reservist must adjust to return to civilian life (GAO, 2005c).

Personal relationships ordinarily do not suffer greatly in the training setting; being gone perhaps 28 days each year, spaced out over a 12 month span, is not normally considered a hardship. Mobilization tours of duty are harder even on NG and reservists, and their families, who are not normally used to being separated for such extended periods. Civilian friendships may become harder to maintain, especially if one's peer groups in the civilian world have no experiences with which to empathize. Divorce rates climb, and higher incident rates of domestic violence may occur (Shellenbarger, 2004; Jowers, 2007).

12.3.4   Costs: Separation

There are many ways to separate from the NG, NGUS, or reserves: death; discharge for medical reasons; discharge for a variety of "honorable" reasons; retirement; and discharge for reasons "other than honorable." Separation means a loss of NG and reserve pay and allowances, either in a training or active-duty mode.

Death has a constellation of final costs, only some of which are borne by military organizations. A standard funeral can easily cost $5–7,000, and usually the stipend associated with service-connected death covers only a portion of funeral costs. Discharge for medical reasons usually removes the NG or reservist from direct military-provided medical care (Tri-Care), and puts him or her on the increasingly-privatized path of veterans' care whose costs are only partly covered by the government (GAO, 2005).

Discharge under honorable conditions, or retirement, usually has no direct financial cost to the individual, save for the adjustment period of returning to civilian life and a civilian lifestyle. If the individual attains "veteran" status, as defined by U.S. Code (Office of Personnel Management, n.d.) or by various state statutes, many benefits still accrue. Discharge under less than honorable conditions can result if a forfeiture of future pay and benefits, including medical care.

Often, a discharge or retirement from the NG or reserves can take one or two months to process. The cost of this time may be small, or might represent another lost opportunity as the NG or reservist must delay the transition to a purely-civilian life.

Changes to personal relationships in this transition can either be a benefit or a cost to the individual—more time becomes available for civilian family and friends, but at the same time there is the separation from coworkers and teammates from an environment of close and dependent associations. Leaving fellow service members the NG or reservist has depended upon in life-or-death situations can represent a substantial personal loss.

12.3.5 Benefits to the Individual

A variety of benefits and inducements are utilized to recruit, retain, and reward for service separating NG and reservists. From a public personnel standpoint, it is perhaps most useful to distinguish between the financial, service and other benefits offered by the federal government and those offered by state and local governments.

The listing that follows is not exhaustive. Each year federal, state and local governments find new and innovative ways to attract and reward people who join the NG and reserves. Most local jurisdictions do not report what types or forms of benefits (if any) are made available to NG and reserves for serving or having served, just within that jurisdiction.

12.3.5.1 Federal Benefits to the Individual

The following Table 12.1 summarizes the federal benefits made available to NG and reserves who are called to active duty in federal service, in addition to issuance of equipment and materials, and providing transportation, quarters, and food or per diem payments. SGLI is the Servicemen's Group Life Insurance policy; USERRA is the Uniformed Services Employment and Reemployment Rights Act; SCRA is the Servicemembers' Civil Relief Act; "Executive Orders" are presidential and federal departmental orders; and veterans' benefits are those administered by federal Executive Departments and offices, such as the Office of Personnel Management and Department of Veterans' Affairs.

This table does not include incentive or re-enlistment bonuses paid by the NG and reserves for members with certain skills targeted by those components, which change in time and focus as different needs arise.

12.3.5.2 State Benefits to State Employees and Others

The following Table 12.2 summarizes state benefits made available to NG and reserves who are called to active duty in federal service. Each state sets eligibility requirements, usually in terms of consecutive days of active duty and combat status. Counties and cities in states without home rule delegation may follow the state's lead as it treats its own state employees, if directed. State and local employees are covered by the provisions of the federal SGLI, USERRA, and SCRA.

Table 12.1   Federal Benefits for National Guard, Reserve Members

Authority	Benefit
SGLI	Life insurance for military members up to $400,000 for premium
USERRA	Protects reemployment rights for employees of all employers over minimum size, prohibits employer denial of benefits because of military membership or service
SCRA	Suspends certain payments, caps interest rates on credit cards and mortgages while on active duty, protects against eviction, suspends civil court actions
Executive order	Departments pay employees' share of health insurance premiums for member, family while on active duty
Veterans' benefits	Veterans' administration healthcare, pharmacy services, pensions, education and training, vocational rehabilitation, home loans, life insurance, employment preference points, burial plot and payment, and survivor benefits

Covering a pay differential means that if the NG or reserve state employee would suffer a pay cut after being called to active duty, the state will make up the difference. Tuition waivers, assistance, and reimbursement are within that state's education system. COLA is a cost-of-living adjustment. Military leave means the state considers the employee to be on leave, and under state pay, for the stated period at the beginning of a call-up. SGLI is the Servicemen's Group Life Insurance policy.

12.4   Summary

Any handbook which seeks to inform the human resources/human capital professional can at best provide a snapshot of then-current events and trends. Following the end of the so-called "Cold War," the downsizing of the active U.S. military—perfectly capable of addressing a single threat or action in a single theater—was a transition caught up in the events of the early 2000s.

In the absence of a strategy of maintaining a large standing military force, a next logical step was to increasingly draw on reserve forces to provide sufficient strength to address the multiple challenges facing the military. Reserve forces in the United

Table 12.2 State Benefits for National Guard, (In-State) Reserve Members (See Especially Governors' Association 2006)

State	National Guard and Reserve	State Employees	Education	Other
Alabama	28,200	Pay differential covered	Tuition waiver, scholarships	Family support, ESGR week
Alaska	4,500	Health/life insurance continued, military leave 15 days	Tuition assistance, reimbursement	USERRA enforcement, $100/month upon retirement, pay SGLI premium (Alaska 2006)
Arizona	12,000	Retain vacation/seniority rights, no time lost	Tuition reimbursement	Vehicle license exemption, jury duty exemption
Arkansas	13,250	COLA although active, protect leave accrual, eligible for recognition pay		
California	61,100	Pay differential covered, military leave 30 days, preference points for any civil service for NG or spouse or survivor (California Assembly 2006a).	Academic leave, loan assumption	Home loan program, immediate reinstatement of healthcare coverage upon demobilization (California Assembly 2006b).
Colorado	17,500	Military leave 15 days, pension rights	Tuition assistance	Property tax deferral, fishing/game licenses

State				
Connecticut	7,100	Paid leave (30 days) and insurance, pay differential thereafter, activation time toward pension	Limited tuition assistance	$1500 property tax, some income tax exemptions, licensing exemptions, $50/mon bonus up to $500 max. for NG, USERRA protections while on state duty (Connecticut Legislature 2006)
Delaware	5,250	Pay differential, military leave up to three years toward pension, continue state health ins. up to two years w/co-pay	Tuition reimbursement	Reimbursement of SGLI premiums, space-available travel, commissary use
Florida	33,400	First 30 days on state pay, pay differential thereafter	Family benefits, forgive out-of-state tuition	Some counties forgive property tax, one-time renter's grant
Georgia	27,600	Pay differential, military leave 18 days (with possible of 12 additional), buy up to five years of state pension	Priority for tuition assistance, in-state, loans, scholarships	Exempt combat pay from taxation, six-month extension automatic, free NG license plate, grace periods on state licenses, low-cost state group insurance, one-year hunt/fish, jury duty excused
Hawaii	9,400		Tuition assistance	Suspend income tax while in combat zone, $1750 income tax exemption
Idaho	5,400	Heirs receive state benefits if employee dies while called up	Freeze educational status, tuition and fee assistance up to 100 percent	Protect custody/visitation rights, extend state driver's license, USERRA for state duty

(continued)

Table 12.2 (continued) State Benefits for National Guard, (In-State) Reserve Members (See Especially Governors' Association 2006)

State	National Guard and Reserve	State Employees	Education	Other
Illinois	25,300	Pay differential, state health and other benefits continue	Tuition grant	No tax on military pay, grants; head-trauma screening; 24-hour PTSD hotline
Indiana	18,700	Military leave 15 days	Tuition supplement, remit for certain dependents	Income tax deduct, extension, family support, drivers' license deferrals, parks and recreation pass
Iowa	13,300	Pay differential	Tuition refunds, tuition assistance	Military pay exempt, death gratuity, vet status at 90 days, license extensions, free counseling, tax extension automatic
Kansas	12,200	Pay differential, $1000 bonus if over 180 days, credit for service time, state life insurance premium paid, optional added life insurance (available)	Tuition grants, dependents'/survivors' benefits	Military retirement pay exempt from tax, vehicle tax waived, licenses extended, hunt/fish license, programs get lottery receipts

Kentucky	12,100	Retirement credits 1 for 6, military leave ten to fifteen days, pay differential	Tuition assistance absence protection	Lump sum death benefit, tax credit, license renewals by mail, exempt from toll payments, legal help
Louisiana	21,500	Pay differential, raises for military police at same rate as sheriffs, state police	Protection from academic fines and penalties	Income tax relief, other jurisdictions encouraged to pay differential, waiver of legal proceedings
Maine	7,300	Military leave 17 days, retirement credits		Professional license CE waivers or deferral
Maryland	24,000	Pay differential		Family support
Massachusetts	14,400	Pay half of premium for SGLI or same amount toward other life insurance premium	Fee exemption	Death benefit increase, $1000 combat bonus, $500 noncombat bonus, Bonus for decedents' spouse and parents, legal support
Michigan	19,400	Limited pay differentials, protected job rights, salary step increases		
Minnesota (Minnesota House 2006)	19,600	Military leave 15 days, pay differential	80–100 percent tuition, refunds, tuition assistance and reimbursement extension of deadlines	Nonresident tax status, family support, refund able tax credit if in combat zone, parks permits
Mississippi	17,900			Family relief fund

(continued)

Table 12.2 (continued)   State Benefits for National Guard, (In-State) Reserve Members (See Especially Governors' Association 2006)

State	National Guard and Reserve	State Employees	Education	Other
Missouri	22,100			Child support on military pay, professional license exemption and vehicle fees, tax extensions, delay of criminal and civil actions
Montana	4,600	Military leave 120 hours	Tuition refunds	Property tax suspension, military pay exempt from tax, retirement pay partial exemption, legal aid, vehicle license fee waiver, professional license CE suspensions, special hunting rights
Nebraska	7,100	Military leave 120 hours tuition reimbursement, survivor's 100 percent tuition assistance	Education leave	Income tax exemption, family support, driver's license validation, reimbursement of health insurance premiums
Nevada	4,500	Military leave 15 days, partial pay differential	Tuition waiver certain terms	

State				
New Hampshire	3,700	Special leave with partial pay differential for 18 months, maintain health and dental coverage for dependents		Driver's license renewal for free; state pays for $250,000 of life insurance (Conference of State Legislatures 2006)
New Jersey	20,300	Military leave 90 days on state duty		Militia has same NG reemployment rights, workers' compensation for injuries in line of duty, legal aid
New Mexico	5,600	Military leave 30 days, use other leave for benefit maintenance, reinstatement of insurance on return if lapsed, preference points	In-state tuition	Spousal unemployment, $250,000 life insurance at state cost for NG
New York	30,500	Supplemental leave	Refund or credit, scholarship programs for survivors	$6,000 burial benefit, SCRA provisions, professional license extensions, free hunt/fish licenses, park pass, tax exemption for NG of NY if on federal duty in NY, spouses allowed ten days' unpaid leave
North Carolina	22,800	Pay differential	Tuition assistance, in-state status	Family support, legal support, state equipment supplements to federal deploys, tax exemption in combat zone

(continued)

Table 12.2 (continued) State Benefits for National Guard, (In-State) Reserve Members (See Especially Governors' Association 2006)

State	National Guard and Reserve	State Employees	Education	Other
North Dakota	4,800		Special enrollment	Family support, special hunting provisions
Ohio	30,000	Pay differential, military leave 22 days, maintain seniority and longevity pay, make-up deferred compensation, purchase retirement credit	Tuition assistance	Combat pay exempt from taxation, tax extensions, license renewal without test, workers' compensation for state duty, $100,000 death benefit on state duty, SGLI premium reimbursement on state duty, injury relief fund
Oklahoma	16,200	Pay differential, military leave 20 days, seniority and longevity pay increases, deferred comp participation, retirement contributions	Fee waiver	
Oregon	11,000	Continued healthcare first 12 activation months, leave donation program	Tuition assistance	$170 uniform allowance, limited income tax exemption, $60,000 property tax value exempt., workers' compensation for state duty injuries

Pennsylvania	32,900	Paid benefits while on military leave	Tuition costs and fees for survivors (Conference of State Legislatures 2006)	Health and other benefits first 30 days of deployment, legal protections
Rhode Island	5,100		Tuition exemption	Income tax extension, legal protections, small business assistance, driver's license extension, state pays premium for up to $400,000 of life insurance for mobilized NG (Conference of State Legislatures 2006)
South Carolina	18,000	Annual leave 45 days, sick leave 90 days, military leave 30 days, can continue state health and retirement plans by continued pay of share	Tuition reimbursement	Family support
South Dakota	5,000	Pay differential	Tuition reduction, free tuition for survivors	$500 bonus for combat tour, $240 for noncombat service, readjustment briefings, reduced hunt/fish licenses
Tennessee	20,000	Limited pay differential, accrue leave balances, longevity pay, retirement time credit	Tuition assistance	Free license plate for NG enlisted, discrimination for NG employment status a Class E felony
Texas	52,200	No loss of benefits, pay differential, military leave 15 days	Tuition reimbursement, certain requirements waived	Property tax deferral, free specialty license plates for NG and Reserve, family support

(continued)

Table 12.2 (continued) State Benefits for National Guard, (In-State) Reserve Members (See Especially Governors' Association 2006)

State	National Guard and Reserve	State Employees	Education	Other
Utah	9,500		Tuition waiver for wounded	License/certification extensions
Vermont	4,200	Military leave 11 days, pay differential, continued healthcare coverage for member and family for state duty, retirement service credit, preference points	Paid tuition for survivors	Emergency family assistance fund
Virginia	25,300	Pay differential, local pay supplements, carry-over annual leave accrual, credit military time toward retirement	Tuition credits, Web site, War Orphans Education Act	Death gratuity untaxed, legal protections, license extensions, Web site, focused employment programs
Washington	21,000	Leave donation program	Tuition waivers, preserve class standing/grades	Driver's license extension, excludes NG pay for unemployment compensation

West Virginia	8,700	Military leave 60 days, state-paid health and life insurance premiums	Up to 100 percent tuition and fees, in-state status, tuition matching	Workers' compensation for state duty injuries, civil legal help, supplemental life insurance
Wisconsin	17,400	Pay differential, continued sick/vacation leave accrual, carry-over of unused leave	Tuition reimbursement	Income tax exemption of military pay, license/certification extensions, legal protection, expedited absentee ballot process
Wyoming	2,100	Military leave 15 days, pay differential, state pays employee's share of health insurance premium, leave accrual, deferred compensation	100 percent tuition assistance	Family support, pay to maintain health insurance, excludes NG pay for unemployment, extra year of reemployment rights, $100,000 death benefit in combat zone
Capitol District	1,200 est.	(DC Government 2006)		
Guam	Unk	Military leave 15 days	75–100 percent tuition for NG	Vehicle license designation for NG and reserve
Puerto Rico	1,150	Pay differential, Christmas bonus eligible within 12 months	Tuition assistance	Combat pay income tax exempt, counseling
Virgin Islands	750	Pay differential		Pay differential (under court challenge)

States means activation of citizen–soldiers, those civilians who train and hold themselves ready for the challenges of active duty. This chapter has summarized the costs and benefits to both the society and the individual faced with the prospect of being mobilized, and to the organizations impacted by those mobilizations.

To keep current, the HR/HC function needs to monitor the financial, legal, and sociological impacts of mobilization of NG and reserve members on the workplace. An even greater impact is felt by public agencies in the United States, from which 40 percent of the NG and reserve strength is drawn.

The author suggests that it may be useful to monitor a variety of Web sites relevant to costs and benefits of a particular agency. For state and local agencies, there will be state-level Web sites for the State Department of Veterans' Affairs, State Military Department, Governor's Office, and Legislative bodies.

On a more global scale, the following Web sites track broad trends in military benefits, and often touch on and analyze costs as well:

U.S. Department of Defense	http://www.Defenselink.mil
U.S. Department of Veterans Affairs	http://www.va.gov
U.S. Department of Labor	http://www.dol.gov
U.S. Office of Special Counsel	http://www.osc.gov
Government Accountability Office	http://www.gao.gov
USDoD National Guard Bureau	http://www.ngb.army.mil
Employer Support of the Guard and Reserve	http://www.esgr.org
National Governors Association	http://www.nga.org
National Conference of State Legislatures	http://www.ncsl.org
Council of State Governments	http://www.csg.org
Reserve Officers Association	http://www.roa.org
National Guard Association	http://www.ngaus.org

References

Alaska Legislature, *Chapter 80, Statute Laws of 2006*, 2006 (Alaska Legislature: Juneau).

Amos, C., Advocate: Reservists Disproportionately Filling IA Jobs. *Navy Times.co*, 2006, Number 24.

Blue Ribbon Commission, *Financial Analysis of "Don't Ask, Don't Tell": How Much Does the Gay Ban Cost?* 2006 (University of California: Santa Barbara).

Brown, D., Guard Unprepared for Crisis, Panel Says. *The Oregonian*, March 2, 2007, Main Section, Sunrise Edition.

Burns, R., Guard, Reserve Lose Active Duty Ceiling. *The Oregonian*, January 12, 2007, Main Section, Sunrise Edition.

California Assembly, *Assembly Bill 2550 codified as Chapter 494 California Laws*, 2006a (State of California: Sacramento).

California Assembly, *Assembly Bill 2884 codified as Chapter 622 California Laws*, 2006b (State of California: Sacramento).

Commission on the National Guard and Reserves, *Second Report to Congress*, 2007 (Commission on the National Guard and Reserves: Arlington).

Congress, *U.S. Code Chapter 10, Sections 101(a)(5), 1209, 12301 et seq., and 12406*, 2005a (Congress of the United States: Washington, DC).

Congress, *U.S. Code Chapter 32, Sections 106 and 501 et seq.*, 2005b (Congress of the United States: Washington, DC).

Congress, *U.S. Code Chapter 38, Sections 101*, 2005c (Congress of the United States: Washington, DC). http://www.dod.gov/esesec/adr2000/Chapter15.html.

Congress, *Uniformed Services Employment and Reemployment Rights Act*, 1994. (Congress of the United States, Washington, DC).

Connecticut Legislature, *Public Act 06–62, Connecticut*, 2006 (Legislature, Hartford).

Constitution of the United States, 1787 as amended. (Government Printing Office, Washington, DC). Article I, Section 8, Clause 16 and Article II, Section 2, Clause 1.

Department of Defense, *DefenseLink News Articles and Releases*, 2001–2007 (Department of Defense: Washington, DC). http://www.Defenselink.mil.

Durch, J.S. and Larry E.H. Too Much Noise. *Military Medical Technology*, Vol. 9, Issue 8, December 11, 2005.

Goldstein, D., Of Iraq and Afghanistan Vets, 25% have Made Injury Claims. *The Oregonian*, March 13, 2007, Main Section, Sunrise Edition.

Government Accountability Office, *Reserve Forces: Actions Needed to Better Prepare the National Guard for Future Overseas and Domestic Missions*, 2004 (Government Accountability Office: Washington, DC). GAO-05-21.

Government Accountability Office, *Force Structure: Assessments of Navy Reserve Manpower Requirements Need to Consider the Most Cost-Effective Mix of Active and Reserve Manpower to Meet Mission Needs*, 2005a (Government Accountability Office: Washington, DC). GAO-06-125.

——, *Military Pay: Gaps in Pay and Benefits Create Financial Hardships for Injured Army National Guard and Reserve Soldiers*, 2005b (Government Accountability Office: Washington, DC). GAO-05-322T.

——, *Military Personnel: A Strategic Approach is Needed to Address Long-term Guard and Reserve Force Availability*, 2005c (Government Accountability Office: Washington, DC). GAO-05-285T.

——, *Reserve Forces: An Integrated Plan is Needed to Address Army Reserve personnel and Equipment Shortages*, 2005d (Government Accountability Office: Washington, DC). GAO-05-660.

——, *Reserve Forces: Plans Needed to Improve Army National Guard Equipment Readiness and Better Integrate Guard into Army Force Transformation Initiatives*, 2005e (Government Accountability Office: Washington, DC). GAO-06-111.

——, *Military Personnel: DOD and the Services Need to Take Additional Steps to Improve Mobilization Data for the Reserve Components*, 2006 (Government Accountability Office: Washington, DC). GAO-06-1068.

Hicks, K. Many Soldiers are Returning from Combat with Hearing Problems. *The Eagle-Tribune*, April 29, 2007.

Hollingsworth, B. *Presentation to Chairman's Reserve Component Conference* [*Powerpoint presentation*], August 2006. (National Committee for Employer Support of the Guard and Reserve, Arlington, VA). Slide 13.

Jowers, K. Rand: Long Tours make Divorce Less Likely. *Navy Times.com*, April 23, 2007. Available at http://www.navytimes.com/2007/04 /military_divorce_rand_070423/.

Lake, A., The Costs to Those Who Soldier On. *Boston Globe*. January 26, 2007. Web Edition.

Larabee, M., Oregon Units Short Millions in Equipment. *The Oregonian*, March 2, 2007, Main Section, Sunrise Edition.

Loven, J. White House Rebuts Guard Shortage Claim. *AP Newswire* on Yahoo.com, May 8, 2007.

Minnesota House of Representatives, Research Department, *Military and Veterans Enactments by the 2006 Minnesota Legislature*, 2006 (Research Department: St. Paul).

Mortenson, E. Police Chief Files Complaint against City. *The Oregonian*, May 9, 2007.

National Governors Association. *The Nation's National Guard*, 1954. (National Governors Association: Washington, DC).

National Guard Bureau. *National Guard Bureau Fact Sheet: Army National Guard FY 2005.* (National Guard Bureau, Washington, DC).

Office of Personnel Management, http://www.opm.gov/veterans/html/, n.d.

Pelofsky, J., Worries Grow over Mental Health of U.S. Soldiers. *Reuters Newswire*. March 28, 2007.

Phillippe, S. *Fact Sheet: Military Base Closure, Cleanup, and Reuse*, 2000 (California Environmental Protection Agency, Sacramento, CA).

Preiss, Robert A. The National Guard and Homeland Defense. *JFQ*, Issue 36, n.d. http://www.dtic.mil/doctrine/jel/jfq_pubs/1336.pdf.

Reuters. Troops Exposed to Sarin Risk Brain Damage: Report. *Reuters Newswire*, May 16, 2007.

Secretary of Defense. *Operation and Maintenance Overview, Fiscal Year (FY) 2007*, February 2006. (Office of the Secretary, Washington, DC).

Shellenbarger, S. Demographics Factor Heavily in Divorce-Rate Statistics. *The Wall Street Journal Online*, April 23, 2004. Available at http://www.wsj.com.

White House Office of Communications, *President Requests Funds to Strengthen Border Security*, May 14, 2006. (White House Office of Communications: Washington, DC).

Bibliography

Baker, F.W. III., Guard's Lack of Equipment Puts U.S. at Risk, Chief Says, May 24, 2007, http://www.defenselink.mil/articles.

Brockman, J., Report Validates Govs' Worries over Guard. *Stateline.org*, March 4, 2007, http://www.stateline.org/live/details/story?contentId=185875.

California Department of Veterans Affairs, *Legislative Update—October 6, 2006*, 2006 (Department of Veterans Affairs: Sacramento).

Connecticut Legislative Analysis Division, *Veterans' Benefits*, 2006 (Legislative Analysis Division, Hartford). 2006-R-0099.

Council of State Governments, Intergovernmental Affairs Committee, *Resolution on the Role of the Military in Disaster Response*, 2005 (Council of State Governments: Wilmington, DE).

Delaware National Guard, *DNG Benefits*. 2007 (Delaware National Guard: Dover). http://www.delawarenationalguard.com/home/new/content/benefits/index.cfm.

Department of Defense, *A Survivor's Guide to Benefits: Taking care of Our Own*, 2007 (Department of Defense: Washington, DC).

Dion, M., *The Role of the National Guard in Disaster Response and Critical Infrastructure Protection.* 2007 (George Mason School of Law Critical Infrastructure Protection Program, Arlington) http://www.cipp.gmu.edu/research/ NationalGuard_CIP.php.

District of Columbia Government, *FY 2007 Proposed Budget and Financial Plan*, 2006 (District of Columbia: Washington, DC).

Employer Support of the Guard and Reserve, Ombudsman Services and the Law. ESGR, http://www.esgr.org/employers2/thelaw.asp.

Faster, Easier Citizenship for Military Personnel: Both Sides of the Issue. n.d. http://immigration.about.com/od/uscitizenshiprequirements/i/MilitCitizenIss.htm.

Federal Aviation Administration, *Employment Rights and Benefits of Federal Civilian Employees Who Proceed to Active Military Duty*, n.d. (Federal Aviation Administration: Washington, DC) http://www.faa.gov/AHR/military/actvtweb.cfm.

Gershkoff, Amy R., Saving Soldiers' Jobs. *Washington Post*, August 4, 2007, Main Section.

Haskell, MSG B., Reserve Employment Information Program Begins. *Armed Forces Press Service*. Washington, DC: Department of Defense, March 31, 2004.

Indiana Department of Veterans' Affairs, *2006 Directory of Approved Programs for Education Benefits*, 2006 (Department of Veterans' Affairs: Indianapolis).

Injured Vet Wins Re-employment & Back Pay. *Federal Daily,* October 23, 2006, http://www.FederalDaily.com.

Iowa Lawmakers Ask for National Guard Help. *Air Force Times*, March 18, 2007, http://www.airforcetimes.com/news/2007/03/ap_iowa_guardhelp_031807/.

Lett, C., HOVENSA Sues V.I. Government over New Guard Differential Pay. *Virgin Island Daily News*, August 23, 2006, http://www.virginislandsdailynews.com/index.pl/article_home?id=17595669.

Lubold, G., Key US Army Ranks Begin to Thin. *The Christian Science Monitor*, May 2, 2007.

Massachusetts Secretary of the Commonwealth, *Definitions of Massachusetts Veterans*, n.d. (Massachusetts Secretary: Boston) http://www.sec.state.ma.us/cis/cisvet/vetdefin.htm.

National Committee for Employer Support of the Guard and Reserve, *Presentation to Chairman's Reserve Component Conference*, August 8, 2006 (U.S. Department of Defense and Employer Support of the Guard and Reserve: Arlington). Power Point Presentation.

National Governors Association, *State and Territorial Support for National Guard and Regular Military Members and Their Families*, 2006 (National Governors Association: Washington, DC).

National Guard Association of the United States, Governor Signs Bill Expanding State Benefits for Guardsmen. *National Guard*, April 2006.

National Guard Bureau, Office of Legislative Liaison, *National Guard Equipment Requirements,* 2006 (Office of Legislative Liaison: Arlington).

New Mexico Department of Veterans Services, *State Benefits*, 2006 (Department of Veterans Services: Santa Fe). http://www.dvs.state.nm.us/benefits.html.

New York State Division of Military and Naval Affairs, *Benefits of the New York Patriot Plan,* 2006 (Division of Military and Naval Affairs: Albany).

New York State Division of Veterans' Affairs, *2006 Veterans Legislation Update*, 2006 (Division of Veterans' Affairs: Albany).

Office of the Secretary of Defense, *Operation and Maintenance Overview: Fiscal Year (FY) 2005 Budget Estimates,* 2003 (Office of the Secretary: Washington, DC).

———, *Operation and Maintenance Overview: Fiscal Year (FY) 2006 Budget Estimates*, 2004 (Office of the Secretary: Washington, DC).

———, *Operation and Maintenance Overview: Fiscal Year (FY) 2007 Budget Estimates.* 2006 (Office of the Secretary: Washington, DC).

Peterson, K., Govs Want Say on Guard Changes. *Stateline.org,* June 16, 2006, http:/www. stateline.org/live/ViewPage.action?siteNodeId=136&languageId=1& contented.htm.

Slavin, B., Reserve Troops' Job Woes Increase. *USA Today,* December 8, 2006, Section A.

Sullivan, J., Home Front. *The Oregonian,* January 10, 2007, Main Section, Sunrise Edition.

Top Official Describes Reserve-Component Mobilization Policy. *Southwest Nebraska News,* April 17, 2007.

Troops Exposed to Sarin Risk Brain Damage: Report. *Reuters Newswire,* May 16, 2007, reporting on a New York Times Web site analysis of a forthcoming report in the June, 2007 *Journal Neurotoxicology.*

Uniformed Services Almanac, Inc., *National Guard Almanac,* Annually from 1974 (Uniformed Services Almanac, Inc.: Falls Church, Virginia).

Virgin Islands Refinery Sues to Strike Down Troop-Pay Law. http://www.easybourse.com/ Website/dynamic/News.php?NewsID=4401&lang=fra August 19, 2006.

White House, Kansas Governor Argue over Storm Response. *AP News Service,* May 8, 2007. Web Edition.

Chapter 13

Trends in Outsourcing Human Resources Benefits: Opportunities, Challenges, and the Florida Example

Elsie B. Crowell

CONTENTS

13.1   Background

The terms "privatizing," "outsourcing," and "contracting" continue to dominate business and academic literature today. They are the latest buzzwords for both private and public sector organizations. Influenced largely by public choice theorists, many advocates believe that the role of government should be limited, that production and delivery of services should be separate, and that the best method of implementing economic and social reform is via networks of private, for-profit entities. These advocates see public sector bureaucrats as self-interested, motivated by wealth and status, and politicians and interest groups by power and perks, respectively (Self 1993; Batley and Larbi 2004). Downs (1967, p. 57) argues that "we can intuitively postulate that the total amount of waste and inefficiency in society is likely to rise as bureaucracy becomes more prominent." These advocates postulate that the concept of separating the production of goods and services via outsourcing results in less government and more savings. In sum, public choice theorists are advocates of reliance on the private market which is intended to reduce the role of government, increase competition, and improve efficiency.

Furthermore, this assumption is grounded in the new public management (NPM) component of public administration. It emphasizes competition in the private sector, contracting out, decentralization, accountability, and the adoption of private sector management practices (Hood 1990).

Because these words are often used synonymously and with varying definitions, it is essential to distinguish among them and emphasize their context in this chapter. Several notable scholars (Donahue 1989; Starr 1989; Augur 1999; Savas 2000) have provided a framework by which we view the term "privatization." Extracted from these concepts, privatization can be framed as a broad theme or umbrella encompassing many forms of public–private partnerships: contracts, outsourcing, franchises, grants, volunteers, vouchers, and self-service. For instance, Starr (1989, p. 22) defines privatization as the "act of reducing the role of government, or increasing the role of the private sector in an activity or ownership of assets." Savas (2005, p. 107) discusses ten different definitions of privatization, and settles on one that captures the essence of the term: "Privatization is changing from an arrangement with high government involvement to one with less." In its purest definition, privatization is the sale of public assets to a private sector interest.

Privatized programs today are more likely to mean outsourcing and contracting, which are generally seen as a narrower definition of privatization. Outsourcing is contracting with a third party to provide services, normally performed internally, for a negotiated set of services and fees. Contracting out is the process of entering into an agreement with an external supplier to perform specific services over a period of time (Cook 1999). Essentially, these terms mean the same thing; therefore, they are used synonymously within the context of this chapter unless otherwise noted.

The purpose of this chapter is to examine trends and practices in outsourcing human resources benefits in the private and public sectors. Its aims are: one, to share a broad overview of privatization; two, to review outsourcing trends in public and private sector organizations; three, to examine some of the benefits and risks associated with the practice of outsourcing HR functions; four, to offer a close-up view of the state of Florida's "People First" outsourcing program; and five, to discuss safeguards, lessons learned as a result of Florida's experience, and public policy implications. Although this chapter contains a broad discussion of privatization experiences of a variety of programs, the opportunities and risks also apply to the outsourcing of employee benefit programs. Public managers will find the review helpful in considering alternatives for service delivery choices and providing guidance for effective partnerships.

13.2 Privatization/Reinvention

Several of today's movements have their roots in public administration starting with the Pendleton Act of 1883. At least 11 reform efforts were launched before the 1993 *National Performance Review*, later renamed the National Partnership for Reinventing America (NPR), all based on private models and lacking an understanding of public sector problems (Kim and Wolff 1994, p. 73). All embraced a common theme that something is wrong with government and called for action against its unwieldy organization, duplication of services, and costly programs. These administrative reform efforts known as "reinvention" became a dominant paradigm in public administration. Most targeted the federal government and gained currency in the 1990s, thanks to Osborne and Gaebler's book (1992) *Reinventing Government: How the Entrepreneurial Spirit Is Transforming the Public Sector*, not to mention the support of public choice theorists.

The concept of privatization dates back to ancient times, but in the United States, it is most often credited to Peter F. Drucker, an American management professor, who first used the term "reprivatize" in 1968. The following year, it was suggested that "privatization" be used instead (Savas 2000). Today's focus on privatization may be traced to the 1970s, 1980s, and 1990s, when local governments experience economic woes due to recession, federal cutbacks, and citizen tax revolts. Thus, local governments led the charge to privatize, to cut costs and respond to deficits, whereas state governments took a more cautious approach (Augur 1999, p. 435).

After the 1980 election of President Ronald Reagan, who strongly supported the premise that government had become too bloated, too costly, the country's conventional wisdom took on a more philosophical edge. He stated in his 1981 inaugural address that "government is *not* a solution to our problem, government *is* the problem" (January 20, 1981). Also during his tenure, the 1984 Grace Commission Report predicted that the federal government would incur an annual deficit of $1 trillion by the end of the 2000 and called for private sector management strategies to address problems created by the bureaucracy (Worsnop 1992).

Efforts were renewed in the 1990s to present privatization as an alternative delivery of service. For example, on April 30, 1992, President George H.W. Bush signed an executive order aimed at enabling governments to sell or lease infrastructure assets, roads, bridges, and airports to private interests (Worsnop 1992). In 1993, the National Commission on State and Local Public Service (NCSLPS), also known as the Winter Commission, issued a report on the mistrust of government and the state of public management at all government levels, maintaining that market mechanisms may be more efficient.

The Clinton administration (1993–2001) also focused on government cost and efficiency. A report of the National Performance Review, *From Red Tape to Results: Creating a Government That Works Better and Costs Less*, outlined steps to these ends (Gore 1993). A top priority of the Clinton administration was to reduce the number of employees; they pledged to eliminate 252,000 federal positions during his tenure. Congress later increased this number to 272,900, calling for a 12 percent cut. By 1998, the federal workforce had experienced a decrease of 355,500 employees, a 16.2 percent reduction (Jones 1998, p. 3).

Horn (1995) describes a transactional explanation of the country's move toward privatization. He observes that it was not gradual but abrupt, coinciding with the widespread economic and fiscal problems in the early 1980s. Nor was it accidental that this practice was strikingly similar in other countries, particularly the United Kingdom, which placed considerable weight on fiscal and debt reduction goals. Most scholars agree that privatization was mainly influenced by the postwar trends, especially the increase in the size of governments after World War II.

Each of these reform movements had as an underlying theme that market forces, via competition, would reduce costs, increase quality, and deliver more effective services than government. Moreover, governments pursued a broad range of strategies to respond to these demands including decentralization, centralization, downsizing, outsourcing, and public–private partnerships.

Therefore, it is not surprising that cost savings and fiscal pressures have been cited most often as the basis for outsourcing services. Seventy-four percent of respondents in a Touche Ross 1987 survey indicated that outsourcing was more advantageous than internal production (Greene 2002). When asked in a 1992 International City and County Management Association (ICMA) survey why local governments were interested in privatization, 90 percent cited efforts to cut costs, although 53 percent mentioned external fiscal pressures (Savas 2000). Moreover, in a business survey conducted by the American Management Association (AMA) in 1996, 70 percent of respondents believed cost reduction was key, 65 percent sought quality improvement, and 72 percent cited time management as a factor in their thinking. Other incentives included enhanced technology and reduced staffing in HR (Siegel 2000, p. 224). Because cost savings are a high priority and encourage greater incentives for direct benefits, an emphasis on market economics is considered advantageous. Thus, outsourcing became a popular strategy to cut cost and reduce the size of government.

13.3 Trends in Outsourcing Human Resources Benefits

The practice of outsourcing human resources (HR) benefits is becoming more prevalent in the private sector. However, certain types of public HR benefits have long been handled by the private sector. Examples include medical claim processing and payments, investments for 401(k) programs, pension retirement plans, and a variety of insurance benefit options. On the other hand, there is limited empirical research on outsourcing HR in the public sector.

13.3.1 Private Sector

The outsourcing of HR benefits is increasingly widespread and growing rapidly in private sector organizations. Businesses are using this approach to reform the human resources field. The Gartner researchers estimate that the value of HR-related outsourcing reached $24.6 billion in 2006, and HR is the largest segment of the business outsourcing market, 18.6 percent. Payroll and benefits ranked as the most popular tasks to be outsourced (Scardino et al. 2006).

The conference board released findings from a 2004 survey among major U.S. corporations, revealing that 76 percent of respondents outsourced one or more major HR functions; just 9 percent had ruled out the practice, compared with 23 percent one year before (Dell 2004). In a 1996 survey conducted by the Society for Human Resource Management, one out of five respondents reported that their organizations had outsourced one or more functions, previously performed by their own HR departments. Of the 1000 largest publicly traded companies, more than 85 percent had outsourced some of their HR business. Furthermore, in a similar study conducted by the American Management Association (AMA), 94 percent of the respondents said they outsourced one or more HR functions (Cook 1999, p. ix)

Additional support for the phenomenal growth in outsourcing HR functions can be found in a survey of 165 companies that do so. Two-thirds of the respondents outsourced a major HR function: 80 percent, 401(k) programs; 70 percent, pension benefits management; and 69 percent health benefits management. Of the U.S. companies that outsource HR benefits, some two-thirds fully or partially outsource five or more functions; 50 percent of 401(k) programs are fully outsourced and 30 percent partly so. The next highest category is pension benefits with 32 percent fully and 38 percent partly outsourced (Gelman and Dell 2002).

A more recent HR private outsourcing contract was negotiated in March 2007, when IBM announced a $217 million contract to manage the personnel functions of American Airlines. The seven and a half year contract will support HR functions, related to IT and a call center for the airline's 88,000 employees. Mercer HR Services is expected to handle the health benefits and pension payroll management component of the IBM contract. American Airlines representatives expect the company to save $60 million during the course of the arrangement, reducing administrative expenses by $2 million a year. The announcement reinforced other major outsourcing agreements won by IBM, Delta Airlines in August 2006, and CVS Pharmacy (with 55,000 employees), a ten-year agreement with functions similar to those of American Airlines (Hines 2007).

Finally, Deloitte Consulting conducted a study that included some of the world's largest organizations participating in outsourcing a broad range of services, including HR. As the top reasons for choosing to outsource certain business functions, the overwhelming majority of respondents, 70 percent, named cost savings, and 57 percent named best practice/quality innovation. These organizations, both public and private, represent a capitalization of nearly $100 trillion, employ more than one million workers, and spend $50 billion on outsourcing contracts alone (Deloitte Consulting 2005).

In summary, the role of HR managers is rapidly changing in the private sector as core functions are outsourced. The main reasons cited are cost savings, technology innovation, concentration on core mission, lack of specialized expertise, and efforts to streamline the production delivery process.

13.3.2 Public Sector

Survey data confirms some growth in HR outsourcing in the public sector; however, unlike private companies, which outsource most HR functions, government tends to outsource functions that are not core management. These include health and benefit administration, workers' compensation administration, employee assistance programs, drug testing, and HR information systems operations (Siegel 2000; Chi et al. 2003).

The public sector may be hindered by philosophical and controversial differences not found in private industry decision making. Many stakeholders, both for and against privatizing certain public functions, express caution and optimism relative to the increasing number of outsourced contracts of any type with private organizations.

One criticism of the public sector's lag in outsourcing HR benefits is HR does not share the same high level organizational status in the United States that it does internationally; the American public sector is said to be a follower of private sector practices (Koch et al. 2004). On the other hand, a different perspective about the lag behind foreign governments holds that there is much less to privatize because a larger percentage of employees work in state-owned businesses in the United States than in other countries (Worsnop 1992).

According to the Council of State Governments (CSG), privatization in state governments remained level or increased slightly from 1997 to 2002. On the basis of the survey results, some respondents reported small savings from 1 to more than 15 percent, but to most, cost savings were largely unknown or not documented. Connecticut and Michigan reported a savings of more than 15 percent from personnel privatization (Chi et al. 2003).

Although there appeared to be no consensus on the value of privatization through empirical data, most policy makers cite general reasons for privatization in government. These reasons mirror those of the private sector: specialized expertise, technology, and cost savings. The largest privatization example cited is Florida's seven-year, $280 million human resources contract. In the area of personnel, reasons offered for privatization "were a lack of state personnel and expertise, cost savings and high quality private services." Services more frequently privatized by states include workers' compensation claims processing, flexible benefits, training consultants, and information technology services. States privatizing more than 10 percent of their personnel services include Connecticut and Florida. On the other hand, 10 agencies replied that their states did not privatize more than 1 percent of personnel services (Arizona, California, Illinois, New Hampshire, South Dakota, North Dakota, Oregon, South Carolina, and Washington) (Chi et al. 2003, p. 3). Table 13.1 provides an overview of the types of HR services outsourced. Training, staff development, and technology are privatized by more states than other types of HR functions.

Given the rapid pace of outsourcing in the private sector, the conference board examined trends in outsourcing HR functions in public sector organizations. A few public sector organizations, U.S. Transportation Security Administration, state of Florida, Detroit public schools, and the Texas Health and Human Services

Table 13.1   Privatized Personnel Programs and Services

Program of Service	*States*
Training program staff/development	California, Connecticut, Iowa, Louisiana, Michigan, North Dakota, Oklahoma, Tennessee, Washington, Wyoming
Information technology	Connecticut, Florida, Idaho, Illinois, Minnesota, Montana
Workers' Compensation Claims Processing	Connecticut, Iowa, South Dakota
Health insurance claims processing	Montana, South Dakota
General program administration/support	Illinois, Iowa
Consultants	Idaho, Iowa
Collective bargaining negotiations	Florida, Iowa

Source: Adapted from Chi, K.S., Arnold, K., and Perkins, H., *Spectrum: The Journal of State Government*, 76, 12, Table 1, 2003.

Commission are recognized as trailblazers in the outsourcing of HR functions. It is estimated that an additional 10–15 states are planning to pursue outsourcing HR functions, including the Office of Personnel Management, the federal HR agency. An overview of the outsourcing of the public sector organizations in the United States is provided in Table 13.2.

Contracting for certain types of services in municipal governments is growing rapidly as numerous studies have convinced policy makers that clear and compelling evidence indicate cost savings. However, these savings are more commonly associated with solid waste collection, transportation, vehicle towing, and related services. For instance, the most frequently contracted municipal services, at 80 percent, are vehicle towing and storage. Of the most frequently contracted services in large cities, employment and training account for 24 percent, nine out of the top ten services (Dilger et al. 1997, p. 21).

According to Warner and Hefetz (2001), growth in privatization of local government services rose slightly from 22 to 24 percent from 1982–1997. Their findings suggest that changing demands for services and instability in contracts, including "contracting

Table 13.2   Public Sector Human Resources Outsourcing

	Employees	Year of Beginning	HR Functions Outsourced	Cost Savings
U.S. Transportation Security Administration	55,600	2001	Total	20–25 percent (estimated)
Texas Health and Human Services Commission	46,000 (approximate)	2004	Total (excluding policy and planning)	$1 billion first two years of implementation; $63 million in savings over five years (targeted)
State of Florida— Department of Management Services	189,000	2002	Total	$173 million over seven-year contract (targeted)
Detroit Public Schools	26,000	2001	Medical benefits administration	$5 million initially; $1 million per year (direct)

Source: Adapted from Koch, J., Dell, D., and Johnson, L., HR Outsourcing in government Organizations: Emerging Trends, early lessons, Research Report No. E-0007–04 RR. New York: Conference Board Inc., 2004, 26–37.

in—the reverting back to public provision of previously privatized services," may account for this. It is possible that "reverse privatization" reflects public sector problems with the contracting process, limited efficiency gains, erosion in service quality, or the broader community values associated with public services delivery.

13.4 Why Do Organizations Outsource?

On the basis of the previous overview of outsourcing in private and public organizations, some of the top reasons for outsourcing are discussed in more detail in this section and summarized in Figure 13.1. (Williams 1998; Cook 1999; Deloitte Consulting 2005; Power et al. 2006).

Cost savings are ranked as the most important reason why organizations choose to outsource services. Two key reasons why HR functions are attractive for outsourcing are that employee-related expenses average about 70 percent of production costs, and employee benefit programs account for the largest share of the HR department's time. These factors may suggest that it is difficult for HR departments to function as a business partner although effectively meeting the needs of employees (Pringle 1995, p. 61). Furthermore, it is anticipated that the vendor, through economies of scale, will realize significant cost savings to be returned to the organization. Staff reduction will also yield savings in office space, benefits packages, salaries, and other related expenses.

Technology (IT) is identified as a priority concern by organizations both public and private, particularly as it relates to HR functions. Investment in advanced technology and the availability of skilled IT workers are key factors in the decision to outsource. Because benefit programs are complex, diverse, and labor intensive, state-of-the-art technology is needed to stay abreast of this rapidly changing field.

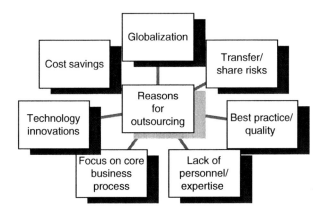

Figure 13.1 Reasons for outsourcing.

Technology is among the largest outsourced functions in both public and private sector organizations, due largely to cost, employee expertise, and changing markets. Instant access to benefits via self-service technology and voice response systems can be made available 24 hours, freeing staff time to become more efficient in more profitable areas.

Moreover, outsourcing technology is booming; growth in federal government contract spending is attributed to two types of services: information technology, which increased from $3.7 billion in fiscal year (FY) 1990 to $13.4 billion in FY 2000; and professional, administrative, and management support services, which rose from $12.3 billion in FY 1990 to $21.1 billion in FY 2000 (U.S. General Accounting Office 2001, p. 3).

Focus on core business process: Services provided by HR staff are viewed as administrative in nature, processing large volumes of paperwork and engaging in time-intensive functions that can readily be outsourced. Elimination of these services will streamline operations and allow HR to become a key business and strategic partner in the organization. For example, staff will be in a position to provide better services in areas such as HR planning, employee relations, career development and progression, and highly sensitive administrative issues. The intent is to explore opportunities to generate profits, reduce cost centers, and increase the overall efficiency of the organization.

Best practices/quality innovation: Organizations seek to improve their services by emulating the best ideas in their respective industries. Through outsourcing, they seek to mimic their counterparts and to maintain a competitive edge in production, creative ideas, and quality of services. The premise of institutional isomorphism or diffusion may prevail even if organizational efficiency cannot be confirmed.

Lack of personnel/expertise: Particularly at the federal level, there are fewer trained HR specialists. This may be attributed to reduced staffing and increased responsibilities, because personnel occupations lost 20 percent of their workforce in the federal government between 1991 and 1996 (Siegel 2000, p. 224). The complexity of benefits, aging workforce, and concurrent increase in retirees are also factors. The aging workforce and retirement trends are affecting some sectors sooner than others. Leading the pack are government, education, healthcare, transportation, and utilities (Young 2003).

Globalization: As organizations seek to remain competitive in today's global economy, offshore outsourcing is an attractive strategy to achieve greater economies of scale. It is a method of tapping into a workforce that will perform low-level, repetitive jobs at effective cost savings. It can also reap the benefits of an educated workforce in the fields of technology, science, and engineering. As more organizations choose to locate facilities in other countries, thus gaining access to international markets, global capabilities are crucial to a successful organization.

Transfer/share risks: Outsourcing offers an opportunity to engage in partnership initiatives. These arrangements are intended to facilitate the goals of both entities in that they may respond to rising costs and financial risks although utilizing competitive markets and increasing profits (Linder and Rosenau 2000, pp. 4–33).

Table 13.3   Advantages of Outsourcing Human Resources Functions

Upgrade HR role from provider services to business partner or strategic role
Reduce production costs
State-of-the-art technology
Response to increased responsibilities and reduced staffing
Focus on core functions
Economies of scale
24 hour access to online benefits information and changes
Integrated delivery service system
Introduction of competition-best service at the least cost
Increased quality/efficiency

Because organizations seek advantages through outsourcing HR services, they anticipate achieving beneficial outcomes. Some of these are listed in Table 13.3.

Although the benefits of outsourcing are numerous, there are many reasons to take precautionary measures. All service delivery options must be carefully evaluated before negotiating the final contract to outsource services. A number of risks can adversely affect both private and public sector organizations. Because cost savings are the predominant reason why organizations choose to outsource (it should never be the sole reason), the value and outcomes of anticipated savings are highly relevant in assessing the attendant risks.

Deloitte Consulting (2005, p. 2) calls for change in the outsourcing market. They assert that organizations have now become more aware of the real costs and inherent risks of outsourcing. Often outsourcing introduces complexity and increased cost requiring more senior management attention and skills than anticipated. "Outsourcing is an extraordinarily complex process and the benefits often fail to materialize." Moreover, many of the expected outcomes did not meet expectations. For example, 70 percent of the respondents in the Deloitte study decided to outsource to achieve cost savings; yet 38 percent paid additional cost for services they believed to be covered in the contract; 57 percent sought best practices, but 31 percent believed vendors became complacent once contracts were finalized. Other concerns, such as access to skilled workers, flexibility, and focus on core functions, were not successfully resolved via outsourcing.

Furthermore, the Gartner Group's (1999) findings revealed that although 70 percent of the companies that outsource technology projects expected to save money only half of them actually did. They predict that to see cost savings a company's cost to do the project internally must be 150 percent or more than the cost of outsourcing. Potential savings are lost in 60 percent of the outsourcing projects.

According to Prager (1994, p. 176), contracting is not a panacea; the public sector must give closer attention to managing and monitoring contracts. True costs must be accurately calculated to determine which alternatives are most efficient, including internal service delivery. Findings suggest that long-term savings will prevail only if a number of conditions coalesce. Moreover, outsourcing does not reduce government outlays nor increase government efficiency unless the decision makes economic sense. On the other hand, opportunities to outsource are evident when a governance structure becomes overgrown; a contractor can benefit from economies of scope and market competition when the government cannot.

Several research studies conducted by an impressive array of scholars, covering the period 1972–1996, find that private sector production is less costly than the public sector. This may be attributed to competition, scale economies, and incentive structure for private sector managers (Brooks 2004, p. 467).

On the other hand, a number of researchers take issue with these findings. Some studies show increased costs (Boyne 1998; Sclar 2000). Other research shows that benefits from privatization fail to consider factors such as the high cost of contracting and monitoring and that some of these savings are short-lived (Stein 1990; Prager 1994; Berry et al. 1999; AFSCME 2006). Contract specifications, nature of the market, and availability of alternative suppliers are all factors.

Starr (1987) questions whether contacting services to private providers results in cost savings. He asserts that privatization transforms public monopolies into private monopolies as successful bidders gain advantages over other bidders. Examples cited are defense, construction projects, healthcare, all of which are areas that have been traditionally private but at a significantly high cost.

According to American Federation of State, County and Municipal Employees (AFSCME 2006), contracting out costs more because hidden costs and service delivery are not included in preliminary estimates. Typically, expenses associated with contract monitoring, administration, conversion costs and other charges for extra work, and the contractor's use of public facilities are not documented.

Finally, Boyne (1998, p. 474) argues that empirical studies do suggest that contracting leads to higher efficiency, which appears to support public choice theorists; however, the methodological critiques are not valid. General problems are absence of control for the following: local preferences, scale effects, and measures of competition.

Given these concerns, organizations must engage in due diligence to minimize the disadvantages or risks associated with outsourcing HR services. Table 13.4 outlines selected areas that require close examination and detailed planning to safeguard the viability of the organization.

13.5 State of Florida: "People First" Outsourcing Program

After Jeb Bush became Florida's governor in 1999, the privatization of government services accelerated. The state entered into 138 private contracts to provide a broad range of services previously performed by state workers. The Reason Foundation

Table 13.4   Disadvantages and Risks in Outsourcing Human Resources Functions

Disadvantages	Risks
Low morale/increased turnover	Lack of vendor performance
Reduction of core staff	Artificial low bids/low balling
Loss of institutional knowledge/expertise	Loss of intellectual property
Dilution of accountability	Security breach/exposure of confidential information
Subcontracting/third-party supervision	Bankruptcy, merger, acquisition
Contract managing/monitoring costs	Escalating costs
Loss of capacity to provide a service	Lack of compliance with governmental
Private monopoly	Statutes, regulations, or directives
Inflexible system (one size fits all)	Contractual disputes
Customer loses control of services	Termination of contractual services
	Governance

(2006) claimed that these projects generated savings of $550 million. Bush believed that Florida's privatization model was an example for other states. In his 2003 inaugural address, Bush famously stated that "[t]here would be no greater tribute to our maturity as a society than if we can make these buildings around us empty of workers, silent monuments to the time when government played a larger role than it deserved or could adequately fill" (Saunders 2003).

Thus, in 2001 Florida embarked on an ambitious agenda to outsource its HR services including the supporting technology component, referred to as Cooperative Personnel Employment Subsystem (COPES). The state has been dubbed a trailblazer among public sector organizations and its contract is cited as being the largest state outsourcing project in the United States (Koch et al. 2004). Commingled with the governor's plans to outsource was the legislative initiative to reform the civil service system, referred to as "Service First." In Florida's case, efforts to reinvent government were not limited to reforming the career service system. They also included outsourcing HR services as a means of increasing efficiency and modernization.

In August 2002, in conjunction with the implementation of service first and the goal of reducing the workforce through privatization, the state signed a seven-year,

$278.6 million contract with Convergys Customer Management Group, Inc., headquartered in Cincinnati, Ohio, to provide an enterprise-wide suite of services for managing the state's human capital. The contracted functions include the administration of payroll, benefits, and staffing through an interactive web-based system called "People First." The Convergys outsourcing contract was touted as saving the state as much as $173.1 million, over the seven-year term. The term has now been extended to nine years and the contract now totals $349.9 million. The Convergys contract was amended six times through July 21, 2004 (Florida Auditor General Report No. 2005-047, 2004).

The implementation of this contract resulted in a 50 percent reduction (949 positions, 480 of which were vacant) in all state agency human resource offices (Florida Auditor General Report No. 2005-047). As a result, employees with the knowledge, expertise, and training to handle personnel and payroll transaction for their agencies were no longer available to provide services to managers, employees, and retirees. Consequently, the remaining staff were barely able to perform existing services and ill-equipped to intervene or troubleshoot any inquiries about Convergys' contractual services.

Florida soon learned that outsourcing a major contract could not be done quickly. The process required meticulous planning, well-thought-out contract negotiations, due diligence, and clear delineation of services to be provided by both the vendor and the state.

In a study conducted by Crowell and Guy, forthcoming, respondents were unanimous in their beliefs that the Convergys contract had made it more difficult to handle personnel functions in the state. A key complaint was that the state failed to include the HR personnel in the planning process. Other factors contributing to the chaotic environment included lack of planning and preparation, unrealistic timelines, and denied requests for adjustments. Although expertise and training are essential elements in such a massive undertaking, Convergys' employees lacked them; they were unable to provide instructions or assist customers. Complicating matters, state employees were not adequately trained to use the new technology. In personnel actions, one of the most common complaints was the increased time it took to process a time and attendance report. A task that had been accomplished in a few seconds under the old system became a 30–45 minute ordeal under the new one. Because time and attendance is also linked to payroll, problems with pay and benefits were abundant. Examples include cancellation of health insurance, over-and-under charges, and unauthorized payroll deductions. According to Doug Darling, Director of Accounting and Audit, the number of electronic fund transfer (EFT) cancellations became four times higher after Convergys began handling payroll (Darling 2005).

Other issues plaguing the People First contract were allegations of identity theft; employees being hired without sufficient background checks; subcontracting to an entity that sent work not only out of state (a violation of the contract), but also out of the country; and a whistle-blower charge pending in the attorney general's office (Caputo 2006a, 2006b; Cotterell 2006a, 2007; Thormeyer 2006).

In short, a one-year delay in implementation, coupled with a lack of compatible software and a user-unfriendly system, contributed to multiple problems that might have been avoided with adequate preparation and planning. Complicating these challenges was excessive turnover in agency heads at the Department of Management Services (DMS), the entity charged with administering and coordinating the People First outsourcing contract.

In an e-mail message to the author on May 31, 2007, Lauren Buzzelli revealed that DMS had six different agency heads between 1999 and 2006.

Audit and legislative reports confirmed many of the concerns expressed by employees. Deficiencies in the Convergys contract are outlined in the Department of Management Services' People First Operational Audit Report No. 2005-047, October 2004.

Seventeen deficiencies are documented in the report, which highlights numerous internal weaknesses with contract negotiators, and in some cases, a total disregard for the integrity of the taxpayer funds. Problems are identified with planning, evaluations and negotiations, contract provisions, deliverables, financial compliance, conflicts of interest, lobbying, and contract administration.

The governor's inspector general also conducted an audit report on contracting in Florida and wrote, "as documented in almost 500 audit findings over a three-year period, controls over contracting are in a state of disrepair." The inspector general's audit was a review of previous audits of seven governor's agencies, performed by agency inspector generals, the State Auditor General, and Office of Program Policy Analysis and Government Accountability (OPPAGA). Inconsistent guidelines and practices were cited as no statewide system of logging for vendor performance existed to share information with all agencies and to determine if contracts should be awarded to a particular vendor. The top two audit problems were performance monitoring and procurement methodology (Harper 2003, p. 1).

Due to these problems with the multimillion-dollar contract, Florida SB 1146 was passed in 2005 to strengthen procurement contracts.* It set forth procedures for state agencies to comply with in outsourcing any service costing more than $10 million, established a Center for Efficient Government, and outlined standards for establishing business cases, contract terms, amendments, renewals, and extensions. Senator Nancy Argenziano, R-Crystal River and chair of the state senate's committee on governmental oversight and productivity, said in an April 2005 press release that SB 1146 addressed "documented examples of poor contract management, cronyism and favoritism in bid awards, questionable official behavior, and wasted use of time and money on failed projects."

Senate Bill 2518, similar to SB 1146, was subsequently passed in 2006, establishing a process to review and evaluate proposed outsourcing projects. It also created the council on efficient government to act as oversight board for all outsourcing initiatives from planning to post implementation.

---

* Governor Jeb Bush vetoed Senate Bill 1146, June 27, 2005.

The implementation of People First began in May 2003. Four years later, a review of the program is now underway. The latest Auditor General Report (No. 2007-087) was released January 25, 2007. The "audit determined that People First, as currently designed and implemented, has made progress in many operational areas. Agencies' knowledge and use of People First continue to grow and, in concert with the implementation of new performance metrics and standards; improvements in project organization, management, and communication; and continued progress in system enhancements, overall functionality has improved. However, significant deficiencies remain, both with People First and with agency use of People First." The majority of 11 deficiencies relate to time sheets, employee pay, and agency payroll actions. The report also noted that "security guidelines were not written and established until March 2006, three years into the project. Moreover all components of the project are not yet available." (Florida Auditor General Report 2007-087, 2007, p. 2). The Auditor General has been unable to document whether the project is saving taxpayers' money (Cotterell 2006b).

In a February 21, 2007, press release, newly elected Governor Charlie Crist ordered a top-to-bottom review of privatization in state government starting with the Convergys People First contract. Created by the legislature in 2006, the council on efficient government will examine the project along with two other major contracts and determine what went wrong.

Also in a May 3, 2007, press release, the newly appointed secretary of the Department of Management Services, Linda South, announced the results of a first ever online survey measuring customer satisfaction. Fifty-nine percent of active state employees surveyed in April 2007 said that People First met or exceeded expectations. The remaining 41 percent said the system fails to meet their expectations. South indicated that the results suggest the need to improve services. However, Bob Nave, vice president of client services for Convergys, stated, "Last year, People First exceeded 95 percent of the established standards for system performance, which exceeds industry standards. Convergys continues to work with the State of Florida to make People First more efficient and easier to use."

13.6 What Can Be Learned from Florida's Experience?

Florida's experience is problematic but perhaps it is exaggerated by its publicness. It is presented in more detail, due to its publicness, timeliness, size, and far reaching impact on the state's public service. It indeed has been a "rocky road." Listed below are lessons, some unique to Florida, others more general in nature:

■ Service First, People First, Convergys—Do not attempt to implement a major outsourcing initiative and reform the civil service system at the same time. Both affect the HR employees on a personal and professional level. They are concerned about job security at the same time they are called upon to implement a major overhaul of the personnel system.

- Obtain a firm commitment from management and include all stakeholders in the planning process from the beginning.
- Complete a risk analysis or needs assessment.
- Develop and complete a cost benefit analysis prior to releasing an invitation to negotiate.
- Establish a system to track cost savings, as well as cost to resume services internally.
- Develop a realistic timeline to implement the project from beginning to end. Rushing through artificial deadlines will not improve the process.
- Demonstrate that viable alternatives, potential hazards, and costs of outsourcing are considered "Prior" to procuring the procurement process.
- Go with a proven vendor; one who has experience doing what you are asking it to do.
- Set specific service levels; establish your expectations up front and include them in the contract as service level agreements including nonperformance penalties and rewards.
- Implement an outsourcing communication strategy; communicate early, often, and in writing.
- Pay close attention to details: If it is not in the contract, you will not get it. Hidden costs reduce projected savings.
- Outline how the project will be managed. Excessive contract monitoring and time-consuming tasks depreciate the value of the service, diminish the savings, and remove managers from their daily responsibilities.
- Always have an exit strategy.

13.7 Public Policy Implications

Although it is difficult to determine the percentage of government contracts spent on outsourcing of HR benefits, public policy concerns about outsourcing are relevant for all public services. As stated earlier, the majority of respondents in surveys indicated that cost saving was the main reason to outsource certain services. By the same token, privatization has been touted as improving service delivery and enabling government to work better and cost less.

A recent series in the *New York Times* points out that the rise in federal spending raises concerns about propriety, cost, and accountability. The *Times'* findings also show that the cost of federal contracts increased from $207 billion in 2000 to $400 billion in 2006 although the number of contracts open to full, competitive bidding decreased from 79 in 2001 to 48 percent in 2005. Moreover, "the top 20 service providers have spent nearly $300 million since 2000 on lobbying and have donated $23 million to political campaigns" (Shane and Nixon 2006, p. 282).

David Cooper, Director, Acquisition and Sourcing Management for the federal government, testified before the House Subcommittee on Technology and Procurement Policy, Committee on Government Reform, that purchases for services now account for approximately 43 percent of all federal contracting expenses—the largest single category. The increase in the use of service contracts coincided with a 21 percent decrease in the federal workforce, which fell from about 2.25 million employees in September 1990 to 1.78 million in September 2000 (U.S. GAO Report 01-753T, 1–4, 2001).

Such revelations highlight concerns both by those who call for outsourcing services to the private sector and by those who take a more guarded position. Thus, public policy makers should consider:

1. Competitive Bidding: The concept of competitive bidding is to create competition, expand the number of suppliers, and secure the best service for the least cost. Cooper's testimony suggested, however, that reduced staffing levels may contribute to workers' failure to seek competitive quotes. The premise of the NPM is that the pressure of competition improves efficiency. In the absence of market dynamics, this trend results in a private monopoly performing the same services without competition.

2. Contract Preparations and Monitoring: Several sources have pointed out that the true cost of outsourcing is unknown because public officials fail to include managing and monitoring contract cost (Prager 1994; GAO 2001; Warner and Hefetz 2001). Should staffing levels show a corresponding decrease as the number of contracts increase, this leaves government with no capability to monitor or assess program objectives or rectify errors created by the private sector (Frederickson 1996, p. 263).

3. Accountability: It is difficult to steer, not row, when power becomes diffused in policy networks and fewer workers are available to perform critical tasks. This fragmented structure creates blurred boundaries, unexpected outcomes, uneven treatment of citizens, and it impairs the ability to take corrective action. Seidman (1998, p. 218) suggests that "by blurring the distinctions between public and private we have permitted the creation of maverick institutions which are able to play both sides, thus making it possible for them to reduce accountability to the government, their shareholders, if any, and the public." Accountability is not limited to program areas but also to legal responsibilities. Metzger (2003, p. 1367) argues that recent privatizations have taken on the government's role, particularly in areas of healthcare, education, and prisons. This type of privatization is sharing authority and delegating responsibilities to private entities. Because the premise of constitutional law is that public and private are distinctive, the law is insufficient to address the delegating of government powers to private organizations. Both Cooper (GAO 2001) and Metzger (2003) question the stance that certain constitutional laws apply to public agencies and employees, but not to private entities and individuals.

4. Human Capital: With the reduction in HR staffing and high number of early retirements, the increased volume of contracting is exceeding the available talent. This results in loss of institutional knowledge, expertise, and a skilled workforce. Therefore, contract training, feasibility studies, cost benefit analysis, and sufficient staffing are key ingredients to ensure that services are delivered in accordance with prescribed standards and contract provisions.

Ironically, as Majone (1994, p. 53) argues, privatization has led to increased regulatory activity which calls for a demand for more employees. Privatization and reduction in government may be connected; however, reductions in staff should be treated as a separate attempt to reform the state (Suleiman 2003, pp. 113–114). Moreover, Fisher and White (2000) assert that broad-based personnel reductions may seriously damage the learning component of the organization if consideration is not given to the impact of downsizing and restructuring on both formal and informal networks.

■ Governance is the relationship between the government and society and the NPM movement has redefined it. Kettl (2002, pp. 5–6) contends that the core of the reform movement debate is about governance: What should government do? What capacity does it need to accomplish its goals? The Federal Acquisition Advisory Panel (2006) expressed concerns about outsourcing trends; they believe that they pose a threat to the government's long-term ability to perform its mission and could undermine the integrity of government's decision-making ability. These are all issues that must be resolved to achieve a successful public–private partnership.

13.8   Conclusion

Although limited empirical research exists on the outsourcing of human resource benefits, we do know that it is occurring at a phenomenal rate in the private sector. Organizations use it to cut cost, focus on core functions, and respond to technology needs of the future. With the exception of a few public sector organizations, government entities have not embraced full outsourcing of core human resources functions. Training and development, and technology services represent the largest percentage of outsourcing services. However, with the continuous influence of reform movements and efforts to reduce the size of government, it is predicted that there will be an increase in HR outsourcing by public sector organizations. Moreover, there are an increasing number of vendors available to offer services for those planning to pursue the outsourcing alternative.

Outsourcing offers several advantages to organizations, given the high personnel cost associated with staffing and related technology. However, it also presents risks and challenges. The Florida experience demonstrates that outsourcing HR is not a panacea. Advanced planning, preparation, and training are vital before considering a major outsourcing program. With such strong economies of scale, why would

Florida engage in so many risks: loss of accountability, confidentiality, and institutional knowledge? These risks increased costs, created low morale, and instill a lack of trust from public servants. Other organizations can take note of Florida's ground-breaking experience and learn from its challenges and consequences.

Because many of the existing HR outsourcing programs are in their infancy, future research is important to track trends, evaluate successes, and learn more about the value of this alternative delivery component. Several scholars argue that it does not matter which sector produces and delivers the service; all organizations perform exceptionally well if human resources are successfully managed, and if appropriate resources are allocated to do the job.

References

American Federation of State, County and Municipal Employees. 2006. *Government for sale: An examination of the contracting out of state and Local government*. Washington, DC. http://www.afscme.org (accessed May 12, 2007).

Augur, D.A. 1999. Privatization, contracting, and the states: Lessons from state government experience. *Public Productivity & Management Review* 22(4): 435–454.

Berry, F., R. Chackerian, and B. Wechsler. 1999. Reinventing government: Lessons from a state capitol. In *Public Management Reform and Innovation: Research, Theory and Application*, (Eds.) H.G. Frederickson and J. Johnston, Tuscaloosa, Alabama: University of Alabama Press. pp. 329–356.

Batley, R. and G. Larbi. 2004. *The Changing Role of Government: The Reform of Public Services in Developing Countries*. Basingstoke: Palgrave Macmillan. Hampshire, England.

Brooks, G.C. 2004. Privatization of government services: An overview of the literature. *Journal of Public Budgeting, Accounting & Financial Management* 16(4): 467–491.

Boyne, G. 1998. Bureaucratic theory meets reality: Public choice and service contracting in U.S. local government. *Public Administration Review* 58(6): 474–484.

Caputo, M. 2006a. State to prosecute contractor. *Miami Herald*. April 11.

———, 2006b. Audit finds vendor work for state below par. *Miami Herald*. April 25.

Chi, K.S., K. Arnold, and H. Perkins. 2003. Privatization in state government: Trends, and issues. *Spectrum: The Journal of State Government* 76(4): 12–21. Lexington, Kentucky: The Council of State Governments.

Cook, M.F. 1999. *Outsourcing Human Resources Functions: Strategies for Providing Enhanced HR Services at Lower Cost*. New York: AMACOM, American Management Association.

Cotterell, B. 2006a. Crist urged to warn workers/personnel data may have gone overseas. *Tallahassee Democrat*. January 18.

———, 2006b. No proof privatization saves money. *Tallahassee Democrat*. December 11.

Cotterell, B. 2007. No evidence of information leak/probe finds discrepancies in People First security. *Tallahassee Democrat*. January 19.

Crowell, E.B. and M.E. Guy. Forthcoming. Florida's HR reforms: Service first, service worst, or something in between? *Public Personnel Management*.

Darling, D. March 2005. *Convergys/People First Update*. Presentation before the Florida Senate Governmental Oversight and Productivity Committee. Tallahassee, Florida.

Dell, D. 2004. *HR Outsourcing Benefits, Challenges and Trends, R-1347-04.RR*. New York: The Conference Board, Inc.

Deloitte Consulting. April 2005. *Calling for a Change in the Outsourcing Market: The Realities for the World's Largest Organizations*. Washington, DC: Deloitte Consulting LLP.

Dilger, R.J., R. Moffett, and L. Struyk. 1997. Privatization of municipal services in America's largest cities. *Public Administration Review* 57(1): 21–26.

Donahue, J. 1989. *The Privatization Decision*. New York: Basic Books.

Downs, A. 1967. *Inside Bureaucracy*. Boston, Massachusetts: Little Brown.

Federal Acquisition Advisory Panel. December 2006 Report. Office of the Federal Procurement Policy & the United States Congress, Washington, DC.

Fisher, S.R. and M.A. White. 2000. Downsizing in a learning organization: Are there hidden costs? *The Academy of Management Review* 25(1): 244–251.

Florida Auditor General. October 2004. Department of Management Services People First Operational Audit. Report No. 2005-047. Tallahassee, Florida.

Florida Auditor General. January 2007. Department of Management Services People First Operational Audit No. 2007-087. Tallahassee, Florida.

Frederickson, H.G. 1996. Comparing the reinventing government movement with the new public administration. *Public Administration Review* (56): 263–270.

Gartner Group. 1999. Market findings: The myth of saving money by outsourcing. *InfoWorld*. 21. 28 (July 12):21 http://find.galegroup.com (accessed June 1, 2007).

Gelman, L. and D. Dell. 2002. *HR Outsourcing Trends*. Conference Board Research Report No. 1321. New York: Conference Board, Inc.

Gore, A. 1993. Creating a government that works better and costs less: Report of the *National Performance Review*. Washington, DC: U.S. Government Printing Office.

Greene, J. 2002. *Cities and Privatization: Prospects for the New Century*. Upper Saddle River, New Jersey: Prentice-Hall.

Harper, D. June 2003. Audit Report: Road Map to Excellence in Contracting. Report No. 2003-3. Office of the Inspector General, Executive Office of the Governor. Tallahassee, Florida.

Hines, M. March 2007. *IBM lands HR outsourcing deal with American*. IDG News Service. *InfoWorld*. http://www.infoworld.com (accessed May 16, 2007).

Hood, C. 1990. A new public management for all seasons. In *Classics of Public Administration* (Eds.) Jay M. Shafritz, Albert C. Hyde, and Sandra J. Parkes, Belmont, California: Thomson Wadsworth. pp. 502–516.

Horn, M.J. 1995. *The Political Economy of Public Administration: Institutional Choice in the Public Sector*. New York: Cambridge University Press.

Jones, V.D. 1998. The pursuit of a better government: Federal government *downsizing in the United States*. Organization for Economic Cooperation and Development (OECD).

Kettl, D.F. 2002. *The Transformation of Governance: Public Administration for Twenty-first Century America*. John Hopkins University Press. Baltimore, MD.

Kim, P.S. and L. Wolff. 1994. Improving government performance: Public management reform and the National Performance Review. *Public Productivity & Management Review* 18(1): 73–87.

Koch, J., D. Dell, and L. Johnson. 2004. *HR Outsourcing in Government Organizations: Emerging Trends, Early Lessons*. Research Report No. E-0007-04 RR. New York: Conference Board Inc.

Linder, S. and P. Rosenau. 2000. Mapping the terrain in public private partnerships. In *Public–Private Partnerships*, (Ed.) P.V. Rosenau, Cambridge, Massachusetts: MIT Press. pp. 4–33.

Majone, G. 1994. Paradoxes of privatization and deregulation. *Journal of European Public Policy* 1(1): 53–69.

Metzger, G. 2003. Privatization as delegation. *Columbia Law Review* 103(6): 1367–1502.

National Commission on the State and Local Public Service. 1993. *Hard Truths/Tough Choices: An Agenda for State and Local Reform.* New York: Nelson Rockefeller Institute of Government.

Osborne, D. and T. Gaebler. 1992. *Reinventing Government: How the Entrepreneurial Spirit Is Transforming the Public Sector.* Reading, Massachusetts: Addison-Wesley.

Power, M., K. Desouza, and C. Bonifazi. 2006. *The Outsourcing Handbook: How to Implement a Successful Outsourcing Process.* Philadelphia, Pennsylvania: Kogan Page.

Prager, J. 1994. Contracting out government services: Lessons learned from the private sector. *Public Administration Review* 54(2): 176–184.

Pringle, E. 1995. The advantages of benefits outsourcing. *Risk Management* 42(7): 61–63.

Reason Foundation. *Annual privatization report 2006.* http://www.reason.org (accessed June 6, 2007).

Saunders, J. 2003. Bush reflects on values, family at inauguration—Governor vows to stress literacy, reducing the size of government. *The Florida Times-Union.* January 8.

Savas, E.S. 2000. *Privatization and Public Private Partnerships.* New York: Chatman House Publishers.

Savas, E.S. 2005. *Privatization in the City: Successes, Failures, Lessons.* Washington, DC: Congressional Quarterly Press.

Sclar, E. 2000. *You Don't Always Get What You Pay for: The Economics of Privatization.* Ithaca, New York: Cornell University Press.

Scardino, L., K. Potter, and A. Young. December 2006. *Gartner on Outsourcing, 2006–2007.* http://gartner.unt.edu (accessed May 15, 2007).

Seidman, H. 1998. *Politics, Position, and Power: The Dynamics of Federal Organization.* New York: Oxford University Press.

Self, P. 1993. *Government by the Markets?: The Politics of Public Choice.* Boulder, Colorado: Westview Press.

Shane, S. and R. Nixon. 2006. *Contractors Take on Biggest Role Ever in Washington. New York Times.* February 4.

Siegel, G. 2000. Outsourcing personnel functions. *Public Personnel Management* 29(2): 224–235.

Starr, P. 1987. *The Limits of Privatization.* Washington, DC: Economic Policy Institute.

Starr, P. 1989. The meaning of privatization. In *Privatization and the Welfare State,* (Eds.) S.K. Kamerman and A.J. Kahn, Princeton, New Jersey: Princeton University Press. pp. 15–48.

Stein, R.M. 1990. The budgetary effects of municipal contracting: A principal agent Explanation. *American Journal of Political Science* 34(2): 471–502.

Suleiman, E. 2003. *Dismantling Democratic States.* Princeton, New Jersey: Princeton University Press.

Thormeyer, R. April 24, 2006. Florida case offers lessons-learned for outsourcing. *Government Computer News.* Online Extra http://www.egov.vic.gv.au (accessed March 18, 2007).

United States General Accounting Office. 2001. *Contract management: Trends and challenges in acquiring services.* Testimony of David Cooper. GAO Report-01-753T, May 22, Washington, DC.

Warner, M. and A. Hefetz. 2001. Privatization and the market role of local Government: Small growth in contracting underscores dominance of service provision by public employees. Paper presented at the Economic Policy Institute's Conference on Privatization: Trends, Issues and Alternatives, January 11.

Williams, O. 1998. *Outsourcing: A CIO's perspective.* Boca Raton, Florida: St. Lucie.

Worsnop, Richard, L. 1992, November 13. Privatization. *CQ Researcher,* 2, 977–1000. http://library.cqpress.com/cqreseacher/cqresrre (accessed December 27, 2006).

Young, M.B. 2003. The aging and retiring government workforce: How serious is the *Challenge? What are the jurisdictions doing about it?* The Center for Organizational Research. Linkage, Inc. http://www.wagnerbriefing.com/downloads /cps_Agebubble (accessed May 1, 2007).

Chapter 14

Accounting and Financial Reporting by Governments for Retirement Benefits: Understanding and Using the Information in Audited Financial Reports

Dean Michael Mead

CONTENTS

The opinions expressed in this article are those of the author. Official positions of the Governmental Accounting Standards Board are established only after extensive public due process.

The retirement benefits of government employees grab the public's attention like few government finance and policy topics can. It is not hard to understand why. States and large cities and counties have long-term obligations for pensions, health insurance, and other retirement benefits totaling billions or tens of billions of dollars each. Even for small to medium sized localities, the total obligation can amount to tens or hundreds of millions of dollars per government. The total outstanding for retiree health insurance alone has been estimated to be $1.5 trillion for all state and local governments in the United States (Zion and Varshney, 2007).

The magnitude of the cost of retirement benefits does not solely explain the public's fascination. Perhaps equally consequential are the headline-worthy instances of shoddy or, occasionally, illegal management of public employee benefits. Although the vast majority of pension plans are relatively well funded, some funds—such as those of the state of Illinois—are notoriously underfunded (Civic Federation, 2006, 2007). The city of San Diego has come under intense scrutiny for the fraud committed by city officials in hiding the true financial status of the city's pension plans (Levitt et al., 2006). Lastly, new requirements that state and local governments report, the full cost and long-term obligations connected with their nonpension benefits, are revealing that practically no money has been set aside to pay for retiree health insurance and other postemployment benefits (Zion and Varshney, 2007).

The widespread concern with public employee retirement benefits is borne out in the broad usage of information about the funded status of pensions. With the possible exception of fund balance and general information about revenues and expenses or expenditures, there may be no more widely used piece of information in the annual audited financial statements of state and local governments than the funded ratio—the actuarial value of assets divided by the actuarial accrued liability (Mead, forthcoming).

The funded ratio is but one part of an extensive set of disclosures that accompany government financial statements prepared under generally accepted accounting principles (GAAP). This chapter discusses the types of information that state and local governments and retirement benefit plans are required to provide in the financial statements, notes, and supporting schedules. The chapter focuses principally on financial reporting by benefit plans and governments that participate in single-employer and agent multiple employer defined benefit plans, because the reporting by governments in other types of plans is less extensive. The initial section discusses GAAP in general, covering briefly GAAP's characteristics, source, and limitations. The second section explains how retirement benefits are viewed conceptually in accounting and, therefore, how GAAP approaches reporting them. The next three sections describe the information a financial report user will find in the financial statements, notes to the financial statements, and required supplementary information, respectively. The penultimate section describes the separate reporting requirements for governments participating in defined contribution plans and cost-sharing multiple-employer defined benefit plans. The concluding section considers the future direction of financial reporting for retirement benefits.

14.1 Background: Financial Reporting by Governments

A typical business transaction involves an exchange of equal value between willing parties. Some transactions in government exhibit the characteristics of a business transaction—a student pays tuition to attend a public university, a homeowner pays a public utility for water, a resident purchases a permit to use the town pool, and so on. Most government activities, however, are not like business transactions at all. It is difficult, if not impossible, to connect the payment of taxes with the receipt of services. The payment of taxes may occur periodically over the course of a year (property or income taxes) or when a separate transaction occurs, such as buying goods or services (sales taxes). The receipt of services may occur steadily over time or only sporadically. For tax-supported services, there also is no clear connection between who pays the taxes (and in what amounts) and who receives the services (and in what amounts). Finally, taxes are not sacrificed willingly—governments impose taxes on the public.

The opaque nature of transactions between taxpayers and governments calls for extraordinary efforts by governments to demonstrate their accountability to the public, to show that they have been proper stewards over the tax dollars they collect. A principal means of demonstrating accountability is the publication of annual financial statements that have been examined by an outside auditor. The auditor confirms that the financial statements have been prepared following a set of standards called generally accepted accounting principles (GAAP). Specifically, the auditor renders an opinion regarding whether the financial statements conform to GAAP and thereby accurately and reliably present the financial status and performance of the governmental entity.

The American Institute of Certified Public Accountants (AICPA)—which is the professional association of the accounting industry and one of the entities that sets standards and practices for financial statement auditors—recognizes the Governmental Accounting Standards Board (GASB) as the body that promulgates GAAP for state and local governments. Governments that prepare financial statements according to GAAP are following the GASB's standards.

However, it is not certain how many of the roughly 88,000 state and local governments in the United States prepare audited financial statements. All 50 state governments issue annual financial statements prepared on a GAAP basis. About half of the states require some or all of the governmental entities within their borders to prepare GAAP financial statements (Icerman, 1996). The vast majority of governments that borrow in the public credit markets prepare GAAP financial statements—buyers and holders of municipal debt clearly prefer GAAP financial statements and borrowers that do not follow GAAP pay a premium on their debt (Gore, 2003; Reck and Wilson, 2005; Plummer et al., 2007).

The accounting and financial reporting practices described in this chapter are those prescribed by GAAP. Separate standards exist for pensions and other postemployment benefits (OPEB), though the standards are identical in most respects. The specific standards are:

■ GASB Statement No. 25, Financial Reporting for Defined Benefit Pension Plans and Note Disclosures for Defined Contribution Plans
■ GASB Statement No. 27, Accounting for Pensions by State and Local Government Employers
■ GASB Statement No. 43, Financial Reporting for Postemployment Benefit Plans Other Than Pension Plans
■ GASB Statement No. 45, Accounting and Financial Reporting by Employers for Postemployment Benefit Plans Other Than Pension Plans
■ GASB Statement No. 50, Pension Disclosures

The simplest manner of determining if a government's financial statements follow GAAP is to read the auditor's report. The auditor's report is a letter attached to the front of the financial statements reflecting the results of the auditor's audit of the statements in accordance with the applicable auditing standards established by the AICPA and the U.S. Government Accountability Office (GAO). This is where the auditor tells you if the government's financial statements are presented fairly in conformity with GAAP and highlights if there are any significant deviations.

14.2   Conceptual Underpinnings of Postemployment Benefit Reporting

The accounting and reporting standards for postemployment* benefits that state and local governments provide are founded on the basic premise that those benefits are a form of deferred compensation given in return for services provided today. The

---

* To this point I have used the more familiar term "retirement" benefits. However, there is a subtle, yet crucial distinction between "retirement" and "postemployment." It is not uncommon for public employees to qualify for benefits after they have left the employ of a government, even if they did not retire from that government or have not yet retired at all. Using the term "postemployment," therefore, encompasses benefits received after employment has ceased, regardless of why or how it has ceased.

standards, therefore, require that the cost of postemployment benefits be recorded as the benefits are earned each year that employees work, rather than in the future when the benefits are actually paid.

The standards also recognize the distinct nature of the governmental environment by taking a "funding friendly" approach. In other words, the standards reflect state and local government finances, which tend to grow relatively steadily and evenly over the long run. For example, the standards allow changes in the unfunded actuarial accrued liability to be eased in over time rather than run through the financial statements immediately. State and local governments typically seek to keep spending and tax growth steady and predictable; large annual swings up and down in tax rates would be very unpopular with the public. Similarly, the standards give governments a choice of six acceptable actuarial cost methods, which allows governments to select a method that is consistent with their approach to funding benefits.

The prime consequence of this conceptual view of postemployment benefits is that defined benefit plans and the governments that participate in them are required to contract with actuaries to establish the numbers that will be reported in the financial statements and accompanying disclosures. In layperson's terms, the actuary calculates how much should be contributed now to ensure that an adequate level of resources is available in the future. Future cash outlays for postemployment benefits are projected using economic and demographic assumptions based on the historical experience of the covered group of employees. These cash outflows are then discounted to their actuarial present value—their estimated value if paid today. The actuarial present value generally is spread over a period that approximates the anticipated years of a worker's employment with the government, utilizing one of the six acceptable actuarial cost methods.

14.2.1 Parameters for Actuarial Valuations

In most cases, the accounting and financial reporting standards do not specify the precise assumptions that governments may make. However, the standards do establish parameters within which governments must reside. Some of the most significant parameters are as follows:

- Frequency of valuation—Actuarial valuations should be conducted at least once every other year, except for retiree health insurance and other nonpension benefit plans with fewer than 200 members, for which actuarial valuations should be conducted at least once every three years.
- Benefits—All benefits provided, whether contractual or not, should be included. This is a significant issue for nonpension benefits, which are sometimes provided without any legal or contractual requirement to do so. Actuarial valuations are based on the substantive plan, the benefit terms as understood by the employer government and the plan members.
- Discount rate—The discount rate used to calculate the present value of the future benefit cash flows should be based on an assumed long-term rate of

return on the investments that are expected to be used to finance the benefits. In general, the greater the degree to which a government is prefunding its benefits, the higher the rate of return and therefore the greater the discount rate. Governments financing benefits on a pay-as-you-go basis use the rate of return on their general investments, which is likely to be much lower than the return on assets set aside in a trust and invested over the long term.

- Actuarial cost method—Governments may select from among six acceptable methods—entry age, frozen entry age, attained age, frozen attained age, projected unit credit, or aggregate.
- Amortization—The unfunded actuarial accrued liability may be amortized or spread over a period of up to 30 years, either in level dollar amounts or a level percentage of the payroll of active plan members.
- Smoothing—Changes in the value of plan assets can sometimes be volatile, rising or falling substantially in any given year. To minimize the effect of this volatility on the actuarial calculations, gains or losses in plan assets are "smoothed" or averaged over several years (usually three to five), producing a more stable actuarial value of assets over time. Although changes in the fair value of plan assets and their actuarial value may not be the same in a given year, over the smoothing period as a whole the actuarial value of assets should closely reflect fair value.

14.2.2 Key Information from the Actuarial Valuation

The portion of the actuarial present value allocated to a particular year is called the normal cost. The portion of the actuarial present value allocated to prior years of employment—and thus not provided for by normal costs in the current or future years—is called the actuarial accrued liability (AAL). If a pension or OPEB plan has cash, investments, and other resources, these may be applied to fund the AAL. The value of these resources is referred to as the actuarial value of assets. The excess of the AAL over the actuarial value of assets is the unfunded actuarial accrued liability (the UAAL or unfunded liability).

The normal cost and the portion of the UAAL to be amortized in the current period together make up the annual required contribution (ARC) of the employer for the period. The ARC is an amount that is actuarially determined so that, if paid on an ongoing basis, it would be expected to provide sufficient resources to fund both the normal cost for each year and the amortized unfunded liability.

The annual pension cost or annual OPEB cost equals the ARC plus or minus certain adjustments if the employer's actual contributions in prior years differed from the ARC. The annual pension or OPEB cost is the pension or OPEB expense that a government would report in its financial statements. Generally, the cumulative sum of differences between an employer's annual pension or OPEB cost and the amounts actually contributed to the plan because the effective date of the standards makes up a liability (or asset) called the net pension obligation (NPO) or net OPEB obligation (NOPEBO) that would be reported in the financial statements as well. If a government funds the ARC each year, then the outstanding unfunded liability never makes its way onto the financial statements.

14.2.3   Plan and Employer Reporting as a Package

Financial reporting on pensions and OPEB is performed by both employer governments and pension and OPEB plans. The financial reporting standards take into account that plans may issue their own financial statements: When a plan issues its own financial statements, the disclosure requirements for the employer government are reduced to minimize duplication of effort. Consequently, the person interested in financial information about pensions and OPEB may need to use the financial reports of the plan and the employer government (or governments, in the case of multiple-employer plans) in tandem to obtain the full complement of note disclosures and supporting schedules. The employer government, in its note disclosures, should tell you whether the plan issues separate financial reports and, if it does, how to obtain one.

14.3   Financial Statements

Pension and OPEB plans present two financial statements—the statement of plan net assets and the statement of changes in plan net assets. If an employer government is the sponsor of a plan, then it will include the plan in two very similar statements in its financial report—the statement of fiduciary net assets and the statement of changes in fiduciary net assets. Figures 14.1 and 14.2 are illustrative statements for a retirement system. The statements that an employer government sponsoring a plan would present would look very similar, with two notable differences. If the government sponsors multiple pension and OPEB plans, they would be aggregated into a single column in the statements. Further, the statements would include columns representing other resources that a government is minding on behalf of others, including private-purpose trusts and agency funds. Chances are good that such a government also will include in its financial report a supporting schedule that breaks down that single column for pension and OPEB plans into its component parts, showing each plan separately.

The statement of plan net assets is essentially a balance sheet, showing the resources a plan holds—its assets—and the amounts it owes—its liabilities. Most assets will be investments, which are shown at their fair market value and aggregated by type. Liabilities typically will be minimal short-term amounts. This is not where you will find the actuarial liabilities, which are amounts owed by the employer government, not by the plan.

The statement of changes in plan net assets is like an income statement, showing amounts added to the plan and amounts deducted. Additions predominantly come

	Pension trust funds	
	SERF	LRF
Assets		
Cash and cash equivalents	$397,530	$246
Receivables		
Members	$1,597,698	$45
Investment sales and other	1,511,344	—
Interest and dividends	770,788	—
Due from other funds	3,434	4
Other program	10,970	—
Total receivables	$3,894,234	$49
Investments, at fair value		
Short-term investments:		
Domestic	$2,118,562	$5
International	759,809	—
Securities lending collateral	38,011,353	—
Equity securities:		
Domestic	85,018,855	40,769
International	44,868,329	13,396
Debt securities:		
Domestic	46,514,538	79,390
International	5,511,716	—
Real estate equities	15,230,979	—
Alternative investments	12,045,147	—
Total investments	$250,079,288	$133,560
Capital assets, at cost, net of accumulated depreciation and other assets	$391,636	$—
Total assets	$254,762,688	$133,855
Liabilities		
Retirement and other benefits in process of payment	$208,113	$207
Investment purchases and other	4,787,920	—
Due to state	1,411	—
Liabilities to brokers for securities lending	38,011,353	—
Due to other funds	309	—
Other program	562,781	17
Total liabilities	$43,571,887	$224
Net assets held in trust for pension benefits	$211,190,801	$133,631

Figure 14.1   Illustrative statement of plan net assets (dollars in thousands).

in two forms—contributions from the employer and employees and investment income. The vast majority of deductions from plan net assets will be benefit payments to plan members, with most of the remainder being administrative costs. The difference between total additions and total deductions is the annual change in plan net assets. This amount is added to the plan net assets as of the beginning of the year

	Pension trust funds	
	SERF	LRF
Additions		
Retirement contributions		
Members	$3,080,879	$160
Employers	6,095,029	—
Total retirement contributions	$9,175,908	$160
Investment income		
Net appreciation in fair value		
of investments	$16,621,497	$3,804
Interest	2,575,346	4
Dividends	2,507,521	—
Real estate	1,221,640	—
Other income	988,904	—
Securities lending income	1,678,675	—
Less investment expenses:		
Costs of lending	(1,520,214)	—
Real estate	(1,113,038)	—
Other	(919,066)	—
Net investment income	$22,041,265	$3,808
Total additions	$31,217,173	$3,968
Deductions		
Retirement, death and survivor benefits	$9,236,073	$7,314
Refund of contributions	170,929	823
Administrative expenses	236,212	290
Other expenses	14,039	5
Total deductions	$9,657,253	$8,432
Increase (decrease) in net assets	$21,559,920	($4,464)
Net assets held in trust for pension		
benefits		
Beginning of year	$189,630,881	$138,095
End of year	$211,190,801	$133,631

Figure 14.2 Illustrative statement of changes in plan net assets (dollars in thousands).

to produce the year-end net assets, which should match what is reported in the statement of plan net assets.

In general, users of these financial statements will be looking to see if the financial status of the plan is improving. They will look to see if additions exceeded deductions, and therefore if net assets increased. Some will compare the numbers with those in the financial statements from the previous year and calculate a percentage change (the prior year number is subtracted from the current year number, and the result is divided by the prior year number and multiplied by 100). They will look for red flags—percentage changes that are out of line with the overall or average change of the plan as a whole. For instance, their attention might be grabbed by a large increase in administrative costs.

Several specific pieces of information in the financial statements are routinely examined. Some people divide the administrative expense by total deductions and track the fraction over time to see whether overhead costs are rising or falling relative to the benefits being paid. Another common calculation is the percentage distribution (a component of a total amount divided by the total amount and multiplied by 100). For example, financial statement users may divide contributions and investment income by total additions and review the results over time to see whether either is becoming a relatively larger source of resources for the plan. Others may divide the value of specific types of investments by the total value of investments to get a general sense of shifts in the plan's investment portfolio.

Although only governments that sponsor a postemployment benefit plan will present the statements of fiduciary net assets and changes in fiduciary net assets, all governments will present other financial statements representing their own financial activity.* These statements will be where you find the costs of a government's postemployment benefits and, if applicable, liabilities. Governments participating in single-employer and agent multiple-employer defined benefit plans will report an expense equal to their annual pension or OPEB cost in the governmentwide statement of activities. It should be noted that this expense represents the cost of benefits and is not necessarily equal to what a government has actually paid in terms of contributions to a plan or direct payments for benefits. If a government is fully funding the ARC, then the expense is likely to be the same as the amount paid. However, governments partially funding or financing benefits on a pay-as-you-go basis will have an expense that may greatly exceed their actual payments. In the governmental funds statement of revenues, expenditures, and changes in fund balances, a government will report expenditures equal to the amount that was due and payable for benefits, which is likely to be much closer to what the government actually paid. The difference between the actuarially determined contributions and the amounts actually contributed or paid by the government equals the NPO or NOPEBO, which are reported as liabilities in the governmentwide statement of net assets.

14.4 Notes to the Financial Statements

Between the financial reports of the pension or OPEB plan and the employer government, you will find extensive notes. All employer governments, regardless of the type of plan they participate in, will present the following information in their notes to the financial statements:

---

* A more detailed discussion of the financial reports of governments, including their fiduciary fund financial statements, can be found in Mead, 2001, 2005.

- Identification and description of the plan.
- Description of the types of benefits provided.
- Identification of the authority under which (1) benefit provisions and (2) obligations to contribute to the plan are established or may be amended.
- Whether the plan issues its own financial report or if it is included in the report of a public employee retirement system or another entity and, if so, how to obtain the report.
- Required contribution rates of employees and the government—if a government has a contribution rate that is significantly different from the ARC, then the note disclosure explains how the contribution rate was determined; governments should also disclose any legal or contractual limitations on the size of their contributions.
- Brief description of the terms of any long-term contracts for contributions to the plan and the amount still outstanding; for example, a government that is not able to make its full contribution in a given year might agree with the plan to make up the shortfall with interest in annual installments over a three-year period.

Figures 14.3 and 14.4 present typical examples of the pension and OPEB note disclosures, respectively, that would be made by a government participating in a plan that issues a separate financial report. Figure 14.5 illustrates excerpted information that would be found in the separately issued financial reports of a pension plan; the remainder of the plan disclosures is left out because they duplicate what is found in the employer government disclosures. The disclosures of an OPEB plan would be very similar; in fact, as plans proceed with implementation of the OPEB, readers may see pension and OPEB disclosures that are consolidated to a degree.

If an employer government includes a pension plan in its financial statements as a trust fund and the plan does not issue its own financial statements separate from those of the employer government, the employer also discloses the following information about the plan (otherwise, you would find this information in the plan's financial report):

- Types of employees covered (such as general employees, police officers, legislators)
- Number of members, sorted by (1) retirees and beneficiaries currently receiving benefits, (2) members no longer working for the government and entitled to benefits, but not yet receiving them, and (3) current employees
- Brief description of (1) the types of benefits provided and (2) provisions for cost-of-living adjustments or other future increases in benefits
- Balances remaining as of the date of the financial report in the plan's legally required reserves, a description of the purpose of the reserves, and whether the reserves are fully funded

Pension plan

Plan description. Hayley Employees Pension Plan (HEPP) is a single-employer defined benefit pension plan administered by the Hayley Retirement System. HEPP provides retirement, disability, and death benefits to plan members and beneficiaries. Cost-of-living adjustments are provided to members and beneficiaries at the discretion of the State legislature. Article 29 of the Regulations of the State of Hayley assigns the authority to establish and amend benefit provisions to the State legislature. The Hayley Retirement System issues a publicly available financial report that includes financial statements and required supplementary information for HEPP. That report may be obtained by writing to Hayley Retirement System, 40 Fremont Road, Anytown, USA 01000 or by calling 1-800-555-PLAN.

Funding policy. The contribution requirements of plan members and the State are established and may be amended by the State legislature. Plan members are required to contribute 7.8 percent of their annual covered salary. The State is required to contribute at an actuarially determined rate; the current rate is 11.9 percent of annual covered payroll.

Annual pension cost and net pension obligation. The State's annual pension cost and net pension obligation to HEPP for the current year ended December 31, 20X5 were as follows:

(dollar amounts in thousands)

Annual required contribution	$137,916
Interest on net pension obligation	2,867
Adjustment to annual required contribution	(2,089)
Annual pension cost	138,694
Contributions made	(137,916)
Increase in net pension obligation	778
Net pension obligation beginning of year	38,221
Net pension obligation end of year	$38,999

Funded status and funding progress. As of December 31, 20X5, the most recent actuarial valuation date, the plan was 85.4 percent funded. The actuarial accrued liability for benefits was $4.3 billion, and the actuarial value of assets was $3.7 billion, resulting in an unfunded actuarial accrued liability (UAAL) of $0.6 billion. The covered payroll (annual payroll of active employees covered by the plan) was $1.2 billion, and the ratio of the UAAL to the covered payroll was 54.2 percent.

The schedule of funding progress, presented as RSI following the notes to the financial statements, presents multiyear trend information about whether the actuarial value of plan assets are increasing or decreasing over time relative to the actuarial accrued liability for benefits.

Actuarial methods and assumptions. The annual required contribution for the current year was determined as part of the December 31, 20X4 actuarial valuation using the entry age actuarial cost method. The actuarial assumptions included (a) 7.5 percent investment rate of return (net of administrative expenses) and (b) projected salary increases ranging from 5.5 to 9.5 percent per year. Both (a) and (b) included an inflation component of 5.5 percent. The assumptions did not include postretirement benefit increases, which are funded by State appropriation when granted. The actuarial value of assets was determined using techniques that smooth the effects of short-term volatility in the market value of investments over a four-year period. The unfunded actuarial accrued liability is being amortized as a level percentage of projected payroll on an open basis. The remaining amortization period at December 31, 20X4 was 23 years.

Three-year trend information
(dollar amounts in thousands)

Fiscal year ended	Annual pension cost (APC)	Percentage of APC contributed	Net pension obligation
12/31/X3	$119,757	99.1	$37,458
12/31/X4	$125,039	99.4	$38,221
12/31/X5	$138,364	99.4	$38,999

Figure 14.3 Illustrative pension note disclosure by an employer government. (From Mead, D.M., *What Else You Should Know about a Government's Finances: A Guide to Notes to the Financial Statements and Supporting Information*, GASB, Connecticut, 2005. Reprinted with permission.)

Postemployment healthcare plan

Plan description. State Retired Employees Healthcare Plan (SREHP) is a single-employer defined benefit healthcare plan administered by the Czerkohnson Retirement System. SREHP provides medical and dental insurance benefits to eligible retirees and their spouses. Article 37 of the Statutes of the State of Czerkohnson assigns the authority to establish and amend benefit provisions to the state legislature. The Czerkohnson Retirement System issues a publicly available financial report that includes financial statements and required supplementary information for SREHP. That report may be obtained by writing to Czerkohnson Retirement System, State Government Lane, Habañero, USA 01000, or by calling 1-800-555-PLAN.

Funding policy. The contribution requirements of plan members and the state are established and may be amended by the state legislature. The required contribution is based on projected pay-as-you-go financing requirements, with an additional amount to prefund benefits as determined annually by the legislature. For fiscal year 20X2, the state contributed $357.7 million to the plan, including $190.7 million for current premiums (approximately 84 percent of total premiums) and an additional $167.0 million to prefund benefits. Plan members receiving benefits contributed $35.4 million, or approximately 16 percent of the total premiums, through their required contribution of $50 per month for retiree-only coverage and $105 for retiree and spouse coverage.

Annual OPEB cost and net OPEB obligation. The state's annual other postemployment benefit (OPEB) cost (expense) is calculated based on the *annual required contribution of the employer (ARC)*, an amount actuarially determined in accordance with the parameters of GASB Statement 45. The ARC represents a level of funding that, if paid on an ongoing basis, is projected to cover normal cost each year and amortize any unfunded actuarial liabilities (or funding excess) over a period not to exceed thirty years. The following table shows the components of the state's annual OPEB cost for the year, the amount actually contributed to the plan, and changes in the state's net OPEB obligation to SREHP (dollar amounts in thousands):

Annual required contribution	$577,180
Interest on net OPEB obligation	90,437
Adjustment to annual required contribution	(95,258)
Annual OPEB cost (expense)	572,359
Contributions made	(357,682)
Increase in net OPEB obligation	214,677
Net OPEB obligation—beginning of year	1,349,811
Net OPEB obligation—end of year	$1,564,488

The state's annual OPEB cost, the percentage of annual OPEB cost contributed to the plan, and the net OPEB obligation for 20X2 and the two preceding years were as follows (dollar amounts in thousands):

Fiscal year ended	Annual OPEB cost	Percentage of annual OPEB cost contributed	Net OPEB obligation
6/30/X0	$497,538	67.4	$1,160,171
6/30/X1	$538,668	64.8	$1,349,811
6/30/X2	$572,359	62.5	$1,564,488

Funded status and funding progress. As of December 31, 20X1, the most recent actuarial valuation date, the plan was 58.1 percent funded. The actuarial accrued liability for benefits was $8.8 billion, and the actuarial value of assets was $5.1 billion, resulting in an unfunded actuarial accrued liability (UAAL) of $3.7 billion. The covered payroll (annual payroll of active employees covered by the plan) was $2.2 billion, and the ratio of the UAAL to the covered payroll was 165 percent.

Actuarial valuations of an ongoing plan involve estimates of the value of reported amounts and assumptions about the probability of occurrence of events far into the future. Examples include assumptions about future employment, mortality, and the healthcare cost trend. Amounts determined regarding the funded status of the plan and the annual required contributions of the employer are subject to continual revision as actual results are compared with past expectations and new estimates are made about the future. The schedule of funding progress, presented as required supplementary information following the notes to the financial statements, presents multiyear trend information about whether the actuarial value of plan assets is increasing or decreasing over time relative to the actuarial accrued liabilities for benefits.

Figure 14.4   Illustrative OPEB note disclosure by an employer government. (From Mead, D.M., *What Else You Should Know about a Government's Finances: A Guide to Notes to the Financial Statements and Supporting Information,* **GASB, Connecticut, 2005. Reprinted with permission.)**

(*continued*)

Actuarial methods and assumptions. Projections of benefits for financial reporting purposes are based on the substantive plan (the plan as understood by the employer and the plan members) and include the types of benefits provided at the time of each valuation and the historical pattern of sharing of benefit costs between the employer and plan members to that point. The actuarial methods and assumptions used include techniques that are designed to reduce the effects of short-term volatility in actuarial accrued liabilities and the actuarial value of assets, consistent with the long-term perspective of the calculations.

In the December 31, 20X1, actuarial valuation, the entry age actuarial cost method was used. The actuarial assumptions included a 6.7 percent investment rate of return (net of administrative expenses), which is a blended rate of the expected long-term investment returns on plan assets and on the employer's own investments calculated based on the funded level of the plan at the valuation date, and an annual healthcare cost trend rate of 12 percent initially, reduced by decrements to an ultimate rate of 5 percent after ten years. Both rates included a 4.5 percent inflation assumption. The actuarial value of assets was determined using techniques that spread the effects of short-term volatility in the market value of investments over a five-year period. The UAAL is being amortized as a level percentage of projected payroll on an open basis. The remaining amortization period at December 31, 20X1, was seventeen years.

Figure 14.4 (continued)

The note disclosures of governments in single-employer or agent multiple-employer defined benefit plans also contain the following information:

- For the current year, the annual pension or OPEB cost and the dollar amount contributed to the plan.
- If a government has an NPO or NOPEBO, it also discloses (1) the components of the annual pension or OPEB cost, (2) the amount of the NPO or NOPEBO, and (3) the change in the NPO or NOPEBO from the prior year.
- For each of the past three years, (1) the annual pension or OPEB cost, (2) the percentage actually contributed, and (3) the NPO or NOPEBO.
- For the most recent valuation, the actuarial value of assets, AAL, UAAL, funded ratio, covered payroll, and ratio of UAAL divided by covered payroll (this is the information presented in the supplementary schedule of funding progress, which will be discussed in the next section).
- Date of the most recent actuarial valuation, the methods and significant assumptions employed in the valuation, and the methods used for amortization.

14.5 Required Supplementary Information

In the financial reports of plans and employer governments, you will find three types of required supplementary information (RSI) in schedules that follow the notes:

- Schedule of funding progress
- Schedule of employer contributions
- Notes to the schedules

Governments present RSI covering the last three actuarial valuations, as long as plans issue their own financial reports. However, if a government includes a plan as

The Kremer Retirement System (KRS) administers three defined benefit pension plans—State Employees Pension Plan (SEPP), School District Employees Pension Plan (SDEPP), and Municipal Employees Pension Plan (MEPP). Although the assets of the plans are commingled for investment purposes, each plan's assets may be used only for the payment of benefits to the members of that plan, in accordance with the terms of the plan.

****

B.   Plan descriptions and contribution information

Membership of each plan consisted of the following at December 31, 20X1, the date of the latest actuarial valuation:

	SEPP	SDEPP	MEPP
Retirees and beneficiaries receiving benefits	15,274	17,337	1,857
Terminated plan members entitled to, but not yet receiving, benefits	1,328	1,508	162
Active plan members	38,292	61,004	3,481
Total	54,894	79,849	5,500
Number of participating employers	1	203	53

****

C.   Funded status and funding progress—Pension plans

The funded status of each plan as of December 31, 20X1, the most recent actuarial valuation date, is as follows (dollar amounts in thousands):

	Actuarial Value of Assets (a)	Actuarial Accrued Liability (AAL) — Entry Age (b)	Unfunded AAL (UAAL) (b–a)	Funded Ratio (a/b) (percent)	Covered Payroll (c)	UAAL as a Percentage of Covered Payroll ((b–a)/c)
SEPP	$3,658,323	$4,284,961	$626,638	85.4	$1,156,346	54.2
SDEPP	$5,269,502	$5,709,764	$440,262	92.3	$1,546,650	28.5
MEPP	$549,696	$559,367	$9,671	98.3	$209,715	4.6

****

	SEPP	SDEPP	MEPP
Valuation date	12/31/X1	12/31/X1	12/31/X1
Actuarial cost method	Entry age	Entry age	Entry age
Amortization method	Level percent open	Level percent closed	Level percent closed
Remaining amortization period	23 years	15 years	Weighted average of 25 years
Asset valuation method	Four-year smoothed market	Four-year smoothed market	Four-year smoothed market
Actuarial assumptions:			
Investment rate of return*	7.5 percent	7.5 percent	7.5 percent
Projected salary increases*	5.5–9.5 percent	5.5–11.5 percent	5.5–11.5 percent
COLAs	None	1/2 CPI increase, maximum of 3 percent	1–3 percent
*Includes inflation at	5.5 percent	5.5 percent	5.5 percent

Figure 14.5   Excerpts from an illustrative note disclosure by a pension plan. (From Governmental Accounting Standards Board, Statement No. 50, *Pension Disclosures,* GASB, Connecticut, 2007. Reprinted with permission.)

a trust fund and a separate report are not issued by the pension plan, then the government presents this RSI for the last six fiscal years. Plans will include schedules covering the past six fiscal years.

14.5.1 Schedule of Funding Progress

The schedule of funding progress provides information that is useful for judging how well funded a pension or OPEB plan is. (Figure 14.6 illustrates a schedule for a pension plan. An OPEB schedule would be identical.) The first column shows the date as of which the information in the following columns was applicable. The third column shows the AAL. As you can see in Figure 14.6, the assets of each of the three pension plans (second column) fall short of the amount necessary to fund pension benefits completely, resulting in the UAAL shown in the fourth column.

Actuarial valuation date	Actuarial value of assets (a)	Actuarial accrued liability (AAL) —entry age (b)	Unfunded AAL (UAAL) (b–a)	Funded ratio (a/b) (percent)	Covered payroll (c)	UAAL as a percentage of covered payroll ((b–a)/c)
SEPP						
12/31/W6	$2,005,238	$2,626,296	$621,058	76.4	$901,566	68.9
12/31/W7	$2,411,610	$2,902,399	$490,789	83.1	$956,525	51.3
12/31/W8	$2,709,432	$3,331,872	$622,440	81.3	$1,004,949	61.9
12/31/W9*	$3,001,314	$3,604,297	$602,983	83.3	$1,049,138	57.5
12/31/X0	$3,366,946	$3,930,112	$563,166	85.7	$1,093,780	51.5
12/31/X1	$3,658,323	$4,284,961	$626,638	85.4	$1,156,346	54.2
SDEPP						
12/31/W6	$2,888,374	$3,499,572	$611,198	82.5	$1,205,873	50.7
12/31/W7	$3,473,718	$3,867,483	$393,765	89.8	$1,279,383	30.8
12/31/W8	$3,902,705	$4,439,761	$537,056	87.9	$1,344,151	40.0
12/31/W9*	$4,323,137	$4,802,700	$479,563	90.0	$1,403,255	34.2
12/31/X0	$4,849,798	$5,236,922	$387,124	92.6	$1,462,965	26.5
12/31/X1	$5,269,502	$5,709,764	$440,262	92.3	$1,546,650	28.5
MEPP						
12/31/W6	$301,305	$342,842	$41,537	87.9	$163,508	25.4
12/31/W7	$362,366	$378,885	$16,519	95.6	$173,476	9.5
12/31/W8	$407,117	$434,949	$27,832	93.6	$182,258	15.3
12/31/W9*	$450,975	$470,512	$19,537	95.8	$190,272	10.3
12/31/X0	$505,714	$513,044	$7,330	98.6	$198,368	3.7
12/31/X1	$549,696	$559,367	$9,671	98.3	$209,715	4.6

*Revised economic and noneconomic assumptions due to experience review.

Figure 14.6   Illustrative schedule of funding progress for a pension plan (dollars in thousands). (From Governmental Accounting Standards Board, Statement No. 50, *Pension Disclosures,* **GASB, Connecticut, 2007. Reprinted with permission.)**

The fifth column divides asset value by the AAL—the funded ratio. A funded ratio can be as low as zero (for a pay-as-you-go system with no assets) and as high as 100 percent or even higher (for a fully funded system, or one that actually has assets that exceed the AAL, respectively). The SEPP plan in Figure 14.6 was 85.4 percent funded as of the most recent actuarial valuation and the MEPP plan was nearly fully funded at 98.3 percent. Each of the plans is better funded in the most recent year than in the first year.

The second-to-last column in the schedule includes the covered payroll—the total payroll of the current employees covered by the plan. The last column then calculates a ratio of unfunded liability-to-payroll—dividing the UAAL by the covered payroll. This ratio declined from 50.7 percent to 28.5 percent for SDEPP.

14.5.2   Schedule of Employer Contributions

A second RSI schedule (Figure 14.7) compares actual contributions to a pension or OPEB plan with the ARC. A government is required to present it only if the pension plan does not issue its own financial report, which would include such a schedule covering the last six fiscal years. The sample schedule shows that the participating government contributed an amount equal to 100 percent of the ARC each year.

14.5.3   Notes to the Schedules

If a government or plan is aware of any factors that have a significant effect on the trend information in the two RSI schedules, such as improvements or reductions in pension benefit provisions, expansion or reduction of the eligible population, or changes in the actuarial methods, it adds an explanatory note to the schedules. If a government reports a cost-sharing plan as a trust fund and the plan does not issue

	Employer contributions					
	SEPP		SDEPP		MEPP	
Year ended June 30	Annual required contribution	Percentage contributed percent	Annual required contribution	Annual percentage contributed percent	Required contribution	Percentage contributed percent
20W7	$100,729	100	$115,935	100	$15,042	100
20W8	$106,030	100	$122,682	100	$15,959	100
20W9	$112,798	100	$129,822	100	$16,768	100
20X0	$118,735	100	$137,378	100	$17,505	100
20X1	$124,276	100	$142,347	100	$18,049	100
20X2	$137,916	100	$157,783	100	$18,653	100

Figure 14.7   Illustrative schedule of employer contributions for a pension plan (dollars in thousands). (From Governmental Accounting Standards Board, Statement No. 50, *Pension Disclosures,* GASB, Connecticut, 2007. Reprinted with permission.)

its own financial report, then the government adds another note to the schedules that describes the methodology and assumptions for performing actuarial valuations for the pension plan.

14.6 Reporting for Other Types of Plans

To this point, the discussion has focused primarily on reporting by plans and by governments participating in single-employer and agent multiple-employer defined benefit plans. The reporting requirements for governments participating in defined contribution plans and cost-sharing multiple-employer plans are less extensive due to the absence of an actuarial valuation—no valuation is necessary for defined contribution plans, and the valuation in cost-sharing plans is performed for the plan as a whole rather than the individual participating governments. The reporting requirements for insured plans also are simpler.

Governments in cost-sharing plans report expenses and expenditures equal to their contractually required contribution. Assets and liabilities would be reported only if there is a difference between the contractually required contribution and what a government actually contributes. They generally do not present any of the actuarial-related disclosures or schedules, though they do disclose in the notes their required contribution and the percentage they actually contributed for the past three years. However, if the cost-sharing plan does not issue its own financial report, then the participating governments each would present the RSI schedules and notes. It should be noted that the RSI would be for the plan as a whole, including all of the participating governments, not just for the government presenting the RSI in its report.

The expense or expenditure for governments in defined contribution plans equals their required contribution according to the terms of the plan. Assets and liabilities result only when there is a difference between the required contribution to the plan and what a government actually contributes. Governments participating in defined contribution plans disclose information about the plan, its provisions, and how it is administered. They also disclose their contribution requirements and the contributions actually made by the government and the plan members.

If a government accumulates resources with an insurance company although employees are in active service, and in return the company unconditionally takes over the obligation to pay the pension or OPEB benefits of the government's employees, this arrangement is called an insured plan. If a government has an insured plan, it makes the following disclosures in the notes:

- Plan description, benefit provisions, and the authority under which the benefits are established and may be changed
- Fact that the obligation to pay the benefits has been transferred to one or more insurance companies

- Whether the government guarantees the benefits in the event the insurance company goes out of business
- Current year pension or OPEB expenditures or expenses and contributions or premiums paid

14.7 Postemployment Benefit Reporting Going Forward

Public employee pensions and OPEB have never been a hotter topic than they are now. The combination of funding and management problems with some pension plans and recent requirements for state and local governments to begin reporting OPEB have spurred two debates. The first and perhaps most clamorous is the debate over the affordability of OPEB. Governments beginning to implement the GASB's OPEB standards are seeing very large obligations and costs in their actuarial valuations and, in virtually all cases, no offsetting resources set aside—essentially, a funded ratio of zero. The second debate has been waged somewhat more stealthily over the sufficiency of the accounting and financial reporting standards.

A variety of issues have been raised about the transparency of financial reporting on postemployment benefits and the usefulness of the information that is provided. Particular sore points for some observers are provisions that allow the effects of annual changes in asset values, for instance, to be reflected over time. These critics would argue that spreading changes in the fair value of plan investments over a five-year period disguises what is truly happening to the financial status of a plan. It may be several years before the reader realizes there is a problem. Likewise, they would believe that amortization of the unfunded liability is equally opaque. Their preference would be to see any changes that affect the obligations and costs of benefits reflected more rapidly.

They may have a point. Smoothing and amortization are intended to minimize year-to-year volatility, which has salutary effects—raising necessary resources to fund benefits is easier when the amounts are relatively stable and predictable. In other words, these methods are conducive to funding. However, they may have unintended consequences. For example, if a government improves its benefits and broadens eligibility to receive them, the immediate impact (all other factors being equal) would be to increase the size of the unfunded liability. The obligation related to the benefits would be greater, but no additional resources have yet been set aside. This is particularly the case in benefit improvements made retroactively for persons already retired. Although the increase in the unfunded liability and concomitant decrease in the funded ratio would be evident in the succeeding reporting period, the impact on the unfunded liability would be amortized and, therefore, have only a marginal impact on the ARC. In layperson's terms, the government might barely feel the financial pain of its benefit promises. Critics have said that this situation provides an incentive for governments to offer benefits that, in the long run, they cannot afford.

The trend in private sector standards certainly is toward faster recognition. At the federal level, the Pension Funding Protection Act of 2004 and the Pension Protection Act of 2006 changed the regulations governing pension funding. Among other changes, they reduced the smoothing of assets and liabilities and required that underfunding be addressed more quickly (Moran and Cohen, 2007). Shortly thereafter the Financial Accounting Standards Board (FASB) issued its Statement No. 158, most notably requiring corporations and not-for-profits to recognize immediately the overfunded or underfunded status of their single-employer defined benefit postretirement plan as an asset or liability in their statement of financial position and to run changes in that funded status through the income statement (FASB, 2006).

Is the same in store for state and local governments? Although the GASB's OPEB standards are relatively new, its pension standards were issued in 1994 (GASB, 1994). Sufficient time has passed to evaluate whether those standards have been effective—to review the experience with implementation of the standards and the usefulness to the public of the resulting information. In fact, the GASB began in 2006 to conduct an initial evaluation of the pension standards, with an eye toward considering in 2008 whether to add a project to amend the standards. The GASB review is significantly different from the effort that led to FASB Statement 158, however. The FASB's clear intention from the start was to speed up recognition of the unfunded liability. The GASB, on the other hand, does not have a particular end result in mind.

Some changes actually have already been made and are reflected in this chapter. With some experience with the pension standards under its belt, the GASB released OPEB standards in 2004 that improved upon some of the pension disclosure and RSI requirements (GASB, 2004). The GASB has since extended those improvements in the OPEB standards to pensions with Statement No. 50, Pension Disclosures (GASB, 2007).

If one were to predict the likely outcome of deliberations over public sector standards for postemployment benefit reporting, it would be a good bet that there will not be any movement toward greater smoothing or amortization. It may also be unlikely that the status quo will be maintained. This only leaves movement in the direction of faster recognition, but the burning question is at what point the resulting added transparency continues to justify the negative implications of greater volatility.

References

Civic Federation 2006. *The State of Illinois Retirement Systems: Funding History and Reform Proposals.* Chicago: The Civic Federation.

Civic Federation 2007. *Status of Local Pension Funding Fiscal Year 2005: An Evaluation of Ten Local Government Employee Pension Funds in Cook County.* Chicago: The Civic Federation.

Financial Accounting Standards Board 2006. Statement No. 158, *Employers' Accounting for Defined Benefit Pension and Other Postemployment Plans—an Amendment of FASB Statements No. 87, 88, 106, and 132(R).* Norwalk, Connecticut: FASB.

Gore, A.K. 2003. The effects of GAAP regulation and bond market interaction on local government disclosure. *Journal of Accounting and Public Policy,* 23, 23–52.

Governmental Accounting Standards Board 1994. Statement No. 25, *Financial Reporting for Defined Benefit Pension Plans and Note Disclosures for Defined Contribution Plans.* Norwalk, Connecticut: GASB.

Governmental Accounting Standards Board 1994. Statement No. 27, *Accounting for Pensions by State and Local Government Employers.* Norwalk, Connecticut: GASB.

Governmental Accounting Standards Board 2004. Statement No. 43, *Financial Reporting for Postemployment Benefit Plans Other Than Pension Plans.* Norwalk, Connecticut: GASB.

Governmental Accounting Standards Board 2004. Statement No. 45, *Accounting and Financial Reporting by Employers for Postemployment Benefit Plans Other Than Pension Plans.* Norwalk, Connecticut: GASB.

Governmental Accounting Standards Board 2007. Statement No. 50, *Pension Disclosures.* Norwalk, Connecticut: GASB.

Icerman, R.C. 1996. *Small Government Financial Reporting.* Norwalk, Connecticut: Governmental Accounting Standards Board.

Levitt, Jr. A., Turner, L.E., and Dahlberg, T.A. 2006. *Report of the Audit Committee of the City of San Diego: Investigation into the San Diego City Employees' Retirement System and the City of San Diego Sewer Rate Structure.* New York: Kroll, Inc. and Willkie Farr & Gallagher LLP.

Mead, D.M. 2001. *An Analyst's Guide to Government Financial Statements.* Norwalk, Connecticut: GASB.

Mead, D.M. 2005. *What Else You Should Know about a Government's Finances: A Guide to Notes to the Financial Statements and Supporting Information.* Norwalk, Connecticut: GASB.

Mead, D.M. (forthcoming). *The Needs of Users of Governmental Financial Information.* Norwalk, Connecticut: Governmental Accounting Standards Board.

Moran, M.A. and Cohen, A.J. 2007. *Pensions: Previewing FASB Phase Two.* New York: The Goldman Sachs Group, Inc.

Plummer, E.H., Hutchison, P.D., and Patton, T.K. 2007. GASB No. 34's governmental financial reporting model: Evidence on its information relevance. *The Accounting Review,* 82(1), 205–240.

Reck, J.L. and Wilson, E.R. 2005. Information transparency and pricing in the municipal bond secondary market. *Journal of Accounting and Public Policy,* 25, 1–31.

Zion, D. and Varshney, A. 2007. *You Dropped a Bomb on Me, GASB: Uncovering $1.5 trillion in Hidden OPEB Liabilities for State and Local Governments.* New York: Credit Suisse.

CONTEMPORARY EMPLOYEE BENEFITS ISSUES

Chapter 15

Work–Life Benefits

N. Joseph Cayer and Charlene M.L. Roach

CONTENTS

15.1 Introduction

The world of work has changed enormously since the 1970s. Among the changes is workplace diversity that encompasses many characteristics including race, religion, culture, national origin, societal effect (e.g. norms, attitudes, or perceptions), global trends, language, gender, age, disability, family arrangement, childlessness, social class, and sexual orientation (Crompton and Lyonette 2006). Among other things, diversity has resulted in changes in quality of work life, healthcare, and the nature of Human Resources Management (HRM) as a field with its policies, missions, and visions (Dick and Hyde 2006; Halpern 2006; Pitts 2006; Wood and Newton 2006). Long gone is the stereotypical traditional arrangement in which the male head of household worked and the female partner stayed home to raise the family and keep house (Graves, Ohlott, and Ruderman 2007). Today there are small signs of a slight reversal of these traditional roles occurring among couples (from diverse backgrounds) where men are choosing to stay at home and provide the nurturing role as homemaker while the women go into the job market and serve as the breadwinners for the households. Although this practice is not common and in the minority, it may be indicative that there is a shift in the status quo of conventional societal norms and roles for men and women. It also appears that one of the main forces driving this trend may be sheer economics. If this continues in the future, it may require radical change in the way society, HR managers, supervisors, and employers view compensation, benefits, and pay packages for all employees.

Employees also differ by whether they are full- or part-time and by educational level and skill sets such as technical training/knowledge or vocational skills. Other forces of change occurring in the landscape of the world of work include managers' and employees' attempts to control the workplace, time schedules, and the ways people work. Additionally, such changes reflect their attempts to shape the nature of boundary management strategies in regard to whether there should be a dichotomy between work and life activities and practices (Kossek, Lautsch, and Eaton 2006). In short, workplaces contain a diversity of individuals with varied interests, motivations, needs, and wants. Not surprisingly, this diversity in employees translates into variations in preferences or concerns about employee benefits. Employers wishing to entice good applicants and retain them find it necessary to offer an array of benefits to fit different needs and expectations and in doing so alleviate some of the congestion that occurs at the junction of balancing life and work roles (Halpern 2006).

Employees work more hours than they did in the past meaning that they have less time for dealing with personal business originating at home, community engagement, life practices, or other matters of everyday life creating conflicts in their work and lives and in some instances resulting in social isolation and psychological problems (Reynolds 2005; Yates and Leach 2006). In 2005, men reported working five hours more and women reported working 3.8 hours longer than they are scheduled to work (Bond et al. 2005; Lingle 2005).

The Bureau of Labor Statistics also reports that workforce trends among mothers indicate a general increase since 2002, including the numbers of mothers of newborns and of infants in the workplace. More specifically, about three-quarters of all mothers are participating in the workforce. There is also a strong trend toward more married mothers with children versus single mothers with children in the workforce (U.S. Bureau of Labor Statistics 2002). The workplace is also more ethnically diverse with 21 percent people of color compared to 12 percent in 1977. It is also older with 56 percent over 40 compared to 38 percent in 1977 and 22 percent in 2002 compared to 37 percent in 1997 of people under 30 in the workforce. Older employees tend to stay employed longer and in new ways representing a shift from past trends (Hudson 2005; Halpern 2006). There is an even split between men and women. Further, women are more predominant than men as managers and professionals, 38 versus 28 percent. Since the post–World War II fertility explosion, women in the West indicate an increasing trend toward childlessness. These statistics show that there may be a positive correlation between women with higher education and their choice to delay motherhood. However, the literature points to several variables that contribute to childlessness such as level of education, marital status, and social and economic status (Wood and Newton 2006).

Dual-career couples increased from 66 to 78 percent from 1977 to 2002 (Bond et al. 2005; Lingle 2005). In recent studies, over two-thirds of employees who have children complain that they do not have time enough to spend with their families (Boots 2004; Galinsky, Bond, and Hill 2004; Galinsky et al. 2005; Stockwell 2006). Reflecting generational differences, younger employees tend to be more focused on family issues and life concerns 41 percent of boomers versus 50 percent of Generation Y and 52 percent of Generation X (Bond et al. 2005; Families and Work Institute 2005; Lingle 2005). On the whole, there is certainly a deviation from the past because more families work for longer time frames than in previous generations.

Work–life benefits reflect the need for adjusting benefit packages to differing needs of employees and to their lifestyle concerns. They also result from a recognition that employees cannot separate their work and nonwork lives (Bailyn 2006; Van Der Lippe, Jager, and Kops 2006). The demands on employees outside of work affect what they do at work and how they do it. Similarly, work has an impact on people's lives outside work (Halpern 2006). Work–life benefits attempt to provide balance between professional and personal lives of employees by accommodating the changing demands faced by employers and employees alike. Some employers use the terms "family-friendly" or "work and family" benefits (Hoyman and Duer 2004; Davis and Kalleberg 2006; Kossek et al. 2006), but we choose work–life benefits as it is more inclusive relating to the stresses that all employees face especially in light of the unique context of the working environment of the twenty-first century (Pitt-Catsouphes et al. 2004; Smithson and Stokoe 2005; Crompton and Lyonette 2006; Gault and Lovell 2006).

Initially, employers tended to adopt work–life benefits in response to increasing numbers of women in the workplace and as a way of creating greater employee satisfaction (Lambert 2000; Carell 2007). In fact, studies have found that work–life benefits are important predictors of job satisfaction (Saltzstein, Ting, and Saltzstein 2001). However, employers also adopt work–life benefits because they have positive impacts on employee behavior and productivity (Lambert 2000). The employee, recognizing support given by the employing organization, develops a greater sense of commitment to the organization. Some research also indicates that managers who show commitment to their family or life responsibilities outside of work develop leadership abilities, a general well-being, greater effectiveness on the job, improved attitudes, and improved overall performance (Graves et al. 2007). Also, in a symbiotic sense, work–life benefits may promote positive spill over effects that enrich both employees' and managers' personal lives and at the same time their professional work lives (Greenhaus and Powell 2006). Other positive enhancements are a reduced interference due to life or family issues in their work lives. Work–life benefits at the same time may enable employees to increase their productivity at work and reduce stresses in their private lives (Wadsworth and Owens 2007).

Work–life benefits vary greatly from employer to employer, but typical of work–life benefit programs are:

Flexibile work schedule
Dependent care benefits
Domestic partner benefits
Career development benefits
Employee Assistance Programs
Wellness programs
Other programs such as legal insurance, lactation programs, etc.

Each of these areas is addressed more fully below.

15.2 Flexible Work Schedules

Flexible work schedules have been a part of employment reality for a long time. Firefighters, for example, long have had nontraditional work schedules. In the 1970s, however, many private employers experimented with work hours that varied from the traditional eight hour workday. The reasons for such experiments included desires and motivation of employees, cost factors associated with more efficient use of facilities, the desire to avoid building more physical facilities, environmental concerns, and traffic congestion, among others. Recognition of the realities of the contemporary workforce diversity also prompts variations in work scheduling. Thus, dual-career couples or people with eldercare concerns, for example, may benefit greatly by having flexibility in their schedules so that they can meet their nonwork obligations. Flexible work schedules include allowing employees to choose their start and end times for work each day, daily flexibility, and compressed schedules.

Approximately 50 percent of employees are eligible for such flex-time as it generally is limited to full-time, permanent employees of employers with more than 50 employees (Galinsky et al. 2004; Stockwell 2006).

Between 1992 and 2002, employees who were able to choose their starting and quitting time rose from 29 to 43 percent (Galinsky et al. 2004). For these employees, it generally means that they have to be at work during core working hours, for example 10 a.m. to 4 p.m., but choose their eight hours anywhere between 8 a.m. and 6 p.m. Of course, the core work hours are defined by the employer and vary by employer. All employees are expected to be at work during the core hours. Managers and professionals and those earning relatively more tend to have more opportunity for flex schedules than those lower in the organizational hierarchy and pay scales. Flex time is used by 70 percent of employees when available; although women tend to use it more highly then men, 79 to 68 percent, respectively. Parents also are more likely (78 percent) than those without children (70 percent) to use it. Employees in service industries also tend to have greater access to flexibility in their work schedules (Galinsky et al. 2004).

Some employees also are able to change their daily schedules. From 1992 to 2002, one survey found that the proportion of employees who could change their schedules daily rose from 18 to 23 percent (Galinsky et al. 2004). Of course, employees with such an option are expected to keep managers and coworkers informed of their work schedules.

Flexible work schedules also include compressed work schedules. It is not unusual to allow employees to work longer hours for fewer days per week. Many people work four ten hour days instead of the traditional five eight hour days. Firefighters traditionally have worked compressed work weeks with the typical schedule being two 24-hour shifts per week for an average of eight 24-hour days per month. This allows an average of five days off per week. Many in the nursing profession now work alternative schedules where they actually have shorter work weeks, but work 12 hour shifts for three days. These schedules are used as recruiting tools and allow employees opportunity to pursue other employment or activities on the extended days off.

Part- or reduced-time scheduling also is very common. Many employers define benefits-eligible employees as working some minimum number of hours per week. Thus, an employee may have to work 35 hours to be benefits eligible. Employers can save a lot of money by avoiding paying benefit costs; thus, they may hire a lot of people for less than the 35 hours or whatever figure they set for benefits eligible. A 2002 study found that only 40 percent of part-time employees have access to benefits compared to 90 percent of full-time employees (Galinsky et al. 2004). Of course, there are many employees who do not want full-time work and part-time employment fits their needs, especially if they have access to benefits elsewhere such as through a spouse's employment or in a few cases through a domestic partner's employment. There are also some employees or professionals who are choosing to give up or sacrifice full-time employment for part-time employment to devote to private interests, personal goals/activities, family, life goals/ambitions, or life demands (Todd 2004). An example may be where one partner in a dual-career relationship chooses to work part-time to devote more attention to lifestyle concerns, unpaid work at home, or family matters. Other reasons for part-time work or flexible schedules include childcare reasons, religious pursuits, mid-career changes (may require retooling), continuing educational training, and personal or business interests.

Statistics also reinforce in the European Union (EU) a greater preference for women working shorter hours of work (30 hour week) than men (37 hour week), especially when there are caring responsibilities at home or unpaid work to balance with employment. Additional statistics in the following areas reinforce these claims that women in the EU may have over men when general comparisons are made of their life demands: about 16 percent of women compared to 8 percent of men have weekly responsibilities for care of the disabled/elderly; 41 percent of women compared to 24 percent of men have daily nurturing and educational duties for at least one hour or more in the household; 63 percent of women compared to 12 percent men have at least one hour or more of daily housekeeping tasks; 85 percent of women compared to 25 percent of men are charged with other household chores or for domestic shopping responsibilities; and in dual income couples with children under five years, women spent more than double the time for domestic or childcare than men (Todd 2004). These findings strongly suggest that women on average may have greater life demands to balance because of their participation in unpaid activities outside the workplace than men, which supports their higher preference for part-time employment to balance their work and life demands. However, the European Foundation for the Improvement of Living and Working Conditions (2003) found that the contemporary society and workforce ideally prefer shorter work hours, where 80 percent of employees who worked more than 50 hours preferred a shorter work week simply because of life concerns and matters that put added pressure on their schedules. One may assume that if these concerns were not bearing so heavily on employees that they may be willing to work longer work hours. The U.S. government encourages part-time employment in the federal service through the Federal Employees Part-time Employment Act of 1978. In the case of the national government, benefits are prorated according to the number of hours worked. Many state and local governments have similar policies.

Seasonal or part-year work represents another type of work schedule flexibility. Some work depends upon the season for example, landscaping, snow removal, agricultural workers, and swimming pool attendants and lifeguards. Thus, employers hire those employees for the needed period of time. There are many people who want seasonal work, among them parents of school children and students who want to work during the summer. Approximately 40 percent of part-time workers, however, would prefer stable, year round jobs (Galinsky et al. 2004).

Part-time employment often is used in conjunction with job sharing. In job sharing, two or more employees share one job, usually working different hours to ensure that the workday is covered. Some dual-career couples in the same profession have found job sharing attractive. The sharing arrangement might provide that one works the morning shift and the other the afternoon shift. Or they may split the job by each working two and a half days. The object is to cover the work and accommodate the needs of the individual employees. Benefits can be prorated as in other part-time work. The public sector may also learn from the private sector in finding new ways to enrich certain types of positions using job sharing as an HR strategy to help managers and supervisors find ways to organize work, enrich jobs, reduce costs, and increase productivity. For instance, positions that could be routine or highly specialized could be rotated to share duties. An example may be in the IT field of programming. Job sharing could give other programmers a working knowledge of the big picture versus being ivory towers of specialist programs through rotation of tasks, enabling employees to have a breadth of knowledge and skills that may be customized to the organization's needs and goals. Historically this type of position requires: specialization in specific tasks or programs, long hours of overtime, tedious analysis, and often times working alone. In the private sector employers are using this type of flexibility creatively in the IT programming field which demonstrates a new way of job sharing (Brady 2007).

With the changing demographics of the workplace, employees often need flexibility to attend to personal or family concerns. The need often arises without a lot of notice and may require only a short time away from the job. Parents often have to attend parent–teacher conferences or be available to take children to dental and medical appointments. Similar issues arise for those with eldercare responsibilities. The employees also have home emergencies such as a heating or air conditioning problem or plumbing or electrical problems or other personal issues or events. Although formal policies cannot cover every contingency, employees do find it important to have flexibility from their supervisors in allowing them to deal with such situations. It appears that more than one-third of employees find a lack of flexibility on the part of their employers to be able to handle such concerns (Galinsky et al. 2004; Stockwell 2006).

Although flexible schedules provide both employees and employers with great benefits as we discussed, there are challenges to this type of benefit. There may be a downside because there are managers and supervisors who view it as less attractive. With this perspective, employees may lose career footing while gaining time for their personal and life practices. This point introduces a cost factor based on the orientation of their managers and supervisors or even the culture of the organization. It is more prevalent in private companies versus public and nonprofit organizations. Some firms reported that flexible policies were not supported by management. Those with this negative attitude tend to see it as a practice for a few, such as useful for women who pursue family or personal life activities (such as charitable work) as their priorities over work (W.P. Carey School of Business 2007). These concerns point to the need for careful training of management and supervisors in the way they evaluate employees' performance using these flexible schedules and correcting suspicions about its drawbacks to one's future career in organizations.

Telework (sometimes called telecommuting) is a trend that allows employees to work from home or some other location different from the office. Sometimes, employers develop satellite sites to facilitate telework. Telework helps the employee to reduce the stress of traveling to and from the work site, increases opportunity for family time, and increases flexibility of schedule. Employers may see increased productivity, greater job satisfaction, and lower overhead costs among other benefits. A mixed method study consisting of 157 employees who telecommute with 89 traditional employees who work set hours at the office showed more productivity for the employees who telecommute and other studies revealed similar results with about 10 and 30 percent productivity increases respectively (Hil et al. 1998).

Telework also allows employees to have some control over their jobs, enabling a sense of psychological empowerment and a development of boundary management strategies (Kossek et al. 2006). Boundary management strategies refer to the guidelines that may be utilized in organizing and maintaining specific distinctions between roles performed for work and at home or in one's personal life within a flexible schedule (Kossek et al. 2006). For instance, employees are able to create clear boundaries for tasks at home such as childcare and work-related tasks such as working on reports and statements for one's specific position. Other techniques include practical steps such as restricted use of their organizations' cell phones, pagers, blackberries, hand held devices, or accessing the Internet or e-mail after the work schedule is completed or not during weekends or holidays as the position may define. Others create home offices with a door or secured space to control interference or interruptions by family members. There is no hard and fast rule. Some employees attempt to integrate both personal and work-related calls while at work. However, it depends on one's preference or orientation to synthesizing work–life roles (Kossek et al. 2006).

Employers also see telework as a very important recruiting tool (Telework Coalition 2005). Although telework offers benefits to employees and employers alike, it also requires clear communication of expectations, normally with a contract between the employer and employee. Of course, it also requires monitoring to ensure that it is working well. There are some positions that are not suitable for telework, such as those requiring customer services or involve work that may be too sensitive or confidential in nature to take out of the office. Thus, employers' would need to use their discretion before authorizing employees to work remotely.

Telework is now common in both the private and public sectors. Among private companies, 37 percent allow telecommuting (World at Work 2007). However, only about 2 percent of employees seem to take advantage of the option (International Public Management Association for Human Resources HR Center 2007). Large public employers increasingly offer the option, especially in urban areas. In the West, five states, Arizona, California, Oregon, Texas, and Washington, joined together in the Telework Collaboration to study and encourage telework initiatives. The initiatives work with both private and public sector employers to facilitate telework with the hope of decreasing traffic and pollution as well as reduce employer costs.

Leave is another benefit that has changed dramatically as the demographics of the workplace changed. Traditional leave policies covered vacation and sick leave and perhaps bereavement leave. Rigid rules governed these policies with such requirements as having to be employed for at least a year before being able to use them or requirements that vacation be taken all at once or that sick leave be supported by a doctor's note. Leave became more flexible as expectations of workers changed. Consequently, employees often now take vacation leave a day at a time or even in shorter increments. Sick leave typically no longer requires documentation of the illness.

Other forms of leave also have emerged. Of course, family leave has become a prominent form of leave with the passage of the national Family and Medical Leave Act of 1993 that requires employers to provide 12 weeks of unpaid leave for illness and care of ill family members as well as care of a newborn, newly adopted, or foster child. Although the leave is unpaid, many policies do allow use of sick leave as part of the leave. For example, the Federal Employees Family Friendly Leave Act of 1994 allows use of up to 13 days of sick leave to care for family members by federal government employees. The state of California provides for up to six weeks of partial pay for family medical leave. The state of Washington adopted a law in 2007 providing five weeks of partially paid leave for the birth or adoption of a child. Family and medical leave has subsumed most maternity and paternity leave that had been provided by employers in the past.

Holidays also represent a form of leave. Governments tend to be more generous than private sector employers in providing holiday leave. Private sector employers provide employees an average of six holidays (usually paid) per year although the public sector generally gives ten to twelve paid holidays annually.

Some employers have gone to paid time-off (PTO) programs to simplify their leave policies. PTO plans add to the flexibility of leave and help accommodate the diverse needs of employees. With traditional plans requiring documentation for sickness or other reasons, employers found themselves spending much time monitoring and judging employees, often with inconsistent results. Typically, PTO plans take the traditional sick, vacation, and bereavement policies and put them together. The total number of days of leave may be less than the sum of all three types of leave, but there is greater flexibility. The employee just has to provide notice and get approval but does not have to justify the leave. Employees can use the time for anything they want.

Other leave includes such things as leave for volunteer activities or to give blood. Sabbatical leaves are common in colleges and universities and, increasingly, are being used in other organizations. Sabbaticals allow employees to refresh their knowledge or learn new things that will be useful to the organization.

The United States lags behind other nations on virtually all leave policies. Although it is praised for protecting employees in the workplace on employment rights and safety, it is often criticized for its level of leave available for vacation, illness, childbearing and childcare, and eldercare (Crompton and Lyonette 2006; Heyman, Earle, and Hayes 2007).

15.3 Dependent Care

Employees with children or eldercare responsibilities have particular concerns in balancing work and personal lives (Todd 2004; Business and Legal Reports Inc. 2007; Crompton and Lyonette 2006; McPherson 2007). In particular, parents of teenagers indicated in a 2002 study that they feel stressed by parental responsibilities and would like help (Galinsky et al. 2005). A survey of federal government employees found that about 54 percent had dependent care needs and that another 19 percent expected to have such needs in the future (U.S. Government Accountability Office 2007). Dependent care issues lead to employee absences, stress, fatigue, and lower productivity. For employees, dependent care programs provide peace of mind, pleasure with work–life balance, and job satisfaction. For employers, in addition to cost and productivity factors (e.g., increased quality of work, reduced negative spill over effects from home to work), dependent care may lead to better recruitment and retention outcomes and boost the image of the organization (McPherson 2007; Todd 2004).

Employer provided childcare takes two forms, no or low cost and direct cost to the employer. A 2002 survey found that between one-third and one-half of employers provided the low cost or no cost programs. Dependent care assistance plans were provided by 45 percent of the employers in the survey (Bond et al. 2005). Dependent care assistance plans sponsored by employers qualify employees for tax exemption up to $5000 in childcare expenses. The pretax money is put in a flexible spending account for the employee thus reducing the employee's tax burden but not costing the employer except for administrative costs (Coe 2002). About a third of the employers in the 2002 survey provided resources and referral for childcare (Bond et al. 2005). Only 7 percent provided direct cost childcare on site or nearby.

For parents of teenage children who indicated they feel particularly stressed, only 7 percent of employers in the 2002 survey with 50 or more employees offered any program for them (Bond et al.). In particular, they tend to offer Employee Assistance Programs and various forms of counseling.

With eldercare, 79 percent of the employers in the 2002 survey say they offer employees time off without adversely affecting their jobs (Bond et al. 2005). Most employers make available resources or referrals for eldercare. Direct subsidy of eldercare is rare (6 percent). Services may include adding an adult family member to healthcare insurance as McGraw-Hill does. Others such as Toyota and Prudential Financial Inc. provide access to a geriatric care manager to help in arranging services, and Bank of America offers group rates on long-term care insurance. Some employers also support day care for elders thus helping to alleviate some of the stress employees experience with eldercare. In comparative studies some governments in the EU are playing a more proactive and beneficent role than the United States through deliberate policies that promote education and awareness of various types of care facilities, wellness practices, and promotion of good models of parenting through the involvement of fathers and mothers (Todd 2004). For instance, the Swedish government has actively promoted, through printed material and advertisement, the positive impact that the fathers' roles have on their child-rearing practices. They highlight the benefits of both parents to claim these parental benefits. As such, parental benefits are given to parents with sick children under their care who are up to 12 years and in some cases up to 16 years. This policy enables both male and female employees in the workforce who are eligible to 120 benefit days per annum. Records indicate that, on an average, employees may take about seven days for a child in a year (Todd 2004).

Dependent care programs can be expensive to provide; consequently, many employers have joined consortia to spread the cost. Employers in Boulder, Colorado; Austin, Texas; New York City; and many other places have established consortia to provide childcare or eldercare services. Employers often pay a membership fee and services are available to their employees, normally at a fee. Of course, employers may subsidize the employee's fee as well. These arrangements are especially attractive to smaller employers because of the cost. However, many large employers such as Citigroup, IBM, the Internal Revenue Service, and the Department of Treasury participate in such consortia. In some cases, unions also help fund the programs.

15.4   Domestic Partner Benefits

Domestic partner benefits generate a lot of interest and controversy, largely because they are associated with homosexuality for much of the population. Gay, lesbian, and transgender groups are the primary supporters of extending domestic partner benefits thus the tendency of people to link them. Domestic partner benefits extend benefits similar to those of traditional family dependents to domestic partners of employees. Domestic partners may be same sex or opposite sex partners in a committed relationship.

Although employers increasingly offer domestic partner benefits, they still are provided by a small minority of employers. The Human Rights Campaign Fund reported in 2007 that 9375 employers (8657 being private companies) offered domestic partner health benefits, the most common employee benefit. Among private employers, large employers are the most likely to offer the benefits. Thirteen states, 145 city and county governments, and 303 colleges and universities provided benefits to domestic partners of employees (Human Rights Campaign Fund 2007). The national government does not offer domestic partner benefits. In many cities, and in the state of California, government contractors are required to extend the same benefits to same sex partners as are provided to married opposite sex partners (Human Rights Campaign Fund 2006).

The increase in coverage of domestic partners reflects a change in family arrangements in U.S. society. The policies recognize that households of unmarried adults in committed relationships are now common. Employers face challenges in determining what is a domestic partnership as most states do not provide legal status for them although that is changing. Massachusetts courts went so far as to determine that same sex couples could marry under the state's constitution. This decision set off a frenzy across the country as opposition groups pushed antigay marriage laws including an effort to amend the constitution in Massachusetts. In some cases, antidomestic partnership policies also were pushed. In addition to determining when a domestic partnership exists, benefit policies also have to provide for when such a partnership is terminated.

In the past, employers often resisted domestic partner benefits partly on the basis of cost. Various studies have found that benefit costs do not increase much at all, usually less than 1 percent but ranging from 0 to 5 percent as a result of domestic partner benefits (Human Rights Campaign Fund 2006). Employers find that the benefits have positive effects in terms of employee satisfaction and a positive image with the gay, lesbian, and transgender community who spend a lot of money in the economy. (see Chapter 17 for a full discussion of domestic partner benefits).

15.5 Career Development Benefits

Employers often assist employees in career development through a variety of practices and programs. Employers benefit as employees match their professional goals with the mission of the organization. Employees develop greater capacity and acquire new competencies in a carefully conceived career development program. The care shown to employees in such a program also often results in greater loyalty to the employing organization. Obviously, the employee is primarily responsible for the progress of a career development plan, but the employer can do much to help the employee to operationalize the plan.

Career development plans include many components such as training and development opportunities, learning on the job, mentoring, and educational assistance. Organizations also need to portray to their employees an ethic of care by becoming an ally or partner with their employees in helping them to create career planning and paths that provide them with the work schedule that will be most helpful to them in balancing their work and life demands. These career development plans that are pro-work and life balance may incorporate benefits that give them flexibility and diverse training (in some cases cross training) for them to hone in on skills and knowledge that can be used to accomplish the organization's missions and objectives. Such plans may allow employees to cross train or act in different positions allowing various types of work schedules and flexibility (Friedman and Greenhaus 2000; Halpern 2006).

Some universities such as Arizona State University have created new approaches in their benefit packages to help maintain the retention and recruitment of sterling faculty members who may be of childbearing age while under tenure review and allow them the flexibility to take time for child birth and redeem time they lost to secure their tenure. These benefits may reduce attrition rates of junior faculty members who are forced out of their tenure track because of these constraints of work and life demands. They also help to alleviate costs associated with committee searches for new faculty and increase the intellectual capital from the expertise of their research contributions to their universities.

In the future, these types of work–life benefits may continue to evolve as employees face unique conflicts in their efforts to balance work and life demands. Helping people cope with the stress of the workplace also is an important part of keeping people on a career track. Overwork and stress can lead to reduced career aspirations among employees, sometimes leading to people opting out of the workforce (Lingle 2005). Employers benefit by programs that help people cope at work so that they are more likely to stay in the workforce. Of course, employers are attempting to deal with the retirement of large parts of their workforces as the baby boomers reach retirement age. Succession plans become a big part of employer planning including focusing on the development of employees already in the organization.

Training and development is a key element of career development of employees and helps the employer develop the capacity to compete and assure achieving its mission. Most large employers have internal training and development programs providing employees the opportunity to enhance skills and learn new ones as well as to prepare for ever-increasing responsibilities. Although smaller employers often cannot afford in-house training and development programs, they have many options. External training and development programs are offered by a variety of vendors, including for profit consultants, nonprofit organizations, college and university training centers, and other government organizations. Employers can send their employees for very specific training and development that fits their needs. Professional associations and conferences offer another opportunity for learning new things relevant to the employee's work.

Employers may set aside a specific amount of money for each employee to use on professional development. For example, the Phoenix Police Department budgets a fixed amount for each employee to use for professional development. The employee then can use that money to attend workshops, institutes, or other training programs. Or, the employee may use the money to pay tuition for college or university classes either as a nondegree student or for work toward a relevant degree. The money may also be used to attend professional conferences. Sabbaticals, common to colleges and universities, are now used by many employers to allow employees extended time away from work to refresh and learn new skills important to the organization (Bond et al. 2005). They are most likely to be available to high level managers and executives.

Employees learn on the job through shadowing others and by experiencing different jobs and parts of the organization. Some employers allow employees to move around the organization, especially as part of supervisory or management training programs. In the early 2000s, Arizona's Maricopa County government introduced a new performance management system and was able to coordinate successive training for managers and supervisors in their training programs for this level of their workforce. In so doing, leaders were exposed to strategies to avoid pitfalls in the new system: such as identifying knowledge gaps, duplication, misconceptions, and poor monitoring techniques. Accountability was maintained as training enforced clear standards for implementation of quality performance management systems and identified systemic flaws. Overall, training programs provide a positive atmosphere for organizational learning, on-the-job training, and a better understanding of the big picture of the organization policies, missions, visions, and objectives. The employee learns about the larger picture and how the various units of the organization work together to achieve the mission. Rotation programs are used both to develop specific new skills and to help build rapport within the organization. Management intern programs are good examples of efforts to expose individuals to various parts of the organization and to prepare them for upper level management positions as well. Mentoring programs provide one-on-one personal support for individual employees as they pursue careers in the organization.

Often forgotten in career development programs is the end of the career. Many people are unprepared for retirement. A benefit offered by many employers is retirement counseling so that employees are prepared for what they face in retirement. Thus, employers offer consultation on financial and legal issues associated with retirement as well as on the social needs of people as they leave the work scene. Many employers offer phased retirement to ease the transition into retirement. Phased retirement also benefits the employer in that it helps new employees to transition to the work using the institutional knowledge of the persons retiring.

15.6 Employee Assistance Programs

Employee assistance programs (EAPs) attempt to help employees whose jobs are being affected by personal issues. Starting as efforts to help employees with substance abuse problems, they have evolved to address virtually any kind of problem employees have. EAPs may offer some services directly or they may provide referral and access to services externally. Large employers typically offer some direct services such as limited duration counseling. Services beyond the capacity of the EAP staff are provided under contract with external providers. Smaller employers usually offer services by referral to outside vendors. EAPs also try to prevent problems through offering stress reduction programs and other such programs so that employees do not get to the point where they are unable to perform their jobs well. Stress reduction programs also help alleviate accidents and injuries at work, absences, and illness. Alleviating these problems also helps reduce workers compensation costs.

Family problems including marital difficulties and problems with children are among the most common issues employees have to deal with. EAPs help in counseling and finding resources to deal with such issues as well as those involving single employees who may also experience difficulties in their personal or private lives (e.g., issues with relationships or personal psychological concerns). They also help address financial and legal issues that arise for employees. Other strains on family or personal life include relocation and jobs for spouses or domestic partners of new employees. EAPs often help deal with these issues as well. As employees resolve these problems, they are able to concentrate on their work thus benefiting themselves and the employer. A contemporary issue that evolved for EAPs since 2001 is the psychological impact of terrorist attacks or violence on employees. Services may include counseling for handling potential exposure to trauma including that related to family victims serving in the military or by exposure through the media's reporting. It is something to consider for future concerns of EAP practitioners in the public, private, and third sector (NGOs), especially for military personnel policies (Mankin and Perry 2004; Cadigan 2006).

15.7 Wellness Programs

Wellness programs encourage employees to develop healthier life styles and to prevent illness and disease thus reducing the pressure on healthcare benefits. The Department of Health of the Commonwealth of Massachusetts estimates that 95 percent of the money spent on healthcare is spent on diagnosing and treating diseases although half of the deaths in the country could be prevented (Massachusetts Department of Public Health 2007). Research studies consistently demonstrate that wellness programs reduce healthcare costs and provide excellent return on investment for employers (Goetzel and Ozminkowski 2006). One study found that 25 percent of all healthcare expenditures result from ten health risk factors that can be reduced or alleviated by wellness programs (Anderson et al. 2000). Workers with risk factors such as tobacco use, hypertension, obesity, high blood sugar, and lack of activity among others tend to be less productive, have higher absenteeism, and more disability and thus add immensely to the cost for employers (Aldana 1997; Goetzel et al. 1998; Halpern 2006). Among the many studies that have demonstrated the cost effectiveness is one at Citibank that found that its investment of $1.9 in a wellness program led to $8.9 million savings in healthcare expenditures, more than 4.5 times the cost (Ozminkowski et al. 1999).

In some cases, employers pass on the savings to employees. For example, employees of the Sabre Holdings Corporation in Dallas, Texas, can get a $10 per month discount on their healthcare premiums just by participating in the company's wellness program. They get an additional $10 if their spouse participates. Turner Construction Company offers employees as much as a $30 discount monthly on premiums for participation in the wellness program plus another $30 a month if their spouses participate. Employees earn credits based on getting physicals, improving fitness, and other actions and those credits translate into discounts on healthcare premiums.

Wellness programs include fitness programs, smoking cessation programs, and onsite fitness facilities including locker rooms, showers, and gyms. Many offer nutrition counseling and information programs. For instance, university campuses such as Arizona State University provide their faculty and staff with wellness programs that offer an array of services in regard to healthcare ranging from health screenings on campus, health awareness and education sessions (some offered during lunch hours), flu shots, stress management programs, proper nutrition, exercise, and generic information about health management (Arizona State University 2007). Other wellness programs may simply provide healthy snacks in their vending machines or organize more sophisticated seminars relating to parenting skills, childcare, and eldercare practices (Recruiters World Special Reports 2007). Some provide incentives beyond the healthcare discounts mentioned above. Sarasota, Florida, for example, allows employees to earn up to six leave days per year for meeting specific fitness goals.

15.8 Other Work–Life Benefits

Some benefits provided by employers do not easily fit into the categories outlined above. Nonetheless, employers tout them as benefits of working in their organizations. For example, many employers offer group life insurance coverage thus allowing employees to purchase life insurance at a reduced premium. Many employers provide a fixed amount as a base and the employee can then purchase more. For example, university employees in Arizona receive a life insurance policy equal to their annual salary and then can purchase more at group rates. Other types of insurances such as automobile or home insurance also may be available at group rates through agreements between the employer and the insurance provider.

Breast feeding has become an issue in many communities as it is considered by many to be important to the health of the child. Some employers have developed programs to allow for lactation and breast feeding of infants on employer premises. Thus, they allow breaks and a private space for breast feeding mothers. State laws often protect the right of a mother to breast feed as in Minnesota where employers are required to provide break time and a private space for lactation. Studies have indicated that such policies and programs lead to reduced absenteeism, reduced healthcare claims, and better morale among employees (Armour 2007).

Employers and employees constantly adapt to changes in their circumstances. Any accommodations that employers can make to help employees handle their responsibilities tend to result in better morale among employees. Thus, even things like relaxing rules on use of telephones and e-mail are seen as providing employees opportunities to handle personal business from work and accommodating the demands on their time. Recognitions and rewards also contribute to employee satisfaction with their workplace. Employers constantly strive for programs and activities that will enhance the commitment of their employees, and research suggests that these efforts are well made.

15.9 Implementation

Creating specific programs is one element of work–life benefits. For these benefits to have an effect, the employer needs to plan and organize a way of ensuring that these are delivered. It takes effort to make sure that managers and employees understand the benefits, how to access them, and how they work. Thus, implementation requires a lot of work.

15.9.1 Creating the Culture for Success

Organizational culture consists of those underlying shared assumptions that may include symbols or artifacts, norms, values, attitudes, or belief systems that take root overtime within an organization and are accepted as part of the way things are done or accepted (Schein 1997). It is sometimes subtle and other times clearly communicated. It may constitute some of the unspoken words that are communicated to employees through traditions and become part of the status quo that define the image of organizations (e.g., the way employees are treated, how organizational values are communicated, how employees are promoted, terminated, and disciplined). In essence, organizational culture is the life blood of the organization that gives energy (or power) to policies and creates communication with all employees represented in informal and formal groups.

When dealing with work–life benefits, organizational culture epitomizes those shared underlying values, attitudes, and assumptions about how organizations support or view their employees' ability to balance work and life demands (Working Families 2006). Some of these work–life cultural practices are communicated through but not limited to HRM policies; attitudes of managers and supervisors; nonverbal cues about using parental leave and other work–life benefits; and how they support flexible working schedules and work–life balance initiatives that evolve overtime to constitute the organizations' work–life benefits, conversations, or discourses that prevail overtime through meetings; official memoranda, or the grapevine about how employees' and the organizations' perceptions of employees' efforts to balance work and life demands (Thompson, Beauvais, and Lyness 1999; Kirby and Krone 2002; Todd 2004; Thompson and Prottas 2006; McPherson 2007).

Creating the culture for success in work–life benefits requires the active support of the organizational leadership—directors, senior HRM professionals, managers, and supervisors. It also requires the support of public officials in government to promote a greater awareness through advocacy and public policies. Leaders may play the role of champions and cheerleaders to infuse a culture that embraces and successfully applies work–life benefits as an accepted practice. This sets the tone for the effective implementation of work–life benefits that are available to employees at different levels—societal, governmental, organizational, groups, and at the individual levels. Leaders' roles in actively supporting legislation, policies, and various work–life benefits will determine how effectively work–life culture will enable employees to tap into the resources and benefits that are stated officially in black and white. Their perceptions of a supportive work–life culture according to research are positively correlated to the use of work–life benefits (Thompson et al. 1999). This type of support provides benefits for both employers and employees in terms of productivity increases, high quality of work life and morale, better coping strategies for work, and life demands (McPherson 2007). The challenge for leaders is walking the talk.

Having other organizational backing contributes to the workplace culture that creates success for work–life benefits practices. These may include in addition to but not limited to managerial and supervisory backing, fellow peers/coworkers support, informal, and frequent conversations about the use of work–life benefits that reinforce work–life balance initiatives and their rewards to the all parties. Also, having diverse examples of role models of employees who use these benefits and are successful in their careers and role models of managers who know how to implement such policies and promote or recognize these employees whom they lead will create the environment for successful implementation of a work–life culture. Support from the organization may be factored through focus groups and monthly meetings where employees may get to share their ideas and get some buy into the way benefits are set up and used (Thompson et al. 1999; Kirby and Krone 2002; Thompson and Prottas 2006).

Further, organizations need to be mindful of the barriers that exist in their organizations to the successful implementation of work–life benefits and practices and find strategies to overcome them. Some barriers include highlighting and promoting long-hour-work week and single minded devotion to organizational work and goals, disregarding or shirking personal and life demands outside of the organization, unfriendly and unsupportive work–life culture for those with life/personal demands or conflicts, absence of information, policies, and discourse (formal and informal) about ways of balancing and implementing work–life benefits, lack of diversity in senior managerial leadership, absence of supervisory/line managers' input, poor attitudes to work–life benefits and their usage, lack of creativity in work designs, organizational inaction of policies, and mixed messages communicated through values about using work–life benefits. These barriers are not exhaustive but represent some of what is researched (Kirby and Krone 2002; McPherson 2007; Thompson et al. 1999; Thompson and Prottas 2006). An example may be a faculty member at a university failing to use parental leave because of fear of negative repercussions to their future career for promotion and tenure by the powers that be. All of these issues work in undermining successful implementation of work–life benefits in organizations and to employees.

Effective strategies that promote or improve the implementation of work–life benefit programs entail setting clearly written objectives of these types of policies and communicating them effectively to managers and employees through training and education. Positive reinforcement of model employees using these benefits can go a long way in creating a culture for successful implementation of work–life benefits

(McPherson 2007). Organizations may also establish benchmarks of best practices in implementing work–life benefit programs and model or tailor these programs to suit their work environments. Some may need to reinvent a culture that promotes work–life benefits by reprimanding behaviors, attitudes, and discourses that undermine employees' use of benefits or those who criticize the existence of these programs (Lewis 2001; Sheridan and Conway 2001; McPherson 2007). Further, organizations may promote these benefits for all employees not just for a select few with families and children. Instead, focus communication on the valuable benefits to a diverse workforce of the twenty-first century by encouraging usage, through regular meetings, organizing employee recognition, or award ceremonies to honor model employees. These policies and values need to be integrated into the whole organization supported by managers and supervisors as well as employees. Employees need to be reassured that using flexible work schedules or taking parental leave will not restrict or hinder their career advancement and development. They also need to see role models of employees and managers/supervisors being users of the program as well as good implementers of it. They also need to shift or reorient the way they think about work–life benefits. Misconceptions about fairness, equity, and productivity have to be corrected and reinforced through success stories within and outside the organizations (McPherson 2007).

There is no short cut to creating a work–life culture that is successful. There is also no one best method of doing this. Rather, there are various approaches and strategies that may be considered. Managers and supervisors may need to be equipped with different types of skills that can be learned and applied to situations. There is also a wealth of resources available through training and education that may be used to support a work–life culture throughout organizations. A successful work–life culture for the twenty-first century workforce is one that continues to look for ways to keep abreast of changes occurring inside and outside of the organization that may help employees cope with work and life demands and conflicts. In so doing, it will reap the rewards of employee and employer commitment, increased productivity, total work–life well-being for all and initiative and discretion (Todd 2004; McPherson 2007).

15.9.2 Assessing Needs

Work–life benefits should address real needs of the organization. Therefore, it is important to determine what the needs are. What does the employer want to accomplish? Are the benefits intended to enhance recruitment and retention? Are they intended to reduce costs and improve performance? Is the desire to do the right thing? The employer needs to prioritize its reasons for providing work–life benefits. Once it has prioritized the reasons, it can then design programs in such a way that the priorities are met.

It is also important to understand who the employees are and what they believe is important. Thus, employers will need to assess employee demographics. These demographics will indicate what types of benefits are going to be important. More specifically, employee surveys address the issue directly. Employees will explain what is important to them and what benefits are particularly important. Employee exit interviews and focus groups also help clarify what employees would like. If the employer negotiates with employee unions or associations, those groups also are good sources of information on employee desires. Once the interests of employees are understood, the employer needs to consider them in relationship to the employer goals for a work–life benefit program and to organization mission. It is also important to consider other benefits the employer already provides whether a part of a work–life benefit program or not. Then, appropriate elements can be consolidated with the work–life benefit program.

The employer also needs to consider what it is willing to spend on benefits. Then the cost of various alternative programs needs to be assessed. Costs of alternatives and current programs then can be used to determine what fits with the planned budget for benefits.

The employer also needs a plan for introducing the program. Will it be implemented all at once or will it be phased in benefit by benefit. Sometimes, costs and physical resources preclude adoption of a comprehensive plan all at once. Employees understand the realities of implementing such plans. Gradual introduction of each element can help in a smooth transition to a new work–life plan.

Work–life benefits fit well into cafeteria benefit plans in which employees can pick and choose those benefits they want. Typically, employees are given a number of dollars to spend on benefits and then choose they want up to the amount of money available. Normally, there are some limits such as every employee having to have healthcare coverage or retirement coverage. Beyond the required coverage, employee choose how to spend the remaining benefit dollars.

15.9.3 Communication and Training

Communication is essential to ensure that all employees including supervisors and managers are clear on what the benefit policy is. Often people do not understand what the term "work–life benefits" means; so, it is important to explain exactly what the organization means by it and what is included in the program. Explaining all the elements as part of a comprehensive plan helps everyone to understand the importance of thinking about work–life balance. Communication also means that employers must listen to employees as they have concerns with implementation of programs. Addressing concerns and answering questions demonstrate the commitment of the organization to the program.

Training of supervisors and managers is essential. Often, adoption of work–life benefits reflects a significant shift in the culture of the organization. It is important for training programs to emphasize how the work–life benefit program is integrated into the values and culture of the organization. Especially with older supervisors, the idea of worker-centered policies is likely to be challenging. Training must address the need to respect the change in policy and accept the employee's right to access the programs. Similarly, managers must learn that accessing the benefits cannot be used in making decisions about promotions and development of employees. Especially difficult to change is the fact that performance and not time spent in performing is to be rewarded. Thus, the focus needs to be placed on outputs and results, not the rules of the organization. It is important to get supervisors and managers to help employees understand that access of available programs will not be used against them. Clearly, supervisors and managers need to recognize the reality that work and personal lives of employees are integrally intertwined and that work needs to accommodate the challenges employees face.

Supervisors and managers also must learn that work–life benefit success is built into the rewards system of the organization. Thus, supervisor and manager evaluation should include how well they integrate the work–life program into their management of employees and organizations. By building the success of the benefits into their rewards systems, employer organizations ensure that they will take implementation of the programs seriously.

15.9.4   Work Design

Many elements of the work–life benefit programs require consideration of work redesign. Flexible working hour arrangements, for example, have many implications for work. Thus, employers need to review their job classification systems and job structures to see if they present barriers to alternative work schedules, job sharing, or other creative ways of getting the work done. Employers, in consultation with employees, can develop approaches that lead to effective integration of work–life alternatives with the needs of the organization to get the work done.

15.9.5   Costs/Benefits

In assessing the costs and benefits of work–life benefits, research generally has indicated that additional costs of such benefits are minimal for employers (Gault and Lovell 2006). There are often direct costs for development and launching of programs. Some programs such as telework or day care facilities require initial equipment and facility costs. Any change also involves some disruption in the flow of work and thus must be considered as well.

The literature also reports that benefits can be substantial in financial and other terms (Gault and Lovell 2006; Hand and Zawacki 1994; Yasbeck 2004). Financial savings are realized in reduced recruitment and training costs because work–life benefit programs result in better retention of employees because of reduced stress and improved employee satisfaction (Demby 2004). When they do recruit, employers with work–life benefit programs are more competitive thus are more successful in attracting the employees they want. Work–life benefits also lead to less absenteeism and sick leave usage thus saving the employer money. Employers experience a reduction in accidents often associated with fatigue and stress. Productivity tends to increase with work–life programs (Baughman, DiNardi, and Hol-Eakin 2003). Employers may be able to increase hours of operation because of flexible schedules and are likely to improve their image with employees and the public.

15.10 Balancing Work and Life—A Reality Check

Ultimately, employers and organizations within the public, private, and nongovernmental sectors will need to prepare themselves for a twenty-first century workforce, which is continually diverse within an extremely complex environment. Such mindsets will enable leaders to be flexible and responsive to these pressures, changes, and needs of a diverse workforce.

Another reality check is to create a new perspective or vision of management. Conventional management informs that it is about getting the job done through others. However, contemporary management should be about helping employees meet their needs as they work to accomplish organizational goals and objectives. It demands a shift in thinking about time expectations for work, work designs, boundary management, life and personal interests, and their impact on work life. This new type of management will enable managers and HRM professionals to lead in the public interest—meeting their employees' work–life balance concerns through work–life benefit programs that are implemented effectively and clearly.

Gone are the days of the stereotypical employees of the workforce where women stayed home with children and men served as the breadwinners for the families. It is a new work–life culture with a very diverse workforce with complex needs and life demands. Contemporary work–life benefits must embrace the changes of this century (e.g., global trends, use of information and communication technology, family arrangements, and increasing longevity) and create a new quality of work life that enables employees to balance work and their personal/private lives effectively and maintain successful career paths. In so doing, organizations and their leaders will be more flexible to an array of work–life benefit programs. They will encourage their employees to use them and reduce stress and increase work life well-being. If public, private, and nongovernmental organizations in the United States resist these changes or are slow in making the necessary adjustments, they will undermine their workforce's greatest asset which is human capital, undermine productivity, increase costs, and possibly lose some of their best and most talented employees. However, there is no quick fix. This type of transformation takes time and requires the support of government officials, public policies, HRM professionals, and managers at all levels to lead by example and champion work–life benefits practices that can be successfully implemented. It may be possible to also tailor what other countries are doing based on benchmark studies for best practices.

References

Aldana, S.G. 2001. Financial impact of health promotion programs: A comprehensive review of the literature. *American Journal of Health Promotion*. 15: 296–320.

Anderson, D.R., R.W. Whitmer, R.Z. Goetzel, R.J. Ozminkowski, J. Wasserman, and S. Sexner. 2000. The relationship between modifiable health risks and group-level health care expenditures. *American Journal of Health Promotion*. 15: 45–52.

Arizona State University. 2007. Employee wellness and work/life balance. http://www.asu.edu/hr/employee_wellness/index.html.

Armour, S. 2007. More nursing moms get lactation programs at work. Available at http://usatoday.com/money/workplace2007-05-14-nursing-usat_N.htm.

Bailyn, L. 2006. *Breaking the Mold: Redesigning Work for Productive and Satisfying Lives*, 2nd ed. Ithaca, New York: Cornell University Press.

Baughman, R., D. DiNardi, and D. Hol-Eakin. 2003. Productivity and wage effects of 'family-friendly' fringe benefits. *International Journal of Manpower*. 24: 247–259.

Bond, J.T., E. Galinsky, S.S. Kim, and E. Brownfield. 2005. *National Study of Employers*. New York: Families and Work Institute.

Boots, S.W. 2004. The way we work: How children and families fare in a 21st century workplace. The New America Foundation. http://www.newamerica.net/Download_Docs/pdfs/Doc_File2146_1.pdf.

Brady, R.L. 2007. 'Extreme programming'—A new twist on job sharing. http://hr.blr.com/news.aspx?id=75504.

Business and Legal Reports Inc. 2007. EEOC examines legal issues surrounding work/life balance. http://hr.blr.com/news.aspx?id=75740.

Business and Legal Reports Inc. 2007. Fatigue in the workplace costs $136B in lost productivity. http://hr.blr.com/news.aspx?id=75301.

Cadigan, J. 2006. The impact of family-friendly compensation: An investigation of military personnel policy. *Review of Public Personnel Administration*. 26: 2–20.

Carell, M.R. 2007. Workforce diversity: 20-year perspective, programs and practices. *IPMA-HR News*. April: 1, 3, 5.

Coe, T.S. 2002. Cost benefit analyses of employee dependent care assistance plans. *Financial Services Review*. 11: 277–287.

Crompton, R. and C. Lyonette. 2006. Work–life 'balance' in Europe. *Acta Sociologica*. 49: 379–393.

Davis, A.E. and A.L. Kalleberg. 2006. Family-friendly organizations? Work and family programs in the 1990s. *Work and Occupations*. 33: 191–223.

Demby, E.R. 2004. Do your family-friendly programs make cents? *HR Magazine*. 49 (January): 74–78.

Dick, P. and R. Hyde. 2006. Line manager involvement in work–life balance and career development: Can't manage, won't manage? *British Journal of Guidance and Counseling*. 34: 345–364.

European Foundation for the Improvement of Living and Working Condtions. 2003. Working-time preferences and work–life-balance in the European Union: Some policy considerations for enhancing the quality of life. http://www.eurofound.europa.eu/publications/htmlfiles/ef0342.htm (download in EN).

Families and Work Institute. 2005. *Generation and Gender in the Workplace*. Newton, Massachusetts: American Business Collaboration.

Friedman, S.D., and J.H. Greenhaus. 2000. *Work and Family-Allies or Enemies?* New York: Oxford University Press.

Galinsky, E., J.T. Bond, S.S. Kim, L. Backon, E. Brownfield, and K. Sakai. 2005. *Overwork in America: When the Way We Work Becomes Too Much.* New York: Families and Work Institute.

Galinsky, E., J.T. Bond, and E.J. Hill. 2004. *Workplace Flexibility: What Is It? Who Has It? Who Wants It? Does It Make a Difference?* New York: Families and Work Institute.

Gault, B. and V. Lovell. 2006. The costs and benefits of policies to advance work/life integration. *American Behavioral Scientist.* 49: 1152–1164.

Goetzel, R.Z., D.R. Anderson, R.W. Whitmer, R.J. Osminkowski, R.I. Dunn, and J. Wasserman. 1998. The relationship between modifiable health risks and health care expenditures. *Journal of Occupational and Environmental Medicine.* 40: 843–854.

Goetzel, R.Z. and R.J. Ozminkowski. 2006. What's holding you back: Why should (or shouldn't) employers invest in health promotion programs for their workers? *North Carolina Medical Journal.* 67: 428–430.

Graves, L.M., P.J. Ohlott, and M.N. Ruderman. 2007. Commitment to family roles: Effects on managers' attitudes and performance. *Journal of Applied Psychology.* 92: 44–56.

Greenhaus, J.H. and G.N. Powell. 2006. When work and family are allies: A theory of work–family enrichment. *Academy of Management.* 31: 72–92.

Hand, S. and R.A. Zawacki. 1994. Family-friendly benefits: More than a frill. *HR Magazine.* 49 (October): 79–84.

Halpern, D.F. 2006. How organizations can alleviate the traffic jam at the intersection of work and family. *American Behavioral Scientist.* 49: 1147–1151.

Heyman, J., A. Earle, and J. Hayes. 2007. *The Work, Family, and Equity Index: How Does the United States Measure Up?* Montreal, Quebec, Canada: McGill University Institute for Health and Social Policy.

Hill, J.E., B.C. Miller, S.P. Weiner, and J. Colihan. 1998. Influences of the virtual office on aspects of work and work/life balance. *Personnel Psychology.* 51: 667–683.

Hoyman, M. and H. Duer. 2004. A typology of workplace policies. *Review of Public Personnel Administration.* 24: 113–132.

Hudson, R.B. 2005. *The New Politics of Age Policy.* Baltimore: Johns Hopkins University Press.

Human Rights Campaign Fund. 2006. The state of the workplace for gay, lesbian, bisexual and transgender Americans. Human Rights Campaign Fund. http://www.hrc.org/Template.cfm?Section=Get_Informed2&CONTENTID=32936&TEMPLATE=/ContentManagement/ContentDisplay.cfm.

Human Rights Campaign Fund. 2007. Employers that offer domestic partner health benefits. Human Rights Campaign Fund. http://www.hrc.org/Template.cfm?Section=Search-the-Database&Template=/CustomSource/WorkNet/srch.cfm&searchtypeid=3&searchSubTypeID=1.

International Public Management Association for Human Resources HR Center. 2007. *Personnel practices: Telecommuting policies.* Alexandria, Virginia: International Public Management Association for Human Resources.

Kirby, E. and K. Krone. 2003. "The policy exists but you can't really use it": Communication and the structuration of work-family policies. *Journal of Applied Communication Research.* 30: 50–77.

Kossek, E.E., B.A. Lautsch, and S.C. Eaton. 2006. Telecommuting, control, and boundary management: Correlates of policy use and practice, job control, and work–family effectiveness. *Journal of Vocational Behavior.* 68: 347–367.

Lambert, S.J. 2000. Added benefits: The link between work–life benefits and organizational citizenship behavior. *Academy of Management Journal.* 43: 801–815.

Lewis, S. 2001. Restructuring workplace cultures: The ultimate work–family challenge. *Women in Management Review.* 16: 21–29.

Lingle, K. 2005. *Workers, Workplace and Work: Connecting the Dots at the Speed of Change,* Keynote address. http://www.awlp.org/library/html/Lingle-A.pdf.

Mankin, L.D. and R.W. Perry. 2004. Terrorism challenges for human resource management. *Review of Public Personnel Administration.* 24: 3–17.

Massachusetts Department of Public Health. 2007. Wellness at work program. Massachusetts Department of Public Health. http://www.mass.gov/dph/fch/wellness/index.htm.

McPherson, M. 2007. Work–life balance, employee engagement and discretionary effort: A review of the evidence. www.eeotrust.org.nz/content/docs/reports/Employee%20Engagement%202007%20Report.doc.

Ozminkowsi, R.J., R.L. Dunn, R.Z. Goetzel, R. Cantor, J. Murnane, and M.A. Harrison. 1999. A return on investment of the Citibank, NA health management program. *American Journal of Health Promotion.* 14: 31–43.

Pitt-Catsouphes, M., E. Swansberg, J.T. Bond, and E. Galinsky. 2004. Work–life policies and programs: Comparing the responsiveness of nonprofits and for-profit organizations. *Nonprofit and Leadership.* 14: 291–312.

Pitts, D.W. 2006. Modeling the impact of diversity management. *Review of Public Personnel Administration.* 26: 245–268.

Recruiters World Special Reports. 2007. Work–life benefits: Don't recruit without them! http://www.recruitersworld.com/articles/rw/special/worklife.asp.

Reynolds, J. 2005. In the face of conflict: Work–life conflict and desired work hour adjustment. *Journal of Marriage and Family.* 67: 1313–1331.

Saltzstein, A.L., Y. Ting, and G.H. Saltzstein. 2001. *Public Administration Review.* 61: 452–467.

Schein, E. 1997. *Organizational Culture and Leadership,* 3rd ed. San Francisco: Jossey-Bass.

Sheridan, A. and L. Conway. 2001. Workplace flexibility: Reconciling the needs of employers and employees. *Women in Management Review.* 16: 5–11.

Smithson, J. and E.H. Stokoe. 2005. Discourses of work–life balance: Negotiating 'gender-blind' terms in organizations. *Gender, Work and Organization.* 12: 147–168.

Stockwell, M. 2006. Flexible work for strong families. Progressive Policy Institute. http://www.ppionline.org/documents/Family_Agenda_111506.pdf.

Telework Coalition. 2005. *Telework facts.* www.telcoa.org/id33_m.htm.

Thompson, C., L. Beauvais, and K. Lyness. 1999. When work–family benefits are not enough: The influence of work–family culture on benefit utilization, organizational attachment and work–family conflict. *Journal of Vocational Behavior.* 54: 392–415.

Thompson, C.A. and D.A. Prottas. 2006. Relationships among organizational family support, job autonomy, perceived control and employee well-being. *Journal of Occupational Health Psychology.* 11: 100–118.

Todd, S. 2004. Improving work–life balance—What other countries are doing? Labor Program, Human Resources and Skill Development, Canada. www.hrsdc.gc.ca/en/lp/spila/wlb/pdf/improving-work–life-balance.pdf.

U.S. Bureau of Labor Statistics. 2002. Labor force participation rates among mothers. In *Working in the 21st Century*. http://www.bls.gov/opub/working/page16b.htm.

U.S. Government Accountability Office. 2007. An assessment of dependent care needs of federal workers using the office of personnel management's survey. http://www.gao.gov/docsearch/abstract.php?rptno=GAO-07–43R.

Van Der Lippe, T., A. Jager, and Y. Kops. 2006. The paid work–family balance of men and women in European countries. *Acta Sociologica*. 49: 303–319.

Wadsworth, L.L. and B.P. Owens. 2007. The effects of social support on work–family enhancement and work–family conflict in the public sector. *Public Administration Review*. 67: 75–86.

Wood, G.J. and J. Newton. 2006. Childlessness and women managers: 'Choice,' context and discourses. *Gender, Work and Organization*. 13: 338–358.

Working Families. 2006. Moving mountains: The culture change challenge. http://www.workingfamilies.org.uk/asp/employer_zone/e_conf_moving_mountains.asp.

World at Work. 2007. *Telework trendlines for 2006*. Scottsdale, Arizona: WorldatWork.

W.P. Carey. School of Business, Arizona State University. 2007. Flexibility's price tag: Gain time, lose career footing. http://www.knowledge.wpcarey.asu.edu/index.cfm?fa=viewfeatures&id=1371.

Yasbeck, P. 2004. The business case for firm-level work-life balance policies: A review of the literature. http://dol.govt.nz/PDFs/FirmLevel/WLB.pdf.

Yates, C.A. and B.B. Leach. 2006. Why 'good' jobs lead to social exclusion. *Economic and Industrial Democracy*. 27: 341–368.

Chapter 16

Higher Education Benefits: How They Help Employees and Organizations

Joan E. Pynes

CONTENTS

At a time in which higher education has never been more important to the economy, nor the economic returns to its citizens any greater, the current generation of low-income young Americans face diminished educational and economic opportunity as a result of lack of access to a college education.

Advisory Committee on Student Financial Assistance 2001

Public organizations are undergoing a transformation. Over 46 percent of local government employees are 45 years or older, although 30 percent of state government employees nationwide are eligible for retirement in 2006, and by 2008 more than 50 percent of federal employees will be eligible for retirement (Ibarra 2006). The International City and County Managers Association (ICMA) notes that the majority of city managers are approaching retirement and there is a smaller group of professionals ready to replace them (Blumenthal 2007). The impending retirements of public employees combined with today's challenges require that public agencies support increasing the education of their employees.

At a time when the public workforce requires greater skills, fewer low-income students are attending college and those enrolled have acquired a greater amount of federal student loan debt. At the same time the changing demographics of American society have called attention to the inequities in postsecondary education. Black and Hispanic students earn bachelor's degrees at a substantially lower rate than white students. Future college-age cohorts will look different than previous generations of college-age students. It is estimated that 80 percent will be nonwhite and almost 50 percent will be Hispanic (Advisory Committee on Student Financial Assistance 2001, p. 4). Today's knowledge-based economy makes college more important. Nearly 60 percent of jobs today require at least some college. The new economy is making a baccalaureate degree the equivalent of a high school diploma in the old economy. It is estimated that shortages of workers with postsecondary-level skills could grow to 14 million by 2020. In order for the states and the nation as a whole to maintain a competitive economic edge, the workforce must have education and training beyond high school. Six out of ten jobs now require at least some postsecondary education and training (Carnevale and Desrochers 2003). The report *Hitting Home: Quality, Cost, and Access Challenges Confronting Higher Education Today* (2007) notes that to remain globally competitive by 2025, 55 percent of U.S. adults will need to have degrees, compared to 40 percent today. To close the gap, 10 million more minorities must earn college degrees by then.

This chapter will address the importance of higher education, why low-income students are getting left behind, and the organizational improvement accrued to an organization that offers higher education tuition reimbursement benefits to its employees, and how public agencies can support their employees in pursing higher education opportunities.

16.1 Importance of Education

Education has been considered a public good, the public obligation was to provide an elementary–secondary system irrespective of class, race, or status. American public schools were important vehicles for social mobility and social change, immigrants were integrated and assimilated into society through public school systems. It was believed that a liberal education provided the knowledge that free people need to guide them in decision making. The purpose of a liberal education is not a technically trained professional but an educated human being (Lustig 2006). Liberal arts constitute the knowledge free people need to guide them in their decision making at home, at work, as neighbors, and as citizens. The sociologist Mills (1956, p. 317) stated that "the end product of … liberal education is simply the self-educating, self-cultivating man or woman to these essential goals of intellectual clarity, self-discovery, and self-motivation, a democratic society must add the capability of self-government and democratic participation."

A variety of public policies advanced the notion of a public good in higher education. Some of the most familiar policies include: the Morrill Land Grant Act 1862 provided public land for colleges that would specialize in agricultural and mechanical arts; the Servicemen's Readjustment Act of 1944 (GI Bill) provided financial assistance to veterans in education and training programs; The Economic Opportunity Act of 1946 (Pell Grant) provided federal work study grants to students from low-income families; the Montgomery GI Bill of 1985 provided education benefits to veterans entering active duty after 1985 and was extended in 1991; the Taxpayer Relief Act of 1997 created the Hope Scholarship for college students; and Title VII of the Higher Reconciliation Act of 2005, which amended the Higher Education Act of 1965, provided funding for the National Science and Mathematics Access to Retain Talent Grant (National Smart Grant) for full-time college students in their third and fourth years of study who are eligible for the Federal Pell Grant Program and who are majoring in physical, life, or computer sciences, mathematics, technology, or engineering or in a foreign language determined critical to national security are examples of policy decisions that support postsecondary education.

The report *Reaping the Benefits: Defining the Public and Private Value of Going to College* (Institute for Higher Education Policy 1998) discusses the movement away from an emphasis on the public, democratic, and equalizing benefits of education to the private economic benefits for individuals. The authors of the report note that a focus on the private economic benefits of education does not provide a balanced view of the benefits resulting from college experience. What often gets neglected are the social, civic, and democratic benefits of education.

Reaping the Benefits identifies four general categories of benefits: public economic benefits; private economic benefits; public social benefits; and private social benefits (Institute for Higher Education Policy 1998, pp. 13–20).

Public Economic Benefits: defined as benefits for which there can be broad economic, fiscal, or labor market effects. Benefits that result in the overall improvement of the national economy as a result of citizens' participation in higher education are public economic benefits. They include: *increased tax revenues* due to higher earnings; *greater productivity* that is attributed to the overall increased education level of the workforce; *increased consumption* resulting from educational attainment; higher consumer spending in a range of categories such as housing, food, and transportation; *increased workforce flexibility* by educating individuals in skills such as critical thinking, writing, interpersonal communication that can be generalized across a variety of job positions; and *decreased reliance on government financial support* given that individuals who attended college participate in government assistance programs such as TANF, Food Stamps, Medicaid, and housing assistance at lower rates than high school graduates or those who have not graduated from high school.

Private Economic Benefits: defined as benefits that have economic, fiscal, or labor market effects on the individuals who have attended postsecondary education. They include *higher salaries and benefits*. Lifetime and average annual earnings are greater for those with college degrees. Individuals with college degrees also receive greater fringe benefits such as vacation time, healthcare, and sick time. *Employment*, individuals who have gone to college are employed at higher rates and with greater consistency. *Higher savings levels*, those with bachelor's degrees have higher value earning assets, home equity, and their financial assets. College educated *individuals* also contribute at higher rates to retirement plans and other saving devices. Improved *working conditions*, college educated persons tend to work in white-collar positions and with greater technology and conveniences. *Personal/professional mobility*, the ability to change jobs or move to another location is correlated with level of education. Persons with a college education tend to have skills that can be more easily applied to different positions and in different job settings.

Public Social Benefits: defined as benefits that accrue to groups of people, or to society broadly, that are not directly related to economic, fiscal, or labor market effects. *Reduced crime rates*, the lower the level of education, the higher the incarceration rates. The greater the level of education one possesses tends to be related to *increased charitable giving and community service*. Educated individuals also tend to have an increased quality of civic life. Higher educated individuals tend to vote and participate in election activities more than those with less education. Individuals with a college education tend to have a greater *social cohesion* and *appreciation of diversity*. They tend to put more trust in social institutions and participate in civic and community groups at higher rates; they also tend to have a greater appreciation of diversity. Higher education levels have been associated with an *improved ability to adapt and use technology*.

Private Social Benefits: defined as benefits that accrue to individuals or groups that are not directly related to economic, fiscal, or labor market effects. College educated individuals tend to have *higher life expectancies and improved health*. The children of college educated parents are likely to graduate from high school and go to college, and are likely to have higher cognitive development resulting in an *improved quality of life for children.* Individuals with higher education levels are able to make more *informed consumer decisions* in selecting goods and services to purchase. A college education results in increased personal status, this is especially true for first generation college graduates. College educated individuals have more *hobbies and leisure activities.* They tend to visit museums and cultural venues more frequently, read more literature, and participate in recreation activities at a rate that is higher than less educated individuals.

16.2   Student Financial Assistance

The major public purpose for financial assistance has been enabling eligible but needy students to enroll in college. Most of this aid comes from federal and state governments and from colleges and universities. Student financial assistance from all of these sources has increased to $45 billion, an increase of 140 percent since 1991 (The National Center for Public Policy and Higher Education 2006, p. 21). But these increases have not been large enough to keep pace with the increased costs of college attendance—especially tuition.

Low-income students needing financial assistance are offered assistance through the Basic Educational Opportunity Grant (otherwise known as Pell grants) and students eligible for Pell grants are eligible for Smart Grants, Guarantee Student Loans (known as Stafford loans and Federal Perkins loans). There are also provisions in the federal income tax code that provide education tax credits and deductions if students go to school to maintain or improve their job skills.

The nation's largest source of financial aide for low-income students is the federal Pell Grant program. The federal Pell Grant program was established to ensure that students needing financial assistance could attend two-year and four-year colleges. The money students receive from Pell grants does not have to be paid back. In 1975, the maximum Pell Grant covered approximately 84 percent of the cost of attending college; in 1990–1991 the average Pell Grant covered 76 percent of tuition at four-year colleges and universities; five years ago the grants covered 42 percent of tuition and today only 36 percent of tuition (Purchasing Power 2005). The highest grant for a student who has no parental support can reach $4050. Only 22 percent of Pell Grant recipients get the maximum award. The average award in 2003 was $2421 which covered only a quarter of the costs of a four-year public college (College Board, *Trends in Student Aid* 2003).

At the same time there is less financial aid for students, the costs associated with going to college have increased. The College Board (2003) reports average tuition and fees at public universities are up 35 percent from five years ago. Over the years, median family income increased by 137 percent, college tuition and fees by 375 percent. About two-thirds of college students are borrowing; three decades ago, it was just a third, graduating seniors faced an average of $9250 in loans a decade ago, now its more than twice that $19,200 (a 58 percent after inflation). Over the past

20 years, college costs increased more rapidly than inflation, the cost of prescription drugs and health insurance, and family income (Haycock 2006, p. 3). As college costs have increased there have not been proportionate increases in need-based scholarship aid.

Although government aid has declined, loans from banks and other private lenders have soared, climbing to 20 percent of all education borrowing last year, up from 12 percent five years earlier (*New York Times* 2006). Because federal financial aid is less available, many students are going to private lenders for loans and three out of four full-time students have jobs.

Low-income students graduating from high school are academically prepared to enter college but confront significant financial barriers that limit their access to college and their ability to stay in college. As suggested by the chapter's epigraph, educational opportunities for low-income young Americans are diminishing despite the growing importance of higher education to the economy and the economic return to its citizens. According to *Access Denied (2001)*, low-income high school graduates are forced by high levels of unmet needs to abandon plans of full time, on-campus attendance at four-year colleges. Those that do attend often live at home and work long hours to make access possible (5). Sixty-five percent work although enrolled, on average 24 hours a week. Only 67 percent of freshmen complete a bachelor's degree within six years. One out of five borrowers drops out of college with debt and no diploma. Students who attend college on a part-time basis reduce their chances of earning a bachelor's degree by 35 percent (Adelman 2006). The average undergraduate student graduates with nearly $20,000 in debt, and low-income students and students of color take on even higher debt (College Board, *Trends in Student Aid* 2003).

During the 2003–2004 academic year, 78 percent of undergraduates worked although they were enrolled in college. On average, employed students work almost 30 hours per week. Part-time, older students, low-income students and students from under-represented minority groups are spending more time at work than others (King 2006).

Two-thirds of the working students state their primary reason for working is to pay tuition, fees, and living expenses, with upper-income students more likely to work to earn spending money to gain job experience. Younger dependent students work less than older independent students. White and Asian American students are more likely to be traditional college age and come from middle- and upper-income families than are students from under-represented groups. As a result, they tend to work less than African American, Hispanic, and American Indian students (King 2006, p. 3).

Both black and Hispanic students earn bachelor's degrees at a substantially lower rate than white students. The future cohort of college students will look different than previous generations of college students because it will be more diverse. Eighty percent of this cohort will be nonwhite and almost 50 percent will be Hispanic. If under participation and lack of degree completion continues, this will have major implications for the lifetime income of low-income students (Advisory Committee on Student Financial Assistance 2001, p. 4).

16.3   Why College Is Important?

Workers with a bachelor's degree earn 75 percent more than workers with only a high school diploma (Advisory Committee on Student Financial Assistance, *Empty Promises* 2002, p. 2). Real wage and job growth is strongest in the higher skilled service sector, although the real wages of low-skilled workers have declined. The Bureau of Labor Statistics indicates that high-skill jobs that require advanced learning will make up almost half of all job growth in the United States. Jobs requiring an associate's degree or beyond will increase at faster rates than jobs requiring less than an associate's degree between now and 2014 (Reindl 2007, p. 1).

The report *Measuring UP* (2006) compared the proportion of degree-holding adults in the United States and other countries and found that among older Americans (ages 35–64), 39 percent hold degrees, the next highest after Canada, but younger adults (ages 25–34) fall behind those in six countries. The United States falls 16th of the 27 countries surveyed in college completion rates.

The National Leadership Council for Liberal Education (2007) notes the economic, global, cross-cultural, environmental, and civic changes presently taking place in the world. "Scientific and technological innovations, global interdependence, cross-cultural encounters, and changes in the balance of economic and political power all have an impact on higher education. The context in which today's students will make choices is one of disruption rather than certainty, and of interdependence rather than insularity" (pp. 1–2).

The report calls for a liberal education to build a greater understanding of the wider world, the need to develop one's analytical and communication skills, and to foster responsibilities beyond one's self. The report challenges the conventional view that liberal education is by definition "nonvocational" (p. 4). The LEAP National Leadership Council notes that narrow learning is not enough; organizations need graduates who are broadly prepared and who possess the analytical and practical skills essential for innovation and effectiveness. The ability to apply learning to complex and unscripted problems is needed in every life including the workplace, in all fields of study including professional and occupational fields (p. 14). Employers reported that they do not want "toothpick" graduates who have learned only technical skills and who arrive in the workplace deep but narrow. These workers are sidelined early on, because they cannot break out of their mental cubicles (pp. 15–16). Employers want students with broad skills that can help them adapt to the changing job market. This holds for even technical professions such as engineering. In an article discussing the education of engineers, King (2006) notes that many societal trends call for engineers to broaden their outlooks, have more flexible career options, and work closely and effectively with persons of quite different backgrounds. Yet, the general education and general orientation of engineers have been directed inward toward the profession, rather than outward to the rest of the society and the world. He recommends moving accredited professional engineering degrees to the master's level and building upon a liberal education that is analogous to premedical education.

16.4 Why Education and Not Training?

As noted above, often the knowledge and skills employees possess become too specialized. To adapt to a constantly changing environment, organizations need employees with analytical and problem-solving skills, ethical reasoning, intercultural knowledge, civic and global knowledge, and the ability to synthesize information across general and specialized studies. Training has been defined as "the acquisition of knowledge and skills for present tasks, which help individuals contribute to the organization in their current positions.... To be successful, training must result in a change in behavior, such as the use of new knowledge and skills on the job" (Fitzgerald 1992, p. 81). Training can be targeted to help employees learn new job-specific skills, improve their performance, or change their attitudes. Organizations should encourage, financially support, and promote training, realizing at the same time the narrow focus of training when compared to the broader goals of education.

An education prepares employees for the future. Encouraging employees to pursue or complete a college education can be combined with career development plans. Higher education and career development planning should be used to improve the skill levels and provide long-term opportunities for the organization's present workforce. The combination provides incumbents with advancement opportunities within the organization so that they will not have to look elsewhere. Spending resources to develop employees signals to them that they are valued by the agency. As a result, they become motivated and assume responsibility for developing their career paths (Fitz-enz 1996). Whereas, training is typically associated with improving the performance, knowledge, or skill of employees in their present positions; career development is viewed as a continuous process consisting of evaluating abilities and interests, establishing career goals, and planning developmental activities that relate to the employees and organization's future needs. The companies identified on the 100 Best Companies to Work For list inculcates developing employees into their corporate cultures. The turnover rates for the 100 Best Companies to Work For are lower than other companies (Drizin 2005).

16.4.1 Current Practices in Educational Assistance

The Promise & Practice of Employer Educational Assistance Program: 2004 State of the Field: Strategies & Trends [Council for Adult and Experiential Learning (CAEL) 2004] surveyed 1304 human resources management professionals across the United States about the educational assistance benefits available at their organizations. Results were obtained from 1304 organizations. Nearly 86 percent of organizations agree that education/tuition benefits are important as a strategic investment. The respondents cited increases in employee retention and productivity as the two most important reasons for offering education/tuition benefits. Tables 16.1 through 16.8 show the variety and scope of tuition and education benefits offered by the organizations surveyed.

Table 16.1   Types of Educational Benefits Being Provided

Benefit Option	Percent Provided
Reimbursement after course completion	82
Educational leave of absence	11
Educational loan assistance	9

Table 16.2   What Kinds of Individual Courses are Covered by Your Company's Educational/Tuition Benefits Program?

Course Type	Percent Covered
Academic courses related to employees' current positions with the company	83
Academic courses related to employees' future positions in company	71
Academic courses related to the company's business (regardless of employee position in the company)	62
Academic courses required by a degree or certificate program	45
Any academic course, even if not required for a degree for certificate program	24
Nonacademic courses or workshops, e.g., ESL, toastmasters, Cisco certification	22

Table 16.3   Education Related Expenses Covered

Types of Expenses	Percent of Companies Covering
Tuition	92.8
Registration fees	46.7
Textbooks	43.6
Lab fees	33.6
Enrollment/admission fees	31
Test preparation courses; fees to test out of courses	12–13
Fees for education and career advising	10.4
Other fees	<10

Table 16.4   Eligibility Criteria

Employee Type	Percent of Funding Eligible
Full-time salaried	93
Full-time nonunion hourly	63
Full-time	31
Part-time salaried	24
Part-time nonunion hourly	21
Part-time union	10
Former employees	2

Table 16.5   Service Requirements

Length of Service Requirement	Percent of Employers Reporting (N = 803)
3 months or less	3.5
4–6 months	29.3
7 months to 1 year	29.6
>1 year	34.3
Other	3.3

Table 16.6   Reimbursement

Dollar Limit	Percent of Employers Reporting (N = 724)
$1–2500	38
$2501–$4000	15
$4001–$5250	11
>$5250	5
Varies by eligible employee group	10
Varies by some other factor	21
Other kinds of set limits	11

Table 16.7 Typical Minimum Student Performance for a Course to Be Eligible for Coverage

Performance Requirement	Percent of Employers
Completion of the course	9
Passing grade in course	26
Minimum grade equivalent to "C"	38
Minimum grade equivalent to "B"	17
Requirements vary	6
No requirements	5

16.5 What are Some County Governments Offering in Regard to Education and Tuition Reimbursement?

Education and tuition reimbursement benefits are often associated with private for-profit sector organizations. Public sector organizations are not usually noted as 100 Best Companies to Work For. However, that is misguided because many public sector organizations have implemented progressive human resources management planning and the development of human capital into their workforce development

Table 16.8 Reasons Your Company Offers Education/Tuition Benefit Programs

Reason for Providing Educational Benefit	Percent of Employers
Employee retention aid	70
Improve productivity	69
Increase qualifications to do new work	61
Develop promotable employees	57
Recruitment competitive edge	48
Improve employee morale	50
To be an employer of choice	38
Tradition and culture of the company	42
Enhance company's PR image	28
Other	3

and succession plans. Many public sector organizations encourage their employees to pursue a postsecondary degree. A review of 16 general purpose county governments was made to see the variety of tuition and education benefits offered. The population of the counties ranged from a high of 3,635,528 to a low of 57, 525. The type of support varies across the counties but it is important to note the support of educational benefits. Educational benefits are not just offered by private sector employers. Table 16.9 presents the findings.

16.6 Education Benefits and Human Resources Management

Given the changing demographics and the propensity for many working adults to have not finished college, employers, if they have not already done so, should integrate education benefits and career development activities into their human resources management plans. Human resources planning is the implementation of human resource activities, policies, and practices to make the necessary changes to support or improve the organization's operational and strategic objectives. To be competitive, organizations must be able to anticipate, influence, and manage the forces that impact their ability to remain effective. In the service sector, this means they must be able to manage their human resource capabilities. All too often agencies have relied on short-term needs to direct their human resource management practices. Little thought is often given to long-term implications. By encouraging their employees to obtain a college degree or finish a college degree they may have started, organizations are laying a foundation for their future needs.

Section 127 of the Internal Revenue Code is a tuition assistance program that makes it possible for employers to provide up to $5250 per year to their employees in tax-free reimbursement for tuition, books, fees, supplies, and equipment for job- or non-job-related education as part of a "Qualified Assistance Program." Section 127 allows employees to improve their skills to advance in their current position or to train for other work in the community. As part of the Economic Growth and Tax Reconciliation Act of 2001, which became law on June 7, 2001, section 127 of the Internal Revenue Code was extended permanently for both graduate and undergraduate courses, beginning January 1, 2002.

16.7 What if the Organization Cannot Afford Tuition/Education Benefits?

Although some smaller or under capitalized organizations may not be able to afford to offer tuition and education benefits to its employees, most employers are able to assist their employees in other ways. Employers have the discretion to establish flexible work schedules to accommodate an employee's class schedule. For example, if an

Table 16.9 Select Counties Offering Tuition Assistance

		Maricopa County, AZ	Fairfax County, VA	Hillsborough County, FL	DuPage County, IL	Montgomery County, MD
Benefit option	Reimbursement postcompletion		Y			Y (for new employees)
	Advance payment tuition assistance					Y
	Educational leave of absences					
	Educational loan assistance					
Course type	Courses related to current position	Y	Y	Y	Y	Y
	Course related to future positions			Y		Y
	Course related to business	Y	Y	Y	Y	Y
	Course required by degree					Y
	Any courses		Y			Y
	Nonacademic courses					Y
Expenses	Tuition		Y	Y		Y
	Registration fee		N	N		Y

(continued)

Table 16.9 (continued) Select Counties Offering Tuition Assistance

		Maricopa County, AZ	Fairfax County, VA	Hillsborough County, FL	DuPage County, IL	Montgomery County, MD
Benefits available	Text books		N	N		N
	Other fees		N	N		Y
	Full-time salaried		Y		Y	Y
	Part-time					Y
	After 3 months or less				N	Y
	4-6 months				Y	
	7 months to a year					
	More than one year					
Funding limits	$1–$2,500			Y	Y	Y
	$2,501–$4,000					
	$4,001–$5,250	Y				
	>$5,250					
	Other	Up to $5,000 a year	100 percent up to $1,169 per year	$2,000 per year for graduates and $1,000 for undergraduates	$3,000 per year	$715 for PT and $1,430 for FT
Performance requirement	Completion of course		Y			Y
	Passing grade					Y

	C1	C2	C3	C4	C5	C6	C7	C8	C9	C10
Other — Minimum of a C			Y							
Other — Minimum of a B										
Other — Requirements vary										
Other — No requirements										
Other — (notes)					Florida schools only				Must remain with county for one year after course completion	
Source (www)	maricopa.gov		fairfaxcounty.gov/hr		hillsborough-county.org		dupageco.org/HR		montgomerycountymd.gov	
Population (Retrieved from U.S. Census Bureau 2005)	3,635,528		1,006,529		1,132,152		929,113		927,583	
County		Westchester County, New York		Baltimore County, Maryland		Wake County, North Carolina		San Mateo County, California		St. Charles County, Missouri
Benefit option — Reimbursement postcompletion	Y	Y	Y		Y	Y		N		
Benefit option — Advance payment tuition assistance								Y		
Benefit option — Educational leave of absences					Y			Y		
Benefit option — Educational loan assistance								N		

(continued)

Table 16.9 (continued) Select Counties Offering Tuition Assistance

		Westchester County, New York	FBaltimore County, Maryland	Wake County, North Carolina	DSan Mateo County, California	St. Charles County, Missouri
Course type	Courses related to current position	Y	Y	Y	Y	Y
	Course related to future positions				Y	Y
	Course related to business	Y	Y	Y	Y	Y
	Course required by degree				Y	
	Any courses	N			W/A	
	Nonacademic courses				W/A	
Expenses	Tuition			Y	Y	
	Registration fee				Y	
	Text books			Y	N	
	Other fees				N	
Benefits available	Full-time salaried		Y		Y	
	Part-time		N			
	After 3 months or less	Y			Y	
	4–6 months				Y	
	7 months to a year				Y	
	More than one year				Y	

		weschestergov.com/HR	co.ba.md.us	wakegov.com/employment	co.snamateo.ca.us	sccmo.org
Funding limits	$1–$2,500					Y
	$2,501–$4,000					
	$4,001–$5,250					
	>$5,250					
	Other	Based on a percentage on a total amount approved for all applicants	70 percent to 80 percent reimbursement		$263 for <3 units, $438 <3 units	
Performance requirement	Completion of course		Y		NS	
	Passing grade					
	Minimum of a C	Y				
	Minimum of a B					
	Requirements vary					
	No requirements					
Other						
Source	(www)	weschestergov.com/HR	co.ba.md.us	wakegov.com/employment	co.snamateo.ca.us	sccmo.org
Population	(Retrieved from U.S. Census Bureau 2005)	923,459	786,113	748,815	699,610	329,940

(continued)

Table 16.9 (continued)   Select Counties Offering Tuition Assistance

		Collier County, Florida	Loudoun County, Virginia	Durham County, North Carolina	Carroll County, Maryland	Delaware County, Ohio	James-City County, Virginia
Benefit option	Reimbursement postcompletion						
	Advance payment tuition assistance						
	Educational leave of absences						
	Educational loan assistance						
Course type	Courses related to current position	Y			Y		Y
	Course related to future positions				Y		Y
	Course related to business	Y			Y		Y
	Course required by degree	Y					
	Any courses						
	Nonacademic courses						

Expenses	Tuition					Y
	Registration fee					Y
	Text books					Y
	Other fees					Y
Benefits available	Full-time salaried	Y		Y		Y
	Part-time					Y
	After 3 months or less	N				
	4-6 months	N				
	7 months to a year	N		Y		
	More than one year	Y				
Funding limits	$1-$2,500	Y	Y			
	$2,501-$4,000					Y
	$4,001-$5,250					
	>$5,250					
	Other	100 percent for 6 hours per semester	$2,200 per year	Up to $500 per year	100 percent	$3,000 per year
Performance requirement	Completion of course					Y
	Passing grade	Y				Y
	Minimum of a C					

(continued)

Table 16.9 (continued) Select Counties Offering Tuition Assistance

	Collier County, Florida	oudoun County, Virginia	Durham County, North Carolina	Carroll County, Maryland	Delaware County, Ohio	James-City County, Virginia
Minimum of a B						
Requirements vary						
No requirements						
Other						
Source (www)	jobs.colliergov. net	loudon.gov	co.durham.nc.us	cgovernment. carr.org	co.delaware. oh.ud	james-city. va.us
Population (Retrieved from U.S. Census Bureau 2005)	307,242	255,518	242, 582	168,541	150,268	57,525

Y, The county does require or offer this option.
N, The county specifically states they do not offer this benefit or option.
W/A, The county allows this option or benefit with approval from supervisor.
Blank, No information was provided.

employee is attending classes at night, allow the employee to leave earlier that day to travel to class. Some employers may not be able to afford college tuition, however, they may be able to afford to purchase textbooks that can become the property of the organization once a class is completed. When appropriate, an employer can substitute tuition for attending conferences out of town. Often the cost of a college class for a semester of learning is less than a conference registration fee, hotel, meals, and transportation expenses not to mention the employee's time away from work.

When employers disseminate information on health insurance, supplemental healthcare plans, retirement plans, and other life enhancement opportunities they can provide information to their employees on the tax credits and deductions sanctioned by the IRS that are available to help offset the cost of higher education. For example, the Hope Credit provides up to $1650 credit per eligible student, available only until the first two years of postsecondary education are completed. Students must be pursuing an undergraduate degree or other recognized education credential; students must be enrolled at least half time for at least one academic period during the year and there can be no felony drug conviction on students' record. The Hope Credit may be limited by the amount of a student's income and the amount of tax liability.

The lifetime learning credit provides up to $2000 credit per return and there is no limit on the number of years a lifetime learning credit can be claimed based on the same student's expense. It is available for all years of postsecondary education and for courses taken to acquire or improve job skills. It is available for an unlimited number of years, students do not need to be pursuing a degree or other recognized education credential, it is available for one or more courses, and the felony drug conviction rule does not apply. The lifetime learning credit may be limited by the amount of a student's income and the amount of tax liability.

A student loan interest deduction is allowed for paying interest on a student loan used for higher education. If a student's modified adjusted gross income (MAGI) is less than $65,000 ($105,000–$135,000 if filing a joint return) there is a special deduction allowed for paying interest on a student education loan. This deduction can reduce the amount of one's income subject to tax up to $2,500.

The tuition and fees deduction can reduce the amount of a student's income subject to tax by $4000. This deduction may be beneficial to a student if the student is not eligible for either the Hope or Lifetime Learning Credit because a student's income is too high. This can be limited by the adjusted gross income.

16.8   Conclusion

In today's rapidly changing environment, employees need the capacity to develop new knowledge and skills, and organizations need a workforce prepared for future changes, society also needs educated citizens willing to engage in the civic, social, and democratic fabric of their communities.

The number of younger workers without college degrees threatens the United States' ability to maintain its economic competitiveness, build a labor force ready to take on high-skilled jobs, and close racial and ethnic disparities in earnings.

At a time when the public workforce requires greater skills and fewer low-income individuals are attending college, organizations should be at the forefront of encouraging employees to obtain college degrees. Higher education broadens one's perspective; it provides benefits to the individuals, the organizations they work for, and the society at large.

References

Adelman, C. 2006. *The Toolbox Revisited: Paths to Degree Completion from High School through College.* Washington, DC: U.S. Department of Education.

Advisory Committee on Student Financial Assistance. 2001. *Access Denied: Restoring the Nation's Commitment to Equal Educational Opportunity.* Washington, DC: Author.

Advisory Committee on Student Financial Assistance. 2002. *Empty promises: The Myth of College Access in America.* Washington, DC: Author.

Blumenthal, R. 2007. Unfilled city manager posts hint at future gap. *The New York Times,* January 11, nytimes.com, http://www.nytimes.com/2007/01/11/us/11managers.html?ei=5094&en=a5f8bcfecfcc 850&hp=&.

Carnevale, A. and Desrochers, D. 2003. *Standards for What?: The Economic Roots of K-16 Reform.* Princeton, NJ: Educational Testing Service.

College Board. 2003. *Trends in Student Aid 2003.*

College Board. *2005–2006 College Costs.* http://collegeboard/student/pay/add-it-up/4494.html/.

Council for Adult and Experiential Learning (CAEL). 2004. *The Promise and Practice of Employer Educational Assistance at Programs: 2004 State of the Field Strategies & Trends.* Chicago, IL. Available at www.cael.org retrieved 2/21/07.

Drizin, M. 2005. Training isn't a cost; it's an investment in your agency's future. *IPMA-HR News* October 2005: 7–8.

Economic Opportunity Act of 1946. Public Law 88–452.

Fitzgerald, W. 1992. Training versus development. *Training and Development Journal* 5: 81–84.

Fitz-enz, S. 1996. How to Measure Human Resource Management. 2nd edition. NY: McGraw Hill.

Guarantee Student Loans (Perkins and Stafford). Public Law 89–329.

Haycock, K. 2006, August. *Promise Abandoned: How Policy Choices and Institutional Practices Restrict College and Opportunities.* Washington, DC: The Education Trust.

Ibarra, P. 2006. The myths and realities of succession planning. *IPMA-HR News* August, 13,15.

Institute for Higher Education Policy and Scholarship America. 1998, March. *Reaping the Benefits: Defining the Public and Private Value of Going to College.* Washington, DC: Author.

King, J.E. 2006. *Working their Way through College: Student Employment and Its Impact on the College Experience.* Washington, DC: American Council on Education.

King, C.J. 2006, June 1. Engineers Should Have a College Education. *Center for Studies in Higher Education. Paper CSHE-8–06.* Available http://repositories.cdlib.org/cshe/ CSHE-8–06.

Lustig, J. 2006. From art to alienated labor: The degradation of academic Work. *Thought and Action* 22: 143–158.

Mills, C.W. 1956. *The Power Elite*, NY: Oxford University Press.

Purchasing Power of the Pell Grant Maximum Award 1974 to 2006. *Postsecondary Education Opportunity.* 2005. Number 162. December 2005.

The National Center for Public Policy and Higher Education. 2006. *Measuring up 2006: The National Report Card on Higher Education.* Author retrieved www. highereducation.org.

The National Leadership Council for Liberal Education & America's Promise. 2007. *College Learning for the New Global Century.* Washington, DC: Association of American Colleges and Universities.

Reindl, T. 2007, March. *Hitting Home: Quality, Cost, and Access Challenges Confronting Higher Education Today.* Lumina Foundation for Education: Making Opportunity Affordable.

Serviceman's Readjustment Act 1944 (GI Bill). Public Law 78–284 (58 Stat.284).

Taxpayer Relief Act of 1997 (Hope Scholarship). Public Law 105–34.

Chapter 17

Transitioning to Defined Contribution Retirement Plans: The Importance of Financial Literacy Development in the Workplace

Joseph H. Holland and Doug Goodman

CONTENTS

The private sector has slowly been shifting from defined benefit (DB) retirement plans to defined contribution (DC) retirement plans. Many nonprofit and public sector organizations are also beginning to make this transition. This article explores differences between DB and DC retirement plans, the implications of transitioning to DC retirement plans, the different motives and needs between public and private sector employees, and the importance of financial literacy. We then show the importance of financial literacy development for employees, especially because DC plans require employees to manage their own retirement portfolios.

17.1 Defined Benefits versus Defined Contributions

In 1974, the Employee Retirement Income Security Act (ERISA) was enacted to protect the assets of individuals who participate in a pension plan at their workplace. ERISA, along with the IRS tax code change in 1978 that enabled employees to contribute to tax-deferred accounts, enabled employers to provide retirement plans to employees in addition to the DB plans, which had primarily been used before the enactment. Retirement benefits from a DB plan are calculated on a formula and are based on an employee's salary and tenure with an organization. ERISA was not enacted to mandate employers to develop pension plans for their employees, but it was enacted to create guidelines for employers to follow who do offer pension plans. Within the policy enactment, the guidelines enabled employers to continue to offer the DB plans, or they could create DC plans. Moreover, they could offer both the DC and DB plans. Retirement benefits from a DC plan are based on the assets that are contributed by the employee. Mostly, the assets are considered tax-deferred until the funds are distributed from the retirement account.* Furthermore, in many circumstances, the employer will match the employee's contributions. Usually, the match is between 0.50 and a dollar, up to 6 percent of an employee's salary. These assets are invested into various financial instruments which are chosen by the employee from funds within the retirement plan. Munnel and Sunden (2001) explain, "...the nature of pension coverage has changed sharply. The DC plan, in which retirement benefits depend on contributions and the earnings on those contributions, has to a large extent replaced the DB plan, in which benefits are provided as a lifetime annuity based on final average salary and years of service" (p. 323).

---

* Some DC plans allow after-tax contributions.

With the shift to DC plans, the responsibility of planning for retirement also shifts. Organizations that offer DC plans establish a relationship with a third party trustee to administer the plan offered to the organization's employees. This relationship does not limit the organization's attention to the plan, but it does enable the organization to reduce their expenses, which are substantial when comparing the administrative cost of operating a DB plan. In other words, the organization does not need staff members to manage the assets in the funds, which can be an immense expense. However, when an organization develops a DC plan, the employee assumes more responsibility for his or her retirement planning. Muller (2003) argues that traditional pension plans saddled the employers with decision making whereas DC plans shift the decision making to the employee.

An important question must be asked in regard to the shift in responsibility. Are employees competent and capable of managing their retirement? In other words, do they understand the complex world of investing? Many individuals shy away from discussions relating to financial planning. They do not understand concepts such as risk tolerance, mutual funds, stocks, bonds, or yield comparison analysis, which are pertinent in developing a sound retirement plan. This lack of planning and knowledge base has been documented in several studies. Dickemper and Yakoboski (1997) indicate that only 36 percent of the sample they studied knew how much they needed for retirement. Furthermore, Employee Benefit Research Institute (ERBI) (1996) reports that individuals were not knowledgeable of the difference between stocks and bonds. These examples are evident that employees are not yet capable of assuming the task of planning for retirement, which can suggest serious problems for the public and for the government in years to come. For example, if the Social Security program continues to offer limited benefits and if individuals do not invest, then many scenarios may occur. First, individuals will not have the resources to care for themselves during their latter years of life. This will cause a demand for more governmental assistance, which due to budgetary constraints, may not be feasible. Second, older individuals will have to work longer than past generations. These problems are beyond the scope of this discussion, yet they need to be addressed in future research.

Regardless of potential social problems with DC plans, there are many public sector and nonprofit sector organizations that offer a DC plan for many reasons. First, DC plans provide a fast accumulation of assets, compared to DB plans. In other words, the assets grow quicker, especially if they are invested correctly. Furthermore, it gives the employee the ability to choose the investments they want to select. Of course, the investment choices are limited to only the funds that the employer allows in the portfolio (Garman, Young, and Love, 2000). Finally, DC plans are portable. In other words, when an employee terminates from his or her employer, they have the option to move the money that is in the DC plan. ERISA allows the employee some options regarding portability. First, they can take a cash withdrawal from the plan, which is taxed at 20 percent, and if the employee is under the age of 59½, they are taxed another 10 percent as a penalty for not using the money for retirement. Second, they can leave the money in the current employer's plan as long as the balance is greater than $1,000. Third, they can elect a direct transfer of the funds to be sent to an IRA. Fourth, they can elect a direct transfer of the funds to be sent to a qualified plan with another employer. If employees are not educated on investment options, portability options, and other important issues concerning their DC plan, they may make bad decisions regarding their retirement planning.

17.2 Employment Sector Differences

Are there differences in retirement planning initiatives regarding employees who work in the private sector, nonprofit sector, and public sector? The question is important because there is expansive literature indicating that private sector organizations are adopting DC plans. However, only recently there has been the discussion that more public sector organizations are adopting DC plans. For example, "In 1998 the state of Michigan switched from a traditional DB plan for new state government employees to a DC plan" (Papke, 2002). Alaska enrolls all new employees in a DC retirement plan (State of Alaska, 2007). Also, Governor Arnold Schwarzenegger proposed the intent to transfer state workers to a DC plan instead of a DB ("*Economist*," 2005, p. 34). These examples indicate that public sector employees have or will eventually have to assume the responsibility of retirement planning.

17.2.1 Motives

Research questions emerge concerning differences between public sector and private sector employees. What needs, values, and motives do public employees have? Are these needs, values, and motives different, compared to private sector employees? Furthermore, once a foundation is framed regarding the differences in each sector, a more pressing question must be asked, do these differences affect public sector employees' ambition to plan for retirement?

Classical theories express the motives of individuals. Although most of these are limited in some perspective, they have been cited and discussed for years. First, Murry (1938) offered a list of 19 identifiers of human needs.* Maslow's (1954) hierarchy of needs identified that when a person's need is satisfied, another need will develop. For example, a worker who is in need of a salary increase to maintain a lifestyle will change his or her need if they are laid off from their current job. Instead of needing a salary increase, they will be in need of a mere income to keep the lights on at home. In other words, needs change as needs are satisfied. Maslow,

---

* Abasement, achievement, affiliation, aggression, autonomy, counteraction, defendance, deference, dominance, exhibition, harm avoidance, infavoidance, nurturance, order, play, rejection, sentience, sex, succourance, and understanding.

furthermore, expressed a temporal order for needs. The hierarchy begins with physiological needs (i.e., food and water) and ends with self-actualization (achieving the apex of one's capacity).

Frederick Herzberg (1968) further refined motivation into two factors: hygiene and motivator factors. Hygiene factors are generally tangible rewards that focus on job context such as policies, supervision, working conditions, interpersonal relations, money, status, and security. Motivator factors are usually intrinsic rewards that focus on job content. These include achievement, recognition, challenging work, responsibility, growth, and development. Motivator factors, according to Herzberg, are linked to job satisfaction although hygiene factors are linked to job dissatisfaction.

Alderfer (1972) surmised Maslow's needs into three factors: growth needs, relatedness needs, and existence needs.* These theorists produced seminal works within the community of human needs. However, are these needs consistent among public sector employees, and if so, does this indicate there are different ambitions when comparing public and private sector employees?

Crewson (1995) found that two groups emerged when investigating the motives of employees within public organizations. Lower-level employees valued job security and pay, and upper-level employees and executives were focused more on challenges and impacting the public.

Understanding values among employees within an organization can enable a manager to increase motivation among employees. Rokeach (1973) developed a list of human values that differentiate between terminal values and instrumental values.† These values were later used by Sikula (1973) to distinguish if industry workers' values were different from public-service workers' values. Although public managers rated higher on some values than industry workers, the findings are not conclusive because the sample size was too small.

Another motive that has been theorized to exist among public managers is a keen sense to serve the public or public-service motivation (PSM). The foundation of PSM surmises that public employees are working to better society and will self-sacrifice to accomplish a mission for the betterment of others. However, this motive must not be generalized among all civil service workers, but research has found that public employees complete tasks that are dissatisfying to improve society (Kilpatrick, Cummings, and Jennings, 1964; Crewson, 1995).

---

* Growth needs: internal and self-actualization; relatedness needs: social and external esteem; existence needs: physiological and safety needs.

† Terminal values: comfortable life, exciting life, sense of accomplishment, world of peace, world of beauty, equality, family security, freedom, happiness, inner harmony, mature love, national security, pleasure, salvation, self-respect, social recognition, true friendship, wisdom.

Instrumental values: ambitious, broadminded, capable, cheerful, clean, courageous, forgiving, helpful, honest, imaginative, independent, intellectual, loving, logical, obedient, polite, responsible, self-control.

Furthermore, researchers have expanded on the concept of PSM by identifying categorical motives for public employees. Perry and Wise (1990, pp. 368–369) postulate that there are three categories in which public employees can identify: rational motives, norm-based motives, and affective motives. Rational motives reflect the idea that the people seek employment with government to participate in the policy-making process. Those with norm-based motives seek government employment out of "a desire to serve the public interest." Affective motives include people who seek government employment because of a "genuine conviction about its social importance." Brewer, Selden, and Facer (2000) found the following four categories in their research that public workers identified with: Samaritans, communitarians, patriots, and humanitarians.

The above research and theories offer a snippet of insight into the needs, values, and motives among public employees. However, a question still remains unanswered, do these needs, values, and motives limit public sector and nonprofit sector employees from investigating retirement planning, compared to private sector employees? This question will be addressed later in this discussion.

17.2.2 Economic Wealth

A number of research studies have been conducted and these studies conclude that public sector employees place less value on financial wealth compared with private sector employees. Does this also mean that public sector employees place less value on planning for financial security? In other words, logically, if research indicates that public sector employees put less value into their current pay, would they be less prone to plan for their retirement, which will indicate their income during their retirement years? Although the above literature presents a framework that indicates that public and private sector employees have different motives in regard to work, does that indicate that they have different motivations in regard to other values, especially economic wealth? At this point, we must narrow the framework of the literature to develop a foundation that supports the assertion that private sector employees and public sector employees have differences in relation to economic wealth.

Rawls, Ullrich, and Nelson (1974) found that there is a difference in values between employees entering the private and nonprofit sector. They administered a myriad of tests to business school graduates who intended to enter either the profit sector or the nonprofit sector. Follow-up data collection confirmed that many of the research participants actually did enter their intended fields. The results of the study indicate that profit and nonprofit sector employees "...differ significantly on a number of personality and value system dimensions" (p. 618). Moreover, the authors state, "they (nonprofit employees) placed less value on obedience, responsibility, ambition, a comfortable life, cleanliness, and economic wealth, and placed greater value on helpfulness, cheerfulness, and forgiveness" (p. 620). Conversely, private sector employees emphasized economic wealth as a greater value. The implications of this study are significant in developing a framework that suggests private sector employees are more apt to develop a retirement plan because they place more emphasis on economic wealth and a comfortable lifestyle.

Furthermore, Karl and Sutton (1998) investigated an exploratory design that found significant differences in job value in regard to public and private sector employees. Karl and Sutton discuss the shift in job value from the turn of the twentieth century to today. As scholars logged the changing values, the literature was limited in investigating comparative models between public and private sector employees' job values. However, because of the implementation of the new public management, scholars needed to look closer at the values held by public employees.* Thus, Karl and Sutton conclude that private sector employees do value wages and economic rewards more than public sector employees.

Another study conducted by Khojasteh (1993) supports previous literature that indicates private sector employees are more motivated by money and economic wealth, compared to public employees. He administered surveys to employees in 25 different organizations (seven public and eighteen private). The survey asked the employees to rank various intrinsic and extrinsic rewards that they held in high value. He concluded, "Unlike the public sector managers, those of the private sector were motivated more by money to obtain an enjoyable and pleasurable life" (p. 397). Futhermore, the research identified that, "public sector managers have a significantly higher degree of satisfaction with pay than private sector managers" (p. 397). In addition, the study indicated that, "pay and job security were found to be significantly less important rewards by public sector managers than by those in the private sector" (p. 395).

Houston (2000) presents an additional study that further confirms the assertion that private sector employees prefer pay more than public sector employees. He frames his work around public-service motivation and tests the difference in intrinsic and extrinsic motives. Moreover, his sample consists of 101 public sector employees and 1356 private sector employees. The research found that public and private sector employees have comparable outlooks regarding meaningful work. In other words, both groups desire work that brings meaning to their life. However, the research presents a stark difference between the groups regarding income, shorter work hours, and job security. The findings indicate that private sector employees are more likely to value high income and shorter work hours, compared to public sector employees. However, public sector employees are more like to value job security, compared to private sector employees.

Do differences in the desire to obtain economic wealth between public sector and private sector employees also translate into less financial literacy for public sector and nonprofit sector employees, compared to private sector employees? The exploration of this question is extremely important because of the constant change to DC plans in public organizations. Public executives who are responsible for

---

* Managers can not assume that all public and private employees have the same values.

implementing DC plans should take a hard look at the literature to determine if public sector employees will take the initiative to educate themselves on their retirement planning because DC plans place more responsibility on the employee, instead of the employer. Therefore, this article seeks to identify the effects of a financial literacy program regarding public sector employees. Comparing both sectors is beyond the scope of this study.

17.2.3 Financial Literacy

Since the enactment of ERISA and the shift from DB to DC plans, many scholars have called for an increase in financial literacy within the workplace (Bernheim and Garrett 1995; Joo and Grable, 2000; Kim, 2003). Although there is literature that focuses on the effects of financial literacy in the workplace, the question remains, how effective is it? Furthermore, there is a gap in the research pertaining to non-profit employees and the effects of a financial literacy program within a workplace setting. A review of workplace financial literacy literature is necessary to understand the issues and results that are currently present.

Loibl and Hira (2005) present data from 1420 questionnaires regarding self-directed learning of financial literacy and the relationship with career satisfaction. Although this study does not emphasize workplace education, it does report a causal relationship that effects career satisfaction. The authors conclude that employees who use self-directed financial learning methods are significantly more "satisfied" with their career, compared to employees who do not use self-directed financial learning methods. Thus, the results indicate that financial knowledge can increase an employee's career satisfaction level. Furthermore, Kim and Garman (2004) found that employees who are financially stressed report an inverse relationship regarding attitudes and behaviors at work.*

Another study conducted by Joo and Grable (2000) surveyed 220 clerical workers. Their results indicated that the workers, who were the best-off financially, desired counseling regarding retirement planning. This study identifies that employees indicate a lack of knowledge and understanding of pertinent retirement planning information that they need to successfully acquire a sensible level of economic wealth.†

Bernheim and Garrett (1995) surveyed 2055 individuals to determine the consequences of financial education in the workplace. The authors find that "education is strongly related to retirement wealth and flow saving" (p. 24). Furthermore, their research indicates that when financial education is offered there are more employees

---

* The research findings indicate that workers "who are financially stressed are more likely to have lower levels of pay satisfaction, spend work time handling financial matters, and be absent from work" (p. 74).

† Information that would help the employee understand risk tolerance, asset allocation, investment options, and identify projected retirement income.

enrolled in the organization's retirement plan, and the employees' DC plan balance is larger. The authors, further, argue that education can have a "spillover" effect to an employees' spouse or significant other. In other words, as a husband or wife receives financial knowledge and increases their financial literacy, they share the information with other members of the household. Moreover, the authors' conclusion "raises the prospect that a serious national campaign to promote savings through education and information could have a measurable impact on behavior" (p. 35).

Finally, the literature addresses the effects of financial education programs in the workplace. However, the body of literature lacks empirical research investigating the effects of a financial education program within a nonprofit organization and how the information affects the employees within this sector. Kim and Garmen (2004) call for a more comprehensive workplace financial literacy program. In other words, some employers offer retirement seminars for employees. This training can increase employee participation in the DC plan, but so many employees feel inadequate regarding other financial issues. A comprehensive workplace financial literacy program would encompass topics related to budgeting, debt management, investments, insurance, retirement and college plan, and mortgages. In addition, a recent General Accountability Office forum (2007) called for employers to offer training in financial literacy to employees so they will be better prepared when they reach retirement age.

17.3 Methods

Regional Mental Health* is a state sanctioned nonprofit organization that provides mental health services to citizens of northeast Mississippi. The organization employs over 300 employees in 7 counties. Administrators in Regional Mental Health were concerned about the number of employees who cashed out their DC plans upon termination or shortly after termination. The organization piloted a financial literacy program with administrators to determine if the program should be offered across the organization to all of its employees. The purpose of this research is to determine if the program causes a change in the attitudes, the behaviors, and the financial well-being of employees regarding personal financial management.

17.3.1 Procedures

The financial literacy pilot program presented an excellent opportunity for an experimental research design. This experimental research design evaluates an

---

* Regional Mental Health is a pseudonym.

experiment group and a control group and compares the pre- and posttest means to determine if the treatment* causes any changes in knowledge, behaviors, and well-being of personal financial management.

The financial literacy program, which has been administered to over 300,000 people in the United States, used in the treatment presented 11 different concepts, which were taught in a one and half hour setting over 11 weeks beginning in September 2006. The concepts covered by the training included saving money, budgeting, emotions and money, bargaining power, debt reduction techniques, investments, insurance, retirement and college planning, consumer awareness, real estate and mortgage information, and collection practices and credit bureaus. These concepts were taught by a nationally recognized financial coach via DVD, which was followed up with a 20 minute group discussion led by a certified program trainer.

The purpose of the financial literacy program is to change the behavior and knowledge of employees so they can be empowered to succeed with money and money-related issues. The principles are described as common sense approaches to handling personal finances.

The pilot program consisted of 15 executives and supervisors from Regional Mental Health. The experimental group was administered a questionnaire prior to the training program to determine their financial knowledge, behavior, and well-being. The questionnaire was readministered at the conclusion of the training program. Completing the questionnaires was voluntary; questionnaires were not coded or linked to individuals. Ten people completed both the pre- and the posttest for a response rate of 67 percent.

The control group was randomly selected among a list of employees from Regional Mental Health. Those selected to participate were also administered a pre- and posttest survey; however, they were not subjected to the treatment. Nine individuals completed the pretest and 18 individuals completed the posttest for completion rates of 23 and 46 percent, respectively ($N = 39$).

17.3.2 Questionnaire

The survey collected demographic data that included age, gender, race, education, family size, and the income of each participant. The questionnaire was adapted from Kim (2004). The first measurement was a self-assessed financial knowledge instrument developed by Kim (2000). The financial knowledge scale consisted of the following ten items that were measured on a Likert-type scale:

■ Families should really concentrate on the present when managing their finances.

---

* The financial literacy program.

- Financial planning for retirement is not necessary for assuring one's security during old age.
- Having a financial plan makes it difficult to make financial investment decisions.
- Having a savings plan is not really necessary in today's world to meet one's financial need.
- It is really essential to plan for the possible disability of a family wage earner.
- Planning is an unnecessary distraction when families are just trying to get by today.
- Keeping records of financial matters is too time-consuming to worry about.
- Saving is not really important.
- It is important for a family to develop a regular pattern of saving and stick to it.
- Thinking about were you will be financially in five or ten years in the future is essential for success.

The next two scales measured financial attitudes (Godwin and Caroll 1986) and financial well-being (Joo and Garman, 1998).

Behavior scale:

- Thinking about where you will be financially in five or ten years in the future is essential for financial success.
- I have a weekly or monthly budget that I follow.
- I review and evaluate spending on a regular basis.
- I live from paycheck to paycheck.
- I regularly set aside money for saving.
- I write down where money is spent.
- I create financial goals.
- I make plans on how to reach my financial goals.
- I developed a plan for my financial future.
- I regularly review my total financial situation.
- I often spend more money than I have.
- I usually pay the credit card bills in full.
- I get myself into more debt each year.
- I compare my credit card receipts with monthly statements.
- I evaluate my risk management (insurance) strategies.
- I am comfortable managing my retirement account.

Well-being:

- How well off are you financially?
- How do you feel about your current financial situation?

- How stressed do you feel about your personal finances?
- How secure do you feel about you personal finances for retirement?
- How satisfied are you with your present financial situation?
- How would you rate your financial knowledge?

17.3.3 Findings

17.3.3.1 Control Group

The control group consisted of a random sample of employees who did not participate in the treatment. Descriptive statistics were used to analyze the demographic information provided by the participants. The group was mostly female (70 percent) and African-American (77 percent). They were more apt to be married (63 percent) with a bachelors degree (48.1 percent). The control group is highly educated with only 22 percent of the participants not holding a college degree. Forty-eight percent have a bachelor's degree and 30 percent have a graduate or professional degree. The income disbursement ranged from <$20,000 to above $80,000. For instance, 19 percent had an income of <$20k, 11 percent had an income between $20k and $29, 29.6 percent had an income between $30k and $39k, 7 percent had an income between $40k and $49k, 11 percent had an income between $50 and $59k, 7 percent had an income between $60k and $69k, 7 percent had an income between $70k and $79k, and 7 percent had an income of $80k or higher. The control group was younger than the experiment group. Thirty-six percent of the participants' ages ranged from 20 to 29, 40 percent from 30 to 39, 8 percent from 40 to 49, and 16 percent from 50 to 59.

17.3.3.2 Experiment Group

The experiment group consisted of executives and supervisors in the agency. Descriptive statistics were used to analyze the demographic information provided by the participants. The group was mostly female (55 percent) and white (80 percent). They were more apt to be married (65 percent) with a graduate degree (70 percent). The income disbursement ranged from $30,000 to above $80,000. For instance, 5 percent had an income between $30k and $39k, 30 percent had an income between $40k and $49k, 20 percent had an income between $50k and $59k, 5 percent had an income between $60k and $69k, 10 percent had an income between $70k and $79k, and 30 percent had an income of $80k or higher. Forty-five percent of the participants' ages ranged from 30 to 39, 25 percent from 40 to 49, and 30 percent from 50 to 59.

Demographically, there were statistical differences between the control and experimental groups in terms of age, race, and income. The experimental group was older, contained less African-Americans, and earned more money than the control group. Because this was a pilot program, the organization decided to experiment with management and then open up the program to all employees. The experiment group is not random. Managers were given the opportunity to enroll in the program.

17.3.3.3   Data Analysis

Three areas concerning financial literacy (knowledge, behavior, and well-being) were analyzed using a one-way ANOVA procedure within SPSS. The statistical method was used to determine if there was a statistical difference between the mean responses of the survey instrument between the control and experiment groups and between pre- and postsurveys. First, differences between the control group and the experiment group in the pretest were analyzed. There were statistical differences on five nondemographic survey items. The experiment group disagreed more with the following survey statement than those in the control group: "Thinking about where you will be financially in five or ten years in the future is essential for financial success." The experiment group agreed more than those in the control group with the following items:

- I live from paycheck to paycheck.
- I create financial goals.
- I make plans on how to reach my financial goals.
- I regularly review my total financial situation.

Table 17.1 reports the means for the financial knowledge scale for the pre- and posttest for both the control and experiment groups. First, the table reports one statistically significant relationship between the experiment and control groups for the pretest that was discussed in the preceding paragraph. There are statistically significant differences between the experiment and control group for the postsurvey for nearly all survey items. The control group reported more disagreement than the experiment group in that families should focus on the present, financial planning is unnecessary, financial planning makes investing difficult, a savings plan is not necessary, financial record-keeping is too time-consuming, and savings is not really important. The differences between the control and experiment groups on the survey items demonstrate more financial knowledge or understanding on the part of the experiment group when compared to the control group. In other words, the financial literacy training program increased the knowledge of those in the experiment group, compared to those in the control group. Table 17.1 reported one statistically significant difference between the pre- and postsurveys for each of the groups. The experiment group reported less agreement with the statement: "thinking about where you will be financially in five or ten years in the future is essential for financial success." The difference is less than one point on the survey, but that difference is statistically significant. The control group reported more agreement with the following statement in the postsurvey than they had in the presurvey, "families should really concentrate on the present when managing their finances." This difference could be explained because the posttest was administered during a December holiday season, which means most consumers are concentrating on the present to pay for the items they may purchase during the holiday time. However, the experiment group did not record the stark change in direction regarding financial knowledge.

Table 17.1 Knowledge Scale Differences between Pre- and Posttest and Control and Experiment Groups

Survey Item	Survey	Experiment Group Means	Control Group Means
Families should really concentrate on the present when managing their finances	Pre	3.30	3.67[b]
	Post[a]	3.56	2.28
Financial planning for retirement is not necessary for assuring one's security during old age	Pre	4.70	4.56
	Post[a]	4.90	4.17
Having a financial plan makes it difficult to make financial investment decisions	Pre	4.30	4.22
	Post[a]	4.80	4.06
Having a savings plan is not really necessary in today's world to meet one's financial need	Pre	4.90	4.22
	Post[a]	4.90	4.28
It is really essential to plan for the possible disability of a family wage earner	Pre	1.60	1.56
	Post	1.40	1.89
Planning is an unnecessary distraction when families are just trying to get by today	Pre	4.44	4.56
	Post	4.60	3.89
Keeping records of financial matters is too time-consuming to worry about	Pre	4.30	4.22
	Post[a]	4.70	3.94
Saving is not really important	Pre	4.80	4.78
	Post[a]	4.90	4.39
It is important for a family to develop a regular pattern of saving and stick to it	Pre	1.50	1.44
	Post	1.60	1.83
Thinking about where you will be financially in five or ten years in the future is essential for financial success	Pre[a]	1.00[a]	1.33
	Post	1.70	1.83

Note: Asterisks in the survey column represent significant differences between the experiment and control groups for the pre- and posttests. Asterisks in experiment and control columns represent statistically significant differences between the pre- and posttests. Coded: 1 = strongly agree, 2 = agree, 3 = neutral, 4 = disagree, 5 = strongly disagree.

[a] $p < .05$
[b] $p < .01$

The next portion of the survey focused on financial behaviors; the results of which are reported in Table 17.2 that shows statistically significant differences between the experiment and control groups for the presurvey for four survey items: I live paycheck to paycheck, I create financial goals, I make plans on how to reach my total financial situation, and I regularly review my total financial situation. The experiment group reported more disagreement than the control group with each of the items. Also, Table 17.2 reports statistically significant differences between the experiment and

Table 17.2 Financial Behavior Scale Differences between Pre- and Posttest and Control and Experiment Groups

Survey Item	Survey	Experiment Group Means	Control Group Means
I have a weekly or monthly budget that I follow.	Pre	3.00[b]	2.22
	Post[a]	1.90	2.78
I review and evaluate spending on a regular basis.	Pre	3.00[b]	2.11
	Post[a]	1.60	2.33
I live from paycheck to paycheck.	Pre[a]	3.30[b]	2.11
	Post[b]	4.33	2.94
I regularly set aside money for savings.	Pre	2.40	2.56
	Post	1.90	2.50
I write down where money is spent.	Pre	3.10[b]	2.44
	Post[a]	1.40	2.57
I create financial goals.	Pre[a]	3.10[b]	2.00
	Post[a]	1.70	2.67
I make plans on how to reach my total financial situation.	Pre[a]	3.20[b]	2.00
	Post	1.90	2.39
I developed a plan for my financial future.	Pre	2.90[b]	2.22
	Post[b]	1.60	2.61
I regularly review my total financial situation.	Pre[b]	3.30[c]	1.78
	Post[a]	1.70	2.61
I often spend more money than I have.	Pre	3.60	3.00
	Post[a]	4.30	3.05

(continued)

Table 17.2 (continued)   Financial Behavior Scale Differences between Pre- and Posttest and Control and Experiment Groups

Survey Item	Survey	Experiment Group Means	Control Group Means
I usually pay the credit card bills in full.	Pre	3.67	3.25
	Post	2.67	3.38
I get myself into more debt each year.	Pre	3.56	3.11
	Post	3.40	3.50
I compare my credit card receipts with monthly statements.	Pre	3.33[b]	2.50
	Post[a]	1.89	3.0
I evaluate my risk management (insurance) strategies.	Pre	3.10[b]	2.78
	Post[a]	2.00	3.11
I am comfortable managing my retirement account.	Pre	3.60[b]	2.68
	Post[a]	2.10	3.18

Note: Asterisks in the survey column represent significant differences between the experiment and control groups for the pre- and posttests. Asterisks in experiment and control columns represent statistically significant differences between the pre- and posttests. Coded: 1 = strongly agree, 2 = agree, 3 = neutral, 4 = disagree, 5 = strongly disagree.

[a] $p < .05$
[b] $p < .01$
[c] $p < .001$

control groups for 11 postsurvey items. The experiment group reported more disagreement with the following two items than the control group: I live from paycheck to paycheck and I often spend more money than I have. They reported higher levels of agreement with the other nine behavioral items. These include:

- I have a weekly or monthly budget that I follow.
- I review and evaluate spending on a regular basis.
- I write down where money is spent.
- I create financial goals.
- I developed a plan for my financial future.
- I regularly review my total financial situation.
- I compare my credit card receipts with monthly statements.
- I evaluate my risk management (insurance) strategies.
- I am comfortable managing my retirement account.

Table 17.2 reports a statistically significant change in behavior for 11 survey items for the experiment group and none for the control group. This overwhelming improvement in behavior supports Kim's finding in 2004 and provides evidence that the treatment (a workplace financial education program) positively changes employee's behavior. Members of the experiment group were more likely to agree that they have a budget and follow it, review their spending, write down where money is spent, create financial goals, make plans to reach their financial situation, develop plans for the future, review their financial situation, compare credit card receipts with statements, evaluate their risks, and are more comfortable managing their retirement. It is interesting to note that the experiment group disagreed with each of the nine items more than the control group in the presurvey. After the literacy course, members of the experimental group indicated a positive change in behavior.

Members of the experiment group are also less likely to agree that they spend more money than they have and live paycheck to paycheck. The changes in these two survey items were more dramatic than those in the control group.

Table 17.3 displays the data collected for the third variable, which is financial well-being. There were no differences between the experiment and control groups for any survey item in the presurvey. There were differences between the groups for two items in the postsurvey: How secure do you feel about your personal finances for retirement and how satisfied are you with your present financial situation? The data indicates that within the experiment group, there was a significant change for all questions. The responses indicated that they were better off financially, they feel better about their financial situation, participants acknowledged less stress regarding their finances, they felt more secure about their retirement, and they were more satisfied with their present financial situation. Moreover, they rated their financial knowledge higher than they did in the presurvey.

Table 17.3 reports one statistically significant difference for the control group. The control group reported that they were better off financially in the postsurvey. This improvement can be explained because of the agency's holiday bonuses that were received prior to the postsurvey. The posttest was administered to the control group and the experiment group the week after employees received their yearly bonuses. This event could have increased the control group's perception of being financially well-off. More importantly, the other indicators did not change in any positive significant manner pointing to an improvement in the control group's financial well-being.

17.4   Discussion and Conclusion

This study uses an experimental design to determine if a financial literacy program affects employees in the workplace. Previous literature indicates that the way employees prepared for retirement in the past has changed dramatically over the past two decades. This change places more responsibility for managing retirement planning on the employees. This added responsibility suggests that employees need to become familiar with their financial world.

Table 17.3 Financial Well-Being Scale Differences between Pre- and Posttest and Control and Experiment Groups

Survey Item	Survey	Experiment Group Means	Control Group Means
How well off are you financially?	Pre	2.40[a]	2.00[a]
	Post	3.40	2.65
How do you feel about your current financial situation?	Pre	2.40[a]	1.89
	Post	3.40	2.71
How stressed do you feel about your personal finances?	Pre	3.00[a]	3.33
	Post	2.20	2.94
How secure do you feel about your personal finances for retirement?	Pre	2.90[a]	2.33
	Post[c]	3.80	2.35
How satisfied are you with your present financial situation? (scaled from one to seven)	Pre	4.10[a]	3.11
	Post[a]	6.00	4.00
How would you rate your financial knowledge? (scaled from one to ten)	Pre	3.10[b]	3.44
	Post	4.70	3.59

Note: Asterisks in the survey column represent significant differences between the experiment and control groups for the pre- and posttests. Asterisks in experiment and control columns represent statistically significant differences between the pre- and posttests. Scale rating on a continuum, 1 not very well off and 5 very well off.

[a] $p < .05$
[b] $p < .01$
[c] $p < .001$

This study uses an experimental design to evaluate any perceived changes in attitudes and behaviors over a three month period. The experiment group was subjected to an 11 week financial literacy program in the workplace, and the control group was not. The findings indicate that the program did not improve the experiment group's knowledge, but it significantly improved the members' behavior and their perceived financial well-being. Furthermore, the study shows there was not a significant improvement or change in attitudes of the control group's knowledge, behavior, or financial well-being during the same time with several minor exceptions.

This study supports several other studies that indicate the importance of financial literacy in the workplace. However, the previous studies lacked the experimental design, which enables a more precise measurement and allows one to assert causality.

Public and nonprofit sector managers and policy makers should be aware of the importance of a financial literacy program in the workplace, especially in organizations with DC retirement plans. The change in behavior may have a spillover effect into the employee's job function, which may be directly beneficial to the organization.

Finally, the study fills a gap that exists in the public sector literature regarding financial literacy and its effect on employees. If public employees are motivated intrinsically instead of extrinsically, then public sector employers must understand the importance of educating their employees if their organization switches from DB plans to DC plans. Furthermore, future research should expand the investigation to include state and local government employees to determine if a financial literacy program will have an effect on these employees' financial knowledge, behavior, and well-being.

References

Alderfer, C.P. 1972. *Existence, Relatedness, and Growth: Human Needs in Organizational Settings*. New York: Free Press.

Bernheim, B. and Garrett, D. 1995. The determinants and consequences of financial education in the workplace: Evidence from a survey of households. Stanford Economics Working Paper #96–007.

Brewer, G.A., Selden, S.C., and Facer, R.L. 2000. Individual conceptions of public service motivation. *Journal of Public Administration Review*, (60), 254–264.

Crewson, P.E. 1995. *The Public Service Ethic*. Washington, DC: American University.

Dickemper, J. and Yakoboski, P. 1997. Increased saving but little planning results of the 1997 retirement confidence survey. *Employee Benefits Issue Brief, 191*(November).

Employee Benefit Research Institute. 1996. Participant education: Actions and outcomes. *Employee Benefits Issue Brief, 169*(January).

Financial Literacy and Education Commission: Further program needed to ensure an Effective National Strategy. 2007. *General Accounting Office Reports and Testimony, Jan.*, GOA 07–100.

Garman, T.E., Young, D., and Love, H. 2000. Success in workplace financial education. *Consumer Interest Annual, 46*, 193–196.

Godwin, D.D. and Caroll, D.D. 1986. Financial management attitudes and behaviors of husbands and wives. *Journal of Consumer Studies and Home Economics*, (10), 77–96.

Herzberg, F. 1968. Onemore time: How do you motivate employees? *Harvard Business Review*, (46), 36–44.

Houston, D. 2000. Public-service motivation: A multivariate test. *Journal of Public Administration Research and Theory*, 713.

Joo, S. and Garman, E.T. 1998. Personal financial wellness may be the missing factor in understanding and reducing worker absenteeism. *Personal Finances and Worker Productivity, 2*(2), 172–182.

Joo, S. and Grable, J. 2000. Improving employee productivity: The role of financial counseling and education. *Journal of Employment Counseling, 37*(1), 2–15.

Karl, K. and Sutton, C. 1998. A comparison of public and private sector employees. *Public Personnel Management, 27*(4), 515–527.

Khojasteh, M. 1993. Motivating the private vs. public sector manager. *Public Personnel Management*, *22*(3), 391.

Kilpatrick, F.P., Cummings, M.C., and Jennings, M.K. 1964. *The Image of the Federal Service*. Washington, DC: Brooking Institution.

Kim, J. 2000. The effects of workplace financial education on personal finances and work outcomes. Virginia Polytechnic Institute & State University: Blacksburg, Virginia.

Kim, J. 2003. Financial education advice changes worker attitudes and behaviors. *Journal of Compensation and Benefits*, *19*(5), 7.

Kim, J. 2004. *Impact of a Workplace Financial Education Program on Financial Attitude, Financial Behavior, Financial Well-Being, and Financial Knowledge*. Paper presented at the Association for Financial Counseling and Planning Education.

Kim, J. and Garmen, T. 2004. Financial stress, pay satisfaction and workplace performance. *Compensation and Benefits Review*, *36*, 69–76.

Loibl, C. and Hira, T. 2005. Self-directed financial learning and financial satisfaction. *Financial Counseling and Planning*, *16*(1), 11–21.

Maslow, A.H. 1954. *Motivations and Personality*. New York: HarperCollins.

Muller, L. 2003. Investment choice in defined contribution plans: The effects of retirement education on asset allocation. *Benefits Quarterly*.

Munnel, A.H. and Sunden, A. 2001. *Private Pensions: Coverage and Benefits Trends*. Paper presented at the Conversation on Coverage.

Murry, H.A. 1938. *Explorations in Personality*. Oxford University Press.

On the march. 2005. *Economist*, *374*(8708), p. 34.

Papke, L. 2002. Individual financial decisions in retirement saving plans: The role of participant-direction. *Journal of Public Economics*, *88*, 36–61.

Perry, J.L. and Wise, L.R. 1990. The motivational bases of public service. *Public Administration Review*, *50*, 367–373.

Rawls, J., Ullrich, R., and Nelson, O. 1974. A comparison of managers entering or reentering the profit and nonprofit sectors. *Academy of Management Journal*, 616–622.

Rokeach, M. 1973. *The Nature of Human Values*. New York: Free Press.

Sikula, A.F. 1973. The values and value systems of governmental executives. *Public Personnel Management*, *2*, 16–22.

State of Alaska. 2007. Alaska Retirement and Benefits. Access from http://www.state.ak.us/drb/employer/hr_dcrplaninformation.shtml, March 25.

Chapter 18

Domestic Partner Benefits

Charles W. Gossett and Eddy S.W. Ng

CONTENTS

18.1   Introduction

As the workforce becomes increasingly diverse, public sector employers, like their private sector counterparts, must expand the relevance of their total rewards and compensation package. This trend can be seen in the increasing prevalence of domestic partner benefits. These benefits include both hard and soft benefits such as medical and dental benefits, life insurance, retirement and pension benefits, family and bereavement leave, as well as other company-sponsored benefits. Employers generally cover extended family members and same- or opposite-sex domestic partners (Martocchio, 2006; Corporate Leadership Council, 2004).

According to the Human Rights Campaign (HRC), 254 of the Fortune 500 companies (51 percent) provided equal benefits to same-sex couples in 2006. A number of public sector employers also offered domestic partner benefits. At the time of writing, 13 out of 50 state employers (26 percent) extended at least some benefits to domestic partners of their employees (HRC, 2006). The same source listed about 150 local government jurisdictions (counties, municipalities, school boards, etc.) as providing these benefits, although this is to some extent an underestimation. In states like California and Vermont which have statewide recognition of domestic partnerships (called Registered Domestic Partners in California and Civil Unions in Vermont and Connecticut) all local governments are required by law to make domestic partnership health benefits available to employees on terms similar to those provided to married couples (Gay and Lesbian Advocates and Defenders, 2005, p. 15; National Center for Lesbian Rights, 2007), so the actual number is much higher than the list indicates. However, it is important to note that the U.S. federal government does not offer its employees domestic partnership benefits, although legislation has been introduced in each congress since 1997 (Domestic Partnership Benefits and Obligations Act, 1997).

Both private and public sector employers recognize that by offering domestic partner benefits, they meet employee interests as well as become more competitive employers. Some observers have claimed that the private sector serves as a model for the public sector with respect to diversity issues, including their provision of domestic partnership benefits (Corporate Leadership Council, 2004; Colvin, 2006; Rubaii-Barrett & Wise, 2007). From a human capital perspective, research suggests that there is a strong return on investment for organizations from more positive results on hiring efforts, improved retention, increased loyalty, trust, and productivity (Cox & Blake, 1991; Corporate Leadership Council, 2004; Reed & Friedman, 2005). However, in the public sector, particularly, the ideas of fairness and equal treatment under the law are also primary motivations for adopting domestic partnership benefits for public sector employees.

Providing domestic partner benefits, however, has also been highly controversial particularly for public sector employers. Berkeley, California, became the first city to offer its employees domestic partnership benefits in 1982 (Gossett, 2007), about the same time the first private sector companies, the *Village Voice* newspaper and Lotus, the computer software company, were also doing so. Gradually, over the next 25 years, the number of jurisdictions—state governments, municipal governments, school boards, and special district governments—has increased, but not without controversy. There are many cities that have debated and rejected the adoption of these benefits, a few who had adopted them under one set of political leaders and repealed them following an election which changed the political leadership, and at least 15 cities that have had to defend their plans against lawsuits challenging their right to adopt such plans (Gossett, 1999). The political debate is comprised of two principal arguments—(1) providing domestic partnership benefits provides recognition to gay and lesbian couples in violation of the wishes of a majority of citizens who view such relationships as morally unacceptable (Chuang, Church, & Ophir, 2005) and (2) the cost of such benefits will place a burden on the taxpayers (Hamrick, 2002; Naff & Kellough, 2003). However, the legal arguments that are used once a plan is challenged in court focus primarily on whether or not the city has the legal authority to create the category of domestic partners or amend their employee benefit plans to include domestic partners (Gossett, 1999). Arguments against the provision of domestic partnership benefits include stigmatization of the organization in the eyes of the public, increased costs (Hamrick, 2002), legal ramifications and tax complications (Shepherd, 2006), accountability to taxpayers, as well as religious and political concerns (Duncan, 2001; Reed & Friedman, 2005; Denike, 2007; Ferguson, 2007).

The purpose of this chapter is to examine the current status of domestic partner benefits among public sector employers. In particular, we will discuss the challenges of

1. creating a definition of the term "domestic partners,"
2. determining who meets the definition and establishing their eligibility for participating in domestic partner benefits, and
3. implementing a domestic partnership version of the standard benefit offerings most employers provide

18.2   Definition of Domestic Partners

For almost all public employers, defining the term "domestic partnership" has been done through a legislative process. Occasionally the benefits are extended through administrative orders or through collective bargaining agreements. Not surprisingly, there are some differences between the definitions from one locality to the other, but they usually have some core elements in common. (Bowman & Cornish, 1992; Gossett, 1994; Hostetler & Pynes, 1995). For the most part, jurisdictions have modeled their legal definitions of domestic partnerships similar to the way marriage is defined. The most common elements include the following conditions: an age requirement comparable to the age for marriage, that neither party be married nor domestically partnered with anyone else, that the parties have a "commitment" to each other, and that the parties not be related by blood in a way that would prevent marriage in that state. Other conditions that are found in such laws include a joint residency requirement, mental competency at the time the partnership is entered into, and a waiting period after the termination of one partnership before another one can be entered. One requirement that is often imposed on parties entering a domestic partnership that is not imposed on couples seeking marriage licenses is a period of cohabitation prior to registering the relationship.

One area of controversy that has emerged is whether or not the ability to enter into domestic partnerships is limited to same-sex couples or if opposite-sex couples should also be allowed to establish domestic partnerships. Most, but definitely not all, public sector employers make domestic partnerships available to both same-sex and opposite-sex couples within the context of designing benefit programs for their employees. Though the specific reasons for this policy may vary from place to place, it is likely that the idea of limiting a benefit like expanded access to healthcare in the context of a law that is designed to expand such access strikes many legislators as contradictory. Also, legislating is the practice of bringing together a coalition of supporters sufficient to get legislation passed and the possibility of losing support by excluding opposite-sex couples might seem counterproductive. One of the ironies of such inclusive definitions of domestic partners is that in a number of jurisdictions, opposite-sex couples far outnumbered same-sex couples in registering for and benefiting from health benefit plans offered to domestic partners (Hostetler & Pynes, 1995, p. 53).

One other definitional debate that has taken place concerns whether or not domestic partners must be "unrelated by blood." Overwhelmingly this requirement is included in the definition, however, at least two jurisdictions have deliberately omitted this requirement. As a result, in Washington, DC and Salt Lake City, Utah, a person may choose a close relative as their domestic partner (or in Salt Lake City, their "designated adult"), although this option is only available to unmarried employees (Gossett, 1994; Thomson, 2006).

It should be noted, however, that when states like Vermont and New Jersey have established civil unions on a statewide basis available to any citizen, such status has been limited to same-sex couples who are not eligible to marry. A partial exception to this pattern is California which limits the status of Registered Domestic Partners (RDPs) to same-sex couples except that opposite-sex couples may also establish a domestic partnership if at least one of the parties is 62 years of age and eligible for Social Security benefits. Thus, as happened at the University of Vermont (Gram, 2000), public employers may choose to offer benefits to married employees and those who are in civil unions or their equivalents, thus eliminating a separate status of domestic partners as defined by the employer itself. In a like manner, in Massachusetts where same-sex couples can avail themselves of civil marriage, a number of private sector employers have abandoned their domestic partnership benefit programs and employees in same-sex relationships are required to get married if they wish to continue receiving health benefits for their partners (Symonds, 2004). Local governments in Massachusetts had been prevented from offering domestic partnership benefits by a state court decision so they did not have to adapt existing domestic partnership programs and could simply continue to offer benefits to married partners (Gossett, 1999).

Unlike the state-recognized civil union and domestic partnership relationships which must usually be dissolved through a court procedure, local domestic partnerships can usually be terminated by one party simply notifying the other party to the partnership, the office at which they registered the domestic partnership, and any party who took an action that relied on the existence of the partnership (e.g., a jurisdiction that offered employee benefits to the nonemployee domestic partner).

18.3 Determining Eligibility, Enrolling, and Tracking Domestic Partners

In many public organizations, employees who wish to enroll a spouse or dependent children in a health benefit program or perhaps take advantage of another benefit such as on-site childcare, simply fill out a form which they sign stating that the relationship exists. Only some jurisdictions required married couples to produce legal documentation proving that they were married, and, even if they did require documentation, they simply accepted a copy of a marriage license from any state in the union. Once a jurisdiction decides that it will offer benefits to the domestic partner and the children of the domestic partner (who may or may not also be the children of the employee entitled to the benefit), however, it must decide how it will determine whether or not a domestic partnership exists. An equity issue also arises as to whether or not employees who are claiming benefits on the basis of being married to someone are going to be required to meet the same kinds of evidentiary requirements as domestic partners must meet (New York City, Office of Labor Relations, 2007).

In states that now have statewide civil union or domestic partnership laws this may be relatively straightforward: the office at which employees sign up for employee benefits simply requires both married employees and civilly unionized employees to produce the state-issued document attesting to their status. Some policy maker will be required to determine whether or not documentation of a civil union or domestic partnership from another state will be recognized as valid in that state, but once the policy decision is made, administration is routine. In states without such statewide recognition of domestic partnerships or civil unions, on the other hand, the situation is more complex. In a number of cities and counties, an independent registry was created as part of the adoption of a domestic partnership ordinance. In those jurisdictions, employees can be required to simply demonstrate that they have registered at that registry; the state or local government has the option to say whether or not they will recognize registration from another jurisdiction or if they will require a couple to reregister in their jurisdiction. But again, once the policy decisions are made, administration of the benefit program is relatively routine.

A not uncommon situation, however, particularly in the years before Vermont became the first state with a comprehensive statewide partnership recognition status in 2000 was that the responsibility fell to the Personnel Office to not only administer the program but also to "officiate" at the creation of the domestic partnership relationship. Persons wishing to qualify for the domestic partnership benefit program had to appear before someone in the Personnel Office and produce any required documentation: e.g., applicants were often required to provide two or more pieces of documentation such as a lease or mortgage showing that the partners shared a residence, joint checking accounts, joint ownership of an automobile, etc. (Becker, 1995). The Personnel Office staff then had to verify the documentation, determine if the age, mental competence, current marital status (i.e., unmarried and unpartnered), and cohabitation requirements were met, and finally administer an oath of some sort that created a legally binding document (e.g., see the procedures established by Portland, Maine [2005]). Such a document then had to be recorded, filed, and maintained, and modified should either of the partners choose to terminate the partnership. Furthermore, when local ordinances required a waiting period between the termination of one domestic partnership before the start of a new one, the Personnel Office would be responsible for ensuring that the requirement was met (Las Cruces, 2007).

18.4 Types of Benefits

Many employee benefits are designed for the employee and his or her family. By recognizing domestic partnerships as a family status, employers need to review their benefit offerings and determine whether or not they will be offered on the same or a comparable basis to those employees with domestic partners. Assuming that the policy decision to recognize these relationships has been made, there are two other considerations that policy makers and employers need to take into account—financial implications and legal implications.

Most organizations generally offer domestic partners a combination of hard (e.g., health and dental, life insurance, retirement and death) and soft benefits (e.g., leave, EAPs) which are reviewed here. Special administrative challenges, costs, and tax implications associated with each type of benefit are also discussed.

18.4.1 Health Benefits

Much of the impetus behind the movement for employers to recognize domestic partnerships was related to the need of some male employees for health benefits for their partners who were suffering from AIDS and who were unable to work (Gossett, 1994). The earliest public and private examples of employers offering domestic partnership health benefits dates from the early- and mid-1980s, the same period in which HIV/AIDS was emerging as a public and private health crisis (Bailey, 1999). Over time it became clearer that there were many employees in unmarried relationships with a partner who lacked access to reasonably priced health insurance either because they were self-employed, or they suffered from a disability that was not covered by any benefit program, or they worked for an employer who either did not offer health insurance benefits, or whose benefits were too costly for the partner to purchase on his or her own.

Public employers, like their private counterparts, take one of two approaches to providing health benefits—self-insure their employees or purchase private insurance for them. Self-insured employers simply had to make up their minds that they would offer such coverage; in a number of jurisdictions, dental and vision benefits were offered to an employee's domestic partner before more general health benefits were because those programs were self-insured, although the general health plan was not. However, in the 1980s, plans that were not self-insured often had difficulty finding an insurer willing to offer the coverage. The lack of any actuarial experience made some insurers skittish and they simply refused to offer the benefit as a product option. However, once some of the earliest employers had a few years experience— and nobody had a horrible financial loss that was attributed to the domestic partnership program—more insurers added a domestic partnership product to their sales list (Hostetler & Pynes, 1995). In at least one state, Georgia, although a local government wanted to provide the coverage and they had found an insurer willing to sell it to them, the State Insurance Commissioner refused to allow the insurance company to sell the product until ordered to do so by a state judge (Croft, 1999).

Frequently, the political debate in states and communities over whether or not to even recognize domestic partnerships centered on a concern that the costs of such benefits would be prohibitive (Hostetler & Pynes, 1995; Gossett, 1999; HRC, 2006). Underlying this concern are two important issues (Employee Benefit Research Institute, 2004). One issue is that most public employers offer two types of plans— employee only and employee plus dependents (often called "family" plans); typically an employee who elects a family plan receives a greater dollar amount subsidy than a coworker who elects an employee only plan (Reddick & Coggburn, 2007). Thus, it would cost the employing jurisdiction more money if more people became eligible for the family plan and if the jurisdiction decided to subsidize it in a manner similar to the way the family plan was subsidized. The second issue is that many public employers, particularly local governments, have "experience-rated" plans which means that the annual price for the health plan is based on the actual usage of plan benefits by the employees and their dependents who are covered. The concern here derives from not knowing whether or not persons who become part of the pool through a domestic partnership will be more or less likely than others added to make use of the benefits. As noted, when domestic partnership health benefits were first being introduced in the 1980s, AIDS was ravaging the gay community and providing medical care to AIDS patients was expensive (Hunt & Rayside, 2000). What has the experience been?

An examination of the frequency of employees registering for domestic partnership coverage suggests that the total number of people using such benefits is not large.

Several studies (Ash & Badgett, 2006; Employee Benefits Research Institute, 2004; Bromer, 2007; Winfield, 2007) have shown that the enrollment numbers are extremely low among same-sex couples and only slightly higher for opposite-sex couples. According to the Human Rights Campaign Foundation, which has been tracking employers with domestic partner benefits, the overall level of domestic partnership enrollment has been hovering between 2 and 3 percent (of the total number of employees electing health benefits from the employer) over the last two decades, with the enrollment rate for same-sex couples being lower, at less than 1–2 percent.*

There are several reasons to believe that same-sex domestic partners are less likely than either married couples or opposite-sex domestic partners to register for their employer's benefit programs. First, both same-sex partners were more likely to be employed outside the home and thus have access to coverage through their employers (Ash & Badgett, 2006). Second, the costs and tax disincentives of receiving domestic partner benefits (see discussion below) for same-sex couples make such benefits unattractive. Furthermore, privacy concerns coupled with the lack of comprehensive laws protecting gays and lesbians from employment discrimination may discourage same-sex couples from taking advantage of domestic partner benefits (Riccucci & Gossett, 1996).

On the other hand, opposite-sex domestic partners have higher enrollment rates in employers' health benefit plans when compared to same-sex couples. A study conducted by Common Ground in the 1990s found that enrollment numbers for unmarried couples are highest for younger, opposite-sex couples (cited in Winfield, 2007). According to the U.S. Census Bureau's Current Population Survey, only 60 percent of opposite-sex unmarried partners were under the age of 35, as compared to 65 percent of same-sex unmarried partners, suggesting that opposite-sex domestic partners tended to be younger. Additionally, opposite-sex couples were also more likely to have children than same-sex couples, and consequently have a greater need for benefits coverage particularly for their children dependents.

Furthermore, employers are concerned with the overall expense incurred for healthcare coverage of domestic partners, particularly for same-sex couples. As noted,

---

* It is important to note that an analysis of the "rate" at which same-sex or opposite-sex domestic partners elect to participate in an employer's health benefit plan is impossible to know at this point. Although most public employers know whether or not an employee is married and are thus able to calculate the rate at which married employees elect no coverage or employee only coverage or family coverage, most public employers do not know whether or not their employees are in a domestic partnership. On the other hand, if it is a requirement that an employee be registered with the government employer to have access to domestic partnership benefits, then it would not be surprising to find that 100 percent of the employees who registered their domestic partnership elected to enroll in the benefits. Once public employers in states that permit same-sex marriages or which register civil unions or domestic partnerships start collecting data on an employee's status, just as they do with marriage, it will be possible for a more accurate assessment of the rate at which domestic partners elect particular employee benefits.

there was initial anxiety with the disproportionate number of HIV/AIDS infections among gay men would inflate healthcare costs (HRC, 2007), although some employers noted that the HIV/AIDS risk for lesbians was much lower than for heterosexual women (Employee Benefits Research Institute, 2004). Moreover, the cost of treating AIDS patients was viewed by many as extremely expensive in the 1980s, even though it was a relatively short-term expense since the time lapse between diagnosis and death was often not very long (Nash et al., 2000). However, such concerns have lessened over time as the actual costs for treating HIV/AIDS proved to be not necessarily more expensive than treating other chronic and life threatening illnesses such as diabetes, cancer, or heart disease (Employee Benefits Research Institute, 2004; Bromer, 2007; HRC, 2007).

On the other hand, some observers expected the benefits cost for opposite-sex domestic couples to be higher, as they are more likely to have children resulting in the need for additional healthcare for the dependent children, as well as for pregnancy and maternity leave (Gochin & Kleiner, 1999). Whether this seeming cost advantage to same-sex couples will persist, however, may need to be reconsidered. Badgett and Gates (2004), using data from the 2000 census, note that lesbian and gay male domestic partner households are raising children at, respectively, three-fourths and half the rate that married heterosexual couples are (p. 3) and are just as likely to have one of the partners at home engaged in full-time childcare (p. 6). Although it is difficult to have an accurate estimate on the costs associated with healthcare coverage, experience suggests that the incremental healthcare costs for both same-sex and opposite-sex couples are less than 3 percent (HRC, 2007).

Several years ago, a report was circulated that predicted dire cost consequences for employers who offered domestic partnership health benefits (Hamrick, 2002). The report was based on the study of small employers in California and it found that the "loss ratio" (healthcare costs to the insurer as a percentage of premiums) was higher for same-sex domestic partners than for opposite-sex partners (married or domestic partners). Such a finding is of concern because it can result in a future rate increase based on past experience. The same would happen to any plan that was experience rated when a single employee in a small employer's plan has a catastrophic health emergency. What the study does not take into account, however, is that because of financial and tax penalties imposed on any employee who elects domestic partnership benefits, domestic partnership couples make a more strategic decision about the costs and benefits of enrolling than married couples. An explanation of the factors that an employee who is considering signing up for domestic partnership health benefits must take into consideration will help make the reasons for this strategic decision making clear.

To begin, it must be recognized that most public employers share the costs of health benefits with the employee regardless of whether or not the employee is enrolling a plan to cover him- or herself only (a single plan) or him- or herself plus a spouse or dependent children (a family plan) (Couch, 2003). As noted, the latter plans usually receive a greater dollar amount subsidy than the former. Under existing federal tax laws and the tax laws of most states, the employer contribution to the employee's health plan of either type, single or family, is not considered part of the employee's salary. However, if the employer elects to provide coverage for a person who is not the spouse or dependent child of the employee, e.g., a domestic partner, the value of that employer contribution towards the cost of the health benefit premium (or value to the employee in a self-funded health plan) must be treated as income to the employee. As income, the value of the benefit is subject to both regular income tax (federal and most state income taxes) and FICA and Medicare taxes (meaning that both the employee and the employer must make higher FICA and Medicare tax payments). One expert estimated the impact:

> Take a person of average income in the country, enrolled in an employer health plan of average generosity. If the plan is covering their domestic partner, the employee is likely to face an additional $1,600 in annual tax liability (income and payroll tax) as a result of that coverage.

Miller [citing James M. Delaplane] 2007

Some employers address this issue by requiring employees to pay the cost of the additional coverage for the domestic partner from their own existing salaries. This avoids the increase in FICA and Medicare taxes paid by the employer, but substantially reduces the take-home salary of the employee electing the domestic partnership coverage (New Jersey, 2006). Another way that these taxes can be avoided is if the domestic partner is in fact dependent on the employee for federal tax purposes which generally means that the employee is providing more than 50 percent of the living expenses of the domestic partner (Crenshaw, 2005). In such cases, additional paperwork must be completed demonstrating this financial dependency. Other public employers, such as the state of California (Hiatt, 2002), have passed tax laws that treat an employer's contribution towards the cost of a health plan covering a domestic partnership health plan in the same manner as the contributions for a married couple's plan are treated. This equal treatment is certainly appreciated by those who benefit from it, but the payroll and management information systems certainly have a programming challenge before them in terms of calculating an employee's taxes because domestic partnership benefits are now taxed for federal purposes but not for state purposes.

Furthermore, most public employers have arranged their health plans in such a way that the employee pays his or her portion of the cost with pretax dollars. To the extent that the employee contribution for the family plan exceeds the contribution for a single plan, the person using the family plan to cover a domestic partner would be required to pay that difference with after-tax dollars. And, unlike the cost of a spouse's or child's medical expenses not paid by insurance (e.g., deductibles, co-payments), the medical expenses of a domestic partner or a domestic partner's children (assuming they were not adopted by nor a legal dependent of the employee partner) cannot be paid with pretax dollars from a Health Benefit Flexible Spending Account (Crenshaw, 2005; Miller, 2007).

Thus, given the significant additional cost to the employee who wishes to enroll in an employer's domestic partnership health plan, it is not surprising to find that only those who anticipate needing to use its benefits rather extensively enroll. The previously referenced study was examining the "loss ratio" only in terms of the value of the premium that the insurance company received from the employer (which was no different from what it received for coverage of a married employee's family) and not what the cost was to the employee who was enrolled for domestic partner coverage. Some members of the U.S. Congress are attempting to address this issue through the "Tax Equity for Health Beneficiaries Act of 2007" (H.R. 1820) which would have federal tax laws amended to allow certain types of beneficiaries, such as domestic partners, to receive the same type of tax treatment that plans provided for married couples and for dependent children currently get (Miller, 2007).

Federal law requires that employers make health benefits available to an employee for certain period of time after employment ends under the Consolidated Omnibus Budget Reconciliation Act (COBRA) of 1986. This law also says that the spouse or dependent children who lose coverage under the health benefit plan in certain circumstances (e.g., divorcing the employee or a child stops being an eligible dependent) must be allowed to extend their coverage under the employer's health plan for a certain period of time. Extending coverage to a person, whose domestic partnership with an employee ends, however, is not mandated by the federal law (U.S. Department of Labor, 2007). The public employer, however, does have the option to extend COBRA coverage to domestic partners and their dependents if they wish (Las Cruces, 2007). As the entire cost of this extended coverage is borne by the person taking advantage of it and the fact that the employer is allowed to recover a 2 percent administrative fee, there is no additional direct cost to the governing jurisdiction, although experience of the COBRA participants is considered as part of the group's overall health experience if that is used in setting premium rates.

18.4.2 Retirement and Death Benefits

The issue of providing retirement benefits for domestic partnerships is often complicated by the fact that pensions are provided through a separate public entity, a state retirement board, for example. In jurisdictions that provide defined contribution retirement plans, this is not usually a problem because, like life insurance, the employee simply names a beneficiary who will receive access to the benefits once the employee has died. And with the recent passage of the Pension Protection Act (2006), tax penalties are no longer imposed for rolling over the benefits of a defined contribution plan into the individual retirement account (IRA) of any beneficiary, not just a spouse as had been true before.

However, for defined benefit plans, many jurisdictions have a statewide pension board that both establishes pension policies (including eligibility policies) and administers the payment of the benefits of state and local government employees and of teachers, as well. Public safety employees, such as police and firefighters, often have pension systems with their own governing boards because the structure of their pension benefits is often quite different from those of other public employees. Most defined benefit retirement plans provide an option for a retiring employee who is married to elect a reduced monthly pension payment in exchange for the right of his or her spouse to receive a survivor's benefit or pension payment should the employee predecease the spouse. The question arises as to whether or not a similar benefit can or should be offered to a retiring employee with a domestic partner. Where the jurisdiction that makes the decision to provide domestic partnership benefits to employees also sets the policy for the pension program the policies can be made consistent, but jurisdictions that rely on a pension system set up by a different level of government may have a difficult time reconciling the retirement benefits of employees in marriages and those with domestic partners.

Public employers generally offer two types of death benefits—a survivor's benefit based on contributions in an employees as-yet-unclaimed retirement account and a death benefit for an employee killed in the performance of his or her job. In both these cases, it is possible for an employee to name anyone as the beneficiary, although the tax consequences of receiving the payment in either case are different if one is the married spouse or dependent child (usually not taxable) or the domestic partner (taxable as gift income). Problems may arise, of course, if the employee has failed to name a beneficiary and state intestacy laws come into play to assign the benefits. If state law does not include a designation for domestic partners in the testation sequence, they will be ineligible to inherit.

18.4.3 Life Insurance

Again, with respect to the employee him- or herself, life insurance is relatively simple because the insured party has the authority to name anyone as the designated beneficiary. A spouse or a domestic partner can be named without much controversy. Failure to make a beneficiary designation, however, can be problematic because the order of who benefits is set by state law rather than the employing jurisdiction. In states with statewide comprehensive civil union and domestic partnership laws, this is one of the issues that is usually addressed making domestic partners or civil union partners an equivalent to a spouse in the intestacy law (typically the order is spouse, children, parents, siblings, nearest next of kin). Thus, in many jurisdictions without statewide laws, an employee's domestic partner would not automatically inherit the life insurance proceeds unless they were the designated beneficiary. This problem can be avoided relatively easily by ensuring that employees make a beneficiary designation and keep it current. A second aspect of life insurance that can arise is family coverage. Some employers offer their employees the opportunity to buy reduced cost coverage for a spouse and children. Because this insurance is usually offered through a third party (i.e., a private insurance company) the issue may become one of creating a contractual requirement that the vendor be willing to insure domestic partners and the children of a domestic partnership in the same manner and on the same terms as they insure members of family created by marriage.

18.4.4   Leave

Some benefits, like annual leave, jury leave, and military leave, are exclusive to the employee and do not involve any particular benefits for family members. Two other types of leaves, however, clearly do involve members of one's family, namely sick leave and bereavement or funeral leave. Although sick leave when an employee him- or herself is ill is not problematic, most sick leave programs offered by public entities allow the use of sick leave to care for a family member such as a spouse or a child. To treat domestic partnerships equitably, the same provisions that apply to families established by marriages need to be extended to families established by domestic partnerships. Likewise, bereavement or funeral leave which authorizes a person to miss work to attend the funeral of a person related by blood or marriage should be extended to a person related by blood or domestic partnership for those employees in such relationships. Some employers, of course, have avoided the need for the distinction among these different types of leaves by moving to a system of "personal leave" that does not ask for reasons or justification for the absence. For many jurisdictions, these leave benefits are the easiest to offer to employees and may be put in place before some of the more complicated and expensive benefit issues are addressed.

There is no inherent additional cost to providing leave benefits to persons who will use the leave to attend to illnesses or deaths within the domestic partnerships because the employer would have offered those benefits to the employee had he or she chosen to enter a marriage rather than a domestic partnership. It is possible that some employees who elect to enter into a domestic partnership might not elect to enter into a marriage if it were available, so in that respect the cost may be higher than it would be if same-sex marriages were permitted and the employer followed the model of some Massachusetts employers who discontinued benefits to domestic partnerships once same-sex marriages were legal.

18.4.5   Other Benefit Programs

Although health benefits, retirement, and leave are the principal employee benefit plans most employees consider when accepting a position, there are some other benefit programs whose design may need to be modified if the employer wishes to be inclusive of employees in domestic partnerships. One of these benefit programs is workers' compensation. Each state has its own workers' compensation program (and the federal government has its own for federal employees). Although the plans are designed to compensate employees injured on the job, some plans determine the amount of compensation the employee (or the employee's heirs in the case of death) will receive on the basis of whether or not the employee is single or has dependents (Whittington, 2005). A spouse or minor children will automatically qualify as dependents and, thus, a higher compensation payment. A public employer who wants to provide a similar benefit for employees with domestic partners will have to adjust the plan, if possible. The tax implications are unclear at this time because most workers' compensation payments to employees are tax free, payments based on treating domestic partners as dependents may not be eligible for the favorable tax treatment provided to spouses and minor children. Again, neither local governments nor private employers may have the authority to make this change on their own (Simpson, 2005).

Another benefit program offered by many public employers is an Employee Assistance Program (Johnson & O'Neill, 1989; Mani, 1991). These programs are designed to assist an employee who finds that problems not directly related to work are interfering with his or her performance on the job. Problems like alcohol or drug abuse, relationship problems, difficulty finding childcare, financial worries, or sometimes legal concerns can distract an employee from his or her assigned duties. By providing Employee Assistance Programs, an employer is able to help direct an employee to appropriate professional services that will, hopefully, reduce the distraction caused by the problem and enable the employee to concentrate on the work at hand. Because so often an employee's problems are related to their life at home, employees in domestic partnership are just as likely to need access to these resources as married employees and it is important that this be recognized in the design of the program and in any direct services contracted by the employing agency (Las Cruces, 2007, §1205).

18.5 Conclusion

There is now nearly a quarter century of experience of public sector employers offering domestic partnership benefits to their employees. Hundreds of local governments, school boards, transportation districts, airport authorities, and other governmental entities now offer these benefits to their employees. In some states—California, Oregon, Vermont, Connecticut, for example—because the state has chosen to formally recognize same-sex partnerships, every public entity in the state is required to offer domestic partnership benefits to employees. Additional public sector employers in other states are considering making domestic partnership benefits available to their employees, but they may be limited by state laws that restrict the authority of local governments and other substate public employers.

The issue of whether or not local governments can offer domestic partnership benefits has reemerged in some states as a consequence of states passing vaguely worded state constitutional amendments that prohibit the state and local governments from treating anything other than a civilly authorized marriage between a man and a woman as if it were a marriage. Despite a long history of cases where courts have found that domestic partnerships were not faux marriages, but a different type of relationship altogether (Gossett, 1999), some public sector domestic partnership programs are facing renewed legal challenges under these new constitutional amendments (e.g., Michigan, see Bell & Witsel, 2007). Jurisdictions must ensure that they are legally able to offer domestic partnership benefits or, at a minimum, that they are not legally proscribed from offering them.

Implementation of health benefit programs for domestic partnerships is not easy. Because of the U.S. system of federalism, all levels of governments affect the implementation process. The federal government's tax laws make administering health benefits particularly challenging. The same is true of state tax laws if the public employer offering the benefits is a lower level of government. Other benefit programs, such as life insurance or retirement plans, especially defined contribution plans, that allow employees to name anyone as a beneficiary are easier to administer. Defined benefit retirement plans and workers' compensation plans will vary in implementation difficulty depending largely on state laws governing them.

There is not good evidence that providing domestic partnership benefits will necessarily result in disproportionately higher costs. In all cases where the jurisdictions choose to subsidize employees with family members at a higher rate than they subsidize single employees, opening programs to employees with domestic partners will make more employees eligible for those higher subsidies. This expense, however, should not be unwelcomed unless the employer had a deliberate policy of trying to keep single employees as a certain percentage of the workforce to hold costs down. Because of the design of many employer health benefit programs and the way in which federal tax laws work to the disadvantage of the employee participating in the program, there may occasionally be some adverse selection (from the insurer's point of view) in those cases. Unlike most married couples who almost automatically elect to enroll in a health benefit plan (the only question being whether the husband's or the wife's plan is the most generous), an employee with a domestic partner has to engage in a much more careful cost–benefit analysis and be prepared to spend far more than his or her married colleague for the same coverage. Benefit program redesign and, more importantly, changes to federal tax laws could reduce this problem substantially.

However, overall the trend seems to be in the direction of more rather than fewer public employers providing coverage for the domestic partners of their employees. The private sector continues to offer the benefits as a way of maintaining a competitive edge in recruiting the best employees. To remain competitive, public sector employers will need to offer similar benefit packages. But personnel policies in government are never designed on purely business principles. Public personnel policies must also reflect community values as expressed through public opinion and through legislation, even if they seem nonproductive from an "efficiency" point of view. In 2006 and 2007, the University of Wisconsin publicly struggled with the conflict between the need to compete for, and retain, the best faculty and the recent passage of an anti-same-sex marriage state constitutional amendment (Foley, 2006; Forster, 2007). Universities in other states are facing the same issue (Gershman, 2007) and local governments, which already have a history of fighting court battles to protect their right to offer such benefits, are likely to do so again if they are told the benefits must be discontinued.

Among the signs that attitudes towards these benefit programs may be changing is the recent passage of the Pension Protection Act of 2006 that allows an employee to assign money from a tax-protected retirement plan to be transferred to a domestic partner (or any other person designated by the employee) without tax penalties if it is rolled over into an IRA. Additionally, domestic partnerships might soon benefit from two pieces of federal legislation introduced and are gaining an increasing number of sponsors—the Domestic Partnership Benefits and Obligations Act of 2007 which would include federal employees and their domestic partners in existing federal employee benefit programs and the Tax Equity for Health Beneficiaries Act of 2007 which would remove the tax penalties currently faced by employees who enroll in health plans that cover their domestic partners.

A final interesting trend in the coverage of domestic partnership benefits concerns the changing definition of the concept as states adopt statewide domestic partnership registries, civil unions, or same-sex marriage policies. As noted at the beginning of the chapter, the majority of public sector entities that offer domestic partnership benefits include both same-sex and opposite-sex unmarried partners. But as states adopt policies allowing a legal relationship short of same-sex marriages, such as civil unions or domestic partnerships, the new relationship status is limited to same-sex couples only. As employers move to requiring that eligibility for employee benefits requires being registered with the state in a civil union, for example, benefits that were previously available to unmarried opposite-sex couples are eliminated. And in the one state that allows same-sex marriages, Massachusetts, the discussion of whether or not public (or private) employers should offer domestic partnership benefits has taken a sharp turn and put advocates somewhat on the defensive. If same-sex couples can marry, will there continue to be a need for domestic partnership benefits (Symonds, 2004)?

References

Ash, M.A. & Badgett, M.V.L. 2006. Separate and unequal: The effect of unequal access to employment-based health insurance on same-sex and unmarried different-sex couples. *Contemporary Economic Policy*, 24(4): 582–599.

Badgett, M.V.L. & Gates, G. 2004. *The Business Cost Impact of Marriage for Same-sex Couples*. A Joint Publication of the Human Rights Campaign Foundation and the Institute for Gay and Lesbian Strategic Studies. Washington, DC: Human Rights Campaign Foundation.

Bailey, R.W. 1999. *Gay Politics, Urban Politics*. New York City: Columbia University Press.

Becker, L. 1995. Recognition of domestic partnerships by governmental entities and private employers. *National Journal of Sexual Orientation Law*, 1(1): 91–104. Retrieved on May 6, 2007 from http://www.ibiblio.org/gaylaw/issue1/becker.html.

Bell, D. & Witsel, F. 2007. Appeal likely in gay case: Battle looms in ruling against same-sex benefits. *Detroit Free Press*, February 3. Accessed from LEXIS NEXIS.

Bennet, L. & Gates, G.J. 2004. *The Cost of Marriage Inequality to Children and Their Same-Sex Parents*. Washington, DC: Human Rights Campaign. Retrieved on May 19, 2007 from http://www.hrc.org/Content/ContentGroups/Publications1/kids_doc_final.pdf.

Bowman, C.A. & Cornish, B.M. 1992. A more perfect union: A legal and social analysis of domestic partnership ordinances. *Columbia Law Review*, 92(5): 1164–1211.

Bromer, Z. 2007. Domestic Partner Benefits: From Marginal to Mainstream. Retrieved on April 12, 2007 from http://www.salary.com/sitesearch/layoutscripts/sisl_display.asp?filename=&path=/destinationsearch/personal/par177_body.html.

Chuang, Y.T., Church, R., & Ophir, R. 2005. Tug of war: The rise of same-sex partner health benefits in Fortune 500 corporations, 1990–2003. Paper presented at the 65th Annual Meeting of the Academy of Management, Honolulu, Hawaii, August 2005.

Colvin, R.A. 2006. Innovation of state-level gay rights laws: The role of Fortune 500 corporations. *Business and Society Review*, 111(4): 363–386.

Corporate Leadership Council 2004. *Prudential Financial: Enhancing the Traditional Domestic Partner Benefits*. Washington, DC: Corporate Executive Board.

Couch, D. 2003. City cuts its share of benefit costs. *Denver Post*, August 19, B-03.

Cox, T. and Blake, S. 1991. Managing Cultural Diversity: implications for Organizational Competitiveness. *Academy of Management Executive*, 5(3): 45–56.

Crenshaw, A.B. 2005. Unexpected expense. *Washington Post*, May 5, p. E01.

Croft, J. 1999. Domestic partner benefits fight ends. *Atlanta Journal Constitution*, October 26, p. A1.

Denike, M. 2007. Religion, rights, and relationships: The dream of relational equality. *Hypatia*, 22(1): 71–91.

Domestic Partnership Benefits and Obligations Act. 1997. H.R. 2761. 105th Congress, 1st Session.

Domestic Partnership Benefits and Obligations Act. 2007. H.R. 4838. 110th Congress, 1st Session.

Duncan, W.C. 2001. Domestic partnership laws in the United States: A review and critique. *Brigham Young University Law Review*, 3: 961–992.

Employee Benefits Research Institute. 2004, March. *Domestic Partner Benefits: Facts and Background*. Retrieved on May 19, 2007 from http://www.ebri.org/pdf/publications/facts/0304fact.pdf.

Ferguson, A. 2007. Gay marriage: An American and feminist dilemma. *Hypatia*, 22(1): 39–57.

Foley, R.J. 2006. UW-Madison deals with fallout over gay marriage amendment. *The Associated Press State & Local Wire*. (November 16). Retrieved on May 31, 2007 from LEXIS/NEXIS.

Forster, S. 2007. UW system makes case for partner benefits. *Milwaukee Sentinel Journal*. (March 23). Retrieved on May 31, 2007 from LEXIS/NEXIS.

Gay and Lesbian Advocates and Defenders. 2005. Some Questions and Answers about the New Connecticut Civil Unions Law. Retrieved on May 29, 2007 from http://www.glad.org/marriage/CT_Civil_Union_Q_and_A.pdf.

Gershman, D. 2007. U-M studies same-sex care options. *Ann Arbor [MI] News* (April 3). Retrieved on May 31, 2007 from LEXIS/NEXIS.

Gochin, G.A. and Kleiner, B.H. 1999. Expanding the family definition: Health care for domestic partners. *Egnal Opportunities International.* 18(516): 111–120.

Gossett, C.W. 2007. Berkeley extends benefits to domestic partners of city employees. In L. Faderman et al. (Eds.) *Great Events from History: Gay, Lesbian, Bisexual, Transgender Events.* Pasadena, California: Salem Press.

Gossett, C.W. 1994. Domestic partnership benefits: Public sector patterns. *Review of Public Personnel Administration,* 14(1): 64–84.

Gossett, C.W. 1999. Dillon Goes to Court: Legal Challenges to Local Ordinances Providing Domestic Partnership Benefits. Paper presented at the annual meeting of the American Political Science Association, Atlanta, Georgia.

Gram, D. 2000. Univ. of Vermont says couples must be civilly unified to get benefits. *Associated Press State & Local Wire,* September 27. Accessed from LEXIS/NEXIS.

Hamrick, M.E. 2002. *The Hidden Costs of Domestic Partner Benefits.* Corporate Resource Council. Retrieved on May 25, 2007 from http://www.corporateresourcecouncil. org/white_papers/Hidden_Costs.pdf.

Hiatt, D. 2002. Domestic partner benefits changes under California law. *Hanson Bridgett Newsletter.* Retrieved on May 25, 2007 from http://hbmvr.com/newsletters/EmployeeBenefitsUpdate/EBenefitsJan02.html.

Hostetler, D. & Pynes, J.E. 1995. Domestic partnership benefits: Dispelling the myths. *Review of Public Personnel Administration,* 15(1): 41–59.

Human Rights Campaign 2007. *The State of the Workplace for Gay, Lesbian, Bisexual, and Transgender Americans, 2006–2007.* Washington, DC: Human Rights Campaign Foundation. Retrieved on November 21, 2007 from http://www.hrc.org/documents/ state_of _the_workplace.pdf

Hunt, G. & Rayside, D. 2000. Labor union response to diversity in Canada and the United States. *Industrial Relations,* 39(3): 401–444.

Johnson, A.T. & O'Neill, N. 1989. Employee assistance programs and the troubled employee in the public sector workplace. *Review of Public Personnel Administration,* 9(3): 66–80.

Las Cruces, New Mexico. Human Resources Department. 2007. §1200—Benefits. Retrieved on May 29, 2007 from http://www.las-cruces.org/HR/per-manual/ sec1200.shtm.

Mani, B. 1991. Difficulties, assumptions, and choices in evaluating employee assistance programs. *Review of Public Personnel Administration,* 12(1): 70–80.

Martocchio, J.J. 2006. *Employee Benefits: A Primer for Human Resource Professionals.* New York: McGraw-Hill Irwin.

Miller, S. 2007. Partnership Benefits Growing; Taxes Dimish Value. Society for Human Resources Management, Compensation & Benefits Library. Retrieved on April 16 from http://www.shrm.org/rewards/library_published/benefits/nonIC/CMS_021128.asp.

Naff, K.C. & Kellough, J.E. 2003. Ensuring employment equity: Are federal diversity programs making a difference? *International Journal of Public Administration,* 26(2): 1307–1336.

Nash, D., Fordyce, E.J., Singh, T., & Forlenza, S. 2000. Trends in mortality rates among reported Acquired Immune Deficiency Syndrome (AIDS) case patients in New York

City, 1990–1998. Paper presented and the International Conference on AIDS, July 9–14, abstract no. TuPeC3385. Retrieved on May 19, 2007 from http://gateway.nlm. nih.gov/MeetingAbstracts/102239345.html.

National Center for Lesbian Rights. 2007. The California Insurance Equality Act How To Use It and What It Means for You and Your Family. Retrieved on May 29, 2007 from http://www.nclrights.org/publications/ab2208_faq_0904.htm.

New Jersey. Treasury Department. 2006. Chapter 246, P.L. 2003—Domestic partnership Act benefits: Frequently asked questions and answers—State Health Benefits Program (SHBP) questions. Updated August 31, 2006. Retrieved on May 17, 2007 from http://www.state.nj.us/treasury/pensions/chapt_246_q&a.htm.

New York City. Office of Labor Relations. 2007. Health Benefits. Retrieved on May 6, 2007 from http://www.nyc.gov/html/olr/html/health/prog_info_enrollment.shtml.

Pension Protection Act. 2006. Pub. L. No. 109–280, §829, 120 Stat. 1001.

Portland, Maine. Human Resources. 2005. Employee Benefits Brochure. Retrieved on May 6, 2007 from http://www.ci.portland.me.us/hr/empbenefits.pdf.

Reddick, C.G. & Coggburn, J.D. 2007. State government employee health benefits in the united states: Choices and effectiveness. *Review of Public Personnel Administration*, 27(1): 5–20.

Reed, L.J. & Friedman, B.A. 2005. Employer recognition of same-sex relationships in the United States: Legal and economic implications. *Employee Responsibilities and Rights Journal*, 17(4): 245–260.

Riccucci, N.M. & Gossett, C.W. 1996. Employment discrimination in state and local government: The lesbian and gay male experience. *American Review of Public Administration*, 26(2): 175–200.

Rubaii-Barrett, N. & Wise, L.R. 2007. From want ads to web sites: What diversity messages are state governments projecting? *Review of Public Personnel Administration*, 27(1): 21–38.

Shepherd, L.C. 2006. Majority of big firms covering domestic partners. *Employee Benefit News*, 20(12): 1, 48.

Simpson, A.G. 2005. N.Y. court denies workers' compensation survivor benefits for same-sex partner. *Insurance Journal*. March 23. Retrieved on May 29, 2007 from http://www.insurancejournal.com/news/east/2005/03/23/52968.htm.

Symonds, W.C. 2004. Gay Marriage's Minefield for Businesses. *Business Week*, May 14.

Tax Equity for Health Beneficiaries Act of 2007, H.R. 1820, 110th Congress, 1st Session. 2007.

Thomson, L. 2006. S.L. Can Offer Benefits to More Than Spouses. Deseret Morning News [Salt Lake City], May 23. Retrieved on May 31, 2007 from LEXIS/NEXIS.

U.S. Department of Labor. 2007. FAQs about COBRA continuation health coverage. Retrieved on May 29, 2007 from http://www.dol.gov/ebsa/faqs/faq_consumer_cobra. html.

Whittington, G. 2005. Changes in workers' compensation laws in 2004. *Monthly Labor Review Online*, 128(1). Retrieved on May 29, 2007 from http://www.bls.gov/opub/mlr/2005/01/contents.htm.

Winfield, L. 2007. Domestic Partner Benefits—A Primer. Retrieved on April 12, 2007 from http://www.common-grnd.com/Domestic_Partner_Benefits.doc.

Chapter 19

Transgender-Inclusive Workplaces and Health Benefits: New Administrative Territory for Public Administrators

Roddrick Colvin

CONTENTS

"There is a growing acceptance of the real-life diversity of people's personal life in the United States, that whatever people's values or beliefs are, diversity exists."

Ellen Galinsky
Work Life Leadership Council

"In order to be as innovative as we have to be and as competitive as we have to be, we have to avail ourselves of all the talent out there. Everyone has something to contribute. Wherever the talent is coming from, we want that."

Joyce E. Tucker
Boeing

19.1   Introduction

In the public, private, and nonprofit sectors, employers are coming to understand that diversity is an inevitable and valuable part of the workplace. Our notions about diversity are constantly changing and expanding as politics, economics, and science influence and increase our understanding of the world. As these perspectives change, the core functions and issues of managing employee benefits become even more daunting for human resources managers as they attempt to ensure and maintain equity among employees while confronting emergent challenges. One such challenge is the efficacious and equitable distribution of benefits for transgender employees.

This chapter explores the efforts of local jurisdictions to manage (from an administrative perspective) the issues that arise when an employee transitions for one gender to the other. In presenting these issues, this chapter highlights current municipal policy adoption and implementation trends, discusses the unique health and medical needs of transgender employees and the associated administrative challenges these needs present, and examines some best practices.

19.2   Background and Definitions

The term transgender refers to people whose gender identity and expression differ from their biological sex (Letellier, 2003). This includes intersexed people, transsexuals, cross-dressers, and others who do not conform to societal expectations of gender (Lombardi et al., 2001). People who are in the process of aligning their gender with their sex are called "in transition." Transitioning can include changing one's name, taking hormones, undergoing surgery to alter the body, and changing legal documents to reflect one's new sex. Although there is very little data, the best estimates are that roughly one in 30,000 adults transitions from male to female and two in 100,000 adults transitions from female to male (Horton, 2006).

Gender identity and expression are often thought of in the context of sexual orientation; however, these concepts should be distinguished and their differences highlighted. Gender identity is a person's internal sense of maleness, femaleness, or something other than these two specific genders. Sexual orientation refers to the gender or sex of the person to whom one is physically or emotionally attracted (Letellier, 2003). Homosexual, bisexual, and heterosexual are all sexual orientations. Because sexual orientation has to do with attraction to someone else, and not one's own gender, transgender people—like the rest of the population—can be homosexual, bisexual, or heterosexual.

Of course, historically and politically, the gay rights movement and the transgender rights movement have been linked. Under the rubric of sexual minorities, both communities have fought to pass more inclusive nondiscrimination civil rights laws (D'Emilio, 1983).

Coming to terms with one's gender identity can be a tremendous inner struggle for self-acceptance. Additionally, transgender people have to manage their identity with family, friends, coworkers, and the broader society. In the process, transgender people may face shame, fear, internalized phobias, fear of disclosing their status, and other self-imposed limitations on self-expression (Currah and Minter, 2000).

Although gender identity may not be clearly visible to others, gender expression is usually visible to family, friends, and coworkers, and may be visible to strangers as well. Given rigid societal ideas about the meanings of male and female and masculine and feminine, is it not hard to imagine the challenges and societal resistance that nonconformists like transgender people must deal with.

19.3   Harassment, Violence, and Discrimination

Transgender people regularly face harassment, violence, and discrimination due to prejudice and others' lack of understanding. Discrimination occurs when governments, institutions, or individuals treat people differently based on their personal characteristics, such as (but not limited to) sex, sexual orientation, gender identity, race, ethnicity, age, or health status (Supateera and Kleiner, 1999). Such discrimination can take a number of forms, including direct discrimination, indirect discrimination, and harassment. Direct discrimination is an explicit policy or law that fosters unequal treatment. The ban on transgender persons serving in the U.S. military is an example of direct discrimination. Indirect discrimination can be an implicit side effect of another policy or decision. An example of indirect discrimination based on gender identity or expression might be found in an employer's dress code. A rule that women must wear skirts potentially discriminates against transgender employees: such a rule might adversely affect biologically female transgender people, for whom trousers may be an important expression of gender identity.

Harassment is behavior that "has the purpose or effect of creating an intimidating, hostile, offensive, or disturbing environment" (Shaffer et al., 2000). Derogatory remarks or jokes could constitute actions contributing to an offensive environment. Most nondiscrimination laws and policies address direct discrimination. Harassment protections, although not as common in laws and policies, has been addressed via court rulings. Few laws and policies address indirect discrimination.

Although researchers and advocates have attempted to document transgender discrimination systematically, anecdotal data and self-reporting continue to be the main sources of information. This does not devalue the reports and surveys that do exist; rather, it highlights the difficulties that exist in gathering accurate and valid data regarding transgender discrimination. To date, little data exists that provides an accurate and reliable picture of transgender-related discrimination.

The limited available research suggests that transgender people face enormous pressure to conform to their birth gender. The lack of conformity to this social pressure helps to generate the discrimination, harassment, and violence they face. Lombardi et al. (2001) offer the most comprehensive study of violence and discrimination against transgender people. In their research, the authors surveyed transgender people through community events and the Internet. With a final sample of 402 valid surveys, the authors concluded that 59.5 percent of the sample had experienced violence or harassment in their lifetimes, and 37.1 percent had experienced economic discrimination. The authors also found a strong link between economic discrimination and violence, leading them to conclude that the workplace can be one of the most dangerous places for transgender people. Their conclusions are similar to several smaller studies, including that of Minter and Daley (2003), who found that nearly 50 percent of their 155-person sample experienced employment discrimination based on gender identity. Oswald, Gebbie, and Culton (2000) surveyed 527 rural lesbian, gay, bisexual, and transgender (LGBT) people and found that coworkers were the most likely perpetrators of sexual orientation or gender-based harassment.

In addition to general workplace violence, harassment, and discrimination, a few studies have explored schools as unique workplace environments. Irwin (1996) explored the workplace experiences of 120 gay men, lesbians, and transgender people employed as teachers, academics, and educators. Irwin found that harassment was widespread in the educational environment. Irwin's conclusions match the results of Sausa (2002), who interviewed transgender students, staff, and faculty about harassment and discrimination and found that schools were often ill-equipped to meet the needs of transgender people on campus—if not ignorant of their needs altogether. As a result, transgender people are often isolated or ignored.

These initial studies point to a disheartening trend and suggest that additional actions are needed to ensure the workplace safety of transgender people. Even without systemic data, a prima facie consideration of transgender people propounds that harassment, violence, and discrimination are real and that corrective policies would benefit them in the workplace.

19.4   Creating a More Tolerant Environment

Given the violence, harassment, and discrimination that transgender people face and the challenges they come up against while in transition, efforts to create a supportive workplace require organizational changes on the part of employers. For transgender people and those in transition, there are many personnel, policy, legal, and medical needs that will ameliorate the workplace and lessen the struggles of their employees.

Specifically, employers can add "gender identity and expression" to the organization's workplace-wide nondiscrimination policies, establish guidelines and a contact person for addressing transgender issues, include transgender information in diversity training programs, ensure that an employee's gender status always remains confidential and private, and establish protocols for changing an employee's personnel and administrative records to reflect his or her new gender post-transition.

From a policy perspective, transgender people face an array of challenges in everyday life. From finding housing to accessing social services, many policies systematically discriminate based on gender status. In the workplace, too, there are policies that present challenges for transgender people (Sheehy, 2004). Employers can address some of these workplace policies by developing protocols that grant restroom and locker room access according to an employee's full-time gender presentation and allowing for gender-neutral modes of dress that avoid stereotyping.

Legal and medical issues are not only the most pervasive challenges transgender people face, they are also the most difficult to address. People in transition have to change their legal status as men or women, which includes applying for new birth certificates and drivers' licenses. The status of their marriages, adoption rights, child custody rights, and inheritances are often called into question and can depend on court interpretations of transgender status in their state of residence. Medical services—both routine and transgender-specific—are often denied to people in transition. But for people in transition—from those beginning to receive hormones to those undergoing gender reassignment surgeries—health and medical needs are of tremendous consequence.

There are several workplace-related legal and medical policies that employers can consider, including removing exclusions for medically necessary treatments and procedures from company-provided healthcare, permitting the use of health- or disability-related leave associated with medically necessary treatments and procedures, and allowing equal access to spousal benefits regardless of the gender of the spouse.

Employers who are interested in creating transgender-friendly workplaces must change or implement policies that do not discriminate against these employees. This often means changing internal processes as well as personnel policies and employee benefits. Given the nature and scope of the changes needed, human resource agencies have a primary and central role in implementing and enforcing transgender-inclusive nondiscrimination employment policies.

19.5   Data and Information about Transgender-Friendly Communities

Ideally, employers interested in creating a more transgender-inclusive workplace adopt and implement the necessary personnel, policy, legal, and medical policies. However, there are many constraints that limit the ability of administrators to act on all of these fronts. Nevertheless, there are communities that have attempted to accommodate the needs of their transgender workers.

The most visible effort is the sharp rise in the number of communities adopting nondiscrimination policies directed at protecting transgender people. Different communities have approached this protection differently. Some envelop gender identity protection inside existing sexual orientation language; others provide protection within the context of sex discrimination. Most communities prohibit discrimination by adding a separate category: gender identity or expression. As of 2005, six states and over eighty-nine local jurisdictions had laws that—at a minimum—prohibited discrimination on the basis of gender identity and expression (Colvin, 2007). The coverage provided by the state and local jurisdictions covers 28 percent of the U.S. population (Mottet, 2006). Leading the effort to innovate transgender protections in employment nondiscrimination are cities. From 1975 to 2005, 89 communities adopted transgender-inclusive policies, of these, 74 were municipalities. Universal among these provisions are protections of gender identity and expression in the public workplace.

Even more impressive than the number of adopting communities is the rate at which policy adoption is occurring. From 1975 to 1997, only 16 communities adopted transgender nondiscrimination laws, but from 1998 to 2005, 77 communities did so. This means two-thirds of these adoptions occurred between 2000 and 2006. Although a relatively small number of communities have adopted these policies, something appears to have changed. Table 19.1 shows the rate of policy adoption.

19.6   Current Data about Cities and Nondiscrimination Laws

In 2005, all known cities with laws that prohibited public employment discrimination were surveyed. Seventy-four surveys were distributed to public personnel agencies in

**Table 19.1   Adoption of Transgender-Inclusive Laws
(Cities, Counties, and States)—1975 to 2005**

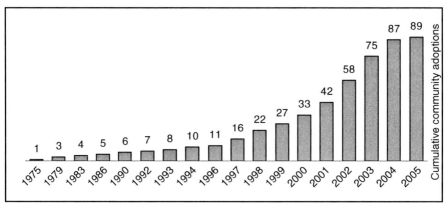

municipalities with employment laws that included provisions for transgender employment (Colvin, 2007). The survey data was collected between June 2005 and September 2005. The results of the survey provide value insights into the efforts of communities.

19.7   Survey Results

Of the 74 surveys distributed, 45 communities responded, for a response rate of 61 percent. The respondents were nearly equally divided in terms of the type of government in each community: 40 percent were mayor-council and 46 percent were council-manager. This suggests that the type of government does not necessarily affect the likelihood that a transgender-inclusive law will be adopted.

The survey also yielded a number of interesting points about the various transgender laws across the country. For example, protections for transgender people are enumerated in laws in diverse ways. These variations might have an effect on the implementation of transgender policies. Four broad categories were used to specify transgender protections: gender (11 percent), gender identity (36 percent), gender identity and expression (20 percent), and sexual orientation (16 percent).

In the responding communities, actual claims of transgender discrimination—of any type—were very low. Seventy percent reported no claims of transgender discrimination. Ninety-five percent of communities reported five or fewer claims of discrimination.

Sixty-two percent of the laws had confidentiality provisions. Of those communities with provisions, 38 percent reported that the confidentiality provision provided "good" or "very good" coverage. Ninety-four percent of the laws had antiretaliation provisions. Of those with provisions, 68 percent of the public managers thought that the antiretaliation provisions provided "good" or "very good" coverage for employees.

19.8 Implementation

The specific components of the laws that make them transgender inclusive were analyzed, yielding the most interesting results about the efforts of cities to become transgender-inclusive workplaces. Sixty-four percent of communities have changed the wording of existing nondiscrimination laws to explicitly prohibit transgender discrimination. Those respondents that have changed or plan to change their policies account for 81.6 percent of communities.

In addition, 42 percent have designated a contact person to answer employees' transgender-related questions, and 48 percent of communities will change gender designation in employee records and materials at the employee's request. In terms of sex-segregated facilities, implementation is less comprehensive: only 12 percent of communities have written policies about restroom and locker room use, and even fewer—only 7 percent—have written shower policies.

Implementation is more varied when it comes to healthcare: 32 percent and 26 percent of communities allow sick leave and disability benefits, respectively, to be used for transition-related medical issues—yet only 8 percent have healthcare benefits that actually cover such issues.

The communities surveyed were asked whether they were considering, planning, or already implementing each of the provisions needed to create a transgender-inclusive workplace environment. Graph 19.1 synthesizes this data and represents the level of implementation for each provision.

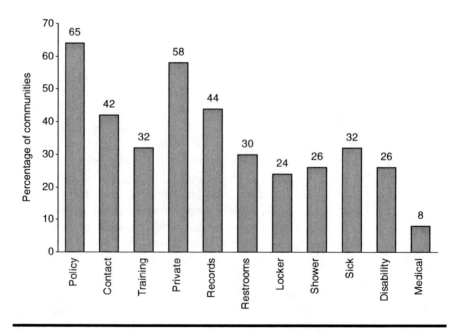

Graph 19.1   Implementation for Each Transgender-Related Provision.

19.9   Health Disparities

As Graph 19.1 indicates, the lowest levels of implementation occur with regard to sick leave, disability leave, and medical leave. These areas have such low levels of implementation because they are expensive to provide due to the cost of healthcare, because of the administrative challenges related to coordinating them with independent health providers, and because of the potential political controversy surrounding providing such benefits. Ironically, these are often the most essential issues for transgender people, because they encounter a number of medical and mental health-related necessities.

19.10   Health Costs

The health needs of transgender workers are intertwined with the health needs of the general workforce. The consensus among health professionals is that healthcare costs are of critical or significant concern to the overwhelming majority of organizations (SCHRAMM, 2005). In 2004, analysts projected a 12.6 percent increase in the national average costs for healthcare and forecast that costs would continue to rise at an average annual rate of 14 percent (SCHRAMM, 2005). In such an environment, employers are hesitant to take on more health-related risk by providing additional benefits to a small and marginalized employee population.

This resistance to broadening coverage may be, in part, due specifically to the costs associated with gender transition. The average cost for male to female surgery is about $11,000 (Horton, 2006). Beyond the cost of the surgery, there are the associated health and medical costs, including the costs for psychotherapy, hormone treatments, and follow-up medical visits.* These costs are reoccurring and extend over the life of the employee. And beyond these core costs there are often additional costs that may concern employers who provide health benefits. For example, a person may need plastic surgery, or opt for hair removal procedures to enhance his or her appearance (Horton, 2006).

19.11   Finding Insurers

Even for those employers willing to provide such benefits, finding insurance providers to cooperate may prove difficult. Many transgender people's health insurance applications are denied when they disclose their transgender status or transition-related medical history (such as hormone-level tests) to a potential insurer. Denials of coverage are most common in applications for private individual plans, but also occur in

---

* Sex reassignment surgery is the operation that matches the body to the mind. Male-to-female operations are more common than female-to-male, since the latter operation is perceived as having less than ideal results by patients. Therefore, the standard operations for female-to-male transgender individuals are usually mastectomy and hysterectomy (Horton, 2006). The costs identified by Horton ranged from $4,500 to $26,000 for male-to-female and $4,000 to $60,000 for female-to-male.

applications for employer-sponsored and other group plans. When considering the breadth and depth of coverage, five categories are usually considered: hormone therapy, mental health counseling, prescription drugs, sex reassignment surgery, and office visits. Insurance providers often assess the reason for an office visit as a method for determining coverage eligibility, including office visits related to hormone therapy, mental health counseling, postoperative reconstructive surgeries, and postsurgery complications.

A cursory search for private insurance companies in California that offer some coverage of transgender-related services identified seven providers.* Of the seven private insurers identified, all providers covered hormone therapy, mental health counseling, and prescription drugs; none of the providers covered the sex reassignment surgery itself. Curiously, all providers but one covered postoperative follow-up visits.

19.12   Administrative Implementation

Currently, a nexus of administrative issues, including but not limited to changing your sex on personnel and organizational files, establishing restroom or other sex-segregated policies, gaining status in a protected group, and changing marital status, are triggered by sex reassignment surgery. But no significant administrative actions can be taken until such surgery has been completed.

Even then, one of the major challenges for human resources managers is establishing health and medical policies that are effective, efficient, and equitable for all employees. But there is a paucity of data about the health and medical needs of transgender people—and a lack of available patterns from which administrators can draw innovations. Without time-tested patterns and sufficient data, even the best-intentioned plans and procedures may be inadequate—for employer and employees alike.

In addition to variable costs for surgery health benefits, concerns about level access for the surgeries is of concern; employers believe they will become a magnet for transgender people who join the organization just for its insurance coverage. There are two private sector organizations that have begun covering transgender surgeries: Lucent Technologies and Avaya. The experiences of these communications firms offer instructive insights about costs and access. Since 2000, Lucent has had three claims from its workforce of 150,000 (Horton, 2006). The three surgery claims totaled less than $20,000 combined. As of 2000, Avaya has had no claims for sex reassignment surgeries from its 40,000 employees (Horton, 2006).

19.13   Politically Charged Issue

Using the public treasury to pay for sex-change operations is an easy target for political opportunists. Despite the enactment of nondiscrimination laws, politicians often

---

* There are other providers and self-insured entities in the United States. These are the known providers in California. The small number of known providers in California suggests a potential challenge in terms of coverage for other—smaller—communities.

balk at the notion of equitable benefits as an antidiscrimination measure. Jurisdictions might be hesitant to proffer healthcare as a benefit because it may draw negative attention and put other components or organizational changes in jeopardy. The recent decision of the city of Largo, Florida, to fire its city manager of 17 years for announcing his intentions to transition suggests a charged social and political environment surrounding the issue (Helfeld, 2007).

Because relatively few organizations have developed a full range of transgender-related administrative changes, little formal or informal knowledge about how to offer benefits to this group of employees exists. This lack of patterns or frameworks means that each employer that considers providing benefits must conduct its own research on the issues. Social learning theories suggest that public administrators with limited resources would rather wait for innovations than develop their own (Colvin, 2007).

19.14   Innovating City: San Francisco

The city of San Francisco stands as the first major city in the United States to provide transgender health benefits. Although several nonprofit and private organizations have embarked on benefit equity, San Francisco offers the most informative model for public administrators.

In 1996, the San Francisco Human Rights Commission began to explore policy options to increase benefit equity for transgender employees, establishing a policy panel that included, among others, people from the transgender community. The panel's goal was to establish efficacious, equitable options for increasing access to procedures related to transition that would also be meaningful to other employees.

The initial efforts of the commission and the policy panel stalled due to a number of important concerns raised by the Health Services System Board (HSSB) and some members of the city council.* Those concerns included justifying coverage for medically unnecessary and cosmetic benefits for people in transition, the level of benefit access for current and past employees and their dependents, the costs associated with providing expensive sex reassignment surgery, and how to address the potential "flocking" that might occur by offering benefits.

Over the next several years, the commission and the panel worked to address these concerns. In 2001, San Francisco began a one-year pilot project to collect more data on offering such a benefit. The pilot project provided sex reassignment surgery via the city's self-insured plan and hormone treatments and psychotherapy through the city's health management organizations (HMOs).[†] With limited

---

* HSSB is responsible for overseeing the administration of the city's employee benefit program.
† The HMOs providing coverage in San Francisco are Blue Cross/Blue Shield, Kaiser Permanente, and Health Net.

information on costs, San Francisco health plan administrators projected that 35 people would access the benefit during the first year at an average cost of $50,000, for a total cost of more than $1.75 million. To cover the expected cost, the plan increased the required employee contributions by $1.70 per month, or about $20 per year (Jost, 2006).* The benefit was also restricted to employees who had worked in the city for one year or more (Harmon, 2006).

During the year of the pilot project and the subsequent two years, the health plan collected $4.6 million to cover the benefit and paid out only $156,000 on seven claims for surgery. On the basis of this experience, the $50,000 cap on benefits has been raised to $75,000 and the one-year exclusion was eliminated. In addition, the three HMOs that offer coverage to city employees are also now offering similar benefits.

In July 2006, the transgender health benefits provided by the city changed again. After collecting valuable data about costs and access, the employee contribution requirement was dropped, and HMOs now cover sex reassignment surgery the same way they cover other procedures.† Sex reassignment and related surgeries are covered like other procedures that are determined to be medically necessary by medical officials.

San Francisco's experience highlights several important facts about establishing new policies. First, the use of professionals and community advocates proved invaluable in helping the commission to understand the issues and the universe of possible solutions. Second, incrementalism—both in policy development and benefits offered—allowed the commission and city council to better manage the implementation process. This also allowed for constant monitoring of the policy and program, which ultimately provided important data. Finally, embracing equity gave the commission a framework for providing coverage. By allowing medical officials to determine the procedures that were medically necessary, the city equalized the healthcare system. For example, hormone treatments are covered by health insurance for transgender employees—and for menopausal employees as well.

19.15 Conclusion

If the trends are correct, work environments will continue to become more diverse, and the demands for more specialized benefits to meet the needs of all employees will increase. The realm of gender identity and expression represents one of the many new frontiers for specialized benefits. Creating transgender-inclusive workplaces

---

* The city insures about 37,000 employees, 21,000 retirees, and thousands of dependents (Buchanan, 2007).

† Transitioning employees are still required to complete the appropriate health, medical, and social requirements prior to sex reassignment surgery, including a psychological assessment, hormone treatments, and living as the appropriate gender prior to surgery.

that include equitable health benefits is no easy task. But it is not impossible. In the same way that organizations have learned to innovate in the work environment to become more friendly and equitable to women, older workers, gay and lesbian workers, temporary and contract workers, and disabled, part-time, and religiously observant workers, it can also innovate to accommodate transgender workers.

Communities that decide to become more transgender-friendly are in a better position to do so than their predecessors. The continual rise in the number of communities with transgender-inclusive nondiscrimination policies can provide the critical information that public administrators need when developing their own local policies and programs. These innovating jurisdictions, in conjunction with local advocates, are critical to the developing of equitable work environments.

Public administrators can look to both the private sector—where there are many examples—and to San Francisco as models of innovation. As the data suggests, health and medical benefits for transgender employees remain the most underutilized component of a comprehensive transgender-inclusive workplace. Organizations that venture into this area of benefits gain the competitive edge for recruiting the best and brightest, as well as retaining those whose see inclusiveness as a beneficial part of the workplace.

Appendix A: Survey Methodology

Each public personnel administrator was first contacted by telephone to confirm that the jurisdiction had, at a minimum, a transgender-inclusive public employment law and that he or she was the most knowledgeable person in the agency to answer questions about the law. After confirmation, the appropriate public personnel administrators were mailed a survey packet explaining the project, an instruction sheet, a questionnaire, a consent form, and a self-addressed stamped envelope.

The survey questions were divided into three major categories: background information, implementation questions, and effectiveness questions.

Background

To provide suitable background information, administrators were asked to explain the process for filing a discrimination claim and the number of claims filed to date. Additionally, information about the nature of these claims was ascertained, including the area of discrimination (hiring, firing, promotion, etc.), the outcome of the claims, and the remedies sought by claimants.

Implementation

Administrators were asked a number of questions related to the implementation of their transgender-inclusive laws. The implementation questions corresponded to the unique organizational changes needed to make the workplace more friendly, including: changing the employment nondiscrimination statement, establishing a contact person who could be contacted about transgender issues, training, procedures for making changes in administrative records, policies regarding sex-segregated facilities, and transgender-inclusive sick leave, disability, and medical policies.

Respondents had several options for rating the level of implementation. The categories included:

No, we have not considered this change (no)
We have considered, but have no plan to implement the change (consider)
We have a plan to implement this change (plan)
We are implementing this change (implementing)
Yes, this change is fully integrated into our operations (yes)

Respondents could answer "no" or "consider" when they had not yet implemented components. They could respond "plan," "implementing," or "yes" to indicate that implementation was occurring or had occurred for their law. Respondents were also given the opportunity to distinguish between whether they had never considered the organizational change or, having considered the organizational change, decided not to implement it. This distinguished between organizations that might implement after being influenced by the study and organizations that had already made a decision about implementation prior to their involvement in the study.

Finally, respondents were given the opportunity to indicate if they had unwritten policies regarding their sex-segregated facilities. Communities might be more likely to address their most pressing organizational changes—restroom, shower, and locker room policies—first. However, lack of guidance might lead to the creation of ad hoc or unwritten policy about these issues.

Effectiveness

Administrators were asked to gauge the effectiveness of the confidentiality and anti-retaliation provisions in the laws, because both the existence of these provisions, as well as their efficacy, could influence the application of the laws themselves. Claimants might be less likely to file discrimination claims if they fear that their confidentiality might be breached or that filing a claim might result in retaliation from other employees.

References

Buchanan, W. 2007. More U.S. employers cover sex transition surgery: Large corporations follow city's lead in offering benefit. *San Francisco Chronicle*, Wednesday, January 31, p. B4.

Colvin, R. 2007. The rise of transgender-inclusive laws: How well are municipalities implementing supportive nondiscrimination public employment policies? *Review of Public Personnel Administration*. Forthcoming.

Currah, P. and Minter, S. 2000. *Transgender Equality: A Handbook for Activists and Policy-makers*. Washington, DC: National Center for Lesbian Rights and the National Gay and Lesbian Task Force Policy Institute.

D'Emilio, J. 1983. *Sexual Politics, Sexual Communities*, 2nd ed. Chicago: University of Chicago Press.

Harmon, V. 2006. *San Francisco City and County Transgender Health Benefit*. San Francisco: San Francisco Human Rights Commission.

Helfeld, L. February 28, 2007. Largo officials vote to dismiss Stanton. St. Petersburg Times. Accessed June 1, 2007 http://www.sptimes.com/2007/02/28/Tampabay/Largo_officials_vote_.shtml

Horton, M.A. 2006. The cost of transgender health benefits. *International Journal of Trans-genderism*. *9*(1).

Irwin, J. 1996. Discrimination against gay men, lesbians, and transgender people working in education. *Journal of Gay and Lesbian Social Services*. *14*(2): 65–77.

Jost, K. 2006. Transgender issues: Should gender-identity discrimination be illegal? *CQ Researcher*. *16*(17): 385–408.

Letellier, P. 2003. *Beyond He and She: A Transgender News Profile*: The Good Times. January 9. http://www.tgcrossroads.org/news/archive.asp?aid=584 (accessed November 2007).

Lombarde, E.L., Riki, A.W., Dana, P., and Diana, M. 2001. Gender violence: Transgender experiences with violence and discrimination. *Journal of Homosexuality*. *42*(1): 89–101.

Minter, S. and Daley, C. 2003. *Trans Realities: A Legal Needs Assessment of San Francisco's Transgender Communities*. San Francisco: National Center for Lesbian Rights and Transgender Law Center.

Mottet, L. 2006. *State Nondiscrimination Laws in the U.S.* Washington, DC: National Gay and Lesbian Task Force.

Oswald, R., Gebbie, E., and Culton, L. 2000. Report to the community: Rainbow Illinois survey of gay, lesbian, bisexual, and transgender people in central Illinois. Champaign-Urbana: University of Illinois.

Sausa, L. 2002. Updating college and university campus policies: Meeting the needs of trans students, staff, and faculty. *Journal of Lesbian Studies*. *6*(3/4).

Schramm, J. 2005. *SHRM Workplace Forecast*. Washington, DC: Society for Human Resources Management.

Shaffer, M.A., Joplin, J.R.W., Bell, M.P., Lau, T., and Oguz, C. 2000. Gender discrimination and job-related outcomes: A cross-cultural comparison of working women in the United States and China. *Journal of Vocational Behavior*. *57*(3): 395–427.

Sheehy, C. 2004. *Transgender Issues in the Workplace: A Tool for Managers*. Washington, DC: Human Rights Campaign Foundation.

Supateera, C. and Kleiner, B.H. 1999. Discrimination in government. *Equal Opportunity International*. *18*(5/6).

Index

G